Things Which Soon Must Come to Pass

A Commentary on the Book of Revelation

By

PHILIP MAURO

AUTHOR OF

The Gospel of the Kingdom; The Hope of Israel; The Seventy Weeks; The Chronology of the Bible; Ruth, the Satisfied Stranger;

Hess Publications
1983 Lockes Mill RD
Berryville, VA 22611
www.hesspublications.com

Printed in the United States of America

"O, EARTH, EARTH, EARTH, HEAR THE WORD OF THE LORD."

Jer. 22:29

Contents

Chapter		Page
	Foreword	i
	Introductory Remarks	1
I	Outlines and Major Divisions of the Book	11
II	The Vision of the Son of Man	46
III	The Letters to the Churches of Asia	83
IV	The Vision of the Throne in Heaven	140
V	The Opening of the Seals	179
VI	The Trumpet Series	265
VII	The Mighty Angel With the Little Book	324
VIII	The Two Signs in Heaven	360
IX	The Vision of the Two Wild Beasts	390
X	Seven Visions of the Time of the End	432
XI	The Seven Vials	454
XII	Rejoicings in Heaven. The Marriage of the Lamb. The Battle of Armageddon	505
XIII	The New Heaven and New Earth. The Bride. The Holy Jerusalem	528
XIV	Conclusion—Where We Now Stand	554
XV	The Millennium	577

ANNOUNCEMENT

"And he said unto me, Write ..."

THE major part of the contents of this volume was published in 1925 under the title "THE PATMOS VISIONS". Subsequent studies of the Scriptures and observance of recent developments in the spheres of world politics and economics, while strongly confirming the main principles and nearly all the details of the interpretation presented in that volume, have indicated the need of certain revisions and additions, particularly in respect to the exposition of *"The Thousand Years"* (Rev. 20:1-10). That portion of the former work has been allowed to stand in order that the reader may see the position taken by the author seven years ago, for comparison with his present understanding of that important subject, as set forth in an additional chapter (XV). A Foreword, prompted by recent political and economic developments throughout the world, has also been supplied.

FOREWORD TO REVISED EDITION

"*O Earth, Earth, Earth, Hear the Word of the* LORD" (Jer. 22:29).

THE message of the Book of "The Revelation of Jesus Christ, which God gave unto Him to show unto His servants", is of supreme importance to those "servants" and indeed to all mankind in this present hour of crisis, an hour that is characterized in marked degree by "distress of nations, with perplexity". It is under the stress of this conviction that the present volume is written; and the writer's purpose and desire are—not to supply interested readers with a complete scheme of interpretation, but—primarily to awaken and stimulate interest in the Book itself, and secondarily to demonstrate its intelligibility and its special applicability to this present time by explaining and exemplifying the principles whereby its symbols and visions are to be rightly interpreted.

At the time of the writing of these pages social conditions of an altogether anomalous and unprecedented character are, and for several years have been, prevalent throughout the world. In the words of an economist of international renown, Sir Arthur Salter, it is a time of "unprecedented financial crisis", of "the collapse of the credit system, revealing the anatomy of the world's economic structure", coupled with "political impotence, the inability of government to govern"

(*Foreign Affairs*, October, 1932); which tallies with the comment of another observer, who says of a recent utterance by President Hoover, that it disclosed incidents of "those terrifying two weeks when the financial structure of the United States seemed about to crumble into an abyss, dragging the welfare of civilization with it in its imminent fall".

Above all it is a time of bewildering economic paradox. Starvation stalks the streets and highways of the civilized nations because—the experts tell us—of the existence in markets and storehouses of an over-plus of food supplies. Dire destitution is the lot of their populations—approximately forty millions of good workers being unemployed or on only part-time employment—and that by reason of the overproduction of those very commodities whereof the unemployed and their families are in need. Acute distress is everywhere felt and not because of the lack of a sufficiency of the things upon which human life and comfort depend, but—because of the lack of buyers of the existent over-plus thereof; or, in the inspired language of the Book, "because no man buyeth their merchandise any more". There is "merchandise" a-plenty and in excess, but buyers are lacking.

Men's hearts everywhere are failing them for fear and for looking after those things that are coming to pass on the earth, whereof the ominous portents are increasingly evident. It may be said that in every community the civilized world over the whole head is sick and the whole heart faint; for the heavens above are dark with menacing storm-clouds and the earth beneath seems to tremble under foot. The present state of the civilized nations is well expressed by a secular writer who says: "What do we see when we look abroad today? We see a world writhing as it were in a purgatory of its own making".

It is to be expected that, at such a time of crisis, the book of Revelation—the only book of the New Testament that is occupied wholly with the foreshowing of things to come—would claim special attention from, and be diligently studied by, all those who, having discerned that the Bible is indeed the Word of the living God, are desirous of knowing, upon the authority of Him Who sees the end from the beginning:—first, how those evil conditions came to be; and second, in what they will eventuate.

Moreover, it is not unreasonable to believe that the Spirit of God, Who inspired the writing of "the book of this prophecy" (Rev. 22:19), will be graciously pleased at this dark hour to afford to them who diligently seek it an understanding of "the things which are written in this book" (*id.*).

THE TITLE OF THE BOOK

That book bears a divinely given title:—"The Revelation (literally UNVEILING) of Jesus Christ," which title has special significance because of the fact that, as is emphasized in the Epistle to the Hebrews, the Lord Jesus Christ, after having accomplished eternal redemption by the sacrifice of Himself, passed

"WITHIN THE VEIL" (Heb. 6:19, 20; 9:24). The title reminds us that, since the moment when He was parted from His disciples "and a cloud received Him out of their sight" (Acts 1:9), He has been concealed behind that veil from the eyes of men; so that, even to His own people, He is present by faith, not by sight. To them, as to all mankind, He is "The King—invisible" (1 Tim. 1:17).

This final book of the Bible assumes to draw aside the veil, so to speak; for it records visions of happenings in that "heaven itself" which Christ has entered and other visions also, which reveal things that were to come to pass thereafter on both sides of that veil, the heavenly and the earthly, visions that cover the entire period from the time of His ascension into heaven down to His coming again.

The things thus revealed, both those on the heavenly side and those on the earthly side of the intervening veil, are embraced in the category of "things which must shortly come to pass" (Rev. 1:1); and the Book itself shows that those things were to eventuate in the coming again of the Lord from heaven, when every eye should see Him (1:7) and in the new heavens and new earth (21:1). Specially is it to be noted in this connection that all the things that are written therein are closely connected with Jesus Christ Himself as the Redeemer of men and as the duly invested Owner and Sovereign Lord of the universe. Hence the peculiar fitness of the inspired title: *The Revelation* of JESUS CHRIST.

Because of this unique feature of the book of the

Revelation it should have possessed, throughout the history of the Kingdom of God on earth, a supreme interest for His people and also a supreme value in their eyes. But unhappily this has not been the case. On the contrary, that wonderful book seems to have been regarded by the many as a collocation of weird and unintelligible visions, and hence has suffered neglect. This misconception concerning the book and its consequent neglect have doubtless been caused mainly by the confusing, contradictory and often fantastical, interpretations that have been put forth of its "signs" and visions. But there is good reason to believe that the hour is now come for a diligent and prayerful study of the book with the confident expectation that a clear understanding will be given of "those things which are written therein".

Visions of Christ in Person

It is of importance for the purpose of the present study to notice at the outset the several guises—so different one from another—in which the glorified Redeemer was revealed to the eye of His servant John in the Patmos visions. In the first of those visions He was seen as "one like unto the Son of man" (1:13) and as encircled by seven golden lamp-stands, which, according to the explanation from His own lips (ver. 20), signified seven churches. Those churches were located one in each of the seven cities designated by name; those cities being all situated within the small pro-consular province of "Asia", and forming an irregular circle following one another in the precise order in which they are here named. This vision and the seven letters of Chapters II and III make it plain that the risen Christ, though veiled from the sight of men, is ever keeping a watchful eye upon His churches throughout the era of His bodily absence; and there is immense comfort, as well as wholesome admonition and information of transcendent value in this feature of the revelation of Jesus Christ.

Who is Worthy to Open the Book?

That the next vision (Chap. 4:1) is of special importance may be inferred from the fact that "a door was opened in heaven" and the seer was bidden to "Come up hither"; whereupon he beholds the throne of God in heaven and One that sat thereon, One Who so transcended verbal description that John could only say He was to look upon like two precious stones, a jasper and a sardius. This indescribable One holds in His right hand a book (or scroll of parchment) inscribed on both sides and sealed with seven seals (5:1). The interest of heaven centers upon that book, and it is apparent that issues of stupendous importance, of such character and scope as to affect the whole creation of God, depend upon an answer being found to the question which is now proclaimed throughout the universe, "Who is worthy to open the book, and to loose the seals thereof?" (ver. 3). The proclamation of this question by a strong angel with a loud voice suggests that the answer had been awaited in heaven for a long time, perhaps during the entire era of the Old Testament.

It is recorded in the preceding chapter that the four and twenty elders had prostrated themselves before the throne, exclaiming, "Thou art worthy, O Lord, to receive glory and honour and power: for Thou hast created all things, and for Thy pleasure they are and were created" (4:11). But it is manifest that the worthiness evidenced by the creation of all things does not qualify the omnipotent Creator "to take the book and to open the seals thereof?" It would seem that the progress of the divine program was arrested at this point and that nothing further could be done until one should be found who could rightfully open the book. Therefore heaven waits in breathless expectancy, while John "wept much because no man was found worthy to open and to read the book" (5:4).

Up to this point Christ has not been seen in this vision; but now John is bidden by one of the elders to dry his tears and to look, for that "The Lion of the tribe of Judah hath prevailed to open the book, and to loose the seven seals thereof". (Note that the word, "prevailed", is the same that the Lord applied to Himself when He said, "Even as I also overcame and am set down with My Father in His throne," 3:21). Thereupon John beheld, "and, lo, in the midst of the throne ... stood a Lamb as it had been slain ... and He came and took the book out of the right hand of Him that sat upon the throne" (vv. 6, 7).

CREATION AND REDEMPTION

Here is a crucial point. If the creation of the universe did not confer upon its Creator the special worthiness or competency required for the opening of the book and the loosing of the seals thereof, what then? The answer is found in the *new* ascription of praise from the four living creatures and the four and twenty elders, who now fall down *before the Lamb* and sing "a *new song*, saying, THOU ART WORTHY to take the book and to open the seals thereof, *for* THOU WAST SLAIN AND HAST REDEEMED US TO GOD BY THY BLOOD".

God's two mighty works, Creation and Redemption, are celebrated in these two anthems. Every creature in heaven and earth who has learned the first principles of the oracles of God can sing, with the spirit and with the understanding also, both those ascriptions of praise to God, and say: "Thou are worthy, O Lord, as Creator of all things to receive glory, and honour and power"; and "Thou are worthy, as the Redeemer of the world, to take the book and to open the seals thereof".

It is of interest to note that once again in the Book we are studying the four and twenty elders raise an anthem of praise to God. The record is found in Chapter XI, verses 16-18, following the proclamation by great voices in heaven that "the kingdoms of this world are become the kingdoms of our Lord and of His Christ". Upon hearing the announcement of this tremendous event, the elders leave their thrones, and fall on their faces before God, saying, "We give thee thanks, Lord God Almighty, Which art and wast and art to come; because Thou hast taken to Thee Thy great power, and hast reigned".

Thus the theme of the third anthem is the kingdom. Doubtless much instruction may be had by comparing the records of these three anthems of the elders, but we cannot pursue the subject.

In each of the first two anthems the Lord is acclaimed as "worthy to receive" something ("receive" in 4:11 being the same word as "take" in 5:6); and it is apparent that what He receives because of redemption is represented, in some way which we shall seek to discern, by the seven-sealed book written on both sides. This is a capital point, for if apprehended it puts us on the track of the true interpretation of the symbol of the seven-sealed book.

We reserve the details of interpretation to the appropriate place, our desire at this point being merely to impress upon the reader's mind the need of laying hold of the meaning of the scene depicted in Chapters IV and V, for the purpose of understanding the contents of the chapters that follow. *For here begins the train of events consequent upon the accomplishment of eternal and world-wide redemption by the sacrifice of the Lamb of God.* If so, then to go forward with an erroneous interpretation of this vision must needs entail error throughout; whereas on the other hand, if we grasp the significance of this scene we shall find it a relatively easy matter to apprehend the meaning of subsequent visions.

What we hope to make evident is that there is no need for the diligent seeker after truth to be in error, or even in uncertainty, as to the significance of the main features of this symbolic vision. We know with absolute certainty just when the crucified and risen Redeemer, "the Lamb as newly slain", sat down on His Father's throne; for many Scriptures state that it was immediately upon His ascension into heaven (Acts 7:55; Eph. 1:20; Heb. 1:3; Rev. 3:21). This being understood, it is not difficult to apprehend in the light of the Scripture the significance of the seven-sealed book and of the events symbolically pre-figured by the successive visions that followed the opening of the seals thereof.

THE FOUR HORSEMEN

Again reserving the details for later consideration, we call to mind at this point that, at the opening of each of the first four seals, one of the living creatures, in a voice as it were of thunder, said "Go", and immediately there went forth *a horse and rider*. It is among the greatest certitudes of history that there went forth at that time into the world influences that have continuously and mightily affected the course of human events, and that, after nineteen centuries, are still in vigorous operation; influences whose strength and character can best be visualized by comparing the state of stagnant China or India with that of any of the progressive nations of Europe or North America.

We expect to make it clear that the forthgoings

(whatsoever, whencesoever and whithersoever they were) which those four horsemen represent have exerted determinative influences upon the whole course of history from the beginning of the Christian era, and that the present social, political and economic conditions are among their inevitable results.

THE DESTRUCTION OF THE JEWISH NATION

It may seem a far cry from the subject of the four horsemen of the Apocalypse to that of the destruction of Jerusalem and the attendant break-up of the Jewish nation; but reasons will be found in the present volume for the belief that those seemingly diverse subjects are in fact closely related. Therefore we are urgent to press upon the reader's attention the dominating influence in shaping the history of Christendom that has been exerted by the dispersion of the survivors of the Jewish people amongst the nations of the world.

Further in this connection we would emphasize the immense importance in God's eyes, and the tremendous effect in the execution of His program for the world, of those historical events which, in fulfilment of Old Testament prophecies and also of the Olivet prophecy of Jesus Christ, culminated in the destruction of Jerusalem by the Romans in A. D. 70, and the dispersion of the Jews, thereby creating conditions, which, by the word of the Lord Himself, were to endure "until the times of the Gentiles be fulfilled" (Lu. 21:24).

The influence of those events upon the history of mankind, and particularly the part taken therein by the scattered survivors of the nation, are not matters of conjecture or uncertainty, but are fully attested both by prophecy and by history. And it is most needful to apprehend these facts for a right understanding of Bible prophecy in general and of the Book of the Revelation in particular. As I said elsewhere (speaking of the destruction of Jerusalem)*:

> "The failure to recognize the significance of that event, and the vast amount of prophecy which it fulfilled, has been the cause of great confusion, for the necessary consequence of missing the past fulfilment of predicted events is to leave on our hands a mass of prophecies for which we must needs contrive fulfilments in the future. The harmful results are two-fold; for *first,* we are thus deprived of the evidential value, and the support to the faith, of those remarkable fulfilments of prophecy which are so clearly presented to us in authentic contemporary histories; and *second,* our vision of things to come is greatly obscured and confused by the transference to the future of predicted events which, in fact, have already happened, and whereof complete records have been preserved for our information".

First of all it is to be observed that the break-up of the Jewish nation marked the transition of God's dealings with mankind from the economy of the old covenant to that of the new covenant. For at that era the old covenant—that "of the letter"—with its temple, priesthood, sacrifices, ordinances, and specially its chosen nation, was completely abolished by the instrumentality of a series of sweeping judgments, thereby making room for the new covenant—that "of the

---
* See "The Seventy Weeks and the Great Tribulation" (p. 200). Wm. B. Eerdmans Publishing Co., Grand Rapids, Mich.

Spirit"—with its "spiritual house" (the church of God and of Jesus Christ), its "spiritual sacrifices", and its "holy nation", composed of the elect out of every nation, tongue and tribe of earth (1 Pet. 2:5, 9).

That cataclysmic event was truly of tremendous moment for all future generations, one for which no parallel can be found in human history. For never before or since has a nation been blotted out of existence, whose surviving people have been dispersed throughout the other nations of the world, resisting destruction and amalgamation alike and maintaining for centuries their distinctive racial characteristics and identity. To this unique feature of history and to its dominating effect in determining the character of the Christian era appropriate consideration will be given in this volume. But for the purpose of these introductory comments it suffices to call attention to the fact that there "went forth" at that time out of Judea and Jerusalem "into all the world" *two diverse sort of people—converted* Jews and *unconverted* Jews. For at the time of her birth-pangs it was with Jerusalem as with her prototype, Rebecca, in that "two manner of people were in her womb" (Gen. 25:23). And the analogy goes further. For like as the diverse careers of Jacob and Esau were foretold before their birth, even so the prophecies of the Old and New Testaments foretold the character and effect of the influences upon the Gentile world—for good in the one case and for evil in the other—of those two out-flowing streams of Jewish humanity.

The contrast between Jacob and Esau, as God sees

it, was the greatest possible, as is evidenced by the words: "Jacob have I loved, but Esau have I hated" (Rom. 9:13); and that between the two divisions of the Jewish race was fully as great. Not only so, but the historical order of the birth of those two peoples of common origin corresponds with that of the two sons of Isaac: first that which is natural and afterward that which is spiritual; and eventually the younger is to have the dominion.

"A Division Because of Him"

The words of the apostle, "So there was a division because of Him" (John 7:43) have a significance deeper and wider far than might at first appear. For that "division" produced the greatest possible of all human contrasts. One group comprised regenerated Jews, those who "received Him", and were born of God (John 1:11-13), these being the true "Israel"—"for they are not all 'ISRAEL' that are of Israel"—the "Israel of God". The other group comprised the unregenerate Jews, those who "received Him not", they being the natural Israel, "Israel after the flesh". The greatness of the contrast is impressed upon us by the Scriptures which declare that the one company were "the children of God" and the other "the children of the Devil" (John 1:12; 8:39, 44; Rom. 9:8; 1 Jn. 3:1, 2, 10, etc.). It follows that there needs must have been a difference correspondingly great between the effects exerted upon the gentile peoples and upon their governments and institutions by those two families respectively.

All of which was foreseen from the beginning and was a part of God's plan for the accomplishment of His eternal purpose in Christ Jesus, and for the establishment of His everlasting kingdom. For to Abraham, the human instrument through whom that plan was to be executed, God gave promise that He would bless him and make him a blessing and that through him and his seed all the families of the earth should be blessed; which promise and like promises have been fulfilled through the believing Jews whom Christ commissioned to "go into all the world and preach the gospel to every creature" (Mk. 16:15), these being the true children of Abraham, according as it is written, "they which are of faith, the same are the children of Abraham" (Gal. 3:7). On the other hand it was foretold from the beginning of the nation of Israel and by Moses its founder that, if they should forsake the covenant of their God, He would root them out of their land in anger and in such manner as to cause astonishment to all the nations (Deut. 29:24-28, etc.).

But this subject is too vast and ramified to admit of more than a passing reference to it here. What is of chief importance for the purpose of this exposition is the fact—for which the proof will be given hereafter—that from the impact of those two tides of Jewish humanity upon the stagnant and decaying masses of the Gentiles there have eventuated two vast and potent dominions of a spiritual nature, which, though invisible, are most real and active, namely, the Kingdom of God and the empire of International Finance. Both are invisible and both are international, and there are other points of resemblance which need not to be noticed here.

It is the unique character of the Kingdom of God in this age that, in the words of its Founder, it "cometh not with observation" (Lu. 17:20), that is, its nature during the present era of the gospel is such that its presence is not manifest to the eye by any of the usual accompaniments of government, for it has no visible constitution or administrative machinery; yet it is a real and world-wide dominion, every member of which has been born of God (John 3:3).

Likewise the empire of finance, now existent in the form commonly called "credit capitalism" though its existence is clearly recognized and though the industrial enterprises and the commerce of the whole world are subject to its despotic sway, is "without observation"; for it is, in the Bible sense of the word, a "mystery", but its potency and its universal sway are none the less real.

The co-existence of these two spiritual empires, their world-wide dominion, their mutual antagonism, their competition for the allegiance of men, and the necessity on their part of making a definite choice between them were clearly indicated by the Lord in a pregnant word of admonition to His disciples: "Ye cannot serve God and mammon" (Mat. 6:24; cf. Josh. 24:15).

It is noteworthy that the mission and the social influence of each of those spiritual agencies was to be of age-long duration; for, by the word of Christ Himself, the work of His disciples in propagating the Kingdom of God was to continue "unto the end of the age" (Mat. 28:19, 20); and on the other hand the dispersion of the unbelieving Jews was to last "until the times of the Gentiles be fulfilled" (Lu. 21:24).

WHAT SHALL THE END BE?

The human material upon which those two diverse spiritual forces were to exert themselves was the population of the Gentile world, which was in a state of corruption, darkness and gradual decay. Those forces were to encounter Greek philosophy, Roman cynicism and barbaric idol worship; these being but different developments of the corrupt human nature common to all those whom God had given up to their own desires and to a reprobate mind, "because they did not like to retain God in their knowledge".

And now, in Christendom of to-day, is manifested the result of nineteen centuries of the impact upon the heathen world of those mighty spiritual agencies that went forth from Judea in the first century of our era. What has been the outcome thus far? Confining our observation to the christianized part of the world, we find that in our day the preoccupation of the great majority of human beings is with Economics, or to use the more familiar term, Business. This is, and for several generations has been, the object of supreme human interest, to which even religion and politics are subordinated. The reason is apparent; for the prime necessities of human life, as well as all comforts, luxuries, rank and position in society, and other things dear to the heart of man are involved. And at this hour of economic depression the deep conviction of the vast majority is that the welfare of mankind, if not the very existence of "civilization", depend upon the speedy restoration of business prosperity. Moreover, at the present time the interest of mankind in the prospects of business is greatly accentuated by reason of a "business depression" of unprecedented extent and severity, or what Sir Arthur Salter terms "an unprecedented financial crisis" (*Foreign Affairs*, October, 1932).

Conditions are such that, in the thought of the average man who thinks of such things at all, the salvation of the world from anarchy and ruin depends upon the speedy revival of manufacture and trade; while among those who delve into the mysteries of economics there are many who predict the near-by collapse of the whole system of "credit capitalism", by which the industries and commerce of the nations are controlled.

In that vast heterogeneous conglomerate of nationalized and industrialized humanity, which constitutes the Christendom of to-day and extends its fringes into the domains of heathendom, the conservative element, whence it derives all its stabilizing, preservative and invigorating influences, is the unorganized but vitally coherent "Israel of God", with its gospel of salvation and healing for all men—the little leaven, dispersed throughout the mass which leaveneth the whole lump, "the salt of the earth", which preserves the decaying mass from utter destruction; whereas the ravaging, disintegrating, disruptive element, which eventually will compass the downfall of the whole system of international "credit-capitalism", is the well organized, though widely scattered, "Israel after the flesh", which long has occupied all positions of economic vantage and controls all the sinews of production and commerce.

THE NEAR-BY CATACLYSM

It is a notable fact and pertinent to our subject that the serious literature of to-day—especially the writings of those who specialize in sociology, political economy, eugenics and the like—teems with volumes and articles which undertake to show from past history and present conditions and tendencies that a universal social catastrophe is imminent. As conspicuous examples, mention may be made of the "Decline of the Western World" by the eminent German philosopher, Spengler, and Gassett's "The Revolt of the Masses". To these writers and to many others it is apparent from what is happening before our eyes that "the doom of our civilization" cannot be long deferred unless adequate preventive measures are speedily taken.

Some of these prophets of doom see the end as issuing in devastating wars, involving the destruction of life on a colossal scale, for which man's inventive genius has already supplied the effective instruments. Others see it as eventuating in world-wide uprisings and revolts of the masses attended by bloody revolutions. To others the complete and irremediable collapse of the world's *economic system*, involving utter and irretrievable ruin, is a matter of a relatively short time. Still others see the end of "Christian civilization" (so-called) in the gradual decadence of the white races from causes now actively in operation, which it is the mission of the recently born science of "Eugenics" to oppose.

To the class last referred to belongs Major Leonard Darwin, son of Charles Darwin, author of the theory of evolution. Major Darwin, now in his 82nd year, was president of the First International Congress of Eugenics (held in London in 1912) and he has recently addressed to the Third Congress of that society (held in New York in August, 1932) a communication in which he declares his "firm conviction" that, unless "wide-spread eugenic reforms"—such as limitation of human parentage to the physically and mentally "fit", the sterilization of the "unfit", etc.—are adopted without delay, our Western civilization is destined to speedy decay. Inasmuch as the specified "reforms" are as likely to be universally adopted as the statutes of Omri, it is apparent that evolution has no hope for mankind.

This despairing outlook is confirmed by the opinion of Dr. Henry Fairfield Osborn, the eminent man of science, who is the honorary president of the Third Eugenic Congress. Prof. Osborn declares that all existing means, methods and schemes of reform, "are merely palliatives" which "may for a time gloss over the cataclysm", but which *"cannot permanently cure it or avoid its recurrence".*

Analyzing the present world-crisis, in view of observations on a recent tour around the world, Professor Osborn says the situation resolves itself into six abnormalities each of which he designates by a compound word whose first element is "over"—viz., over-destruction of natural resources; over-mechanization of industry; over-construction of means of transport; over-production of food and other commodities; over-confidence in future demand and supply; and over-production of manufactures with consequent permanent unemployment for the least efficient workers. (Paper submitted to the Third Eugenic Congress, August 22, 1932.)

The premises upon which this learned man bases his conclusions are patent to all observers. The Western nations in general, and preëminently the United States, have erected vast industrial works and equipped them with the most highly developed machinery designed for the mass production of manufactured articles, with the definite object of *reducing prices* to a minimum, so that that ideal condition of human existence might be attained in which there would be no lack of any desirable thing but an abundant supply of everything for everybody. With the same utopian object in view, agriculture has been tremendously stimulated by means of fertilizers, power-driven planters, cultivators, harvesters and other machinery, whereby the production per acre of wheat, corn, cotton and other staples, has been enormously increased and the earnestly sought desideratum of greatly reduced prices has been finally achieved. For has it ever been doubted, or could be doubted, that the existence of plentiful supplies of all needful and desirable things at minimum prices would mean prosperity, contentment and happiness, with ample leisure for recreation or amusement, for all classes of society?

But now that the wise plans and well directed efforts of our industrialists and financiers have achieved an amazing success, the result is—not the ideal social conditions of prosperity and contentment that were confidently expected, but—just the reverse, a state of distress, suffering, social upheavals and diversified miseries, without precedent in the history of mankind; a condition such that the efforts of governments and auxiliary institutions, aided by specially created agencies are being exerted to the very utmost to reverse the process, and to raise the prices of all farm products and manufactured articles. In fact, it is agreed by "the best minds" in government, science, industry and finance, that not only the return of prosperity, but also the very existence of our civilization, depend upon the raising of the prices of the prime necessities of life and of all products and commodities that are in general demand.

"The Specific Task of Our Age"

Another exceptionally competent observer of world conditions, Sir Arthur Salter, the eminent British economist and financier, has recently stated his convictions upon "The Future of Economic Nationalism". In an article under that title (in "Foreign Affairs", October,

1932), characterized by great sobriety of expression and by deep solemnity, Sir Arthur impressively warns his fellowmen that:

> "The world is now at one of the great cross-roads of history. The system, usually termed capitalist, but I think better termed competitive, . . . has developed deep-seated defects which will threaten its existence unless they can be cured. We need to reform, and in larger measure to transform this system." He points out the desperate need of the reorganization "of industry, of credit, and of money. . . . This is the specific task of our age. If we fail, the only alternatives are chaos, or the substitution of a different system inconsistent with political and personal liberty, perhaps after an intervening period of collapse and anarchy".

A dread outlook surely; and indeed a hopeless one. For where are the supermen or super-agencies that are to cope successfully with this stupendous "task of our age"? Having premised so much, this judicious student and observer of civic affairs goes on to furnish, unconsciously, of course, a striking illustration of that "perplexity", which was to be, according to the Lord's Olivet prophecy, the distinctive characteristic of the era of "distress of nations" at the time of the end. Sir Arthur says:

> "Now, in every aspect of this great task *one fundamental issue constantly occurs*. Upon what basis are we to plan, at what goal should we aim? Are we to move more and more towards a system of closed units, with political and economic boundaries co-terminous . . . ? Or are we to aim again at building up world trade within the framework of a world order?" And notwithstanding the discouraging certainty that "no complete realization of either ideal is of course practical", we are nevertheless to realize that "it is *now* that we must decide towards which we shall move".

The article presents a careful and conscientious, but scarcely illuminating, discussion of this momentous issue, upon which the very existence of human society is said to depend. In it the writer refers bitterly to

"political impotence at home and abroad", to "the inability of government to govern," to "the corrupting influence of a policy of changing tariffs", and to the effect upon legislatures of "competitive —or corruptly concerted—pressures"; and tells us that, "after many years of international negotiations on commercial policies", he has "come to the deliberate conclusion that the greatest and most fundamental difficulty was—not an international one at all, it was the impotence of the national governments"; for what determined the attitude of delegates to such international conferences "was not a conception of national policy but a calculation of political pressures". In other words, what effectually bars the adoption of those economic measures that are absolutely necessary for the preservation of human society, are the most deep-seated and ineradicable traits of human nature.

True it is that "lessons taught by the past are rarely learned; but immediate suffering is a more effective schooling; and world trade is now demonstrating its real value by its disappearance". But to what conclusions do these clear sighted observations bring us? Thus speaks this eminent authority and international expert:— "A world order *must be* established"—but how, and by whom?—"the conditions of secure intercourse must be assured. Economic nationalism must be a passing phase in the world's history"—but how is it to be brought about?—"The immediate answer is doubtful. We may drift on till natural forces at last compel a solution after decades of intervening anarchy and disorder. Or we may, by deliberate policy anticipate the conclusion and avoid the intermediate period of suffering and destruction. The issue depends upon a few great countries, upon their recognition that they cannot abdicate their responsibilities for the fate of a world". And the final word is, "Nationalism is the abuse of nationality, which now threatens all that it has given or promised with destruction. The present situation is the greatest challenge ever given to the constructive and collective intelligence of man".

This is truly a lame and impotent conclusion; but it affords an illustrious example of the utter futility of all human efforts at devising a remedy for the present desperate condition of mankind, and at the same time it is a striking testimony to the fact that those long foretold days of "distress of nations with perplexity" are now upon us. For surely the world-wide "distress" is patent and acute, while the "perplexity" has the aspect of utter bewilderment.

Happily we are not bidden at this crisis period to look for deliverance to "a few large countries", but to "look *up* and lift up your heads; for your redemption draweth nigh" (Luke 21:25-28).

Thus—however it may be explained—the experience of mankind, by actual trial and upon a world-wide scale, has demonstrated, despite all seemingly obvious a priori theories to the contrary, that while on the one hand, a scarcity of commodities and high prices therefor mean privation for the many, a low scale of living for the workers, with the limitation of the good things of life to the enjoyment of a favored few, on the other hand, *a superabundance* of all needful and desirable things at minimum prices means a condition far worse, for it brings about unprecedented destitution for the workers and their families, a loss of resources or greatly diminished income to the well-to-do and the middle classes, acute governmental anxieties, violent social upheavals and desperate political expedients—a condition which is described with marvellous exactitude by the brief phrase of Jesus Christ—"distress of nations with perplexity"; the state of human affairs the world over being such that thoughtful men, though unenlightened by the Scriptures, see in them clear portents of the approaching doom of Christendom.

What is the explanation of this anomaly? this contradiction by actual experience of the most assured and well-founded expectations of mankind as to what must needs result from a plenitude of food supplies and commodities—should that ideal condition ever be attained? The shining goal of our marvellous, world-transforming age of science, invention and machinery was the multiplication of the products of farms, mines and factories to the point where there should be enough of everything for everybody—and to spare. For it was axiomatic that, if ever that goal should be reached, the utopian state of universal wealth and satisfaction would have arrived. What then is the explanation of the stupefying fact of current history that, when the day of superabundance, so long striven for, came at length, the results were just the reverse of what was so confidently and so reasonably expected? The pursuit of that inquiry would take us beyond the scope of this volume. Moreover, it is unlikely that any concise answer could be found; though to one observer at least the question, "What is the trouble with our economic machinery" is distressingly simple; for he offers the following explanation: "The farmer has no money to buy the products of the factory because the factory worker has no money to buy the produce of the farmer because the factory is idle because the farmer has no money". And it must be admitted that many current explanations which are far more voluminous are not a whit more satisfactory. On the other hand, we may point to the view which finds favor with many writers that the purpose which motivates production, in the era of capitalism, is—not the supply of human needs, but—the making of profits for investing capitalists; that that system can never adjust the balance between production and distribution; and that, as tersely expressed by Prof. Laski:— "the essence of a capitalist society is its division into a small number of rich men and a great mass of poor men". If that be indeed inherent in the system itself, then its utter overthrow can be only a matter of time.

It may, and likely will, turn out that those who have only their natural intelligence and the light of human experience whereby to shape their conclusions are mistaken in believing that the downfall of civilization is immediately at hand; for there may be, as in the past, brief periods of partial revival of "business". In fact, there are indications that such a period is even now beginning. But nevertheless there is every assurance to those who give heed to "the sure word of prophecy", that the time is now come, whereof the Saviour said— "And when these things begin to come to pass, then look up and lift up your heads; for your redemption draweth nigh" (Lu. 21:28).

The Thousand Years

The former edition of this work contained but brief

and general comments on the Millennium, the reason being that the writer had not been enabled, up to that time, to obtain answers, satisfactory to himself, to the questions, what? where? and when? is the period designated in Chapter XX by the phrase, "the thousand years". But now the case is different and in Chapter XV, which has been added to this present volume, will be found an attempt to set forth answers, derived wholly from the Word of God, to those deeply interesting and important questions. It will be found that the writer is not in agreement with the post-millennialists, who hold that there will be a thousand years of earthly peace and prosperity before our Lord's second advent; nor with the pre-millennialists, who hold there will be such a period following His second advent and preceding the new heavens and new earth; nor with the a-millennialists, who hold that there is no millennium at all. The view-point of this exposition is neither preterist, nor historicist, nor futurist. So much as to what it is *not*. As to what it *is*, we trust that they who shall have read thus far will be disposed to read further and ascertain for themselves. To them, and to all, we say in the words of the book, "Come and see".

Introductory Remarks

I THINK it not amiss to state that I have felt *impelled* to the writing of this present book. I was most reluctant to undertake it; for whenever the thought presented itself, such mountains of difficulty arose before my mind, that I shrunk from the attempt with a deep consciousness of my insufficiency. Yet the pressure to which I have referred persisted, and with increasing force, until at last I made a beginning truly "in weakness, and in fear, and in much trembling". But confidence came as I went on; for it seemed evident that help was being given from above, in that difficulties vanished, and passage after passage, previously dark or obscure, opened up clearly to my view.

When the significance of the four horses and their riders dawned upon me and was confirmed by abundant evidence from the Scriptures; when the meaning of the great "signs in heaven" of Chapter XII was perceived; and particularly when the trumpet visions showed forth their transcendently important meaning —all in the clear light of other Scriptures— I could no longer doubt that these studies, however defective as to details, were correct as to the main lines of the prophecy, and that they should be given to my companions in the kingdom and patience of Jesus Christ.

The reader will understand that I am not giving the above experience as a reason why anyone should accept the explanations set forth in this book, but only as my own reason for publishing it.

A good test of the explanation of any part of the Apocalypse is its agreement, or otherwise, with the design of the Book as a whole. If it be seen in the first place that the interpretation of a particular passage explains the symbols thereof consistently with the scriptural usage of those symbols, and without straining, forcing, or in anyway manipulating them; and if it then be found to be in harmony with the design of the Book as a whole, and specially with that of the particular group to which it pertains, it may be safely accepted as correct. For the true solution of every complicated problem proves itself by the fact that it explains and agrees with every feature thereof.

Take for example the trumpet series. All the visions in that group should have a common character, in agreement with the biblical significance of a trumpet. So the explanation of every trumpet vision must first of all meet *that* requirement. Then it must agree with the explanation of each of the other trumpet visions, and stand in proper chronological order with respect thereto. And finally, the entire trumpet series must be so explained as to be in agreement with all the other groups, in such wise as to constitute with them a complete and harmonious design, answering to the declared purposes for which the Apocalypse was written. I think the explanations given herein can bear this test.

In the preparation of this book I have been guided throughout by the principles, *first,* that the Apocalypse is written not in common speech, like the other Books of the New Testament, but in the *sign language;* and *second,* that every sign, symbol, or figure *is interpreted somewhere in the Bible.* What Hengstenberg said is most true: "The seer of the Apocalypse lives entirely in Holy Scripture". And so is Zullig's remark to the same effect: "The Book hardly ever refers to anything that is not Biblical". Therefore in the Bible itself the explanation of every symbol is to be sought; and there too it may be found, if diligent search be made.

And here we have an exceedingly strong proof of the authenticity of the Book, and that it is the Divine ending to the sacred Volume. For the Apocalypse sends those who would search out its treasures, to *every part of the Bible,* thereby proving its relation to all the other Books, as an essential part of one design. On the other hand, the diverse rays of light that spring up from every part of the Bible, point onward to, and converge upon, this final Book.

In entering upon the study of the Apocalypse, one is met at the threshold by certain questions which he must needs settle before he can advance. These preliminary questions relate to the main divisions of the Book, and to the relations they bear one to another, in respect both to their subject matter, and also to their sequence, that is to say, to the chronological order of the events they severally symbolize. For there are two conflicting systems of interpretation that claim our careful consideration, namely, the *Historicist,* and the *Futurist;* and the difference between them is great.

1. *The Historicist System*

This is the generally accepted Protestant view of the Book, a prominent feature thereof being that it regards the first beast of Chapter XIII as representing the Church of Rome, and the second as representing the Papacy. According to this system, the things seen in the several groups of visions of Chapters VI to XX (from the opening of the first seal to the beginning of the Millennium) are events that were to happen during this present gospel dispensation. Hence, expositors of this school seek the fulfilment of those visions in the historical events of the Christian Era. And generally, though not perhaps unanimously, they regard the several groups as following each other in regular chronological order; that is to say, the seven seals are supposed to begin at the days of the apostles and to carry us along a few centuries; and then the trumpet group begins where the seals leave off; and then the vials in like manner. According to this view, as elaborated by its able exponents, Newton, Birks, Guinness and many others, all or nearly all the prophecies of the Book down to the Millennium have now been fulfilled.

I find certain serious defects in this system; chiefly that it ignores what seems to me a very plain fact, namely, that the visions of the several groups are arranged not with respect to the period of time in which the things they picture are to happen, but with respect to their character, or subject matter. Thus, the things symbolized by the seals have the same general character, so with the trumpets; and so with the vials. For surely, the fact that certain things are grouped together under a certain emblem that is common to them all, whereas other things are grouped together under another emblem, common to them, but very different from the first, is proof that the grouping is *topical* and not *chronological*. Therefore, one of the main conclusions underlying the present exposition is that *each of the several groups is complete in itself,* and that its starting-point in time must be determined without any reference at all to the point in time at which the preceding group ended. Thus the groups may, or may not, overlap; that is to say, one group may take us again over a period of time already traversed by a preceding group, in order to reveal events of a different character, or in a different sphere. This feature of the independence of each group from the others I regard as of prime importance, insomuch that, if disregarded, the interpretation must needs be erroneous. It is a feature that characterizes other parts of the Bible. A conspicuous and instructive instance is found at the very beginning thereof. For the first section of Genesis (Chap. 1:1-2:3), is complete in itself. It gives a consecutive account of the creative acts of the six days, including the creation of man, male and female; and it goes on to the seventh day, upon which God rested from all His work. The next section of the Book, which begins at verse 4 of Chapter II, does not take up the account where the first leaves off, but goes back to the work of the third day, giving particulars concerning the origin of plant life; and then it comes to the sixth day, and gives a detailed description of the creation of the first man and first woman. Precisely the same method is seen again and again in Revelation. Thus, for example, the series of the seven seals gives an account of consecutive happenings up to the day of wrath (sixth seal) and takes us on to the silence in heaven (a sabbath) at the opening of the seventh seal. Then the visions of the trumpet group go back, and give particulars of eras embraced in the preceding visions of the seals. This example is the more noteworthy because of the marked correspondences in other respects between Genesis, the Book of the old creation, and Revelation, the Book of the new creation.

Another objection to the Historicist system is that its explanations are often materialistic, sometimes grotesquely so. It seeks an interpretation of every vision in some historical event—a battle, an invasion, a revolution—or some happening of a purely physical kind; and often it is exceedingly difficult to see any resemblance between the symbol and the thing it is supposed to represent. But to me, the Book is essentially *spiritual* in character; and while it certainly has much to do with human affairs and other happenings on earth, yet it has much to do also with happenings on the spiritual, or unseen, side of creation. This will appear clearly in the course of the exposition.

2. The Futurist System

This system of interpretation has gained the acceptance of many writers and students of prophecy during the past forty years. Apparently its popularity is due largely to Dr. Seiss' *Lectures on the Apocalypse;* for there is little in current writings of the futurists that is not found in those Lectures. According to this view, *all the visions from and including Chapter IV to the end of the Book are yet future; and none will begin to be fulfilled until the resurrection and rapture of the saints* (1 Thess. 4:14-17; 1 Cor. 15:51, 52) *shall have taken place.* It is a distinctive feature of the Futurist system that all the events and eras pictured in Chapters IV to XX. 6, inclusive (*i. e.* to the beginning of the Millennium) are to take place in the short space of seven years; and that this fateful period, into which all these stupendous events are to be crowded, is the last "week" of the seventy weeks of years mentioned in the famous prophecy of Daniel 9:24-27. For it is held by commentators of this school that the seventieth "week" was not continuous with the other sixty-nine, but is to be viewed as a disconnected period of time, which will be fitted in at the end of the Christian Era, filling the interval between Christ's coming *for,* and His coming *with,* His people.

It will be recognized by all who consider the matter with any degree of care, that the Futurist view is a radical one, involving departures of a very material character from the view that has been taken by Protestant expositors in general. For that reason it should not be accepted without a diligent inquiry first as to the foundations upon which it rests. Having held that view for a number of years I was, of course, reluctant to part with it; and the more so because it is the teaching of so many of those who, in these last days, are standing firmly for the truth of the gospel of Christ. But a painstaking examination of the matter has satisfied me that the futurist interpretation lacks the support of scriptural evidence; whereas, for the historical fulfilment of many of these prophetic visions, we have *all the proof there ever can be in such a case;* namely, the correspondence of the event with the thing foretold.

Therefore, to those who hold the futurist view of the Apocalypse, my word is this: You must needs admit upon the proof offered in the following pages, *first,* that the events therein referred to have happened, and the conditions therein described have existed, during this present era; and *second,* that those events and conditions do correspond closely with the prophetic visions of the Book; and that is all I ask. If beyond that you think there is reason to expect a further and more complete fulfilment after Christ shall have come for His people, there is nothing to forbid. I can only say that I do not share that expectation.

One strong objection I now see to the Futurist viewpoint is that it tends to quench one's interest in this wonderful Book, by pushing the things it predicts far away from us, making its transcendently important revelations to be for those of a coming dispensation, the so-called "tribulation saints", and thus virtually detaching it from the rest of the Bible. On an occasion, some years ago, when I raised a question about this with one who held the Futurist view, he suggested that we should not grudge to the "tribulation saints" one Book out of the sixty-six in the Bible. But I do most decidedly grudge it to them, and the more so because I am firmly persuaded that the "tribulation saints" of the Futurist system are altogether an imaginary company; and that we, the Lord's people of this dispensation, are the true "tribulation saints" (John 16:33; Ac. 14:22; and see comments below on Rev. 7:14).

After I had completed my preliminary studies, and had made considerable progress in the writing of the present volume, Hengstenberg's valuable commentary, written more than seventy-five years ago (and previously quite unknown to me) came by chance into my hands. I was gratified to find in it (as will appear by quotations here and there) a confirmation of conclusions I had reached in regard to some of the more important visions. I am indebted also to the author of that exposition for light upon several specific passages. But as to his exposition as a whole, it seems to me that, to use one of his own favorite expressions, "it swims in the air". For his interpretations of the major groups are not attached to any definite events or epochs; and even the Millennium is left floating about, as a thing that has had its fulfilment somewhere in the time past of this present dispensation. This is "postmillennialism" of a sort I had not hitherto heard of.

My expectation is that the present volume will at least serve the useful purpose of awakening fresh interest at this time in the study of the Apocalypse, a thing much to be desired. This I believe the reading of it will do, regardless of whether the reader views the Book from the historicist, or from the futurist standpoint. And my expectation also is that it will prove helpful in the study of Bible Symbology in general. I feel confident that the right lines of interpretation have been followed, and that the various groups of visions have been correctly explained as to their main features. Yet there remain many questions to be answered, affording abundant opportunity for further study in various directions. Particularly is further light to be sought with respect to some of the numerical symbols.

And now, with praise and thanksgiving to Him Who gave us this "Revelation of Jesus Christ," for the hours spent and meditations enjoyed in the study of it, and for the sustaining strength and help therein that could have come from no other source, I commit to His use, and invoke His blessing upon, this humble effort to edify His saints, heartily uniting with all who can say: "Unto Him that loveth us, and hath washed us from our sins in His own blood, and hath made us kings and priests unto God and His Father; to Him be glory and dominion for ever and ever, Amen".

Framingham, Mass., June 30, 1925.

CHAPTER I

Outlines and Major Divisions of the Book

IN ENTERING upon the study of this wonderful Book we should keep always in mind that what we have before us is the Revelation of *Jesus Christ*. It is not the revelation of things to come, though it has to do largely therewith. It is not the revelation of the four horsemen, nor of the woman clothed with the sun, nor of the ten horned beast, nor of the scarlet woman, nor of the fall of Babylon, nor of the New Jerusalem, but—of JESUS CHRIST. Therefore we should be ever on the alert to observe how, and in what various connections, Christ is revealed in the different divisions of the Prophecy. For Christ is central in every part of the Book, and every group of symbols derives its significance from Him.

With this thought in mind, and remembering also that the groupings of the symbols are according to topics, or subject-matter, and not necessarily according to chronological order, let us take a rapid survey of the entire Book, and thus familiarize ourselves in a general way with the several subjects here revealed in their relations to the Lord Jesus Christ.

Chapters I-III. Emphasis is here laid upon the foundation truth concerning Christ that He is the Alpha and Omega, the Beginning and the Ending, the First and the Last (vv. 8, 11). He is here fully identified with "Him which is, and which was, and which is to come, the Almighty" (vv. 4, 8). In these chapters He is revealed as the great Head of the Church (Eph. 1:22; Col. 1:18), giving His message, by the Spirit, to the angels of the seven churches, a special message covering the entire dispensation, and intended for all the churches of Christ (2:7, 11, 17, 29; 3:6, 13, 22). It is easy to see that in this entire vision we have but one general subject, Christ in relation to the churches, and that with the next vision (Chap. IV) there is a complete change of subject. Happenings in a different sphere altogether from that of the churches of Christ are pictured to us from this point on to the end of the Book. Hence the question arises, do these events belong to the same era as that in which the churches of Christ are in the world, or to a subsequent era? Do they run parallel to the history of the churches, or do they lie entirely beyond the last chapter of that history? The latter view is that of the futurist school of interpretation, which is in favor with many students of prophecy in our day. But I have been constrained to reject that view as contrary to the evidence, which points clearly to the conclusion that the design of the Book as a whole is to give to the people of God (Christ's "servants") a foreview of those events of the Christian era which in God's estimation thereof are most important, and would best serve to sustain their faith and patience during the long period of waiting for the coming again of the Lord from heaven. For it seems very clear to me that, as another has said:—

"The Revelation gives no regularly progressive disclosure of the future, advancing in unbroken series from beginning to end; but it falls into a number of groups, which indeed supplement each other, every successive vision giving some other aspect of the future, but which are still formally complete in themselves, each proceeding from a beginning to an end".

Chapters IV-VII. Here we have a vision of heaven and the throne of God therein. Christ is now seen in a very different character, being symbolized as "a Lamb as it had been slain". In that character He takes the throne and receives the book sealed with seven seals. So we here behold the Lord as Redeemer and Heir, receiving the Kingdom He has gained by His redemptive work (Dan. 7:13, 14; Lu. 19:12, 15) including "all power (authority) *in heaven* and *in earth*" (Mat. 28:18). He thereupon proceeds to exercise this authority by opening successively the seals of the book; and as the seals are opened on the throne of heaven, world-embracing events take place on earth, whereby, as will be seen hereafter, the course of history throughout this entire dispensation from beginning to end, was to be shaped.

Chapters VII to XI. 18. The era of this vision (or series of visions) is that of the seven trumpets. It is characterized by visitations in judgment upon the denizens of earth, at first comparatively mild in their nature, but increasing in severity, and culminating in the three "Woe"—trumpets, the last of which ushers in the day of wrath and revelation of the righteous judgment of God (Rom. 2:5). As the purpose of a trumpet is to sound a loud, far-reaching warning (Ezek. 33:3) so the events of this series are warnings to men and nations to take heed to their ways, and to flee from the wrath to come, by submitting to the will of God and the authority of His King. In this series Christ appears, not in the likeness of a Son of man, girt as Head and Lord of His churches, nor as a Lamb newly slain, but as a mighty "Angel". In Chapter 8:3-5, He stands at the golden altar, and "much incense" is given Him, which He adds to *(marg.)* the prayers of all the saints. Inasmuch as no creature could minister at that altar, or offer the prayers of *"all* the saints" to God, or add any merit or worthiness (incense) thereto, it is clear that Christ Himself is represented by this symbol. What this has to do with the action of the trumpets will appear later on.

Again, just before the sounding of the last trumpet, He is seen as a mighty Angel, whose face is as the sun and His feet as pillars of fire (cf. Chap. 1:15, 16); and to the accompaniment of a loud voice, as when a lion roareth, and of the seven thunders, He places His right foot upon the sea and His left on the earth, thereby showing that all things have been put under His feet (Eph. 1:22), and announces the speedy ending of "the mystery of God" (Chap. 10:1-7).

Chapters XII, XIII. "The days of the voice of the seventh angel" (10:7) were to be an era of transcendent importance, that in which the eternal purpose of God in the creation of man (Gen. 1:26) was to be accomplished. That purpose was to be fulfilled not in Adam, the first man, but in the Son of man, and specifically in the woman's "Seed". In keeping with this, Christ is revealed in this vision first as the "Man child Who was to rule all nations with a rod of iron", whom the dragon, "that *old* serpent" (as old as the days of Eden, and older,) sought to destroy, but who was caught up to God and His throne (12:5).

Chapters XIV-XVIII. Another vision, marking another division of the Book, begins at Chapter 14:1, with the words: "And I looked and lo, a Lamb stood on the mount Sion". The period of this vision is the last part of the days of the voice of the seventh angel, marked by the outpouring of the vials of wrath, the overthrow of the Kingdom of the beast, and the fall of Babylon.

In this era the rule of rebellious man, human government in its opposition to God, reaches its culmination in the reign of the beast. After contemplating this development on earth, John looks in another direction and sees on Mount Sion (where God said He would put *His* King, Ps. 2:6) a Lamb, and with Him a hundred and forty-four thousand, having His Father's Name in their foreheads (Chap. 14:1). Christ is also seen in this vision as One like a Son of man, seated upon a cloud, having upon His head a golden crown, and in His hand a sharp sickle, with which He is about to reap the harvest of the earth (14:14, 15).

Here again, as is easy to see, Christ is revealed in characters which are in keeping with the subject of the vision.

Chapters XIX, XX. This vision opens with transports of joy in heaven, amidst which "the marriage of the Lamb" is announced (19:1-7); and then John sees heaven opened, and a wondrous vision of Christ is given as the "Faithful and True" (v. 11), as "The Word of God" (v. 13), and as "KING OF KINGS, AND LORD OF LORDS" (v. 16).

Chapters XXI, XXII. In these last chapters we are brought to the "new heaven and new earth," to the eternal state and the heavenly Jerusalem. There is here no symbolic representation of Christ, but we are told that the Lord God Almighty and the Lamb are the temple of the Holy City, and that "the Lamb is the light thereof" (21:22, 23). And at the end His voice is heard again speaking to John as at the beginning, declaring once more that He is "Alpha and Omega, the Beginning and the End, the First and the Last," and giving the thrice-repeated assurance, "I come quickly."

Thus it will be seen that the Book as a whole is composed of seven distinct groups of visions. This sevenfold structure is one of the prominent characteristics of the Book.

Divisions and Sub-Divisions

Looking at the contents of the Book from another point of view, we observe that the greater part

Outlines and Major Divisions of the Book 17

thereof is composed of five distinct programs or groups, which are easily identified, and marked off from each other and from other portions, by the fact that each comprises a complete series of seven. These are:—

1. The Seven Churches (Ch. II, III).
2. The Seven Seals (Ch. VI-VIII).
3. The Seven Trumpets (Ch. VIII-XI).
4. The Seven Visions of Chapter XIV.
5. The Seven Vials (Ch. XVIII).

Further we observe that, in addition to these five groups, each composed of exactly seven distinct parts, there are other visions, which are introduced at various points, and which have a special bearing upon what follows next after their respective appearances. These are:—

1. The vision of Christ in the midst of the seven candlesticks (Ch. I). This introduces the letters to the seven Churches.

2. The vision of the throne in heaven, the Lamb taking the throne, and receiving the book sealed with seven seals (Ch. IV, V). This introduces the program of the seals.

3. The vision of the sealing of 144,000 of all the tribes of Israel, and of the innumerable company out of all nations (Ch. VII). This vision occurs between the 6th and 7th seals. It plainly pertains to the day of wrath (6th seal), and signifies the restraining of the destroying storm ("four winds") until all the elect are gathered out (Mat. 13:30).

4. The vision of the angel at the golden altar, who offers the prayers of all saints, with much incense added thereto (Ch. VIII). This introduces the program of the trumpets.

5. The vision of the mighty Angel whose face was like the sun, who had in his hand a little book open, and who set one foot on the sea, and the other on the dry land, and swore that the mystery of God should be finished in the days of the voice of the seventh angel (Ch. X). This introduces the immensely important era of the 7th trumpet. And here we find a special group of prophecies, apparently those of the little book which John was commanded to eat. They are found in Chapters XII, XIII, XIV.

6. The vision of the measuring of the temple of God, and of the two witnesses (Ch. XI). This vision also precedes the sounding of the seventh trumpet.

7. The panoramic vision of the sun-clothed woman, the great red dragon and the Man-child (Ch. XIV). This leads into the vision of the ten-horned beast that rose up out of the sea, and of the two-horned beast that rose up later out of the earth (Ch. XIII).

8. The vision of the company standing upon a sea of glass, who sing the song of Moses and the song of the Lamb (Ch. XV). This introduces the program of the vials.

9. The vision of the woman on the ten-horned beast (Ch. XVII). This adds further details of the reign of the beast.

10. The vision of the fall of Babylon (Ch. XVII), giving additional particulars concerning the day of wrath.

11. The vision in heaven acclaiming the approach of the marriage of the Lamb (Ch. XIX). This introduces the coming of Christ in judgment to execute vengeance on His enemies (2 Thess. 1:7-10), and to reign with His saints a thousand years.

12. The vision of the New Jerusalem (Ch. XXI).

The first of the main divisions of the Book, which embraces the messages to the seven churches and the introductory vision of Christ in the midst of the seven golden candlesticks, is different in character from the other four. It is composed mainly of a series of letters dictated by the Lord Jesus Christ, each to a different church. There is no action at all in the three chapters which make up that first division of the Apocalypse. The other four series of sevens, on the contrary, are all action, and often of the liveliest character.

Then again, the theater of the first series is that wherein Christ is owned as Lord — the churches; whereas the theater of the other four series is the hostile world, by which He is rejected. To that world He has nothing to say in addition to what He has already said, and is saying, through the gospel. There is no new message and no further message for the world; and even when, at the very end of time, an angel flies in mid-heaven with a special word to them that dwell on the earth, even to every nation, and kindred, and tongue and people, that word is none other than "the everlasting gospel" (Rev. 14:6). What the Spirit has further to say in this last Book of the Bible is not to men in general, but "to the churches". Indeed this Book is peculiar in this, among other things, that God gave it to Jesus Christ to show unto His servants—not to any others. No wonder then that to many it appears to be a bewildering jumble of meaningless and ill-assorted objects, animate and inanimate.

We note then that there is one series of sevens which has to do with the spiritual realm—the churches—and is in *plain words* from the lips of Jesus Christ; and then follow four series of sevens that have to do with the physical realm—the world and its inhabitants; and these latter are expressed in *symbols* that serve to hide their meanings from all who are not the servants of the Lord Jesus Christ.

A careful observation of these main divisions and prominent features of the Book, and their relations to one another, will help greatly to an understanding of the details of the several visions.

But we would look a little more closely at the relations which the several major divisions (especially the five series of sevens mentioned above) bear to one another.

1. The first series—the messages to the churches—is in a class by itself; and inasmuch as it is given in

ordinary language, not in symbols (though it contains many figurative expressions), it offers no special difficulty.

2. The program of the Seals is comprehensive; for it embraces all the three subsequent programs. It extends from the time Christ ascended into heaven and occupied the throne of God, taking into His hands the seven-sealed book, down to the sabbath-silence in heaven that ensued upon the opening of the seventh seal.

This series has an important distinction, namely, that each successive stage of it is introduced by an action of the Lamb in Person—the breaking of a seal; whereas in the other programs the successive stages are introduced by the mediation of angels.

3. The program of the Trumpets begins at some period of time prior to the day of wrath (sixth seal) and continues to and into that great and terrible day. Its character throughout is that of *warnings,* in the form of visitations of a calamitous nature, increasing in severity, all with the object of bringing men to repentance.

4. The program of Chapter XIV lies wholly in the latter part of the era of the Trumpets. The events of this series follow one another in rapid succession; and there are clear indications, as will be seen later on, that their location is just before the end, probably between the Sixth and Seventh Trumpets. This series gives us a look behind the scenes, showing us happenings on the spiritual side of creation at the time of the

end, whereas Chapter XIII shows events on the material side.

5. The program of the Vials is the most limited of all. Its period is the latter part of "the days of the voice of the seventh angel". It is the very end of the day of wrath.

As to the Symbols Used in the Book

The language of this Book for the most part is not that of common life. It is the language often used by the O. T. prophets, in which the meaning is conveyed mainly by symbols drawn from nature, or from human affairs. Therefore a knowledge of common language will not carry one very far in the interpretation of this Book. One must know the meaning of the symbols found in it, which are many and of extraordinary variety. The first verse notifies us that the Book is written in the language of *signs;* for it is there stated that Christ sent and "Signified" it, that is, communicated it by *signs,* to His servant John.

These signs or symbols are such as are used in prophetic dreams, as those of Joseph, of Pharaoh's officers, of Pharaoh himself, of Nebuchadnezzar; and in the visions of Ezekiel, Daniel, Zechariah, and other prophets. To these therefore we must go, and we must search them carefully for whatever information is to be had from them concerning the symbols used in Revelation. Some of the symbols are explained in the Book itself (e. g. 1:20; 17:12, 15, 18); and from other parts of the Scriptures, as those just mentioned, all the light we need as to the meaning of the symbols is to be had.

Such being the character of the Book, we must be ever on our guard against looking for literal fulfilments of the symbols, as for the destruction of literal ships in the sea, or of literal trees and grass, and for literal hail, earthquakes, etc. For the sea is a symbol (as we are plainly told), and of course the "ships" therein must also be symbols; and so with other things in all parts of the Book. Many, we believe, have gone astray through not observing this most necessary caution.

But it is possible, and indeed easy, to err on the other side also. For not everything named in the Book is a symbol. Hence it is sometimes a difficult matter to decide whether a certain thing is presented in its own proper character, or as a representation of something else.

Again, we must not expect always to find the things symbolized in the realm of the physical; for there are important happenings which lie wholly in the realm of the spiritual, whereof only the effects are manifest to human senses. Creation has two sides, the visible (to mortal eyes) and the invisible; and the Book we are studying is an account of things that were to happen both in the realm of the seen and in that of the unseen. Angels and principalities and powers, both good and evil, are as much involved in the happenings of this Book, as earthly dominions, nations, and potentates. The book whose seven seals were successively broken by the Lamb on the throne, and which was gradually unrolled by Him, was written on *both* sides, indicating that the things contained in it pertained both to the outer realm of nature, and the inner realm of the spirit.

And furthermore, some of the earthly things symbolized are not of a tangible sort, but are in the nature of a political or religious movement or development, as the rise of the Papacy, the Protestant Reformation, and the like.

These are some of the matters it is needful for us to keep in mind as we seek for the interpretation of the symbols used in this Book.

In What Era is the Fulfilment of These Visions to be Sought?

Out of respect for those expositors who have adopted the futurist system of interpretation and for the many who have accepted their views, I feel called upon, before proceeding to the detailed exposition of the Book, to set forth fully the reasons why I believe that "the words of this prophecy" refer to events that were to happen *in,* and not *after,* this present dispensation. And we have not to seek far or dig deep to find ample reason to warrant that belief; for the very first verse states that God's purpose in giving this revelation to Jesus Christ was that He might "show unto His servants things which must *shortly come to pass*". These words are not at all ambiguous, and the simple-minded would never sus-

Outlines and Major Divisions of the Book 25

pect that they could have been intended to convey any other than their ordinary and apparent meaning, namely, that the things foretold in "this prophecy" were to happen in the era that was just then beginning. The word here rendered "shortly" means *just that*. It is variously translated in other Scriptures by the words *quickly, speedily, soon*. Thus, in Acts 25:4, Festus, after commanding that Paul be kept at Caesarea, said that "he himself would depart *shortly* thither". In Philippians 2:19 Paul writes, "I trust to send Timotheus unto you *shortly*". And so also in 1 Timothy 3:14; Hebrews 13:23; and 2 Peter 1:14. In Galatians 1:6 we have, "so *soon* removed"; in Philippians 2:33, "so *soon* as I shall see how it will go with"; and in 2 Thessalonians 2:2, "That ye be not *soon* shaken in mind."

Such being the invariable usage of the word in the N. T., it is inconceivable that it would have been employed in the first sentence of this Book if the things revealed in it were not to begin to happen until the entire dispensation should have run its course.

Furthermore, the persons that were to be benefited by this "Revelation of Jesus Christ" were God's "servants", and first of all those servants who were living at that time, represented by "His servant John". This should suffice to settle the question; for if the things foreshown in these Patmos visions are not to begin to happen until the servants of Christ, one and all, shall have left this scene, of what possible use could these predictions, so carefully veiled in symbols, be to them? After the rapture of the saints the servants of Christ will all be with Him (1 Th. 4:17) and the happenings on earth at that time will be displayed clearly before their eyes. Symbolical representations thereof would be useless to them. On the other hand we know that, as a matter of fact, the servants of Christ, all down the centuries of our era, have sought to trace the course of historic events in connection with the great epochs and the many vicissitudes of the Kingdom of God by the light of this wonderful Book, not doubting at all that it had been given them for that very purpose. Were they deceived? And if so, were they to blame for taking the words we have quoted as meaning here what they invariably mean wherever elsewhere they are used in the N. T.?

But furthermore, the promised blessing of verse 3 to those that read, hear and keep the words of this prophecy, is predicated expressly upon the fact that "the time is at hand". This statement also is free from uncertainty.

And finally, at the very end of the Book these statements are repeated in emphatic terms. For John records concerning the revealing angel: "And he saith unto me, These sayings are faithful and true: and the Lord God of the holy prophets sent His angel to show *unto His servants the things which must shortly be done*" (22:6); this being a re-affirmation of what is stated in the first verse of the Book. And again: "And he (the angel) saith unto me, Seal not the sayings of the prophecy of this book: *for the time is at hand*"

(22:10). This is an important and an enlightening statement, because it is manifestly intended to be read in contrast with the statement made by the revealing angel to Daniel concerning the visions given to him: "But thou, O Daniel, shut up the words, and seal the book, even to the time of the end" (Dan. 12:4). The visions whereof the angel was speaking were those beginning at Chapter 9:24, and had to do with "the latter days" (10:14) of the national existence of Daniel's people, including the coming of Christ, His rejection and crucifixion, the awful overthrow of the city and sanctuary by the Romans, and "the time of trouble such as never was since there was a nation even to that same time". Those events were yet five hundred years in the future at the time they were made known to Daniel. Hence he was commanded to "shut up the words, and seal the book to the time of the end"; and with this ran the promise "The wise shall understand" (Dan. 12:10); which promise was fulfilled to the disciples of Christ when He "opened their understanding that they might understand the Scriptures" (Lu. 24:25). But John is commanded to seal *not* the sayings of the prophecy of *this* Book, for the express reason that "the time is at hand". I do not see how we can avoid the conclusion that the visions of John differed from those of Daniel in that while Daniel's related to a time that was about five centuries in the future, John's related to a time that was to begin forthwith. And I here anticipate somewhat by pointing out how perfectly this accords with the words of the voice that summoned John to heaven, saying: "Come up hither, and I will show thee things which must be *hereafter*" (4:1).

These statements are one and all so clear and simple, and it is so natural and reasonable to take them in their apparent and ordinary sense, that futurist expositors are faced at the outset with the embarrassing task of explaining them away, and of making it appear that the familiar words "shortly", "at hand", and "hereafter" are used in these passages with special meanings quite different from what they bear elsewhere in the Word of God. As to this I can only say that the best of the reasons that have been given in support of that view seem to me exceedingly unconvincing and I am glad to be relieved of the necessity of explaining away the obvious meaning of familiar words and phrases, and to feel free to accept them according to their common usage both in the Bible and out of it. For as Hengstenberg has observed, the statements upon which we have been dwelling "are opposed to the view of those who would convert the entire Book into a history of the time of the end, and confirm the view which treats it as our companion through the whole course of history." Further he aptly says: "The boundless energy of the Divine Nature admits of no delay. There is nothing of quiescence or indolent repose in God. His appearing often to linger is merely on account of our short-sightedness. He is secretly working for salvation and destruction, when He seems to us, perhaps, to be standing aloof; and only when by the execution of His judgment we are called to enter His salvation, do we learn consequently what is meant by the 'shortly'. . . . God be praised that we are never pointed to the far distant future."

Another weighty consideration may appropriately be mentioned here. It is found in the character of the more prominent symbols of the Book. These are of grand and imposing proportions, such as to demand, for the great events and epochs represented by them, time measures on the scale of centuries. The going forth of the four horses and the accomplishment of their several missions; the great events of world-wide importance that follow the successive trumpets; the history of the sun-clad woman, the Man-child, and the dragon, the war in heaven, the woman's sojourn in the wilderness, and the persecution of her seed by the dragon; the rise, one after the other, of the two great beasts, and the development of their dominion over all the world; the career and overthrow of "Mystery Babylon" (the harlot), and of commercial Babylon (the great city);—all these are things of vast dimensions, requiring for any one of them a correspondingly great stretch of time.

How contrary then to all reason, as well as to the meaning borne upon the face of the symbols themselves, is any system of interpretation that would crowd all these great and expansive prophecies into the space of seven years, and which requires that the most stupendous world-events, events that in their very nature demand long periods of years, should rush at jig-time across the stage of human history, following upon one another's heels so closely as to leave not even breathing-space between!

The space of seven years in which all these tremendous happenings are assumed to take place is less than that which at the date of this writing (1925) already separates us from the late world-war, the effects of which are but just developing. And that was but an episode of world-history. Any one of these visions would require for its fulfilment many times the space of seven years.

The Analogy of Scripture

But there is weightier reason still for the view we are here taking. It is found in the voice of Scripture itself. For the symbols of the horses and of the wild beasts are used in Old Testament prophecy, the former in Zechariah, and the latter in Daniel. The symbols of the beasts are explained in Chapters 7 and 8 of Daniel's prophecy, so there is happily no room for question as to their meaning. The four great beasts that Daniel saw were four Kingdoms or world-powers that were to arise out of the earth (Dan. 7:17). Each one of those empires lasted *many times seven years;* and the last of them (the Roman) more than twice seven centuries. In the case of the Macedonian empire, we have in the meteoric career of Alexander the Great, a conquest of extraordinary rapidity, insomuch that it is represented by a he-goat moving so swiftly that he "touched not the ground" (Dan. 8:5-8). Yet the full development of the small part of human history that is represented by that beast, required centuries of time.

This should suffice to establish the matter; but the evidence is stronger yet. For it has been noticed by all commentators and indeed is too plain to escape attention, that the first beast of Revelation 13 closely resembles the fourth of Daniel 7, and has, moreover, some characteristic of each of the other three. Now practically all expositors are agreed that Daniel's fourth beast represents the Roman Empire, which was slow in its rising and development, and which occupied the stage of history for a period of many centuries. Daniel saw this beast, so "dreadful, terrible and strong" rise up out of the sea (Dan. 7:3); and John too saw a beast of the same description, only delineated more clearly, "arise up out of the sea." Can we close our eyes to these marked resemblances, and go so contrary to the clear indications they furnish, as to assign to the entire career of John's beast but a fraction of the utterly insignificant period of seven years? Would anyone do such a thing unless bound hand and foot by a theory of interpretation which requires it?

But looking further we observe that, as Daniel considered the horns of this fourth beast, a remarkable development took place. Another "little horn" came up among them, having eyes like the eyes of a man, and a mouth speaking great things. And Daniel was particularly impressed "because of the voice of the great words which the horn spake". We are not for the moment concerned with the question who (or what) that little horn represented. Regardless of how that question may be answered, the development was one that required a long period of time, to which must be added the period of the career of the little horn. Now there is just such a development in John's vision; for after giving various details concerning the beast with the seven heads and ten horns—details that suggest extended periods of time for their fulfilment—John speaks of seeing another beast coming up out of the earth, whose speech was that of a dragon. So here is something which, by analogy with Daniel's vision, must require for its fulfilment a long stretch of years.

Further it should be observed that John saw the actual rising up of each of these beasts, one after the other. Therefore the vision embraces in its scope the entire career of each of the two beasts. This fact alone would seem to be fatal to the futurist system of interpretation; for the futurists are agreed that the symbol of the ten-horned beast represents the Roman Empire. True, they say it represents only the *very last stage* of that Empire, the "revived Roman Empire", as it is generally expressed. But that restricted view of the significance of the symbol is not compatible with the statements that John saw the first beast actually coming upon the scene—"rise up out of the sea"—and that later on he "beheld another beast *coming up* out of the earth." These words declare in the clearest way that his vision embraced the actual coming into existence of the things represented by the two beasts respectively.

The futurist system should be tested also by what the Scriptures, both Old and New Testaments, declare to be one of the chief purposes for which prophecies are given, a matter to which the Lord Jesus Himself made repeated reference. Thus, through Moses, this test of true prophecy was given: "And if thou shalt say in thine heart, how shall we know the word which the Lord hath not spoken? When a prophet speaketh in the name of the Lord, if the thing *follow not,* nor come to pass, that is the thing which the Lord hath not spoken" (Deut. 18:21, 22). To the same effect the Lord Jesus said, "Now I tell you before it come, that *when it is come to pass, ye may believe that I am he";* and again, "And now I have told you before it come to pass, that, *when it is come to pass, ye might believe";* and yet again, "But these things have I told you, that *when the time shall come,* ye may remember that I told you of them" (John 13:19; 14:29; 16:4).

Thus prophecy is given that the faith of the people of God may be strengthened by the happening of the thing predicted. It is eminently suited to that end, being as clear a manifestation of Divine action as the working of a miracle. It is hardly necessary to point out that the postponement wholesale of the prophecies of this Book to a yet future dispensation would frustrate this important purpose, if indeed they were to be fulfilled in the christian era. Therefore we should refuse the futurist view until it is established by full and clear evidence.

The "Missing Week" of Daniel's Vision

It is one of the fundamental assumptions of the futurist system of interpretation that the last of the "Seventy Weeks" of Daniel 9:24-27 did not follow the sixty-ninth, but was detached from the others, and put off to the end of this present dispensation, and will fit into the course of time immediately after the catching away of the people of God (the "rapture") to meet the Lord in the air. This is spoken of as the "missing week"; and in this supposed "missing week" (seven years) all the stupendous events, epochs and eras of Revelation IV to XIX are to take place, according to the futurist system. I shall not discuss this fanciful idea in the present volume, having considered it at some length in my book, "The Seventy Weeks and the Great Tribulation".

What John Was Charged to Write

The futurist view rests mainly upon a peculiar interpretation of Chapter 1:19, "Write the things which thou hast seen, and the things which are, and the things which shall be hereafter". The futurists regard John's commission to write, given him in these words of Christ, as having three distinct and separate divisions. They further hold, and this is necessary to their system, that by "the things which thou hast seen" He meant only the vision described in Chapter 1, verses

12-16; that by "the things which are", He meant only what we have in Chapters II and III, the letters to the seven churches of Asia; and that by "the things which shall be hereafter", He meant events which then lay in the *far distant* future, *wholly beyond* this present dispensation.

This is a very artificial interpretation of the passage; and certainly it is far too questionable and too much open to dispute to serve as a foundation for what has been built upon it.

1. *"The things which thou hast seen"*. These words may indeed be limited to the single vision of Christ described in verses 12-18, though many commentators give them a meaning broad enough to include all the visions of the Book. I am not satisfied, however, by the reasoning which gives this clause so broad a meaning, and which requires us to assume that the introduction was written after the main portion of the Book. But we have to take notice of the words of verse 11, spoken before John had turned and seen the vision of Christ in the midst of the candlesticks: "What thou seest write in a book and send it unto the seven churches which are in Asia". This lends strong support to those who hold that the commission our Lord gave to John at this time related only to the messages to the seven churches, that is to say, to the first three chapters of the Apocalypse, and who point out that the letters to the churches contain things then future, as well as things present. So there is a serious question at the very threshold of our present inquiry, though while I

admit the matter is not entirely clear, my opinion is that what we have in Chapter I is intended as the introduction to the entire Book, and not to the first section thereof only.

2. *"And the things which are"*. This clause lends no support to the futurist view. Indeed it would be difficult to find a less appropriate title for the contents of Chapters II and III. What the futurist system, as based on its interpretation of 1:19, absolutely requires is that there should be a clearly marked division of the Book describing matters occurring in this present dispensation, ending with the coming of Christ for His people; and following that, another division describing events that are to happen thereafter. But we find nothing of that sort. What we *do* find is that the two chapters which the futurists arbitrarily designate "things which are", differ from the chapters that follow not as regards *the time* of occurrence of the things they describe, but as regards their *subject matter*. For Chapters II and III have to do exclusively with the churches of Christ. Their scope is limited strictly to things ecclesiastical. On the other hand, the subsequent chapters have nothing at all to do with the churches. Their scope, so far as they relate to matters on earth, is limited to the affairs of the nations of the world. This objection is fatal to the futurist system, since it is evident that, whatever be the nature of the "things which are", the "things which shall be hereafter", are things *of the same kind.* Furthermore, Chapters II and III do not contain *any description*

whatever of things as they were at that time. They are wholly occupied with letters to the angels of the seven churches of Asia. And those letters are not taken up with descriptions of things as they then were, but the contents of one and all consists in commendations, rebukes, promises, exhortations, and threatenings. Then again, they refer not only to the *then present* state of these several churches, but also to things *past,* and things that were *yet to happen.* Furthermore, the references they contain to things as they then were are not to "things which are" in general, but only in respect to the churches of Christ, and not to all of these, but to seven churches in the province of Asia. And finally, if we limit this clause, by reason of the context, to the churches of Asia, then to be consistent we should impose the same limitation upon the words "the things which shall be hereafter", which would be destructive of the futurist system. For it is clear that the clauses "things which are", and "things which shall be hereafter", are *strictly parallel,* the difference between them being not at all in the nature of the "things" themselves, but solely in the time of their occurrence. And since the things of Chapters IV to XXII have nothing to do with the affairs of the seven churches of Pro-consular Asia, or of any churches whatever, it is clear that it is inadmissable to take the words "things which are" as an inspired definition of messages which deal with the affairs—past, present, and future—of the seven designated churches. What also bears heavily against the futurist view of the words "things which are", is the fact that a charge to "write" is given to John at the beginning of each of the seven letters of Chapters II and III. This makes it highly improbable that the words, "write—the things which are", had any relation to those letters. Therefore, in view of all this, I can but give it as my deep conviction that the futurist system fails completely at this point.

3. *"And the things which shall be hereafter"*.

Here is where the futurist scheme is weakest; for it absolutely requires that the familiar and well-understood word "hereafter" be given a novel meaning, one that, so far as I am informed, it never bears. The word as we here find it, is unqualified by other words which might affect its meaning. Hence there is no justification whatever for taking it to mean historical events, all of which lay in a future and far distant dispensation. For to-morrow is just as much "hereafter" as two thousand years hence.

According to the futurist system, the "things which shall be hereafter" are those described in Chapters IV to XXII. That is to say, all that is foretold in those chapters is to be fulfilled in the next dispensation. But it is certain that the word "hereafter" does not have the effect of transporting all those things across the twenty centuries of our era and locating them in the next dispensation; and if the word "hereafter" does not have that effect, we shall look in vain for anything else capable of accomplishing such a prodigious dislocation.

Outlines and Major Divisions of the Book 39

The first verse of Chapter IV ends with the significant word "hereafter". Let us carefully note what it says, for just here is the crux of the matter.

"After this I looked, and behold, a door was opened in heaven; and the first voice that I heard was as it were of a trumpet talking with me; which said, Come up hither, and I will show thee things which must be *hereafter*".

From the last five words of this verse it is reasonable to infer that the visions John was now summoned on high to see were "the things which shall be hereafter", an account of which he was charged in Chapter 1:19 to write. And here again the familiar word "hereafter" is used without any qualifying terms, and with nothing whatever in the context to suggest that it is to be understood in any other than its ordinary sense. The statement is plain and the meaning unambiguous. John was taken up to heaven "in the spirit" (2.2), in order that he might be shown things that were to be thereafter, that is, from that time onward.

So far from there being anything in either the text or context to suggest that the word "hereafter" is to be given an extraordinary and unheard of signification, the fact is that the verse itself contains a sufficient reason for rejecting that idea as altogether untenable. For the phrase rendered "hereafter" *(meta tauta)* occurs also at the beginning of the verse, where it is rendered "After this". Thus the verse *begins and ends with identically the same phrase,* a phrase which is capable of being expressed in English by "hereafter", or "thereafter" or "after this", or "after these things", the last being the most literal rendering.

Now no one would maintain for a moment that the first *meta tauta* means after a lapse of several thousand years; and it is perfectly obvious that the passage affords just as much warrant for locating John's translation in spirit to heaven in the next dispensation, as for locating in that far distant day the things, and all of them, which he was given to see. For here we have a simple adverbial phrase which is *twice used in the very same sentence.* All must agree that where it first occurs it has its ordinary meaning, and that there is nothing whatever to indicate or to suggest a different meaning at its second occurrence. We are therefore bound to give it the same meaning at the end of the verse as at the beginning.

It should be noted that the words of this verse do not state or imply that the visions John was to see contained future things exclusively, but only that they had to do *mainly* with future things. For when the visions themselves are studied it will be seen that some of them start from events that had already taken place, and from those past events as a starting point, they carry us on to future things. In Chapter XII, for example, we have a panorama of a course of events that has its starting point in the first chapter of Genesis. It is true indeed that the design of the Book is to reveal future things; and it will be seen that past events are brought in only in order that the future things may be

Outlines and Major Divisions of the Book 41

set in their proper place in the particular line of historical events to which they severally belong.

Some have taken the words of Christ recorded in Revelation 1:19 as giving to John his complete commission for the writing of the three different parts of the New Testament whereof he was the scribe. They point out that the Gospel of John contains the things whereof John was an eye-witness—"the things which thou hast seen—"; that his Epistles deal with things as they were in his lifetime—"things which are—"; and that the Revelation contains things that were to happen thereafter—"things which shall be hereafter". This suggestion is worthy at least of thoughtful consideration; for there is nothing fanciful about it, it agrees with the facts, and it does no violence to the inspired language.

But, taking the verse as applying solely to the Book of the Revelation of Jesus Christ, we have only to read that verse according to a construction frequently used in the Greek language, and in the New Testament, in order to get a clear meaning. The point to be noted is that where, in English, clauses are connected by the conjunctions "both—and", or "even—and", in Greek it is "and—and". Thus the verse may with perfect propriety be rendered: "Write the things which thou hast seen, *both* (or *even*) the things which are, and also the things which shall be hereafter". This construction is frequently used by the Lord, as recorded by John. Thus in John 4:36 we have, "That *both* he that soweth *and* he that reapeth may rejoice together"; and in 7:28, "Ye *both* know Me, *and* ye know whence I am"; and in 15:24, "But now have they *both* seen *and* hated *both* Me *and* My Father".

Finally as regards this interesting point, we would call attention to the striking similarity between the commission the Lord here gives to His servant John from the glory, and the one which He had previously given Paul from the glory. For the commission given to Paul was likewise divided into two parts, things he had already seen, and things which were to be shown him thereafter. These are the Lord's words to Paul: "For I have appeared unto thee for this purpose, to make thee a minister and a witness *both of these things which thou hast seen,* and of *those things* in the which I *will appear unto thee"* (Acts 26:16).

In this connection there is a distinction which must be carefully observed in order to a right understanding of the plan of the Book. I refer to the difference between the order in which the visions were seen by John and described by him, and the order of the happening of the things revealed in the visions. For the order or sequence of the several visions shown to the seer is one thing, and the order or sequence of occurrence of the events symbolized is another thing; and through failure to observe this, certain commentators have been led into confusion. Thus, because the vision of the trumpets followed that of the seals, it has been assumed by some that the events of the trumpet-program begin where those of the seals left off; and so with the program of the vials. But by careful examination of the several programs it will be seen that the distinction between the several groups is topical, rather than chronological. That is to say, under the symbols of the seven seals is grouped a series of events of a certain character, under the trumpets another series of a different character, and under the vials another of a still different sort. It is evident, of course, that the events of each program follow in regular order, corresponding to the order in which their respective symbols appear. That is to say, the events symbolized under the first trumpet are followed by those symbolized under the second, and so on to the end of the seven. But it does not follow that the events of the first trumpet come next in order after those of the seventh seal. On the contrary it is quite plain that the sixth seal brings us to the day of wrath ("For the great day of *His wrath* is come", 6:17), whereas in following the line of developments under the trumpets, the day of wrath is not reached until we come to the days of the voice of the seventh angel, when we have the announcement, "And *Thy wrath* is come, and the time of the dead that they should be judged" (11:18). Since therefore the seventh trumpet ("the last trump", 1 Cor. 15:52) synchronizes with the sixth seal, it is clear that the two programs overlap, and that we must look for the events of the preceding six trumpets in the period of the first five seals.

This important feature of the plan of the Book first came to my knowledge when I noticed that a distinct topic begins at Chapter XII, namely, *God's purpose in the creation of man,* and that the panoramic vision of that chapter traces the development of that purpose, and the various attempts of the great Adversary to defeat it, from the beginning to the end. I was thus led to see that in other divisions of the Book the events symbolized are grouped with reference to their *character,* rather than with reference to *time*—that is to say, topically rather than chronologically. This will appear as we proceed; and it will be seen, I think, that the recognition of this feature of the plan of the Book, which has been pointed out by many commentators before myself, affords material help toward the understanding of its entire contents.

THE DATE OF THE APOCALYPSE

As to the time of the writing of the Book there is no need of a review of the evidence. While there has been some dispute about it, there appears to be ample support for the generally accepted view that the Book was written near the end of the first century, and that John's banishment to the Island of Patmos was during the persecution that broke out in the reign of the emperor Domitian, A. D. 81-95. Those who, like the Romanist expositors, wish to find the fulfilment of the judgments foretold by John in the destruction of Jerusalem, seek support for the view that John's banishment to Patmos, and the writing of the Apocalypse, were during the persecution that broke out in the reign of Nero (A. D. 54-68). But the available evidence lends no support to that view, the motive for which is quite apparent.

CHAPTER II

The Vision of the Son of Man

THE divisions of the first chapter of Revelation are clearly marked.

Verses 1, 2 give the inspired title of the Book, and its source. They also declare its purpose; and tell how it was communicated to John, the instrument chosen for writing it.

The title is, *The Revelation of Jesus Christ.*

The source of this Revelation is God the Father, who gave it to Him.

The Divine purpose or end to be accomplished by it was to show to the servants of Jesus Christ things which were shortly to happen.

The channel of communication was an angel ("His angel") of whom no particular description is given. That this angel was a being of exalted rank and dignity is evident from the fact that, when his mission in respect to John had been completed, John fell down to worship before him. For in Chapter 22:8, John says: "And I, John, saw these things and heard them. And when I had heard and seen, I fell down to worship before the feet of the angel which showed me these things. Then saith he unto me, See thou do it not; for I am thy fellow servant, and of thy brethren the prophets, and of them which keep the sayings of this Book: worship God". Again in 19:10, and a third time in 22:8, 9, John falls down before this revealing angel, to worship him, and is rebuked by him in words similar to those here recorded. There is yet another reference to this revealing angel in verse 16 of Chapter 22, where the Lord Jesus Himself says: "I Jesus have sent *Mine angel* to testify unto you these things in the churches".

The human writer of the Book gives his name, "John", and clearly identifies himself as he who bore record of the Word of God, and of the testimony of Jesus Christ, and of all things that he saw. Thus we have the assurance that this Book is by the same John that wrote the fourth Gospel.

There are several links in the chain whereby this Book reaches us. The Father gave it to Jesus Christ; Who commissioned His angel to bear it to John, to whom the angel communicated it by signs; and John was commanded to write it in a Book, which Book is now before us.

The Promised Blessing. Verse 3.

The book is of a character so strange, so unlike the other Books of the New Testament, and so difficult to understand, that the people of God might be disposed to turn away from it, and might even think it was not to be read by the simple believer. Therefore at the very beginning is a promise of blessing to him that readeth, and to them that hear the words of this prophecy, and to them that keep those things that are written therein.

This blessing is a striking and important feature of the Book, and careful heed should be given thereto.

The language of the verse suggests the thought that the Book would ordinarily be read aloud by one person ("him that readeth") and that others ("they that hear") would listen to the reading. Such would be, of course, the usual procedure at the beginning, and for many centuries thereafter; for copies of the Scriptures (all made by hand until the 16th century) were scarce; and the many would know their contents only by hearing them read aloud. In such a state of things there would be a natural tendency to read only favorite portions; hence arises the likelihood that this Book would suffer neglect. So we see good reason for this special encouragement to both reader and hearers.

The blessing is also for them that *keep* the things written herein; the word "Keep" signifying to guard as by having one's eye upon the thing to be kept, to hold fast to it, and not to let it get away.

Adam Clarke makes a suggestion, in regard to the purpose of the Book, that is worthy of consideration. It is this: "That the Book of the Apocalypse may be considered as a prophecy continued in the Church of God, uttering predictions relative to all times, which have their fulfilment as ages roll on; and thus it stands in the Christian Church in the place of a *succession of prophets* in the Jewish Church; and by this especial economy prophecy is still continued, is always speaking, and yet a succession of prophets rendered unnecessary. If this be so, we cannot too much admire the wisdom of the contrivance which still continues the voice and testimony of prophecy, by means of a very short Book, without the assistance of any extraordinary messenger, or any succession of messengers, whose testimony at all times would be liable to suspicion, and be subject of infidel and malevolent criticism, howsoever unexceptional to ingenuous minds the succession might appear."

If this be indeed the design of the Book, it is clear that it is frustrated in large measure by postponing the fulfilment of the major part thereof (all after Chapter III) to a time when the people of God will be no longer on earth.

Furthermore, it is evident that neglect of the Book would have been of little moment if the fulfilment of the prophecies written therein was not to begin for several thousand years. Hence the exhortation to read, to hear and to keep the things written in this Book, is coupled with a reason which seems to have been added for the very purpose of dispelling the idea that there was to be delay in the fulfilment of the words of this prophecy; the reason for the exhortation being that "the time is *at hand*".

In these words there is a manifestly intended contrast with the command given to Daniel concerning the visions seen by him. For he was bidden to "shut up the words and *seal the book,* even to the time of the end" (Dan. 12:4). But John is not to seal the description of his visions, for the time thereof was not far off; it was near.

What might be the nature of the promised blessing of verse 3 is not stated; but the fact that the promise is not specific makes it all the larger. The blessing is repeated at Chapter 22:7 in the words: "Behold, I come quickly: blessed is he that keepeth the sayings of the prophecy of this book".

This "Blessed" is the first of a complete series of seven beatitudes found in this Book, which marks it as a characteristic feature of the Book, and adds to its impressiveness. This is the series:—

Chap. 1:3, "Blessed is he that readeth" etc.

Chap. 14:13, "Blessed are the dead that die in the Lord from henceforth".

Chap. 16:15, "Blessed is he that watcheth and keepeth his garments".

Chap. 19:9, "Blessed are they which are called unto the marriage supper of the Lamb".

Chap. 20:6, "Blessed and holy is he that hath part in the first resurrection".

Chap. 22:7, "Blessed is he that keepeth the sayings of the prophecy of this book".

Chap. 22:15, "Blessed are they that do his commandments".

The Address to the Seven Churches. Verses 4, 5.

This is most impressive. Never was a communication from Deity itself given with such a setting forth of the majesty and glory of the Source whence it came. John conveys to the seven churches which are in Asia "Grace and peace"—*grace,* the largeness of God's

The Vision of the Son of Man 51

favor in all its manifold expressions; and *peace,* the Divine security, tranquillity and prosperity—from the Triune God. This benediction proceeds from—

"*Him which is, and which was, and which is to come;* and from—

"*The Seven Spirits which are before His throne;* and from—

"*Jesus Chirst, the Faithful Witness, the First-begotten of the dead, and the Prince of the Kings of the earth.*"

This solemn and majestic presentation of the Persons of the Godhead as the Source of the benediction, standing as it does at the forefront of the Book, should deeply impress our hearts with the awful majesty of the Supreme Being, and cause us to realize that here we are indeed upon holy ground.

1. God is here presented as the eternally self-existent One, the words, "He Who is, and Who was, and Who is to come", being an amplified statement of the ineffable Name of Exodus 3:14. It is there rendered, "I AM THAT I AM"; but the sense of eternal existence, past and future, is implied in the original Hebrew words.

"The idea of pure, absolute, unchangeable existence, as expressed in the name Jehovah, is quite a practical one. The people of Israel, in asking for His name, were to find in it a pledge and security for what was to be performed by Him, for His wonderful help in the most distressful circumstances; not what would merely satisfy their metaphysical curiosity. The name Jehovah comprises in itself the fulness of all consolation, and the treasures thereof are here brought up from their depths and are placed before the eyes of believers, the seer's companions in the Kingdom and patience of Jesus Christ. Against this Rock of the pure, unchangeable, absolute Being of God, dash all the despairing thoughts of those happy ones who can call this God their own, as also all the proud thoughts of the world which has Him for its enemy" (Hengstenberg).

2. The Holy Spirit, Who is next mentioned, is set forth as "The seven Spirits which are before His throne" (see Chap. 4:5). Inasmuch as the Lord Jesus Christ is the immediate Source of this revelation, He puts the Father and the Holy Spirit before Himself. That the Holy Spirit, the "One Spirit" (1 Cor. 12:13; Eph. 4:4) is here, and also in Chap. 4:5, referred to as the "Seven Spirits," reminds us that numbers, as well as other familiar things, are used in this Book not in their ordinary sense, but as *symbols;* and we must be careful to read them as such. This caution is most necessary.

The significance of the number *seven,* which occurs so often in this Book as to make it one of the distinguishing features thereof, is easily perceived. It signifies fullness or completeness. Here it is the fullness of the Holy Spirit. The third Person of the Godhead, in the plenitude of His Being, unites with the Father and the Son in this message of grace and peace to the churches. "The sevenfoldness does no violence to the unity. It merely points to the fullness and variety of the powers that are embraced in the unity".

Such being the significance of the phrase "seven Spirits", we are warranted in assuming that the paral-

The Vision of the Son of Man

lel phrase, "seven churches", in the same verse, is to be taken as embracing all the churches of that time and of all times subsequent; these making in their totality "one body". For in Ephesians 4:4 mention is made of the "one body", as well as of the "one Spirit".

3. The Lord Jesus Christ is presented in a three-fold way: *first,* as the "Faithful Witness", which refers to what He was in the days of His flesh (John 1:18; 17:25; 18:37 etc.); *second,* as the "First-begotten of the dead", which refers to what He now is in resurrection; (1 Cor. 15:20; Col. 1:18); *third,* as "the Prince of the Kings of the earth" (Psa. 89:28), which refers to the character in which He will be manifested at His second coming (Chap. 19:16).

All these three designations of our Lord describe Him in His *humanity,* and in His relation *manward.* It is "the Revelation of Jesus Christ" we are studying; and that Revelation begins with a three-fold presentation of the "One Mediator between God and men, the *Man* Christ Jesus" (1 Tim. 2:5). As Man He was the Faithful witness; as Man He is the First-born from the dead, the First-fruits of them that slept; and as Man He will reign over men, both over the nations, and over the kings of the earth (Rev. 21:24). But this Revelation of Jesus Christ does not stop with what He was, and is, and will be as Man. It goes on immediately, and in no uncertain terms, to reveal Him in His *eternal Deity* (vv. 8 and 11).

The Ascription of Praise. Verses 5, 6.

The ascription does not in terms embrace the Father or the Holy Spirit, but is addressed to Christ alone. For its theme is *redemption*. Like the description of the Lord Jesus Christ, it is three-fold: "Unto Him that loved us (or better, *loveth us*), and washed us from our sins in His own blood, and hath made us kings and priests unto God and (or *even*) *His Father;* to Him be glory and dominion forever and ever. Amen."

These words, apart from their immediate purpose, which is to lead out our hearts in worship and adoration to Him who has done such great things for us and at such cost to Himself, are of much value in the interpretation of the symbols of the four living creatures and the four and twenty elders of Chapters IV and V. Hence they give light as to the entire scene pictured to us in those chapters. This will appear later on.

The Outlook of the Prophecy. Verse 7.

"Behold, He cometh." The coming of Jesus Christ in visible power and glory is everywhere in the New Testament presented as an impending event, a thing for which His people were to be ever looking, waiting, and watching. The added words, "with clouds", are in the first place indicative of His Deity. Again and again it is written, "The LORD went before them in the pillar of a cloud"; "the LORD appeared in the cloud"; "the cloud of the Lord was upon the tabernacle" (Ex. 13:21; 16:10; 40:38 etc.). So at the Transfiguration, "A bright cloud overshadowed them, and behold, a

voice out of the cloud" (Mat. 17:5). Furthermore, those words recall His own saying as to His coming again "in the clouds of heaven" (Mat. 24:30; 26:24 etc.). And finally they identify Him as the Being seen by Daniel—the One like a Son of man, coming with the clouds of heaven (Dan. 13). But the clouds also are a shadow of judgment to come; and that thought is prominent here, as the succeeding clauses of the sentence clearly show.

"And every eye shall see Him". It is a part of God's plan for the future that every child of Adam's race shall have at least *one look* at Him who gave Himself a ransom for all. That sight will be the supreme bliss of those who have believed on His Name; but it will be a moment of indescribable terror for those who have despised such dearly bought mercy as that which the gospel offers free to all. This is indicated by the dismay of those unrepentant and unpardoned ones who, at the opening of the sixth seal, are seen seeking a hiding place in the dens and rocks, and crying to the mountains to fall upon them and hide them from the wrath of the Lamb (6:15, 16).

"And they which pierced Him". These are singled out for special mention; and it is added that *"all kindreds of the earth shall wail because of Him"*. For to every nation of earth the offer of salvation through His Name will have been made, and by all refused. We have here a repetition of what was prophesied by the Lord through Zechariah, in the words, "And they shall look upon Me whom they have pierced, and they

shall mourn for Him as one mourneth for his only son" (Zech. 12:10); and of what the Lord Jesus Christ Himself predicted: "And then shall appear the sign of the Son of man in heaven; and then shall all the tribes of the earth mourn; and they shall see the Son of man coming *in the clouds of heaven,* with power and great glory" (Matt. 24:30). The words, "all kindreds of the earth," show that it is the final judgment of the whole world which is here in view.

The Lord and His Servant. Verses 8 and 9.

In verse 8 the Lord declares His Name (as He declared it to Moses in Exodus 3:14, to which passage we have already referred) saying: "I AM Alpha and Omega, the Beginning and the Ending, which is, and was, and which is to come, the Almighty". In assuming this Name He claims what is declared of Him in Colossians 1:16, 17; and 2:9: "For by Him were all things created, that are in heaven, and that are in earth, visible and invisible, whether they be thrones, or dominions, or principalities, or powers; all things were created by Him, and for Him: and He is before all things, and by Him all things consist (*i. e. stand together;* cf. Heb. 1:3, "upholding all things by the word of His power"). "For in Him dwelleth all the fulness of the Godhead bodily" (Col. 2:9).

These words of the risen Lord Jesus Christ are an unqualified claim to completest and supremest Deity. And considering them particularly as a part of "the revelation of Jesus Christ", we would specially note two things:

1. The Lord here reveals Himself as the eternally self-existent One, that being the force of the words "I AM", or (as here more fully expressed) "Who is and Who was and Who is to come". None but the self-existing God can say "I AM" in this sense; for no creature exists of himself, or has life in himself. Every creature's life is dependent upon that which is outside himself, and which he can lay hold of only by the will of God. Thus the life of a man, which is the highest form of life known to us, is dependent moment by moment upon the oxygen of the atmosphere, and from day to day upon food and drink; it being entirely beyond his power to supply himself with these essential things. Man's life is both *derived* from an external source, and is also *dependent* upon regular supplies from an external source. But Jesus Christ has "life in Himself" (John 5:26). Hence that profound truth, "He that hath the Son *hath life;* and he that hath not Son of God *hath not life"* (1 J. 5:12).

2. In the verse we are considering, the Lord declares Himself not only as the self-existent One, but also as the Revealer. Alpha and Omega are the first and last letters of the alphabet of the language in which the New Testament is given to us. Therefore as the whole of the writing known as "The New Testament of our Lord and Saviour Jesus Christ" is embraced and comprehended between those two letters, so God's revelation of Himself, and of His purposes, and of His mind for us, is embraced and comprehended, and is brought within our reach in the Person of the

incarnate, crucified and resurrected One, Jesus Christ. He is "the Word of God". In Him God is "manifested".

Verse 8 begins "I AM Alpha and Omega, the First and the last"; whereas verse 9 begins, "I, John, who also am your brother, and companion in tribulation, and in the kingdom and patience of Jesus Christ." What a contrast is presented by these two verses! And what a difference is put between the Lord of glory and that beloved disciple who, in the days of His flesh, leaned upon His breast! Have we not in this contrast and in this great difference indeed a "revelation of Jesus Christ"?

That most favored servant and beloved disciple is but *one of ourselves;* and the Holy Spirit would have us to realize this and enjoy the comfort of it. The man who was given to see those wonderful visions is our "brother," and our "companion in tribulation". Indeed it was in the very season of his sufferings that Christ appeared to Him. And is it not in the times of our tribulation also, rather than in seasons of earthly ease and enjoyment, that He draws near to us? Would any of those who love Him shrink from even the sorest trial if he knew that the Lord was waiting to reveal Himself in the midst of it?

John was also inspired to describe himself as our companion "in the kingdom and patience of Jesus Christ". This phrase is deeply significant, and it has an important bearing upon the design of the Book as a whole. It brings home to us our personal interest and share in the revelations here given us. A "companion" (a word found only in the writings of Paul, and here in this passage) is one who shares or partakes of something along with others. We are the fellow-sharers with John in tribulation, and in the kingdom and patience of Jesus Christ. The Kingdom of Jesus Christ existed in the days of John, and it exists today. John and those whom he addressed directly were in it then. We are in it now. It has existed on earth from that day until now. And *this Revelation of Jesus Christ has to do with the history of that Kingdom and the experiences of those who are in it.*

It is deeply to be regretted that the company of the people of God in the world has come to be spoken of almost invariably as "the church of God". We read and hear of the history of the church, the trials of the church, the conflicts of the church, the triumphs of the church, etc., etc. But the Scripture does not so speak. That which has a continued existence on earth throughout this dispensation, is not "the church of God", but "the Kingdom of God" and the misapplication of the name *church* for *kingdom* is not only a great mistake, but a great misfortune; for the truth has suffered much in consequence. Let it be noted, then, in the interest of verbal accuracy and of all that depends thereon, that the Church of God *in the collective sense* (Mat. 16:18, Eph. 1:22 etc.) is not on earth, indeed is not in existence as a complete thing in this dispensation. For it is in process of formation; and furthermore but a tiny fraction of its membership is on earth at any one time. What *does* exist on earth in this era is, *collectively, the kingdom of God* (into which every saved person is immediately translated, Col. 1:12) and *locally* the numerous *churches of God* (note the plural). May it not have been in anticipation of this very error in the use of the word *church,* that we have the sevenfold repetition of the words, "what the Spirit saith unto (not the *church,* as nearly everyone would now say, but) the *churches?"* And that in Chapter 22:16, the Lord says, "I Jesus have sent mine angel to testify unto you these things in the *churches"?* Certainly there is a great difference between the church (in the collective sense) and the churches. And certainly also we can avoid much confusion and error by the simple rule of using the words of Scripture always with their scriptural meanings.

In considering the passage now before us, it should be noted that the same three things so singularly joined together here (tribulation, kingdom, and patience) are similarly united in Acts 14:22, where it is recorded concerning Paul and Barnabas that they confirmed the souls of the brethren, exhorting them to *continue* in the faith, and that through much *tribulation* we must enter into the *Kingdom* of God. So likewise in setting before us the Kingdom in which grace reigns, Paul says that *tribulation* worketh *patience* (Rom. 5:3; 8:23, 25).

"The things mentioned are singularly woven together. The *Kingdom* stands in the middle, the *tribulation* before, and the *patience* after. This is the form of Christianity in this life.

Through the tribulation the Kingdom is pervaded with the patience of Christ, till the tribulation shall have been overcome, and no more patience shall be required. With carnal men, who have not entered into the Kingdom of Christ, tribulation brings no patience, but rather causes irritation. A wild beast, if not irritated, may be as quiet as a lamb; but when anything has excited it, it breaks forth in its fury" (Bengel).

The vision on the Lord's Day. Verses 10-16.

We now come to John's description of the first of his visions. It is, most appropriately and significantly, a vision of the Lord Jesus Christ Himself, and in His glorified humanity; for He appeared as one "like unto the *Son of man*". This was a "revelation of Jesus Christ" indeed, and such as the eye of mortal man had never beheld.

As to the circumstances in which this wondrous vision was seen, John mentions two things. *First,* he was "in the spirit", that is to say, he had passed out of the state or condition of normal human consciousness, into that supernormal state wherein spiritual things are perceived. It is an experience known to the prophets of old (Ez. 2:2 etc.). In that state Peter beheld the vision of the great sheet let down from heaven, (Ac. 10:10-15). In that state Paul was caught up to the third heaven, and there heard unutterable words (2 Cor. 12: 1-4). So likewise it was with John's second vision (Rev. 4:2); and hence presumably with all the rest.

Second, it was "on the Lord's day". Those who hold the futurist system would make this mean *the Day of the Lord.* That is, they would understand

John as saying that he was carried forward in the spirit into the future era in order that he might behold things which are to happen in that great and terrible day. So likewise the Seventh Day Adventists expound it; though for a different and obvious reason. But against this there is, first of all, the objection that it is a strained construction; and further the expression is a different one from that which is everywhere used to designate the Day of the Lord (Ac. 2:20; 1 Cor. 1:8; 5:5; 2 Cor. 1:14, 2 Pet. 3:10; 1 Th. 5:2). This difference must be regarded as decisive. But in addition, the vision which John then beheld does not belong to the Day of the Lord. Beyond all question, and as all are fully agreed, the vision of Christ in the midst of the candlesticks is a vision of *this present dispensation,* wherein the churches of Christ are set as lights shining in the spiritual darkness of the world. This is a fatal objection to the idea that "the Lord's day" is equivalent to "the Day of the Lord". On the other hand, it is known from early christian writings that the first day of the week received the designation "the Lord's day" from a time very close to the beginning of the era; and we have in this verse a proof that it had begun to be so designated ere the last of the apostles and scribes of the Bible had finished his labors.

"The key to the right understanding of *the Lord's day,*" says Hengstenberg, "is supplied by verse 5, where Christ is called the *first begotten from the dead,* and by verse 18, where likewise reference is made to the resurrection as the pledge that He will quicken His people out of death. These passages prove (1) that the Lord's day is the day of resurrection, that being the day on which Christ was manifested above all others as *Lord* (Comp. Rom. 1:4); (2) that it was so named not because of what the church should do on that day, but because of what the Lord did on it".

Being thus " in the spirit on the Lord's day," John heard behind him a great voice, as of a trumpet. That voice, having the loudness and clearness of a trumpet, he heard again when summoned to heaven to behold the succeeding visions (4:1). It reminds us of the great happenings at Mt. Sinai, when the Lord appeared in a vail of cloud and fire, and when "the voice of the trumpet exceeding loud" struck terror to the hearts of those that heard it (Ex. 19:16; 20:18; Heb. 12:19).

The Voice was that of the Lord Jesus Himself; and the words John heard were these: "I AM Alpha and Omega, the First and the Last"; and then came the command: "What thou seest, write in a book, and send it unto the seven churches which are in Asia; unto Ephesus, and unto Smyrna, and unto Pergamos, and unto Thyatira, and unto Sardis, and unto Philadelphia, and unto Laodicea".

The word "what thou seest, write in a book" should be taken as inclusive of all that John was to see in supernatural vision; for the "book" he was to write is presumably this Book of the Revelation of Jesus Christ.* The seven churches of Asia, already men-

---

* But some take this command of the Lord to John as covering also his Gospel and Epistles, and this view has something to commend and support it. Others again would limit it to this present vision, and claim that ''the book'' means merely the messages to the churches.

tioned in verse 4, are now named individually. Upon referring to a map of Asia Minor it will be seen that the seven cities thus designated, when regarded as a group, form a sort of irregular circle; and that if we go from one to another, beginning at Ephesus, they occur geographically in the precise order in which they are here named, this being also the order in which they are severally addressed in Chapters II and III. This presents to the mind's eye a most impressive and significant picture. There stands "in the midst" the glorified Redeemer. He is solitary in His grandeur and majesty. The seven golden candlesticks that encircle Him represent all the churches of all the centuries, and of all parts of the world. And as He turns from one to the other, beginning at Ephesus and ending at Laodicea, He sends the message—"what the Spirit is saying to the churches"—to every point of the compass, and to every part of the world. It is a picture of incomparable grandeur. May the reader and the writer be among those "blessed" ones that have "an ear to hear".

That this scene is laid in the midst of the province of Asia is significant. The center of God's dealings had been the earthly Jerusalem; and the first of "the churches of God", whence the word had gone forth to all the world, was there. But when this vision was given, Jerusalem on earth was no longer the center of God's interests and operations in the world. In fact it had been blotted out by the armies of Rome, which executed the vengeance of God upon the apostate city.

For at the time of this vision, the prophecy of the destruction of Jerusalem, which Christ had spoken in His parable of the wedding supper (Mat. 22:7), had been fulfilled. According to that parable, the Jews would reject the invitation of the gospel, and some would ill treat the bearers of the gospel message, even putting them to death. And the parable ends with the prophetic words: "But when the King heard thereof, he was wroth; and he sent forth his armies, and destroyed those murderers, and burned up their city" (Mat. 22:7).

Furthermore, we observe that this circle of churches lay in what had been the theater of the principal labors of the apostle Paul. They were the earliest recipients of the teaching which the Lord had given through that chosen vessel, first by word of mouth, and then by letters. That group, therefore, was, in actual historic fact, *the center* from which the doctrine of Christ, "the whole counsel of God", that Paul had been prompt to declare, spread to every part of the world. A good many years had now passed since Paul had finished his course, probably forty or thereabouts; and from Christ's message to Ephesus can be seen the spiritual decline that had already taken place. Indeed, as we read the seven messages to those churches of Asia, we cannot fail to realize that the freshness and spirituality of apostolic days were already past, and that the Lord was here speaking in full view of conditions that have prevailed down to our own days. Hence these messages are by no means obsolete.

The great Voice which John heard was *behind* him; and continuing, he says: "And I *turned* to see the voice that spake with me. And *being* turned, I saw seven golden candlesticks; and in the midst of the seven candlesticks one like unto the Son of man, clothed with a garment down to the foot, and girt about the breasts with a golden girdle".

Stress is laid upon John's change of attitude. It was only after "being turned" that he saw the wondrous vision and received the Lord's message. The thought this suggests is that we, too, have our spiritual gaze turned often in the wrong direction, and hence do not see the Lord in His majesty. We recall the gracious promise, "And thine ears shall hear a word *behind thee,* saying, This is the way, walk ye in it" (Isa. 30:21).

From this point onward the Book is written in the language of symbols; and this we must keep ever in mind, else we shall quickly lose our way and find ourselves in a region of mysteries. The seven golden candlesticks that John saw were the symbols of things which, in appearance, bear no resemblance at all to candlesticks. But as to this particular symbol we have the explanation from the Lord Himself (v. 20); and His explanation of the meaning of candlesticks (or lampstands) and of stars, serves also to indicate the principle upon which all the symbols of the Book are to be explained.

The Lord Jesus Christ as here seen by John was "like unto a Son of man". This refers to Daniel 7:13,

The Vision of the Son of Man

where the seer says: "I saw in the night visions and behold, one *like the Son of man*"; and he goes on to say, "And there was given him dominion, and glory, and a kingdom, that all people, nations and languages should serve him". Thus He is seen in His glorified humanity; and the expression implies His Deity; for if He was *like* a Son of man, then in His true Being He must be far higher.

The garment in which He appeared, a robe flowing down even to the feet, was the sign not only of the priestly office, but of the kingly as well; and the whole of the description that follows exhibits Christ as King and Judge. Both the long robe and the golden girdle have reference to the one seen by Daniel, whose body was like the beryl, his face as the appearance of lightning, his eyes as lamps of fire, and his voice like that of a multitude (Dan. 10:5, 6). On this passage Bengel remarks: "A King is more exalted than a priest. Hence Scripture speaks much oftener of the kingdom than of the priesthood of Christ". And as regards the girdle about the breast, he says: "One who is busy girds himself about the loins (Isa. 11:5). But he who girds himself about the breast must be in a state of dignified repose. Jesus, by His sufferings and death, has overcome all. What profound reverence should fill our hearts before this incomparable majesty!" We recall the Scripture: "For he (Christ) that is entered into his rest, he also hath ceased from his own works"—those necessary for our salvation—"as God did from his" (Heb. 4:10).

We gather, therefore, that the manner of the Lord's appearance to John was designed not to indicate His present office of intercessor, but rather to impress upon the seer, and upon all who should read and ponder this description, the transcendent importance of the things revealed in these visions. God's messages to the prophets were commonly brought and communicated by angels (Heb. 2:2); but this was brought by the glorified Lord in all His royal dignity and glory. Its importance therefore is correspondingly great.

The description given of Christ is wholly in symbolic language; moreover it consists of seven distinct items. Therefore it is highly mystical; and in meditating upon its several features we must exclude from our minds all thought of *physical* resemblance, and seek for a perception of *moral* likenesses only.

Of the Lord's appearance in the days of His humiliation we have no description at all; no, not so much as a line. It is one of the marvels of the Gospels that with all the intense love and the devotion the writers had for Christ, not one line did they write concerning any detail of His personal appearance. This would have been impossible if their writing had not been divinely controlled and inspired. All pictures of Jesus of Nazareth are therefore wholly the work of the human imagination. We have not the faintest idea as to His appearance in the days of His flesh. God has seen to it that there should be no representation of Him as He looked when "He took the form of a servant", and was "found in fashion as a man". But

The Vision of the Son of Man

here, as risen from the dead and glorified, a description is given, whereof the completeness is indicated by its seven-fold character.

The order in which these seven features of our Lord's appearance are presented is noteworthy. The following arrangement will represent them to the eye; and it will be seen that they are in pairs, grouped about the Voice, which has the central place, like the central stem of the seven-branched candlestick of the Tabernacle and Temple in its relation to the three pairs of branches.

1. HEAD and HAIRS white like wool, white as snow;
  2. EYES as a flame of fire;
    3. FEET like fine copper glowing in a furnace;
      4. VOICE as the sound of many waters;
    5. RIGHT HAND holding seven stars;
  6. MOUTH from which issues a sharp sword;
7. COUNTENANCE as the sun, shining in full strength.

Next to the Voice, of which John makes special mention, we have on one side the Feet and on the other the Right Hand; next to these on one side the Eyes from which issued a flame of fire, and on the other the Mouth from which issued a sharp sword; and next to these on one side the Head and Hairs, lustrous white, and on the other the Countenance shining as the sun in the fullness of its strength. It is a picture far beyond the power of the human imagination to conceive. Small wonder that John, upon seeing it, "fell at His feet as dead".

Much time could be profitably occupied in meditating upon these seven descriptive symbols; but inasmuch as their significance has been often pointed out by writers gifted with spiritual discernment, we limit ourself to a brief word on each feature.

1. The whiteness of the Head and Hairs symbolizes the eternal Being of God. The same symbol is used of the "Ancient of Days", seen by Daniel on the throne of heaven, "Whose garment was white as snow, and the Hair of His Head like pure wool" (Dan. 7:9). The color *white* is itself a symbol, the identical word being used sixteen times in the Apocalypse, and as a derivative once. It signifies invariably something pertaining *to Christ or to His people*. It is the dazzling whiteness of light. It gives the idea of glittering splendor. It is the symbolical representation of the glory. The words, "O Father, glorify Me with Thine own self, with the glory which I had with Thee before the world was" (Jn. 17:5), correspond in meaning.

2. The Eyes like a flame of fire indicate Him as the One from whom nothing is hid, "Who searcheth the reins and heart" (2:24; Jer. 17:10 etc.). This is a strong assertion of His Deity.

3. Feet like unto fine brass (or copper), glowing as with the intense heat of a furnace, mark Him as the One who in judgment will tread the wine-press of the wrath of God and trample His enemies under His feet (19:15; Isa. 63:3). Brass (*i. e.* copper) is associated with the judgment of God, as in the case of the brazen altar. When the Lord appeared to Ezekiel in visions

foretelling judgment on Jerusalem, the feet of the cherubim which supported His throne were "like the color of burnished brass" (Ezek. 1:7).

4. When the glory of the God of Israel appeared to Ezekiel "His voice was like the noise of many waters" (Ezek. 43:2). So we have in this feature a mark that identifies the Lord Jesus Christ as the God of Israel, the One whose voice produced such fear and awe in the hearts of the people of Israel at Mount Sinai. There is an indescribable majesty, and a tone of irresistible might and authority in the sound of the rush of waters.

5. The Right Hand is the hand where a man's strength and skill reside. In the song of triumph at the Red Sea, Israel sang: "Thy right hand, O LORD, is become glorious in power; Thy right hand, O LORD, hath dashed the enemy in pieces" (Ex. 15:6; Ps. 118:15, 16). Many other scriptures show the significance of this symbol. The Lord saves by His right hand (Psa. 17:7). It is the hand "of power" (Mat. 26:64). In Bible language, to have a thing in one's hand means to have it under one's power. To Noah and his sons God said, concerning all the beasts, fowl, and fishes: "into your hand are they delivered" (Gen. 9:2). Moses in his final blessing said: "All His saints are in Thy hand" (Dt. 33:3). David addresses the Lord in these terms: "But I trusted in Thee, O LORD: I said, Thou art my God; my times are in Thy hand" (Ps. 31:14, 15). And Christ says of His sheep: "Neither shall any man pluck them out

of My hand" (John 10:28). Therefore, by the vision of the Lord Jesus Christ holding the seven stars, which represent the angels of the seven churches, in His right hand, we are given to understand that all His churches are ever in His protecting care, as well as under His absolute power; and that He will both preserve and also govern them.

6. His Mouth out of which goes a sharp two-edged sword.

The reference here is primarily to Isaiah 49:1, 2, where the Spirit of Christ, speaking through the prophet, says: "From the bowels of My mother He hath made mention of My name. And He hath *made My mouth like a sharp sword*". There is a clear reference to this passage in the Lord's message to Pergamos: "Repent; or else I will come unto thee quickly, and will fight again them with *the sword of My mouth*" (Rev. 2:16). The word of God is called in Ephesians 6:17 "The sword of the Spirit"; and in Hebrews 4:12 it is declared that "The word of God is quick (*i. e.* living) and powerful, and sharper than any two-edged sword". The Word of His Mouth is spirit and life to them that receive it (John 6:63); but to them that reject it, it is a sword of judgment; for He has said, "The word that I have spoken, the same shall judge him in the last day" (John 12:48). In agreement with this, the vision of Chapter 19:11-21 shows Him coming forth for judgment; and there again it is recorded that "His eyes were as a flame of fire", (penetrating all "the secrets of men" Rom. 2:16), and that "Out of His mouth goeth a sharp sword, that with it He should smite the nations".

7. His Countenance as the sun shining in his strength. The sun is the supreme light-giver of the physical world. So Christ is the supreme Light-giver of the spiritual world. In the description of the eternal city it is said that "the city had no need of the sun, neither of the moon to shine in it; for the glory of God did lighten it, and the Lamb is the light thereof" (Rev. 21:23). This is "the true Light" (John 1:9). It is the Light that shines *in the heart* of the man who repents and believes the gospel. "For God", says the apostle, "Who commanded light to shine out of darkness, hath shined *in our hearts* to give the light of the knowledge of the glory of God *in the face of Jesus Christ*" (2 Cor. 4:6). The one who wrote the words last quoted tells of the occasion when that Light shone in full strength upon him; for in his defence before King Herod Agrippa he testified, saying: "At midday, O King, I saw in the way a Light from heaven, *above the brightness of the sun,* shining round about me" (Ac. 26:13).

Such, in rapid summary, is the seven-fold description of the glorified Son of man, the like of which is not to be found in any book, in any language. For the heart of man could not have conceived of such a blending and grouping together of transcendent powers and glories. Indeed the heart of man cannot even receive the picture when presented to him, any more than the eye could bear the glory of that light. For this is the Holy

Spirit's portrait of Him who is the effulgence of the Father's glory, and the express image of His Person (Heb. 1:3). Various features of this sevenfold portrait appear in different connections in subsequent parts of the Book. But only here are they all presented together.

There are, of course, no words of our language whereby the glories and beauties of the risen Redeemer could be described, and nothing within the sphere of human knowledge to which He could be compared. For the question still remains without answer, "To whom then will ye liken God? or what likeness will ye compare unto Him?" (Isa. 40:18). This, men are forbidden even to attempt; and the Holy Spirit knows the impossibility of doing it. Hence He puts before us this amazing group of *symbols,* that *they* may speak to us, so far as we can receive it, of the ineffable glories which will be revealed in that day when, transformed into His own likeness, "we shall see Him as He IS" (1 Jn. 3:2). For "when Christ, who is our life, shall be manifested, then shall ye also be manifested with Him in glory" (Col. 3:4).

The effect upon John, and the Mandate given him. Verses 17-19.

The effect of this vision upon John was overpowering. He states it in few and simple words, which bear the plain impress of truth, the words being very different from what would be used by one who was describing an imaginary event:—"And when I saw Him I fell at His feet as dead". Thereupon the Lord laid His right hand, that same hand of power, upon him, and uttered the divine, "Fear not".

Here again is a marked likeness between John's experience and that of Daniel, the differences being just sufficient to show that the beloved disciple of the New Testament was not copying from "the man greatly beloved" of the Old. For when Daniel saw the One clothed in linen and girded with gold, whose face was as lightning and His eyes as lamps of fire, and the voice of His words like the voice of a multitude, he too was completely overcome. "There remained no strength in me", he says; "yet I heard the voice of his words; and when I heard the voice of his words, then was I in a deep sleep on my face, and my face toward the ground. And, behold, *a hand touched me,* and set me upon my knees, and upon the palms of my hands" (Dan. 10:7-10). And Daniel too heard the quickening words, "Fear not; peace be unto thee; be strong, yea, be strong" (v. 19).

And now again, for the third time in this short chapter, the risen Christ asserts His eternal Being saying, "I AM the First and the Last; He that liveth, and was dead; and behold, I am alive forevermore, Amen". And after this reiterated assertion of His right to the incommunicable Name, He declares His victory and lordship over death and the nether world, saying, "And have the keys of hell and of death".

The words, "I AM the first and the last", express what is included in full Godhead, as appears from Isaiah 44:6, "I am the first and the last, and beside

Me there is no God". The assertion that He is the *first* refers to the creation of the world (Isa. 48:12, 13). He is the *first,* for "In the beginning was the Word, and all things were made by Him" (John 1: 1-3). So also He is *the last;* for all created things shall wax old as a garment, and as a vesture He shall change them; but He is *the same,* whose years are without end (Heb. 1:10-12).

He also asserts His supreme authority over death and hell, that being the force of the words, "and have the keys of hell and of death". His power therefore is absolute and universal. It not only embraces heaven and earth (Mat. 28:18), but extends also to the infernal regions.

Then comes the mandate to John: "Write the things which thou hast seen, and the things which are, and the things which shall be hereafter". As to these words there is no need of further comment.

The Lord's explanation of the stars and candlesticks. Verse 20.

The last verse of the chapter is of peculiar importance because of the light it throws upon the Book as a whole, and the clear indication it gives of the principle upon which the Book is to be interpreted. The Lord states that the seven stars are a "mystery", and the seven candlesticks likewise; and of these He gives the explanation. But He does not explain any of the other symbols found in this chapter. This, however, is quite enough to tell us that the other distinguishing features of the vision, and those of other visions as well, are also mysteries; that is, they stand for things of another kind than themselves, things to which they bear no physical resemblance at all, but to which there is a moral likeness that we can perceive when once it is pointed out. This verse, therefore, puts us on the right track for the true interpretation of the Book.

By "mystery" in the N. T. is always meant a secret of such a nature that it can be known to human beings only by means of a Divine revelation, a thing which is inaccessible to the natural man, and can be apprehended only by those who are in fellowship with God. The nature of a "mystery" is such, moreover, that even after it has been explained, it yet remains beyond the apprehension of those who have not received the Holy Spirit. For, as Hengstenberg remarks: "in spite of the revelations given through John, the fleshly and impenitent in the seven churches still continue to grope in darkness in regard to the stars and the lampstands, entertaining concerning them the most earthly and superficial views". And he goes on to say: "The angels are God's messengers, and therefore the angels of the churches could only be the angels whom God had sent to the churches, and whom He had entrusted with the charge of them". And he cites the words of Christ in Matthew 18:10, saying, "according to which the angel of any one is the particular angel to whom the charge of that one has been entrusted" (Acts 12:15).

Specifically the verse we are considering explains two symbols whereof, without it, we should have sought the meaning in vain; for I know of nothing in the Bible whereby it could have been ascertained that the candlesticks represented churches, and that the stars represented the angels of the churches. But with the help of this explanation of the "mystery", it is easy to see the fitness of these symbols. Christ's people are appointed to be the light of the world during the darkness of His absence (Mat. 5:14); and their responsibility is to "shine as lights in the world" (Phil. 2:15). But the light they have is not from themselves, but from Christ, the true Light; for "the spirit of man is the candle of the Lord" (Prov. 20:27), and it remains unlighted until he is brought to Christ, by conversion, when it is ignited from His light, even as life is imparted from His life. But Christ Himself has said that men do not "light a candle and put it under a bushel, but *on a candlestick*" (Mat. 5:15). And now we learn that the "church", or local gathering of saved people, is the candlestick; and that when Christ saves sinners and so changes their nature that they are no longer "darkness but light in the Lord" (Eph. 5:8), He intends that they should be congregated into churches, to the end that they may collectively "give light unto all that are in the house".

Nor could we have known, apart from this verse, that the stars of this vision represent the angels of the churches. Indeed we should not know otherwise that there is an angel assigned to special duty, and charged with special responsibility, in connection with each of the churches of Christ. The explanation therefore adds much to our knowledge concerning the ministry of the angels, those wondrous celestial beings, whose numbers are infinite, who excel in strength, who fight the battles of the Lord, who execute His commandments, hearkening to the voice of His word (Psa. 103:20; Mat. 26:53; Heb. 12:22 etc.). But once we have this most valuable explanation, we can easily see how it accords with other passages of Scripture. The Lord had made known incidentally that to every one on earth who enters the Kingdom of heaven an angelic guardian is assigned (Mat. 18:10); and the early disciples understood this (Ac. 12:15). Then in Hebrews 1:14 it is revealed that the angels are *"ministering* spirits", that is to say, servants of the Lord ("angels and authorities and powers having been made subject unto him", 1 Pet. 3:22); and that they are "sent forth" to serve on behalf of those who, by their heavenly birth, have become the "heirs of salvation".

Furthermore, from the closely related Book of Daniel it appears that the various nations have each a mighty celestial being who in some mysterious way presides over its destinies. Thus, Michael the archangel was the "prince" who stood for the nation of Israel (Dan. 10:21, 12:-); and mention is made also of other angelic princes, as for instance "the prince of Persia", and "the prince of Grecia" (Dan. 10:20). But these latter are evidently *rebel* angels, for they resisted the One who appeared to Daniel; and moreover He declared to Daniel that "There is none that holdeth with Me in these things, but Michael, *your* prince".

From all this we may assuredly gather that just as there was a mighty angel who "stood for" the people of God in the past dispensation, so now there is an angel who *stands for* each of the churches of Christ, and who is so identified with it before Him as to be held responsible for the spiritual state thereof. For every church is a society, a sort of principality or commonwealth distinct from every other, and linked to the others solely through Christ, the Head of all. He recognizes no federation of churches, and of course no sects nor denominations; for each "church" is complete in itself, and is responsible to no authority on earth but the Word and Spirit of God. There is no person, committee, board, synod, council or convocation, that has jurisdiction from Christ over a group of churches. It clearly appears from Chapters II and III that each "church" is independent of every other, and that each "angel" is responsible only for *that particular church* to which he has been assigned.

This information concerning the angels and their relation to the churches is of great value, and should be prized accordingly. But, sad to say, this explanation of the stars which John saw in Christ's right hand, has been by many expositors completely set aside, and the stars have been made to represent, not angels, but human ministers, such as are in our day installed in the various churches of Christendom. There are, however, several fatal objections to this view. The strongest is, of course, that by the Lord's own word the stars are symbols of *angels,* not of *men.* Further than that, the institution of the now almost universal one-man ministry (the clergyman or pastor of the church) was wholly unknown in New Testament times. The messages could not have been addressed to such, for they did not exist. Each church had its elders, overseers (bishops) and deacons, and also prophets and teachers, but never the one-man "minister" or "pastor" as now (Acts 11:30; 13:1; 14:23; 15:2, 4, 6; 20:17; Phil. 1:1; 1Tim. 3:1, 8; Jam. 5:14; 1 Pet. 5:1, 2; etc.). Moreover the elders, deacons, etc. of those days, were simply members of the congregation, who, by reason of ripe age and other qualifications and spiritual gifts, were able to exercise care over the flock in various ways. They were not an official or clerical class. They did not answer in any wise to the symbol of a star. Such a thing as one individual in a position of authority over the church was not only unknown, but would have been contrary to the expressed will of the Lord as regards the constitution of His churches.

We must here call to mind a caution that has been already given, namely, that in this Book are found symbols not only of things visible, but of things invisible; not only of things on the outer or material side of creation, but also of things on the inner or spiritual side. For it is the revelation, or unveiling, not only of things that were to happen on earth in the time then future, but also of things existing and going on in heaven. There have been many mistaken interpretations of parts of this Book, due to the idea that the symbols one and all represent things visible and material, and events on earth. Let us keep in mind, therefore, that we are here studying a Book that is written on *both* sides.

It is true indeed that the explanation given us of the "mystery" of the stars, leaves many things unexplained. For we are told nothing of the manner in which the angels of the churches exercise their ministry and discharge the responsibilities of their office. We should like, of course, to know about these matters. But the fact that God has seen fit to leave us in ignorance of them is no reason why we should set aside the explanation, which, though but partial, is certainly clear as far as it goes. Yet what chiefly impresses me in certain comments I have read on this verse is that they are mere efforts to explain away the divine explanation, some of them being attempts of the most laborious kind to make it appear that the stars are not angels, as Christ plainly stated, but persons of another order (human beings). To me, however, the explanation as given from the lips of the glorified Lord is not only clear and simple, but also exceedingly satisfactory.

CHAPTER III

The Letters to the Churches of Asia

SEEING that the symbol God has chosen as the representation of the local church of this dispensation is a candlestick (or lampstand) we may infer that the main purpose of its existence is to hold aloft, for the benefit all around, the light of God's truth. In other words, the church is the appointed *witness* for Christ. Its members are gathered into one body to the end that by their collective testimony, not in word only but chiefly in their distinctive manner of life after a pattern utterly foreign to this present evil world, they may show forth the reality, and the saving and life-transforming power, of the gospel of Christ who died and rose again. For Christ's people are in the world, not for themselves or for what they can get out of it, but strictly to "occupy", that is to carry on business, *for Him.* They are first *called out** of the world, and then are *sent back into it,* as "ambassadors for Christ" (2 Cor. 5:20). The risen Lord declared the great business of their lives in a few comprehensive words when He said, "Ye shall be witnesses unto Me" (Acts 1:8). And in this high calling they are co-workers together with the Holy Spirit (John 15:26,27; Acts 1:8; 5:32). The word spoken by the

---
* The word "church" *(ekklesia)* by its derivation signifies a *called out* company. See in this connection John 17:6, 16-18; for the words of Christ there recorded declare the *calling out,* and also the proper constitution of every church.

Lord and recorded in Matthew 5:15 throws clear light upon this subject, and is itself interpreted by His explanation that the candlesticks represent the churches: "Neither do men light a candle, and put it under a bushel, but *on a candlestick;* and it giveth light unto all that are in the house".

Such being the main purpose of Christ for His churches, it would follow that when He walks in the midst of them and searches them with those eyes that are like flames of fire, His chief concern would be as to the things that affect their testimony. For if a church fails in its testimony, if it be not maintaining a clear witness for Christ, it is a failure in the very thing for which it was called into being. Therefore, every church of God is to be judged as to its efficiency and faithfulness as a light-bearer; and it is primarily with respect to that supremely important matter that their condition and their behaviour are reviewed by the Lord Himself, with the results set forth in these seven letters. Let us therefore keep that fact in mind in our study of them; remembering also that the scene here put before us is not a thing of the long ago, but of this entire age, during which our Lord is ever walking in the midst of His churches.

What then is the testimony the churches are responsible to maintain? Or, to use the figure here employed, what is the nature of the "light" they are expected to shed upon "all that are in the house"? Briefly, the testimony or "light" of the local church is the *conduct* of those who compose it, that is to say, their whole manner of life, in their relations with one another and with "those who are without". Their entire behaviour should be such as to "show forth the praises of Him who has called them out of darkness into His marvellous light". Therefore, their manner of *life* should be as much in contrast with that of the unregenerate, as light is in contrast with darkness.

Light and *love* are closely related. The ruling life-principle of the natural man is *love of self;* that of the Kingdom of God is *love of others.* For in that one word, *love,* "all the law is fulfilled"; for "love is the fulfilling of the law" (Gal. 5:14; Rom. 13:10). The whole world that lieth in the evil one, with all its gigantic enterprises, and all its complex machinery, is organized, maintained and operated upon the basis of the two dominant motives of the natural heart—selfishness and covetousness. If by a miracle those prime characteristics of human nature were suddenly eradicated, the world's stupendous enterprises would come to a standstill; the vast machinery of industry and commerce would cease to operate; for the incentives that impel men into the rush of "business" would be gone. For the world's great motto is "get"; whereas Christ's word to His people is "give". These principles are mutually antagonistic.

The letters to the churches take us on to the new-creation ground. Therefore we do well, before examining them, to glance back to the beginning of the old creation, for the lesson it has to teach us in regard to the general subject of light and darkness. Upon sc doing we find that in the setting of the physical creation in order, one of the most important details was the arrangement for giving light. And we find also that the light-bearers which God set in the physical heavens were His *witnesses* to men (Psa. 19 etc.). So likewise in the spiritual creation. Christ is both "the Sun of righteousness" (Mal. 4:2) and also "the faithful and true Witness" (Rev. 1:5). And furthermore, just as God made "the stars also", He has now set the churches as lesser luminaries in the spiritual heavens.

What then does Christ find to be the state of His churches when they are examined and tested by the general principles stated above? In considering this question we are getting at the very heart of His messages to the churches; and this is what I wish to do, rather than to attempt an exposition of the letters in detail; for there are already available many commentaries on these messages, in which their lessons are unfolded to the profit of all who read them.

THE FRAMEWORK OF THE SEVEN LETTERS

Upon examination of these seven letters it is at once perceived that they are all framed upon the same model, which has a seven-fold structure.

1. Each begins with the words: "Unto the angel of the church of —— write: These things saith", and then Christ, instead of naming Himself by Name, refers to Himself by some one or more of the descriptive symbols whereby He was revealed to John in the pre-

ceding vision, or by some other revelation of Him given in that chapter (except only in the case of the letter to the church in Philadelphia, where He refers to Himself in other terms, as will be pointed out in the appropriate place). Thus, the letters to the churches are closely linked with the vision of Chapter I.

2. Next comes in each case the declaration, *"I know thy works"*. By this we are reminded that every detail of the conduct of every church is fully known to Him; and that it will be righteously judged by Him, whether for praise or blame.

3. Then follows, in all cases but one, a *commendation,* bestowed upon whatever, in the condition or behaviour of the church, Christ finds to be in anywise praiseworthy. Only in the case of Laodicea is the note of praise or commendation altogether lacking.

4. After this is a word of *reproof:* "Nevertheless, I have against thee"; or "But I have a few things against thee"; or "Notwithstanding, I have a few things against thee". However, in the message to Symrna and in that to Philadelphia, there is no word of reproof. It seems that the Lord makes the utmost of everything He can commend.

5. Then we have a word of *exhortation* or *encouragement,* suited to the condition of the church addressed; and in each of the five cases where reproof has been administered, we find in this connection a call to "repent". In this we see the Lord's patience and long-suffering toward His churches, and His longing

desire for the restoration of such as are not maintaining a good testimony to His name.

6. In each message is heard the solemn *call:* "He that hath an ear, let him hear what the Spirit saith unto the churches". This is a characteristic saying of the Lord Jesus Christ. None other makes use of it. He employs it in connection with certain of His utterances in order to impress upon us their peculiar importance. It occurs eight times in the Gospels, where in each case the plural "ears" is used (Mat. 11:15; 13:9, 43; Mk. 4:9, 23; 7:16; Lu. 8.8; 14:35); and eight times also in Revelation (in each of the seven letters, and again in Chap. 13: v. 9), where the singular, "ear", is used in each case. These seemingly undesigned correspondences between Revelation and other Books of the Bible are of great value, in that they tend to establish the authenticity of the former, which some have been disposed to question. Correspondences of this sort are very numerous.

7. Finally, every letter contains a *promise* which is addressed in each case "to him that overcometh". In the first three letters the call to "hear" precedes the promise to him that overcometh. In the last four this order is reversed.

Thus again, in the structure of these letters, we find that *sevenfold* character which, everywhere throughout the Book, bears witness to its completeness and finality. This is most appropriate in that Book which was to complete the revelation of God to men, and which contains in its concluding verses that intensely solemn and threatening warning to any man who should add to, or take from, "the words of the book of this prophecy" (22:18, 19).

I.

To the church in Ephesus. Chap. 2:1-7.

This was a highly favored church. Its foundation had been firmly laid in the labors of Paul, assisted by Apollos, and also by Aquila and Priscilla (Acts 18: 19-28). The Jews in the synagogue at Ephesus gave willing ear to Paul's preaching at his first visit, which was brief (18:20, 21); and they were further instructed by Apollos, whose knowledge of "the way of God", though defective at first, was subsequently perfected by Aquila and Priscilla. At Paul's second visit, when he returned from Jerusalem, he spent three months, disputing in the synagogue, "and persuading the things concerning the Kingdom of God" (Acts 19:8). Some, however, were hardened; and because of their opposition, Paul, and with him those who believed, withdrew from the synagogue; but he continued his preaching *daily,* in the school of one Tyrannus, for the space of two years; and his work was so thoroughly done, and so richly blessed of God, that "all they which dwelt in Asia heard the word of the Lord Jesus, both Jews and Greeks". And not only so, but God wrought miracles of an uncommon sort ("special miracles") by the hands of Paul (Ac. 18:9-12), thus bearing witness with them, according to Hebrews 2:4.

The incident of the Jewish exorcists (vv. 13-16) served also to make known the power of Christ, and to authenticate the preaching of Paul, insomuch that "this was known to all the Jews and Greeks also dwelling at Ephesus; and fear fell on them all, and *the Name of the Lord Jesus was magnified*" (Ac. 19:17).

Moreover, the effect of the truth of God thus manifested at Ephesus was such that those who used heathen books of magic, voluntarily brought them and burned them publicly, to the value of fifty thousand pieces of silver. "So mightily grew the Word of God and prevailed" (vv. 19, 20). Assuredly then, much was to be expected of the church at Ephesus, which had been thus brought into existence, and to which had been given such extraordinary manifestations of the power of the risen Christ in His heavenly kingdom.

But that is not all, for we have in Acts 20 the record of Paul's farewell message to the elders of the church at Ephesus, who met him by appointment at Miletus. The tenderness and warmth of that remarkable utterance, the urgency of the entreaties, and the solemnity of the warnings it contains, show how important to the whole work of Christ it was that the testimony of His church at Ephesus should be maintained. And in view, moreover, of the prominent place given in the Book of the Acts to the work of the Lord at Ephesus, we can well understand why He selected that church as the starting point of His series of messages. Here is another link between the Revelation and the preceding Books of the New Testament.

To the church at Ephesus the Lord presents Himself as "He that holdeth the seven stars in His right hand, who walketh in the midst of the seven golden candlesticks"; in other words, as He Who has sole authority over all His churches, and who keeps them under constant and searching scrutiny. He finds things to commend in this church: "I know thy works, and thy labour, and thy patience, and how thou canst not bear them which are evil: and thou hast tried them which say they are apostles and are not, and hast found them liars: and hast borne, and hast patience, and for my Name's sake hast laboured, and hast not fainted". In not many churches today, we fear, could there be found so much to commend. But there was something lacking, without which the *light* must fail. Let us then pay strict heed to the next words: "Nevertheless I have against thee that thou hast *left thy first love*".*

These few words are most illuminating. They reveal in the first place, what it is that Christ looks for in His people. Works, and labor, and endurance, and zeal for the truth in testing the claims of false apostles (see 2 Cor. 11:13) are things that lie on the surface. But Christ looks deeper. "The Lord looketh on *the heart*". Where is "the *love of Christ*" which at first had constrained some of them to forsake the synagogue, and others to abandon their religion, the worship of the world-famous Diana of the Ephesians, and

---
* The word *somewhat*, after "I have," in the A. V. is an unwarranted interpolation. It greatly weakens the force of the passage.

to sacrifice their costly libraries? It is no longer there; the church has left it behind; and hence the Lord can take no satisfaction in their zeal, and works, and patience. The Lord never forgets that "first love", but is ever saying to us, as to Israel of old, "I remember thee, the kindness of thy youth, *the love of thine espousals*" (Jer. 2:1).

These words reveal also that the mainspring of a true and convincing testimony to the world is the *love of Christ* in the heart. How important to know this! What an incentive is here to a continual scrutiny of our affections, and of the objects upon which we are setting them! Has He this charge to bring against us also, that we too have left our first love? That can never be said of Him; for of Him it is written that, "Having loved His own which were in the world, He loved them *unto the end*" (John 13:1).

Here then is the vital thing. *God is love;* and He "commends His own love toward us, in that, while we were yet sinners, Christ died for us" (Rom. 5:8). It was the perception of that love of God for us that first softened our hard hearts, and awakened in them, for a little time at least, a responsive love for Him. Yes, and it is there still; though it needs to be awakened and called into activity; for still we one and all, do and must ever affirm, "we love Him, because He first loved us". But it is the "*first* love", the affection as it was in its freshness, that He misses. It is as He said to Israel of old, "I remember thee, the love of thine espousals" (Jer. 2:2). And is it so with us?

Then it is vain and useless for us to try to set matters right in other directions. *This* is the all important matter; and it claims our undivided attention. And we need not despair, for the remedy is plainly declared: "Remember therefore from whence thou art fallen; and repent, and do the first works". *Remember.* Let us go back in our thoughts again and yet again to those days of heaven on earth when first we came to the knowledge of Christ, and of His redeeming love. And then *repent*—turn to God in our hearts, confess our failure, and seek love again from its only Source; "for love is *of God*" (1 J. 4:7); and this is His gift to us; "for God hath not given us the spirit of fear; but of power, and *of love,* and of a sound mind" (2 Tim. 1:7). And again it is written: "For the love of God is shed abroad in our hearts by the Holy Ghost, who is given to us" (Rom. 5:5).

This word is supremely important to each one of us; and if we can truly join in the first clause of John's ascription of praise; if we can truly say, "Unto Him that *loved us*" (1:5), we shall give ourselves no rest till we have crucified all the affections and lusts that come between our poor hearts and Him Who can justly claim all our love.

I believe the great lesson of this letter to Ephesus is that *the maintenance of the testimony of the church depends upon love for Christ, to whom the church belongs.* This is made evident again from the warning of what would follow if His call to repentance should be unheeded: "Else I will come unto thee quickly, and *remove thy candlestick* out of its place, except thou repent".

We have no higher revelation of truth than that given in those two short and marvellously simple statements from this same John: "GOD IS LIGHT"; "GOD IS LOVE". Our best attempts at explaining those words to do but serve to weaken their force and obscure their meaning. But our knowledge thereof is enlarged when we put them together and perceive that *Light* is the external manifestation of what God Himself IS in His essential Being. Hence the two statements are one. God is Light *because* God is Love. It is a case of cause and effect. Therefore, the light of the church *must* fail when the love fails; and there is no remedy but to "repent, and do the first works".

The Lord specially commended the Ephesian church because it had tested some who presented themselves as apostles, and had found their pretensions to be false. This recalls the warnings which the true apostles had given. Particularly does it bring to mind Paul's words to the elders of this very church: "For I know", said he, "that after my departing shall *grievous wolves* enter in among you, not sparing the flock. Also of your own selves shall men arise, speaking perverse things, to draw away disciples after them" (Acts 20:29, 30). Yet more definitely he wrote to the church at Corinth concerning efforts that would be made by servants of the evil one to corrupt them from the truth, saying: "For such are *false apostles,* deceitful workers, transforming themselves into the *apostles of Christ*" (2

Cor. 12:13). The words of John Himself are of the same import: "Beloved, believe not every spirit, but *try the spirits* whether they are of God; because many *false prophets* are gone out into the world" (1 J. 4:1). And Peter also gives a like warning (2 Pet. 2:1, 2).

These apostolic warnings all rest upon that of the Lord Jesus Himself, in His Sermon on the Mount: "Beware of false prophets, which come to you in sheep's clothing, but inwardly they are ravening wolves" (Mat. 7:15).

Apparently there is a return to this subject at verse 6: "But this thou hast, that thou hatest the deeds of the Nicolaitanes, which I also hate". For the wording indicates that the Lord is not introducing here a new topic, but is referring back to the false apostles He had previously mentioned, thus pouring the balm of His commendation into the wound His sharp reproof had made. Who these Nicolaitanes were, and what their particular heresy, cannot be determined with certainty. They are mentioned again in the letter to Pergamos, at which point I will offer a suggestion as to their general character. But we need not press the inquiry closely, for these letters are intended for the warning and exhortation of all the churches down to the very end; and there is need to be ever testing the claims of those who come in the guise of true servants of God and teachers of His word.

The promise to him that overcometh is that Christ will give him to eat of the tree of life that is in the midst of the paradise of God. The tree of life figures conspicuously in the vision of the glorified earth with which the Book ends. It would seem to be the figure of eternal blessedness, eternal salvation in its largest sense. At first glance it may appear that this, and some other of the promises of these letters, merely offer to those who overcome that which is secured to all the redeemed. But the Scriptures distinguish in many places between gifts and rewards; and while it was not the will of God to specify definitely the character of the several things promised in these messages, we may be fully assured that they are rewards of surpassing richness and blessedness.

II

To the church in Smyrna. Chapter 2:8-11

This is the shortest of the messages, and it contains no reproof.

The Lord here presents Himself as "The First and the Last, Who was dead and is alive". These words are most appropriate; for the church to which they were addressed was in "tribulation and poverty". They were exposed to the persecution of false brethren (those who said they were *Jews,* but were not, but were the synagogue of Satan); and moreover, they were about to suffer worse things; some of them even unto death. But here is encouragement for them from Him "Who *was dead* and is alive"; Who by His death has destroyed "him that had the power of death, that is the devil" (Heb. 2:14); and has robbed death of its sting, and the grave of its victory.

The great adversary is here mentioned first under the name "Satan" in verse 9, and then under the name "Devil" in verse 10. In verse 9 reference is made to what might be called the ecclesiastical activities of the adversary; for one of his most successful devices against the truth is the organizing of religious societies, and the promoting of religious enterprises, in imitation of, and as a substitute for, those good works which Christ has ordained that we should walk in them (Eph. 2:10). The church at Smyrna was opposed by such an organization. Those who composed it professed to be "Jews"—the symbolic name of God's true people. But they were not. They had only the outward profession and name. But since the Cross, it takes more than the name and outward profession to make one a "Jew". "For he is not *a Jew* who is one outwardly; neither is that circumcision which is outward in the flesh; but he is *a Jew,* who is one inwardly; and circumcision is that of the heart, in the *spirit,* not in the *letter"* (Rom. 2:28,29; see also Rom. 9:6-8). Therefore, every religious gathering or society, even though it take a name that belongs to Christ's redeemed people, and though it conform never so strictly to "the letter", and to all that is "outward in the flesh", yet if it be composed of those who have not been regenerated in heart by the Spirit of God, and have not been washed from their sins by the blood of Christ, that society is not a church of Christ but a "synagogue of Satan".

The apostle Paul likewise employs the name "Satan" in the same connection; for in warning against "false apostles", who sought to pass themselves off as "the apostles of Christ ", he said: "And no marvel; for *Satan himself* is transformed into an angel of light" (2 Cor. 11:13-15). Paul's warning thus covers both the danger disclosed in the letter to Ephesus, and also that disclosed in the letter to Smyrna. The church at Ephesus had tested those *who said* they were apostles, and found them liars; whereas the church at Smyrna was openly antagonized by those *who said* they were Jews, and were not. From the reference to the "poverty" and "tribulation" of the true church of Smyrna, it may be inferred that the "synagogue" of those who claimed to be Jews was rich in this world's goods, and was flourishing and prosperous, in contrast with the "poverty" of the true church; and as it was then, so now. But we note the comforting words in parenthesis, following the word poverty, *"but thou art rich"*. Not only were they the true people of God, but theirs was the true riches.

It is significant that the only other church, besides that at Smyrna, which receives unqualified praise from Christ (Philadelphia), was also opposed by them of "the synagogue of Satan, which say they are Jews, and are not, but do lie" (3:9).

In verse 10 the activities of the adversary take the form of *physical persecutions;* and here he is named "the Devil"; "Behold, *the devil* shall cast some of you into prison, that ye may be tried; and ye shall have tribulation ten days: be thou faithful unto death, and I will give thee a crown of life". Thus warned, and thus encouraged, many, no doubt, faced with fortitude and endured with patience the "tribulation" through which they were to pass.

Some have sought to indentify ten distinct persecutions of christians in general at the hands of imperial Rome as the "ten days" here mentioned. But this is far-fetched. Days do not symbolize persecutions. But the number ten, in Bible symbology, seems to indicate *a complete testing,* or a trial *to the limit.* Thus, Jacob complained that Laban had changed his wages "ten times" (Gen. 31:7, 41). The plagues of Egypt were *ten* in number. Israel was fully tested with *ten* commandments (Ex. 20). When God's patience had been tried to the limit, He said, they had tempted Him now "these *ten* times" (Nu. 14:22). Job complained of his friends saying, "These *ten* times have ye reproached me" (Job. 19:2). Daniel requested that he and his companions be proved or tested (as regards their food) *"ten* days" (Dan. 1:12-15). So we get the thought that the church at Smyrna was to be *fully tested* in the furnace of affliction.

The chief lesson of this passage appears to be that it is by trials, sufferings, and tribulations, that spiritual progress is promoted and eternal rewards gained. We also obtain from this letter the assurance that Christ in a special way draws near and reveals Himself to those who are called upon to suffer for His Name's sake; to the end that in all these things they should be more than conquerors through Him that loved them (Rom. 8:37).

The promise of this letter is: "He that overcometh shall not be hurt of the second death". Here again we find ourselves beyond our depth, and therefore attempt no explanation of this promise. The second death is defined in Chapter 20:14 as the lake of fire.

III

To the Church in Pergamos. Chapter 2:12-17.

Christ here presents Himself as "He which hath the sharp sword with two edges". The bearing of this is seen in verse 16, where, speaking of those whom He had just reproved (verses 14, 15) He says: "Repent; or else I will come unto thee quickly, and will fight against *them* with the sword of My mouth". That "sword", His word, has one edge for His enemies (19:15), and another for the judgment of His own people, when their behaviour, or their condition, requires its use.

Verse 13 contains strong commendation: "I know thy works, and where thou dwellest, even where Satan's seat (*i. e.* throne) is: and thou holdest fast My Name, and hast not denied My faith, even in those days wherein Antipas was My faithful martyr, who was slain among you, where Satan dwelleth".

This church was in a place of peculiar danger, a place of direct exposure to the adversary; for it was where Satan's authority was in some special way acknowledged. His devices in this case did not take the form either of spurious christianity, or of physical persecutions, as at Smyrna; but were of a nature similar to the device employed by Balaam against Israel, when he taught Balac, the king of the Moabites, to cast a stumbling-block before the children of Israel. This was accomplished through the women of Moab, by whom the Israelites were enticed to take part in the idolatrous sacrifices of the Moabites, and to commit fornication (Nu. 25:1-3). The sin which answers to this on the part of "the Israel of God" (Gal. 6:16) is their participation in the formal or ceremonial doings, especially of those of a religious, or quasi-religious character, of this present evil world. As it is written: "Ye adulterers and adulteresses; know ye not that the friendship of the world is enmity against God?" (Jam. 4:4).

The Moabites were the near kin of the Israelites, which would seem to be a reasonable ground for close and cordial relations and intercourse. It is instructive, however, to observe that Israel suffered more damage from their near kinsmen, the Edomites, Moabites, and Ammonites, than from their avowed enemies. And so it is now. The Israel of God has more to fear from the respectable elements of society, from those who assume a benevolent and patronizing attitude to "religion" in general and perhaps to christianity in particular, than from those who are the avowed enemies of Christ.

But Pergamos had previously experienced a season of physical persecutions, such as was awaiting Smyrna;

and Pergamos had stood the test. For it had held fast the Name of Christ, and had not denied His faith, even in those days of fiery trial when the rage of the enemy had been such that Antipas (one of Christ's martyrs not otherwise known than by the Lord's reference to him here) was slain. This steadfastness of the church in those days of persecution was doubtless the reason for Satan's change in tactics, as stated in verse 14. Upon that verse we have sufficiently commented above.

In verse 15 we read: "So hast thou also them that hold the doctrine of the Nicolaitanes, which thing I hate". In the letter to the church in Ephesus "the *deeds* of the Nicolaitanes" were referred to. Here it is their *doctrine*. Whoever these Nicolaitanes were, both their deeds and also their doctrines were hateful to the Lord. The only clue we have to an explanation is found in the meaning of the name itself, and this is worthy of consideration because it finds support in the meaning of the name *Balaam,* which occurs in the preceding verse. The name *Nicolas,* which belonged to the person of whom these Nicolaitanes were the followers, means one who *conquers* (or *lords it over*) *the people.* Now it can hardly be a coincidence in a Book where names and numbers, as well as objects, are used as symbols, that the name *Balaam* in Hebrew has substantially the same meaning as *Nicolas* in Greek, and that here we have mention in verse 14 of the doctrine of Balaam, and in verse 15 of the doctrine of the Nicolaitanes. This would point to the conclusion that

Nicolaitanism was some form of heresy having for its object to bring the people of God into some sort of spiritual bondage. Such was the character of that early heresy against which the Epistle to the Galatians was written. The aim of that teaching was to bring into bondage again those whom Christ had made free from Jewish rites, ceremonies and ordinances, such as circumcision, and the keeping of holy days. That was the work of some whom the apostle called "false brethren", who, said he, "came in privily to spy out *our liberty* which we have in Christ Jesus, that they might *bring us into bondage"* (Gal. 2:4). The term "false brethren" corresponds closely with the words, "who say they are Jews and are not, but are the synagogue of Satan", the author of all that is "false". It would seem that this particular evil had become very general in those early days. For in the passage already referred to where the same apostle utters a strong denunciation of the "false apostles", who, though the ministers of Satan, were representing themselves as the apostles of Christ, he uses the expression "if any man *bring you into bondage,"* and also speaks of having been "in perils among *false brethren"* (2 Cor. 11:13, 15, 20, 26). It is not that circumcision, or the observance of days and the like, matters at all, one way or the other, since Christ by His death and resurrection abolished all the shadows of the law; "For in Christ Jesus neither circumcision availeth anything, nor uncircumcision, but a new creature" (Gal. 6:15). But the attempt to impose upon "the Israel of God" the obligation to observe the abolished ordinances of the law was not only an effort to bring them into bondage to "the weak and beggarly elements" (4:9) from which Christ had made them free, but was also a distortion of the gospel, so great as to make it a *different gospel* (1:6, 9).

The warning in the message to Pergamos is, "Repent; or else I will come unto thee quickly, and fight against them with the sword of my mouth". From the wording of this warning it appears that we have not here the case of a whole church being carried away with evil doctrine, as the whole church at Ephesus was charged with falling away from its first love. For Christ says, "I will come to *thee,* and will fight"—not against thee, but—"against *them*". Yet the call to "repent" was to the entire church, which is, of course, responsible for evils allowed to exist in its midst.

The promise to him that overcometh is twofold: (1) Christ will give him "to eat of the hidden manna". This is in apparent contrast with "to eat things sacrificed to idols" (v. 14). The reference is to some special enjoyment of Christ (of whom the manna is a type) as foreshadowed by the golden pot full of manna, which Aaron was commanded to lay up before the ark of the testimony in the holy of holies (Ex. 16:33; Heb. 9:4). (2) Christ will "give him a white stone, and in the stone a new name written, which no man knoweth saving he that receiveth it". The gift of a new name always carries with it some great blessing or high honor; and the lustrous white stone (probably a diamond) is exceedingly precious. Hence the promise points to something of surpassing value.

IV

To the church in Thyatira. Chapter 2:18-29

This is the longest of the letters, and its message is weighty. It reveals further the methods employed by the adversary, exposing the very "depths of Satan" (v. 24); so that, if we give earnest heed to these things, we shall be able to say with the apostle that "we are not ignorant of his devices"

The revelation of Jesus Christ must needs involve also the revelation of that mighty being who dares to contend with Him, and who wages ceaseless warfare for the possession of "the souls of men" (18:13). Hence various phases of that perpetual warfare are seen throughout the Book we are studying; and its entire course, from its beginning at the dawn of creation, to its final and decisive conflict in the time of the two beasts, which is in "the days of the voice of the seventh angel", is briefly traced in Chapter XII, as will be shown later on.

But in these letters we are given specially to see those tactics which the enemy employs against the churches of Christ. Therefore it behooves us to observe with closest attention the teaching of Christ concerning "the Devil" and "Satan" (see 12:9), as developed in the three successive letters to Smyrna, Pergamos, and Thyatira.

To this last-named church the Lord presents Himself as "The Son of God, Who hath His eyes like unto a flame of fire, and His feet are like fine brass".

The combination of these two symbols is very forceful; and moreover it is most appropriate to what follows. For the symbols strikingly present the Lord as the One whose eyes search out every evil deed, and Whose feet trample in judgment upon all the wicked doings of man.

This address to Thyatira is also noteworthy as being the first and the only time in the Book that Christ is presented by Name as the *"Son of God"*. That there is a special reason for this cannot be doubted; and that reason is to be sought, of course, in the conditions, peculiar to the Thyatira church, as disclosed in this letter. Let us therefore examine the passage with that thought in mind, remembering always that each of these seven churches is but a type, or representative on a small scale, of something in the affairs and history of the churches in general, throughout the world, and throughout the age. Briefly then, our view is that in this letter to Thyatira we are given to see the inception of that masterpiece of Satanic deception, that monstrous heresy, whose fullest development has been manifested in Romanism. Many facts and indications point to this conclusion, as will be seen hereafter; but we only state at this point the conclusion itself, in order that the matters now before us may be examined in the light thereof.

Now one great aim, if not the chief aim, of the enemy of God in propagating the Romish heresy (which is what we take to be "the depths of Satan") is to degrade the Lord Jesus Christ from His place as *Son of God;* for it is under that title that He is presented to men: (1) As the Creator and Heir of all things (Mat. 11:27; Col. 1:13-16; Heb. 1:1-3); (2) As the only Way of access to the Father (John 14:6; Eph. 2:18); (3) As the only Source and Giver of life to perishing men, and hence the only Saviour (John 5:21, 24, 25, 26; 1 J. 5:12); and (4) as the One who has brought to mankind the final and complete message or Word of God (Heb. 1:2; Rev. 22:18, 19).

In direct opposition to each of these features of revealed truth concerning the "Son of God", though the opposition is indeed disguised (so far as possible) with diabolical cleverness, the Romish heresy systematically present Jesus Christ, not as the Son of God, but as the Son of Mary. In all its doctrine, in all its ceremonies, in all its liturgy and books of devotion, in all its pictures and images, and in all its literature, the false church of Rome, with most consummate and satanic craft, and with most deadly purpose, exalts Mary—making her the compassionate one, the efficacious intercessor on behalf of sinners, the real mediator between God and men; and exhibits Christ in a position of subordination; the effect being, of course, that the millions who are thus deluded and blinded by "the god of this world", are led to put their trust in Mary instead of in Jesus Christ the *Son of*

God. It does not in the least affect the truth of what we are now setting forth that in Romish formularies the words of Scripture are often used, and that Christ is often referred to therein by His scriptural titles; for all that is but a part, and a most effective part, of the scheme of deception. The Devil knows the Scripture; and he knows how to quote it to his own ends; and he knows also how to mix in with the pure meal, the deadly poison of his own doctrine. Notwithstanding therefore the orthodoxy of creeds and formularies, the maintenance professedly of the doctrine of the Trinity (though truly it is denied in practice) and all that, the Christ of Romanism is "another Jesus". Hence, in that system chiefly, though in other great systems also (as Unitarianism, and other forms of *Humanism*) is fulfilled the apostolic prophecy, "He that cometh preacheth *another Jesus, whom we have not preached*" (2 Cor. 11:4). And be it carefully noted that, in sounding this warning, the apostle was speaking of what was to be the working in days to come of "the serpent" who "beguiled Eve by his subtlety" (v. 3). The adversary's activity along this line was to head up finally in "that wicked one," whose coming will be "after the *working of Satan,* with all power and signs and lying wonders, and with all deceivableness of unrighteousness in them that perish; because they received not the love of the truth that they might be saved" (2 Thess. 2:8-10).

In Thyatira, as in Pergamos, Christ sees many things to commend. For He says: "I know thy works,

The Letters to the Churches of Asia

and charity, and service, and faith, and thy patience, and thy works; and the last to be more than the first". This is high praise. But He hastens to the subject of the evil thing that had risen up and was developing amongst them, and to that subject the greater part of the message is devoted. "Notwithstanding" I have against thee* that thou sufferest that woman Jezebel, which calleth herself a prophetess, to teach, and to seduce my servants to commit fornication, and to eat things sacrificed unto idols".

The introduction of the name *Jezebel,* as a symbol of the evil seen by those flaming eyes, is very illuminating. Jezebel, whose name signifies *unchaste,* was the daughter of Ethbaal *(with Baal)* king of the Zidonians; and when Ahab king of Israel took her to wife, he became a mere puppet in her hands. Moreover, through her influence the worship of Baal became the State religion of the ten tribes, whence it spread to the kingdom of Judah. It was never completely eradicated till the captivity (1 Kings. 16:30-34 etc.).

Baalism was a licentious religion; and hence it fitly symbolizes that great heresy of christendom whose essential characteristic is spiritual unfaithfulness to Christ, and which fairly revels in gorgeous ceremonials and all that is attractive to the flesh. But the resemblance is even closer; for it has been shown by those who have made a study of comparative religions, that

---

* The words "a few things" are of very questionable authenticity; and they certainly are not in harmony with the context.

many specific features of Romish ritual are derived directly from Baal-worship.

In Biblical symbology, and particularly in the Apocalypse, a woman is the symbol of an elaborate or perfected system, whether religious, political, or industrial. In this instance Jezebel stands for a *system of doctrine*. The context makes this plain; for the words of Christ refer to Jezebel, not as a queen, but as a "prophetess", one who was *teaching* His servants to commit fornication, and to eat things sacrificed to idols. Evidently then there had arisen in the church at Thyatira a system of doctrine so monstrously evil that Christ utters a threatening warning against those who were accepting it, "except they repent of their deeds", saying: "Behold, I will cast her into a bed, and them that commit adultery with her into great tribulation, except they repent of their deeds. And I will kill her children with death; and all the churches shall know that I am He that searcheth the reins and hearts".

The execution of this threat is, I believe, revealed by the vision described in Chapter 17. There is seen a woman of royal rank, but utterly dissolute, one "with whom the kings of the earth have committed fornication, and the inhabitants of the earth have been made drunk with the wine of her fornication" (17:2). And we read that the ten horns (ten kings) "shall make her desolate and naked, and shall eat her flesh, and burn her with fire" (v. 16). This is the "bed" into which God will cast *her;* and her end will be like that of Jezebel, who was cast from an upper window into the street, which became her death-bed; and her flesh was literally eaten by the ravenous street dogs, insomuch that "they found no more of her than the skull, and the feet, and the palms of her hands" (2 K. 9:35). And not only so; but God's judgment upon Jezebel had been foretold "by His servant Elijah, the Tishbite" (v. 36) as that upon her anti-type has been foretold by "His servant John".

The words, "And I will kill *her children* with death," are striking. Rome delights in the name "mother". She has endless terms of endearment for her "children", and countless ways of expressing her motherly fondness for them. But her denial of the Son of God hides from those "children" the one and only source of *life:* Hence ("except they repent") there is nought for them but death, even the awful doom of "the second death".

But not all in Thyatira were involved in this false and ruinous doctrine. For Christ has a special word for "the rest in Thyatira, as many *as have not this doctrine, and which have not known the depths of Satan, as they speak*", *i. e.,* as the teachers of this doctrine of Jezebel teach. His word to those faithful ones is full of encouragement. "I will put upon you none other burden, but *that which ye have* hold fast till I come". That which they had was, as may be inferred from the context, the truth revealed in the New Testament Scriptures concerning *the Son of God* as the Creator and Heir of all things, as the only "Way" to the Father, and only Mediator between God and men, as the completeness of the Word of God, and especially as the only Source of eternal life.

The promise runs thus: "And he that overcometh and keepeth My works unto the end, to him will I give power over the nations; and he shall rule them with a rod of iron; as the vessels of a potter shall they be broken: even as I received of My Father; and I will give him the morning star".

A prominent feature of Romanism is its insistence on "works", and especially upon works wholly unlike those enjoined in the New Testament Scriptures, the "good works which God hath before ordained" for those who are re-created "in Christ Jesus" (Eph. 2:10; Tit. 3:8, 14). The works which "mother Rome" requires of her children are derived mainly from pagan sources, and are often characterized by superstition and triviality. In contrast with these, the Son of God promises a magnificent reward to them that keep *His* works unto the end. For such shall even share the great reward promised *Him* by His Father. This promise takes us back to that great prophecy, the Second Psalm, the only place in the O. T. where Christ is spoken of as the Son of God. It is Christ Himself who here speaks through David, saying: "I will declare the decree: the Lord hath said unto Me, Thou art *My Son;* this day have I begotten Thee. Ask of Me, and I will give Thee the heathen for Thine inheritance, and the uttermost part of the earth for Thy possession. Thou shalt *break them with a rod of iron;* Thou shalt dash them in pieces like a potter's vessel" (Psa. 2:7-9).

We shall have occasion to refer again, in the course of our present study, to this great prophetic Psalm, for there is much in the Apocalypse in the way of the fulfilment of its predictions.

We must bear in mind that the settled purpose of the church of Rome, from which it has never deviated in all the centuries of its existence, has been to acquire and exercise "power over the nations". The pope arrogantly and blasphemously claims the right to exercise that power as "the vicar of Christ". And the attempt of the papacy to rule the nations has had a considerable measure of success. This is symbolized by the picture of the harlot riding the ten-horned beast (Chap. XVII). How appropriate then is this promise to the overcomer: "I will give him *power over the nations*"!

The promise of the Morning Star points to the possession of Christ in some special and exceedingly precious way; for in Chapter 22:16, He says of Himself, "I AM the root and the offspring of David, the bright and *morning star*". These words suggest some connection with His royal authority as Son of David, as is also implied in the context, and in the Psalm of David, which we have quoted. In the resurrection "one star differeth from another star in glory" (1 Cor. 15:41). So the promise points to some pre-eminence among the "stars" in glory. The apostle Peter likewise has this reward in view when he exhorts the people of God to take heed unto the sure word of prophecy (now made "more sure" by the death and resurrection of Christ, and by the confirmation of the New Testament Scriptures) "as unto a light that shineth in a dark place, until the day dawn and *the day star* arise in your hearts" (2 Pet. 1:19).

V.

To the church in Sardis. Chapter 3:1-6.

The character of the last three messages is quite different from that of the four preceding. In those we are given to see the development of a positive evil raised up in the midst of the churches by the enemy of Christ. Its beginning was in "the deeds of the Nicolaitanes", in Ephesus. But the heresy had not made much headway there; for Christ commends the angel of the church of Ephesus for hating the deeds of the Nicolaitanes, "which", He said, "I also hate". But in Smyrna we note a great development of this evil thing. The synagogue of Satan is now in full swing. It is well organized, prosperous, aggressive, and animated by a persecuting spirit. Passing then to Pergamos, we find not merely the *synagogue* of Satan, but his *dwelling place,* and the *place of his throne;* and there we find also them that hold the doctrine of Balaam, and them that hold the doctrine of the Nicolaitanes. In Thyatira this evil reaches its full development; for there we find the very "depths of Satan". Things can get no worse along that line.

Coming now to Sardis we find, not the rise and progress of a system of satanic wickedness, but a state

The Letters to the Churches of Asia

of *decline and decay,* a dying out of spirituality and love of the truth.

To this church Christ presents Himself as "He that hath the seven Spirits of God, and the seven stars". These symbols are easily read in the light of Scripture. As already pointed out, the "seven Spirits symbolize the fullness of the "One Spirit", and the "seven stars" represent the totality of all the churches; Therefore, Christ here presents Himself as the One to whom God has given the Spirit in His fullness, "without measure" (John 3:34; Col. 1:19), and as the One who has supreme authority over all the churches.

The relations of Christ to His churches, as expressed by these symbols, can be profitably studied in Chapters XII-XIV of 1 Corinthians where the One Spirit—"the same Spirit", "the selfsame Spirit", the "one Spirit" (12:4, 8, 9, 11, 13)—is set forth in the diversities of His gifts and the fullness of His operations; and where the authority of the one Lord Jesus Christ, "the same Lord" (12:5), is declared as extending to and over "all the churches of the saints" (14:34, 37). The doctrine of these chapters, and the truth revealed in them, bear directly upon the message to Sardis, therefore it would be well for the reader to refer to them for further light. For the Lord, in addressing this church, (Sardis) calls upon them to remember how they had "received and heard". This must be a reference (1) to the gifts of the Holy Spirit which had been so freely bestowed at the beginning, and which all the churches had "received"; and (2) to "the doctrine of Christ", which had been so faithfully taught by the apostle Paul, who had "kept back nothing that was profitable", but had declared "all the counsel of God" (Ac. 20:20, 27), and which all the churches had "heard", both by word of mouth and by letter.

Christ finds in the "works" of this church nothing that He can expressly commend. For all He says on that subject is: "I know thy works, that thou hast a name that thou livest, and art dead". There is, however, a note of commendation, though rather a faint one, in verse 4.

This Sardis-like condition is very prevalent in our own day. For there be many congregations that have the name of *life* in that they bear the Name of Him that liveth, and in that they have also the name in their respective communities of being a "live church", because of their various activities, and of their numerous enterprises, both social and religious. But, in the eyes of Him whose Name they bear, those activities are but "dead works", whereof they have need to "repent", and from which their consciences need to be "purged" (Heb. 9:14).

So He proceeds at once to deliver His exhortation and His warning. "Be watchful, and strengthen the things which remain, that are ready to die: for I have not found thy works perfect before God. Remember therefore how thou hast received and heard; and hold fast, and repent. If therefore thou shalt not watch, I will come on thee as a thief, and thou shalt not know what hour I will come upon thee".

It is clear that these words do not speak of some evil thing suffered to exist and develop among them, but rather of the languishing and decay of spiritual life, and of the knowledge and love of the truth among them. That decay was plain in His sight, though hidden from human eyes by a cover of religious and other activities.

The exhortations are, *Be watchful; strengthen the things which remain; remember; hold fast; repent.* These all bear witness to a state of spiritual decline. It is as if the church of Sardis were composed of a company such as "the rest in Thyatira", those who did not hold the doctrine of Jezebel, but who had fallen into a very low spiritual condition. They had still something left of the truth of God that had been taught them, and of the things of Christ the Spirit had revealed to them. But these things were "ready to die"; and they too would soon be lost if they did not remember what they had received and heard in days past, and hold them fast, and repent.

The words "I will come upon thee as a thief", are not a reference to the Lord's second advent, but to a sudden visitation in judgment, if they should ignore His warning. And of course, this is a message to every church that is in the Sardis condition.

But there were a few "even in Sardis" whom the Lord could commend, though He could not bestow any praise upon the church as a whole.

"Thou hast a few names even in Sardis which have not defiled their garments; and they shall walk with Me in white, for they are worthy".

Here again we have the descriptive word "white", so often applied in this Book to divine and heavenly things. The garments of the redeemed in glory are "white", lustrous white (6:11; 7:9, 14). The garments of the bride are of "fine linen, clean and white" or *bright* with dazzling radiance (19:8). On the earth man is the only one of the countless species of living creatures that has no natural clothing. Sin stripped him of his garments of glory and beauty, wherein he originally stood in the likeness of God; and so he is the only shabbily dressed creature in the world. If this feature of man's natural condition were better understood, the promises of Scripture relating to the garments of the saints in glory would be more highly appreciated.

The promise to him that overcometh is in these words: "He that overcometh, the same shall be clothed in *white raiment;* and I will not blot out his name out of the book of life, but I will confess his name before My Father, and before His angels". The reference to the white raiment calls for no further comment. The book of life is prominent in the last chapters of the Apocalypse (20:12, 15; 21:27; 22:19). Its mention in the letter to Sardis is appropriate in view of the fact that life and death are the main theme of the letter. The final clause of the verse last quoted recalls the Lord's promise recorded in Matthew 10:32, 33, and

Luke 12:8, 9. Quoting from Luke: "And I say unto you, whosoever shall confess Me before men, him shall the Son of man also confess before the angels of God: But he that denieth Me before men shall be denied before the angels of God".

VI
To the church in Philadelphia. Chapter 3:7-13.

To this church Christ presents Himself in characters not taken from the sevenfold description of Him given in Chapter I; nor from other revelations of Himself given in that chapter. It will have been noticed by the careful reader that to each of the churches the Lord reveals Himself in a character that is in keeping with the condition of the particular church addressed. We should expect therefore, from the distinctive character wherein He presents Himself to the church in Philadelphia, to find there a condition of things quite different from that of every other church. And that is what we do find.

The message begins: "These things saith He that is holy, He that is true, He that hath the key of David, He that openeth and no man shutteth; and shutteth and no man openeth".

There is no reference here to the eyes of flame, nor to the feet that tread down the evil-doers and their works, nor to the sword of His mouth, nor even to the right hand of His power with which He holds the seven stars. The very first words indicate that the church in Philadelphia is in such a state of spirituality as to know

Him who is *holy,* and Who is *true.* Again we have from Christ a strong assertion of His Deity; for only God can say "I AM holy" (1 Pet. 1:16: Lev. 11:44). Isaiah 57:15 is specially in view: "For thus saith the High and Lofty One that inhabiteth eternity, WHOSE NAME IS HOLY; I dwell in the high and holy place, with him also that is of a contrite and humble spirit". Such evidently was the spirit of the church in Philadelphia, to which He now comes, "to revive the spirit of the humble, and to revive the heart of the contrite ones".

The words "He that is *true",* take us to John 17:3; where He says: "And this is life eternal, that they might know Thee, the ONLY TRUE GOD, and Jesus Christ whom Thou hast sent"; and also to 1 John 5:20, where we read: "And we know that the Son of God is come, and hath given us an understanding that we may know HIM THAT IS TRUE; and we are IN HIM THAT IS TRUE, even in His Son, Jesus Christ. This the TRUE GOD and eternal life". These words might be taken as expressive of the spirit of the church in Philadelphia.

The next words of the address, "He that hath the key of David, He that openeth" etc. present difficulty, and have been variously explained. I will presently refer to those passages of Scripture which seem to bear upon this part of the verse, and in the light of which it must be interpreted. The next verse of the chapter we are studying is first of all to be taken into consideration, for it is directly connected in thought: "Be-

The Letters to the Churches of Asia

hold, I have set before thee an *open door,* and no man can shut it: for thou hast a little strength, and hast kept My word, and hast not denied My name".

The meaning of this is clear in part at least. It is because this church has but little strength of its own that Christ says "I have set before thee an open door, and no man can shut it". And this door, opened by the power of Christ, and kept open by His power, is moreover His reward to the church for keeping His Word and not denying His Name. This is of the utmost importance for such a time as this, a time of wholesale denials of His Word and His Name on the part of large and influential "churches", and of prominent, learned, and able "ministers". For whatever may be signified by the "open door", it is beyond question something in the nature of a rich *reward* to the faithful church of "little strength", in a time of great and widespread apostasy.

Some have referred to the "open door" of opportunity of which Paul speaks (1 Cor. 16:9; 2 Cor. 2:12), and have suggested that the door which Christ opened to the church in Philadelphia was of that nature. This would imply that Philadelphia was zealous in missionary effort, and in spreading the gospel. But this suggestion does not agree with the rest of the verse; and particularly does it fail to explain the reference to "the Key of David". This striking phrase will put us on the track of the meaning, for it occurs in one other passage, and only one, namely, Isaiah 22:22. Turning to that Scripture we find that the prophet is there speaking in and of the days of Hezekiah, when the Assyrian was invading the land; when "breaches" had been made in "the city of David", and the defenders were so sorely pressed that they had even torn down the houses in order to repair the breaches in the wall (vv. 9, 10). Yet they were *not looking to the Lord for help*. On the contrary, though He was calling them to weeping, and to mourning, and to sackcloth (*i. e.* to *repent*), they were giving themselves over to mirth and festivity, to joy and gladness, eating flesh and drinking wine, saying, "let us eat and drink, for tomorrow we die" (vv. 11-13). At that time Shebna was the officer "over the house", and to him God sent by Isaiah a message announcing the judgment that was about to fall upon him. And then He says, "And it shall come to pass in that day that I will call my servant Eliakim, the son of Hilkiah—and I will commit thy government into *his* hand—and *the key of the house of David will I lay upon his shoulder; so he shall open and none shall shut; and he shall shut and none shall open* . . . and they shall hang on him all the glory of his father's house" etc. (vv. 20-24).

This passage should be considered in connection with Isaiah's earlier prophecy concerning the birth of Christ, in which occur the well-known words, "And the government shall be *upon His shoulder*; . . . Of the increase of His government and peace there shall be no end, upon *the throne of David*" (Isa. 9:6, 7). And the conclusion I draw from the two passages is that "the key of David" is a symbol for the royal authority of Christ as the promised Son of David, the Messiah, and as the Heir of all the promises made to David and his house, that is to say, of "the sure mercies of David". Briefly then, to have the key of David means to have supreme and absolute authority. Moreover, our Lord, by speaking of Himself as "He that hath the key of David", in effect says that Eliakim was a type of Himself, and that the circumstances in which the key of David was laid upon the shoulder of Eliakim were typical of the circumstances in which the Philadelphian church found itself. 2 Kings 18 tells us what those circumstances were. Jerusalem was threatened by the Assyrian armies; and Rabshakeh had come against the city with a great host, and stood without the wall and cried out an insulting message to be carried to King Hezekiah. Eliakim and Shebna were the representatives of the King who received the message and brought it to him. The sequel was that God, through Isaiah, sent to Hezekiah the promise of deliverance from the King of Assyria, which promise He immediately fulfilled. This was, so to speak a *door of escape or deliverance,* a *way out* of threatened danger, a door which those in Jerusalem could not open for themselves, because they had but a "little strength". This I take to be the nature of the assurance given to the church in Philadelphia.

But who was the enemy that threatened them? The next verse answers this question; and it also enlarges the promise: "Behold, I will make them *of the synagogue of Satan,* which say they are Jews, and are not, but do lie: behold, I will make them to come and worship before thy feet, and to know that I have loved thee".

Referring back to our comments on the message to Smyrna, another weak but faithful church, we find two conditions that are repeated in Philadelphia; first, they in Smyrna were opposed and persecuted by false brethren, who said they were "Jews", but in reality were "the synagogue of Satan"; second, they were about to have great tribulation ("tribulation ten days"). This second condition is found in Philadelphia also; for verse 10 reads: "Because thou hast kept the word of my patience, I also will keep thee from *the hour of temptation,* which shall come upon all the world, to try them that dwell upon the earth". But here is a great difference. Those in Smyrna were to suffer "unto death", and therefore the comfort to the overcomers was that they should "not be hurt of the *second* death". There was no open door of escape for them. But the church in Philadelphia was to be kept from (*i. e.* out of) the impending trial, whatever the nature thereof might be. Christ would exercise His royal authority, the supreme lordship given Him in heaven and earth, symbolized by the key of David, and would open to them a door of deliverance.

The message continues: "Behold, I come quickly, hold that fast which thou hast, that no man take thy crown".

We have no warrant to take the words "I come quickly" as signifying Christ's second advent; for whatever may be the more remote application of the passage, its immediate application was to the church in Philadelphia actually existing in John's day. Christ often speaks of His coming to an individual or a company in a sense quite different from His personal and visible advent in power and glory. John himself had recorded the words, "I will not leave you comfortless, I will *come to you*" (John 14:18); and these, "If any man love Me he will keep My words" (this is what the church in Philadelphia had done) "and My Father will love him, and we will *come unto him*" (id. v. 23). But we have a more direct indication than these of the sense of this promise; for in the preceding letter to Ephesus Christ had said, "Or else I will *come* unto thee quickly", using the same words as here (2:5). Also to Pergamos He had said, "Repent, or else I will *come* unto thee quickly" (2:16); and to Sardis likewise, "I will *come* on thee as a thief" *i. e.* most unexpectedly (3:3).

But while insisting, as we must, upon the first application of the passage to the church in Philadelphia, we believe the promise will have its final and complete fulfilment in the second coming of Christ, when He will open a door of deliverance heavenward for every church and every saint which and who, in a day of dark apostasy, is keeping His Word and not denying His Name. We believe too that this was intended to be at all times during the Lord's absence a bright hope and cheering prospect before the eyes of His true people.

The words, "Hold that fast which thou hast, that no man take thy crown", seem also to point to the case of Shebna and Eliakim as an illustration. Shebna had the "crown", so to speak; that is, he was "over the house", and wore the "robe" and "girdle" of office; but God said, "I will clothe Eliakim with thy robe, and strengthen him with thy girdle, and I will commit *thy government* into his hands" (Isa. 22:15, 20-22). Thus another man took Shebna's crown; and the reason was that *he would not heed the Lord's call to repent* (v. 12).

Reference should also be had in this connection to the Lord's parable of the nobleman, "who went into a far country to receive for himself a kingdom and to return" (Lu. 19:11-27). When Christ sent this message to the Church in Philadelphia He (the "nobleman" of the parable) had already gone to heaven (the "far country") and had received the kingdom, for His own description of Himself is "He that *hath* the key of David", which declares that the kingdom had been given Him. And to this agree the words of Paul, "Remember that Jesus Christ of the *seed of David* was raised from the dead according to my gospel" (2 Tim. 2:8); and again: "And as concerning that He raised Him from the dead, now no more to return to corruption, He said on this wise, I will give you the sure mercies of David" (Ac. 13:34). But the particular feature of the parable that now concerns us is that which relates to the servant who hid his lord's money in a napkin, and who sought to justify himself by casting aspersions upon his lord's character. Of that man it might be said he had not kept his lord's word, and had denied his name. Therefore his pound was taken from him and *given to another*.

Let us then give all diligence to hold that fast which we have; for our Lord's word is, "That unto every one which *hath* shall be given"—a crown;—"and from him that hath not, even *that he hath* shall be taken away from him" (Lu. 19:26).

The promise to him that overcometh, in this letter to Philadelphia, is as remarkable and as distinctive as is the introductory address: "Him that overcometh will I make a pillar in the temple of My God; and he shall go no more out: and I will write upon him the Name of My God, and the Name of the city of My God, which is New Jerusalem, which cometh down out of heaven from My God; and I will write upon him My new Name".

These promises are great beyond the power of words to express. We make, therefore, no attempt to explain them; but this only would we point out, namely, that the entire promise is very suggestive of David, who comes prominently into view in this last Book of the Bible (see 5:5 and 22:16)—who has indeed a place in it such as is given to no other man. David's longing desire was for the house of God (Ps. 23:6; 1 Chr. 29:3), and the "one thing" he desired and sought after was that he might *dwell* in the house of the Lord all the days of his life (Ps. 27:4). How directly responsive to this is the first clause of the promise, "I will make him *a pillar* (something permanent) in the temple of My God; and he shall *go no more out"!* The crown, which speaks of royal honors, has been already mentioned; and now comes a reference to the royal City, the New Jerusalem, which answers to the city of David, the earthly Jerusalem. The promise of the new name also is connected with that City; for in the description John gives of it he says: "The throne of God and of the Lamb shall be in it; and His servants shall serve Him: and they shall see His face; and *His Name shall be in their foreheads"* (22:3, 4).

VII

To the church of the Laodiceans. Chapter 3:14-22.

We come now to the last of the seven letters. It too has a very distinctive character, and conveys a most solemn and impressive message, one that fitly brings to a conclusion this, the very last of the connected discourses of Christ.

This is a church for which the apostle Paul had had great conflict (Col. 2:1; 4:15); and now we find it in a state of extreme spiritual destitution.

The Lord here presents Himself as "The Amen, the faithful and true Witness, the Beginning of the creation of God". These characters are not taken from the sevenfold description of Chapter 1:13-16; but they are taken from other revelations of the Lord Jesus Christ found in that chapter. For He is there presented as the "Alpha and Omega, the Beginning and the ending" (v. 8), and also as "the faithful Witness" (v. 5).

The significance of this address is evident. As I have sought to show above, the churches of Christ were placed in the world primarily to serve as witnesses to Him, and in these letters they are viewed in that capacity. The things which Christ commends are things which testify to Him; and the things He reproves are things which mar the testimony of the churches, and tend to bring dishonor upon His Name. They may fail; but He is ever "the faithful and true *witness*".

He moreover is "the Amen". Here again the Lord Jesus Christ takes to Himself one of the names of God. It is a remarkable name; and the connection in which it occurs should be carefully noted, because of the light it throws upon the Scripture we are studying. It is found in Isaiah 65:16, in the midst of a prophecy wherein God foretells in strong and clear words the overwhelming judgments that were to fall upon the apostate people of Israel, them "that forsake the Lord"; and where He foretells also that He will transfer His favor to another people, of whom He speaks as "My servants", and "My chosen" (Isa. 65:13-15). This great thing which God pledged Himself to do He refers to as a *new creation,* saying, "For behold, I create new heavens and a new earth" (v. 17); and He speaks also of creating another Jerusalem, where "the voice of weeping and the voice of crying" shall be "no more heard" (vv. 18-20). And here it is that we find this remarkable passage:

"And ye"—apostate Israel—"shall leave your name for a curse unto my chosen" (cf. those who say they are *Jews*); "for the Lord God shall slay thee, and call His servants by *another name*" (cf. Rev. 22:3, 4 and the promise to Philadelphia): "That he who blesseth himself in the earth, shall bless himself in the God of Truth"—literally GOD THE AMEN; "and he that sweareth in the earth, shall swear by the God of Truth"—GOD THE AMEN (vv. 15, 16).

This title describes God as the One who accomplishes all His purposes and all His promises. The Lord Jesus Christ is this *God the Amen;* "For all the promises of God in Him are yea, and in Him *Amen*" (2 Cor. 1:20). And most appropriately He presents Himself in this character in the last of the seven messages. It is most fitting too that He should here couple with this revelation of Himself the statement that He is also, "the Beginning of the creation of God". The position in which this last statement occurs would lead us to think that it is the new creation, specifically mentioned in Isaiah's prophecy, that is in view; that is to say, the new spiritual creation begun in the resurrection of Jesus Christ. But whichever it be, the statement is equally true.

The spiritual condition of this church is thus described: "I know thy works, that thou art neither cold nor hot: I would thou wert cold or hot. So then, because thou art lukewarm, and neither cold nor hot, I will spue thee out of My mouth".

These words strikingly describe a condition of indifference. The Laodiceans were not warm in affection for Christ, they were not burning with zeal in His cause; nor yet were they cold and altogether heartless. If they had been in this latter state it would have been easier for Him to deal with them, and there would have been greater likelihood that they would discover their real condition and need. Therefore He says, "I would thou wert cold or hot". It is not easy to see why the Lord would rather they had been actually cold, than lukewarm. Therefore the following comments may be helpful:

"The Lord speaks here only of the condition of those who stand in a relation to Himself. So that we can think of being 'cold' only in such manner as has connected with it the painful sensation that one is cold, and hence has a hearty desire to become hot. . . . In a manner similar to the being 'cold' here the being 'blind' occurs in John 9:41 'were ye blind *(i. e.* did ye but feel yourselves blind) ye should not have sin; but now ye say, We see; therefore your sin remains'. Accordingly the being cold is an absolutely preferable state to the being lukewarm. 'Would that thou wert cold', the Lord is also saying to our Laodicean age. Were it but come to that, the warmth would soon appear of itself" (Hengstenberg).

"One must not estimate what he has of the heat of life by his own feelings. A person in a state of bodily health who has a lively heat in his body may be himself quite unconscious of it, while another who takes his hand readily perceives it. So in spiritual things, one who is accustomed to spiritual ardour may be without much sensibility, such as may appear strange and wonderful to another of little experience in the divine life. It belongs also to the fundamental constitution of the soul, that when it burns with a fervent zeal for God, the fire within shall never say, *'It is enough'* " (Bengel).

Christ now proceeds to declare wherein their lukewarmness consisted; saying, "Because thou sayest, I am rich, and increased with goods, and have need of nothing; and knowest not that thou art wretched, and miserable, and poor, and blind, and naked".

Ignorance of its true condition, therefore, is that which chiefly characterized the church of the Laodiceans; thinking itself rich when in reality it was poor; thinking itself well supplied with all that a church of Christ should have, when in reality it was destitute of the most essential things. The state of this church is just the reverse of that in Smyrna, which was seemingly in poverty and tribulation, but in reality was "rich".

There was no tribulation in Laodicea, no persecutions, no synagogue of Satan to molest them. They were having a very easy and comfortable time. No doubt the church-machinery was of the most approved pattern, the equipment all up-to-date, and the appointed routine of services regularly carried out. Such churches are numerous, and to make them realize their actual spiritual state is ever a matter of stupendous difficulty.

But the Lord does not give them over. First He proffers advice, "I counsel thee"—. Then He calls them to "repent", coupling that call with a most tender word of exhortation. Then He presents to them a

The Letters to the Churches of Asia

wondrous opportunity and possibility (v. 20). And finally He gives a surpassingly glorious promise (v. 21). Thus we find the message to Laodicea full of encouragement.

Christ had declared that they were "poor, blind, and naked"; but in the next breath He offers to supply them with "gold", that they might be no longer *poor;* with white raiment, that they might be *suitably clad;* and with eye-salve, that they *might see.*

1. *Gold tried in the fire.* In Psalm 19:7-11 David declares the value of the Word of God, speaking in detail of the *law* of the Lord, His *testimony,* His *statutes,* His *commandments,* His *judgments;* and he says of them: "More to be desired are they than *gold,* yea, than much *fine (i. e. refined) gold".* Again in Psalm 12:6 he says: "The words of the Lord are *pure* words; as silver *tried in a furnace of earth, purified seven times".* The words of the Lord are little accounted of in the church of the Laodiceans, and have but little part or influence in its doings. The minister chooses a text from the Bible (unless he finds something more appropriate to his discourse in some other book, or in the daily paper); but real ministry of the Word of God, a habitual unfolding of its contents and application of its lessons, a searching of its pages and a laying to heart of its admonitions, have no place in this church. Dross is taken for gold, and pewter for silver. Hence, in the very place where there is the most appalling spiritual poverty, the people are think-

ing themselves rich, and increased with goods, and in need of nothing.

2. *White raiment that thou mayest be clothed, and that the shame of thy nakedness do not appear.* Again we have a reference to that lustrous glistening "white", which is the proper raiment of the saints of God. This is one of the symbols that is explained for us in this Book; for in Chapter 19:8 it is stated that the "fine linen, clean and *white*" represents "the righteousness (or righteous acts) of the saints". The figure of a robe, or garment, is sometimes used (as in Isaiah 61:10; and Mat. 22:11) to represent the righteousness of God, which He bestows as a gift upon every one who believes in Jesus Christ. But here it symbolizes those acts of righteousness which should always adorn the conduct of God's people.

3. *Eye-salve, that thou mayest see.* The advice to "anoint thine eyes with eyesalve", suggests that the church of the Laodiceans was destitute of the gifts of the Holy Spirit, and was dependent upon church machinery for the carrying on of all its work. For John speaks of the Holy Spirit as the Unction (or Anointing) from Christ, "the Holy One" (1 John 2:20); and says: "But the Anointing which ye have received of Him abideth in you, and ye need not that any man teach you: but as the same Anointing teacheth you all things, and is Truth, and is no lie, and even as it hath taught you, ye shall abide in Him" (v. 27).

"Buy of Me". Christ stands ready to supply these things of priceless worth to all who are willing to

"buy". He is saying, as in Isaiah 55:1, "Come ye, and he that hath no money; come ye, . . . *buy* without money, and without price". Yet the word "buy" is used advisedly, for we are to *"buy* the truth; . . . also wisdom, and instruction, and understanding" (Prov. 23:23). Every bit of God's truth that is really ours, every bit of heavenly wisdom, instruction, and understanding that is ours, has *cost us something;* and if we are not willing to make some sacrifice of time, inclination, effort, to forego some indulgence, or some opportunity for earthly gain or enjoyment, in order to enrich ourselves with heavenly treasure, then we have not yet learned the difference in value between tinsel and gold, between colored beads of glass and gems of the deepest mine.

Then comes a word which reveals all of our Lord's tenderness and all of His faithfulness: "As many as I love, I rebuke and chasten: be zealous, therefore, and repent" (v. 19).

Sharp has been His rebuke to this lukewarm church. But it does not mean that He had turned away and abandoned them, or was about to do so. It means *just the reverse.* For He was standing near, and ready to supply their need, and to enrich them with all His treasure; and His rebuke was a proof of His unchanging *love.* Nor will He fail to use the rod of correction, if His "counsel", and His call to "repent" be unheeded. Of this He warns them, and then says, "Be *zealous therefore,* and repent". The call for *zeal* is not found elsewhere. It is appropriate here, because of the prevailing lukewarmness.

But He is not through yet revealing His grace to this church, and His yearning desire for its recovery from its state of spiritual tepidity, poverty, blindness and nakedness. So He adds this final word: *"Behold, I stand at the door and knock: if any man hear My voice, and open the door, I will come in to him, and sup with him, and he with Me"* (v. 20).

The comment we have most frequently seen and heard upon this verse is to the effect that it indicates the well-nigh hopeless state of this church. Christ is *outside*, we are told; and then usually it is added that He is not expecting to be admitted, and so forth.

But there is another view that may be taken of the matter, a view that is more in harmony with the deep concern manifested, the generous offer made, and the unchanging love declared, in the preceding verses. It is not that Christ is *outside* that chiefly impresses me; but that He is *so near*, even at the very door; and not only so, but is ready to enter instantly it is opened. For He is standing close by, not that He may swiftly visit them in judgment, but that He may *come in and sup with them*. And yet more, He is even knocking for admission; and not only so, but He will come in to "any man", who will hear His voice, and open the door. This is very, very far, as I see it, from being a hopeless, or even a discouraging situation.

The state of affairs at the end of this letter reminds us of that at the end of the great parable of Luke XV, generally called the parable of the Prodigal Son, though it would be more properly called the parable of the *Elder* Son, seeing that the climax of the lesson has to do with him. In the parable, the elder son, well satisfied with himself, is *outside* the house, the door is *open,* and his father is entreating him to come in. Here it is the other way. The self-satisfied church is *inside,* the door is *closed,* and Christ is calling and knocking for admission. The point of resemblance lies in this, that in both cases the story is *left unfinished,* so that we do not know how the matter ended. Is not God in each case saying in effect that He has done all that Divine Love could do, and that the eternal issue now rests with those to whom the last appeal has been made, and over whom Divine compassion still lingers?

The message to the church of the Laodiceans is distinctive in that it has a special word to the individual— *"if any man".* In Thyatira the Lord recognizes a remnant of faithful ones, "the *rest* in Thyatira, as many as have not this doctrine" (2:24); and in Sardis there are "a *few names* which have not defiled their garments" (3:4); but in Laodicea there is a word of strong encouragement to the *individual* who, amidst general indifference to the things of God, longs for personal fellowship with the Lover of his soul. For he has only to open the door of his inner being in order to have his desire fulfilled. Such a one need not do even so much as the disciples at Emmaus, who "constrained

Him", ere "He went in to tarry" and to sup with them (Lu. 24:29, 30).

The letter closes with the greatest of all the promises: "To him that overcometh will I grant to sit with Me in My throne, even as I also overcame, and am set down with My Father in His throne". This needs no comment. And now in conclusion, for the seventh time we hear the urgent call (and may we find grace to heed it) "He that hath an ear, let him hear what the Spirit saith unto the churches".

The Seven Letters Viewed as One Discourse

By many able commentators these seven letters are taken as constituting one connected prophecy, foretelling the main developments and principal eras in the history of God's people (or as some call it "the professing church") throughout this age. This idea has been elaborately worked out in a number of ably written books, and it has considerable support in "Church" History. For it does appear as if there had been a succession of periods, more or less clearly marked, corresponding respectively, in a general way at least, to the conditions set forth in these several letters, and occurring in the same order; that is to say, first an "Ephesus" period, (loss of first love) immediately following the days of the apostles; then a "Smyrna" period of fiery persecution, and so on.

We do not, however, attempt to consider the letters from that point of view, partly because it has been thoroughly done in books easily obtainable, but chiefly because that is certainly not the *main* purpose of these last messages of the risen Lord Jesus Christ to His churches. They are given us, not so much to reveal things to come, as to admonish, encourage, warn, guide, and reprove, to the end that we may pass the time of our sojourning here in fear, and may give all diligence to work out our own salvation with fear and trembling, having respect "unto the recompense of the reward". In each letter there are lessons for every church and every saint. For in each the call is to *every one* that hath an ear, to hear what the Spirit is saying, —not to one church in particular, but — to "the churches" in general.

CHAPTER IV

The Vision of the Throne in Heaven

"After this I looked, and behold, a door was opened in heaven; and the first voice which I heard was as it were of a trumpet talking with me; which said, Come up hither, and I will show thee things which must be hereafter. And immediately I was in the spirit; and behold, a throne was set in heaven, and One sat on the throne".

THE words, "Behold, A THRONE!" give us the subject of this superlatively wonderful and supremely important vision. For the throne is the central object of this scene, and every other person and thing embraced in it takes its place with reference to that throne. In these two short chapters the word "throne" occurs seventeen times. Thus is impressed upon us the mighty truth, which is generally ignored on earth, that there is a *throne in heaven,* and that all things are under the authority of Him that sitteth upon the throne. This is the first thing made evident to the consciousness of every man to whom a door is opened in heaven. For to men in their natural condition the heavens are closed, and the god of this world blinds their minds even to the elementary truth that "the Lord God omnipotent reigneth".

But the special purpose of this vision is not to bring to mind the great truth that all things are under the government of God. For the scene pictured in Chapter IV is but introductory to that of Chapter V, in

The Vision of the Throne in Heaven

which is revealed the glory of the risen Redeemer, whose presence upon that throne is what gives to this day of grace and salvation its distinctive character. For we have need at this point again to remind ourselves that the Book we are studying is "the revelation of Jesus Christ". His participation in the government of the universe is concealed from the eyes of men. It is known, and can be known, only by revelation. What is shut to man he cannot by his own efforts discover. But the ministry of the Holy Spirit is to reveal to the eye of faith the hidden glories of the exalted Redeemer. "Look, ye saints, the sight is glorious! See the Man of sorrows *now!*"

The vision of Chapters IV and V is quite disconnected from that of the preceding chapters. For the description begins, "After this I looked"—which means, of course, after the writing of the letters to the churches of Asia. The "first voice as a trumpet" which John had previously heard speaking with him is that of Chapter 1:10: "I was in the spirit on the Lord's Day, and heard behind me *a great voice, as of a trumpet*". That voice now summons John to come on high through the open door which he had already seen. The words "immediately I was (or more correctly *became*) in the spirit", show that a call to "come up hither" is the same as a call to be in the spirit. It summoned John to leave the region of the natural senses, and to be in the region of the supernatural, "the spirit". Those words also pre-suppose that, between the preceding vision and this present one, there was an interval during which John was in his natural state. And it is important to note this; for it is not possible to advance in the understanding of this Book until it is clearly apprehended that it does not give a regularly progressive disclosure of the future, but is divided into a number of groups, each formally complete in itself, and each beginning, *not where the next preceding left off,* but at some starting point (it may be in the distant past) best suited to the special topic of that vision or group.

The words, "Immediately I became in the spirit" are evidently in purposed agreement with those of 1:10, which are the same as here, "I became in the spirit", thus giving us to know that the second vision begins at this point. According to Bengel: "John was at once lifted above all that is natural and placed among divine things, his whole soul being filled, illuminated and occupied by these".

The first part of the description (Chapter IV) pictures the throne, the assemblage of elders surrounding the throne, the seven lamps of fire before the throne, the sea of glass, and the four living creatures. This part closes with the worship rendered by the living creatures and the anthem of praise from the four and twenty elders to Him that sat on the throne, who liveth for ever and ever. The second part of the vision is marked by the presence upon the throne of the exalted Redeemer, seen as "a Lamb as it had been slain, having seven horns and seven eyes". The remarkable circumstances of His introduction to the seer's notice

The Vision of the Throne in Heaven

make it very evident that the main purpose of this vision as a whole is to reveal our glorified Saviour *in the act of occupying His Father's throne,* than which we can conceive of no event more worthy of being thus revealed, or more worthy to evoke the anthem of praise and adoration which bursts forth from those nearest the throne, and then is taken up by the myriads of angels that surround the throne, finally extending to "every creature which is in heaven, and on earth, and under the earth". It is not conceivable that any other event could evoke this outburst of praise from all creation. But we are not left in any uncertainty whatever as to the occasion of this transcendently important scene; for a comparison of the anthem at the end of Chapter IV with that at the end of Chapter V shows that the subject of the former is creation *("for* Thou hast *created all things"),* whereas that of the latter is redemption *("for* Thou wast slain, and hast *redeemed us").*

Beyond any doubt then, we have here the "revelation" of that supremely glorious event by which were fulfilled the greatest of the prophecies, such as "Yet have I set My King upon Zion the mountain of My holiness" (Ps. 2:6); "The LORD said unto my Lord, Sit Thou at My right hand, until I make Thine enemies Thy footstool" (Ps. 110:1); the event declared in the New Testament Scriptures which tell us that the risen Redeemer is "gone into heaven, and is on the right hand of God, *angels and authorities and powers being made subject unto Him"* (1 Pet. 3:22); that God has "raised Him from the dead and set Him at His own right hand in the heavenly places, far above all principality, and power, and might, and dominion, and every name that is named, not only in this world, but also in that which is to come" (Eph. 1:20-23).

In view of these clear indications there is, to my mind, no room for any doubt whatever that the group of visions beginning with Chapters IV and V and embracing the entire program of the seals, has for its historical starting-point *the ascension of our risen Lord into heaven and His occupation of the place of which He alone is worthy at the right hand of the Majesty in the heavens;* and that this group of visions has to do with events which *began to happen from that transcendently glorious occasion.* And this is the conclusion of a large majority, including, I think, far the ablest, of those who have sought to expound the contents of this Book,—though, of course, majorities settle nothing.

Furthermore, the words of the Lord Himself furnish a link which directly connects this vision with the one preceding. For in His message to Laodicea He said, "Even as I also *overcame,* and am *set down* (literally, *sat* down) with my Father in His throne" (3:21). The past tenses of the verbs in this sentence plainly declare that the occupation by Him of His Father's throne *had already taken place* when He appeared to John in that first vision on the isle of Patmos. We have therefore only to connect with this the words spoken by one of the elders to John, as recorded in

Chapter 5:5, in order to have a complete revelation as to the time of the scene described in these chapters. That elder said: "Weep not, behold: the Lion of the tribe of Judah *hath prevailed* to open the book, and to loose the seven seals thereof". And thereupon John looked, and saw in the midst of the throne a Lamb as it had been slain. The word here rendered "prevailed" is *the same as is rendered "overcame"* in Chapter 3:24. Thus it is made plain that the vision begins at the point where the Lord Jesus Christ, having "overcome" by His sacrificial death (Heb. 2:14) the powers of evil, death, and hell, and being raised from the dead by the glory of the Father, "sat down" with Him upon His throne in heaven. It begins at the fulfilment of the words of Psalm 24:7-10: "Lift up your heads, O ye gates; and be ye lifted up, ye everlasting doors; and the *King of Glory shall come in*". It shows us also the fulfilment of Daniel's prophetic vision, who beheld the heavenly courts "until the thrones were set up" (not *cast down,* as the A. V. has it), "and the Ancient of days did sit. . . . And behold, One like the Son of man came to the Ancient of days . . . and there was given Him dominion, and glory, and a Kingdom" (Dan. 7:9-14). But I do not dwell upon this vision of Daniel at this point, for it will be needful to refer to it later on.

On the other hand, I am unable to find in the Scriptures any support at all for the view that the vision of Revelation IV and V shows something that is yet future, and that will not take place until the saints of

God are raised, changed, and taken to heaven. The fact that in this vision are seen four and twenty elders, who are taken (and rightly) to be a representation of the redeemed of the Lord, lends no support whatever to that view, as will be shown when we come to discuss the several details of the vision.

Therefore, as I view the matter, God has given us in this scene a symbolic representation of His two-fold work of Creation and Redemption; the epoch of the vision being that at which Redemption was accomplished as regards the payment of the redemption price, "the precious blood of Christ" (1 Pet. 1:19), when "by His own blood, He entered in once (for all) into the holy place, having obtained *eternal redemption*" (Heb. 9:12). There yet remain, however, many things to be accomplished before "the redemption of the purchased possession unto the praise of His glory" (Eph. 1:14). For "the day of redemption" in that sense, unto which day we have been sealed by the Holy Spirit of God (Eph. 4:30), is yet future. Between these two stages of the work of redemption—the paying of the purchase price by the Lamb that was slain and has redeemed us to God by His blood, and the taking possession of the whole redeemed creation—lay the history of the entire dispensation of the Holy Spirit. And it is to such features of that history as, in the wisdom of God, it most behoved us to know, that the visions of this Book, down to Chapter 20:3, relate. It is of the utmost importance then that we should be clear as to this; for manifestly, if such be indeed the purpose of these visions, we should wholly defeat that purpose, so far as we ourselves are concerned, by postponing their fulfilment to another dispensation.

DETAILS OF THE VISION

The Throne. As already pointed out, the central feature of the vision, dominating and overshadowing all else, is the Throne. That He who sat thereon when first seen by John is God the Father is apparent from the fact that He is distinguished from the Lamb, and from the seven Spirits. "The Kingdom is originally the Father's and remains His. For Christ sits upon the Father's throne" (Bengel). What John saw in this vision is what Peter had proclaimed in Jerusalem on the day of Pentecost (Acts 2:33).

"And He that sat was to look upon like a jasper and a sardius; and there was a rainbow round about the throne, in sight like unto an emerald".

The three precious stones here mentioned are, of course, symbols; and their meaning as such lies, no doubt, in their respective colors. The jasper is of divers colors; but where it is mentioned in the description of the New Jerusalem (21:11) there are the added words, *"clear as crystal"*, which verse also states that it is the "most precious" stone, and is *the light* of the heavenly city. And that light, according to verse 23, is "the *glory* of *God"*, that of His essential nature. This is what is here represented by the jasper. The sardius, according to an authority on precious stones, is "red, as red flesh, dark red". Orpheus speaks of the "blood-colored sardius", and Epiphanius says, "it is of a fiery red appearance and blood-like". This is taken by some to indicate the approach of judgment, which is plainly in view (v. 5) even though at a distance. By others it is thought to suggest the punitive righteousness of God, "the light in its warmth, light in love, or its opposite anger". These are the thoughts that are most prominently associated with the color of blood-red or fiery red. When Ezekiel beheld the glory of the Lord approaching in judgment there was the appearance of "a *fire* infolding itself", and a "brightness", a word denoting the brightest splendour there can be, "the color of amber, out of the midst of the fire" (Ez. 1:4); and this description is repeated in slightly different terms in Chapter 1:27, and 8:2.

The Rainbow. John makes prominent mention of a rainbow, not incomplete as we now see it in the cloud after rain, but completely encircling the throne. The rainbow was the token of the covenant God made with Noah and his sons, and with every living creature, for perpetual generations (Gen. 9:8-17). The space given in Genesis (where stupendous events are related with severest brevity) to the rainbow, testifies to its importance as a symbol. But we need not enlarge upon its meaning. Sufficient for our purpose to state that the rainbow is, for *those who see it,* an evidence that the storm has already passed over the spot whereon they stand. This rainbow that encircles the throne of

God is visible to those, and only to those, who stand under the shelter of the cross of Christ. The storm of God's righteous indignation and burning wrath has already passed over the place where they stand, and *will not visit it again.* In this rainbow the color of the emerald predominates (for we are not to think of it as all green, since a green rainbow would be no rainbow at all) ; and green is the color of earth, as blue is that of heaven. This indicates that the events that are about to ensue have to do with the earth. Moreover, green is the most tender and refreshing of all colors, the most restful to the eye. Its presence here, along with the dazzling white of the jasper, and the fiery red of the sardius, is reassuring to our timid hearts. We need, indeed, to be reminded constantly of the awful majesty and intense holiness of God; but we are not to forget His grace and forbearance toward all who, though deserving the consuming fire of His wrath, have been brought to trust in His mercy and pardoning love. Therefore, the rainbow of emerald color is very comforting, especially in view of the lightnings and thunderings and voices that proceeded out of the throne (v. 5).

The seven Lamps of fire. This is one of the symbols that are explained in the Book; for we are told that these are "the seven Spirits of God". As to the significance of this symbol there is no need to add to what has been already said, except to point out that in it we have one of a number of correspondences between this scene and the appointments given by God to

Moses for His earthly sanctuary. For it is evident, I think, that what John now beheld is the pattern of the sanctuary, which God had shown to Moses in his day, and concerning which He repeatedly and strictly admonished him, saying, "See that thou make all things according to the pattern showed to thee in the mount" (Heb. 8:5, quoting Ex. 25:40). To this deeply interesting aspect of our subject we purpose to return shortly.

The Elders and the Living Creatures.* We view these together because in the description of this vision, and also of later ones, they are joined together in such a way as to indicate that in them we have a composite symbol, and a symbol of something very precious in God's eyes, as is evident from their nearness to the Throne. By attention to the following passages we may gain much information as to the significance of this symbol:—

Chapter 4:8-11. When the living creatures give glory, honour, and thanks to Him that sat on the throne, who liveth for ever and ever, the four and twenty elders fall down before Him that sat upon the throne, and worship Him that liveth for ever and ever.

Chapter 5:7-10. When the Lamb has taken the seven-sealed book from the hands of Him that sat upon the throne, the four living creatures and the four

---

* The term "beasts," applied to these beings is most regrettable, particularly in view of the fact that the same term is used (and properly) to describe those monsters of iniquity (chaps. XIII, XVII, XIX) in which the powers of Satan are finally headed up and destroyed. In the original, the words are totally different. That used for the four creatures in heaven is *Zoa*, meaning *living ones*. Therefore we shall designate them by that name, or by their more familiar name *cherubim* (See Ezek. 1:5 and 10:20).

The Vision of the Throne in Heaven

and twenty elders fall down *together* before the Lamb, *all* having harps and golden vials full of incense, and *together* they sing the new song of the redeemed, saying, "For Thou wast slain, and hast redeemed *us*".

It should be carefully noted that in this passage the four living creatures join with the elders in the song of redemption, and expressly include themselves among the redeemed.

Chapter 7:11. All the angels stand about the throne, and about *the elders and the four living creatures.*

Chapter 14:2, 3. Voices from heaven, and harpers, sing as it were a new song before the throne, and *before the four living creatures, and before the elders.*

Chapter 19:4. After the fall of the mystical city Babylon, Alleluias are heard in heaven, "and *the four and twenty elders and the four living creatures* fell down and worshipped God that sat on the throne, saying, Amen, Alleluia".

In all these passages the elders and the living creatures (sometimes one is mentioned first, and sometimes the other) are not only associated closely together, but both are closely associated *with the throne.* Indeed they have a position with reference to the throne that no angels or other creatures share. These facts will help us in our attempt to ascertain the significance of those symbols.

For let us remind ourselves again at this point that we are not looking at "the heavenly things themselves" (Heb. 9:23), which no mortal eye could behold, and which human language could not describe; and that we are not looking at objects which bear any *physical* resemblance whatever to those heavenly things. No one would for a moment suppose that there is any physical likeness between our glorified Redeemer and "a Lamb having seven horns and seven eyes," or between the Holy Spirit of God and "seven lamps of fire". What we are attempting to do is to decipher a description *written in hieroglyphics,* a description in which the pictures of familiar objects are used as representations of spiritual realities, which may be persons, or which may be moral ideas or truth, the symbols being such as merely to suggest the realities for which they stand, by reason of some *moral* likeness which they bear thereto.

With this in mind, let us recall some passages in other parts of the Bible that throw light upon the scene now before us.

The Vision of Isaiah.

In the year of the death of the leper king of Israel, who had profaned the *earthly* sanctuary of God, Isaiah saw a vision of the *heavenly* sanctuary, and at the same time he received directly from the throne one of the most sweeping and significant of all the prophecies of coming judgments upon the people of Israel. This is his description of the vision:—

"In the year that King Uzziah died, I saw also the Lord* sitting upon a throne, high and lifted up, and His train filled the temple. Above it (the throne) stood the seraphims: each

---
* From John 12:39-41 we know that this was Christ Himself.

The Vision of the Throne in Heaven

one had six wings; with twain he covered his face, and with twain he covered his feet, and with twain he did fly. And one cried to another, and said, Holy, holy, holy, is the Lord of hosts; the whole earth is full of His glory. And the posts of the door were moved at the voice of him that cried, and the house was filled with smoke" (Isa. 6:1-4).

The resemblances between this vision and that of Revelation IV are striking. Isaiah saw the throne of heaven and Him who sits thereon; and above the throne (*i. e.* upon it) were the seraphim, who, like John's living ones, had each of them six wings, and who utter the same *trisagion,* "Holy, holy, holy, the Lord God of hosts". Isaiah mentions also the "door", and that the place into which he was permitted to look was "the temple". John does not state this in Chapter IV or V, but it is implied, as we shall see, and is plainly stated later on. Thus in Chapter 11:19 we read: "And the temple of God was opened in heaven"; And in 15:8: "And the temple of God was *filled with smoke* from the glory of God, and from His power".

The differences in details between the two visions do not indicate that the seraphim, for example, were any different in John's day from what they were in Isaiah's. Those differences in details are to be taken as expressive of some *different aspect* of truth; for obviously the great voice that he heard. Further, Isaiah tells us there are things revealed in John's vision that were not revealed in Isaiah's.

The Visions of Ezekiel.

The same living creatures were seen by Ezekiel in his visions; and at that time also they appeared in connection with the proclamation of Divine judgments upon Israel and Jerusalem. They are described at length in Chapter 1:4-28, the description being very close to that given by John, (though with significant differences). As in John's visions, the living creatures were *four* in number (v. 5). Moreover, they combined in their make-up the likeness of a man, a lion, an ox, and an eagle (v. 10). Their wings are specially mentioned (vv. 6, 8, 9, 23, 24). They were associated with the throne of God (v. 26), with "the voice of the Almighty, like the noise of great waters" (v. 24), and also with a "rainbow" (v. 28).

In Chapter 10:1-22, Ezekiel describes another vision of the throne and the living creatures; and of the latter he says: "This is the *living creature* that I saw under the God of Israel by the river of Chebar; and I knew that they were the *Cherubims*" (v. 20). We have therefore, the clearest warrant for designating these wondrous and mysterious beings as the "living creatures", or "cherubim". Consequently our inquiry is only as to the special relation of the cherubim (or rather, of what they represent) to the Presence and purposes of God.

THE VISION OF GENESIS 3:24.

We note, therefore, that the cherubim are first seen at the gate of the garden of Eden, being there associated with the flaming sword; and that their office was "to keep the way of the tree of life" (Gen. 3:24). Judgment against Adam and his entire race had just been pronounced, and the execution of his long sentence of banishment from the tree of life was just begun. *But in the heart of that sentence of judgment was enshrined the supreme promise of deliverance for sinful man, and for creation itself, through the woman's Seed;* and inasmuch as the function of the cherubim was to "keep", that is, to *guard,* the way of the tree of life, we may assuredly conclude that they symbolize, or pictorially represent, *the sure purpose of God to open again to fallen man* (His *banished and outcast creature) the way to all that is symbolized by "the tree of life".* The final and eternal accomplishment of this purpose is put before us, in symbolical language, in the last chapter of Revelation; and the main object of the entire Book is to present in outline the great events, in the course of God's dealings with the earth, which lead up to the consummation of that supreme purpose.

In the light of these facts of Scripture it is easy to see the reason for the re-appearance of the cherubim in the closing visions, here presented, of earth's long history; and for the prominent place given them therein. But this will become clearer as we proceed. Let us only fix in our minds the thought that the cherubim stand as the sign of *God's everlasting covenant concerning the earth and man, and as the pledge of its accomplishment.* We shall see later on that the thought represented by the elders is involved in this central object of God's work of Redemption, and that it gives definiteness thereto; so that the combined symbol, the four cherubim and four and twenty elders, represent *the full purpose of God concerning the earth and man.*

The fact that the cherubim are *four* in number indicates that they represent, or have to do specially with the material creation; and the fact that their combined make-up embraces the resemblances of the man, the lion (chief of wild beasts) the ox (chief of tame beasts) and the eagle, indicates that the whole creation, now groaning in the bondage of corruption (Rom. 8:21, 22), will share the benefits of the work of redemption.

The Ark of the Covenant

We come now to the Tabernacle, which occupies so large a space in the life and work and writings of Moses. In that remarkable structure, and specially in the Ark, which is its central feature, we have an elaborate and detailed symbol of the work and ways of God in His dealings with men, and particularly of Christ, through whom His mighty plans are carried to completion. On this we cannot now enlarge, but would only point out these important facts: 1, that the tabernacle, in all its parts, was a representation, a working model, so to speak, of what had been shown to Moses in the mount, and hence that *what John saw in heaven was the original from which Moses copied the tabernacle of witness;* (2) that the figures of the cherubim were woven into the fabric of the tabernacle and the vail (Ex. 26:1, 31), and were also made of *one piece with the "mercy-seat"*, which formed the cover of the ark (Ex. 25:18-22). Thus it is impressed upon us by the details of the tabernacle and of the ark that the cherubim are identified in the closest way with *"the eternal purpose" of God* "which He purposed in Christ Jesus our Lord" (Eph. 3:11), their figures being of one piece with that which represents the very heart of His covenant. Furthermore we observe that the gold figures of the cherubim stand in the same relation to the ark as their originals stand in relation to the throne in heaven; that their wings are specially mentioned; and that the token of *judgment already executed* is present in the blood of the sin-offering sprinkled upon the mercy-seat. This latter feature has the same significance as the rainbow in John's vision.

It is appropriate to notice again at this point that the cherubim are *four* in number, this being mentioned several times; which indicates that they represent God's covenanted purpose for the *whole physical creation;* and to notice also that their wings (the power that sustains and moves them) are *six,* just short of the number of Divine perfection, showing that, although so closely identified with the throne of God, they are not Divine. The number of the elders is *twenty-four,* the product of the same two factors *(four* and *six)* that are associated with the cherubim. So the same truth is symbolized there. But the number twenty-four has another significance also, which will be stated presently.

The Temple of God in Heaven

In the light of the Scriptures to which we have briefly referred above, let us now contemplate the picture given us in Revelation of that heavenly Sanctuary, whereof the tabernacle of Moses and the temple of Solomon were the earthly and temporary "shadows" (Heb. 8:2; 9:23, 24; 10:1); and in so doing let us seek help of the Holy Spirit to look *beyond the symbols* He uses, to the spiritual truths and realities represented by them.

At a great crisis-point in the Apocalypse, namely, the sounding of the seventh trumpet, the following incident takes place: "And *the temple of God* was opened in heaven, and there was seen in His temple *the ark of His covenant:* and there were lightnings, and voices, and thunderings, and an earthquake, and great hail" (11:19).

This sudden and dramatic re-appearance, out of the mysterious silence of Scripture that had enshrouded it for centuries, of the ark of the covenant of God, is a very striking indication that at the point of time here specified, namely, "the days of the voice of the seventh angel" (10:6, 7), the accomplishment of all that was associated with that wonderful symbol is close at hand. And this, moreover, is in keeping with the word and oath of the mighty Angel of Chapter 10, that "in the days of the voice of the seventh angel, when he shall begin to sound, *the mystery of God*

The Vision of the Throne in Heaven

should be finished, as He hath declared to His servants the prophets" (10:6).

Therefore, and in order that we may gain a clearer knowledge of these transcendent matters, let us carefully consider the features here revealed of God's heavenly Sanctuary, comparing the earthly "patterns" (Heb. 9:23) with their heavenly counterparts.

1. *The Throne.*

This is what was represented by the ark, for that was the place of God's holy Presence, of whom it was said that "He dwelleth between the cherubim" (1 Sa. 4:4). It is the throne of righteousness and judgment, for these are declared to be "the habitation of His throne" (Psa. 97:2). But that throne becomes the "throne of grace", when the slain and risen Lamb occupies it, after having borne for us the just judgment of God, and having fulfilled all righteousness by His sacrificial death. This is what is shown to us in Chapter 5; and the promise of it is already there in the rainbow.

Nothing more need be said in order to identify the ark of the covenant with the throne of God in heaven.

2. *The Seven Lamps of Fire*

It is clear that the golden candlestick (or lampstand) with its seven branches and seven lamps, supplied with pure olive oil (a type of the Holy Spirit), by whose light *all the service of the earthly sanctuary was accomplished,* answers to the "seven lamps of fire", which John saw before the throne in heaven. The correspondence in this case is so apparent that no one could miss it. Let this then serve to remind us that the things of Christ can be seen only *by the Spirit:* of whom the Lord Himself promised, saying, "He shall glorify Me; for He shall receive of Mine, and shall show it unto you" (John 16:14). For "the natural man receiveth not the things of the Spirit of God; neither can he know them, because they are spiritually discerned " (1 Cor. 2:14).

3. *The Elders.*

To the study of this symbol we should give the closest attention, for much depends upon a right apprehension of it. The elders are twenty-four in number, and are seated upon thrones surrounding the throne of God. They are clothed in white raiment, and have on their heads crowns of gold (4:4). Later, after the Lamb occupies the throne, they are seen with "harps and golden vials full of odors (or *incense,* marg.) which are the prayers of saints" (5:8). These features, along with others, make it clear that the elders are a symbol of *God's purpose for His elect people.* What answered to them in the earthly sanctuary was the *twelve loaves of the shewbread,* which rested upon the table, which *like the ark itself,* was made of the fragrant and imperishable acacia (or shittim) wood, overlaid with pure gold. Thus the table was associated closely with the ark, even as the elders are associated with the throne in heaven (Ex. 25:23-30); and from the identity of the materials we deduce the truth of God's "purpose", that the redeemed should all be conformed to the *image* of His Son (Rom. 8:28,

29) and eventually be changed into His likeness (1 John 3:2); or in other words that they "might be partakers of the divine nature" (2 Pet. 1:4). In the fact that the elders are seated upon thrones and have upon their heads crowns of gold, we read God's purpose that they should be *kings,* sharing with the King of kings the honors and glories of His supreme royalty and dominion; and in the fact that they have vials and offer incense before the throne, we read God's purpose to make them *priests* unto Himself. In a word, we see in these elders a pictorial representation of what John declared in his ascription of praise to Christ Jesus in Chapter I, where he describes Him as "the Prince of the Kings of the earth" and says, "Unto Him that loved us, and washed us from our sins in His own blood, and *hath made us kings and priests* unto God, even His Father, be glory and dominion for ever and ever".

These words speak of this as having been already done; and so likewise the symbol of the twenty-four elders seen in heaven, tells us that God, who sees the end from the beginning, views this purpose of His as already accomplished in Christ.

The number twenty-four is twice twelve, which is the product of the factors *three* and *four,* the former being the numerical symbol of Divine Being, and the latter that of the earth. Therefore the numerical symbols agree with what these elders say concerning themselves; namely, that they are "redeemed to God out of every kindred, and tongue, and people, and nation"

(5:9); and they also witness to the close union of God with His redeemed people.

The number twenty-four is also the product of the factors twelve and two. Now the government of God is represented in the Old Testament by the heads or elders of the *twelve* tribes of Israel, and in the New Testament by the *twelve* apostles. We see also the recurrence of the number *twelve* and its multiples in connection with the people of God (7:4-8; 12:1; 14:1), and in connection with the Holy City. In the description of the latter, mention is made of "the *twelve* tribes of Israel", and of "the *twelve* apostles of the Lamb"; the city having *twelve* gates and *twelve* foundations, and at the gates *twelve* angels; its dimensions being *twelve* thousand furlongs, and the thickness of its walls a hundred and forty-four cubits (twelve times twelve) (21:12-21). From these indications the significance of *twelve* as a numerical symbol is clear; and therefore we may take the number twenty-four as representing *the redeemed of both dispensations.*

The term "showbread" means literally *bread of the face,* signifying that which is placed as a memorial before the Face of God. Hence the suitability of this symbol to represent those who are "before the throne of God and serve Him day and night in His temple" (7:15).

With all these facts before us it should cause us no surprise that when John was given to see the temple of God in heaven at the time of the ascension and enthronement of the Lord Jesus Christ, he should have seen there the symbols of God's eternal purpose for us, His redeemed people, and symbols also (the cherubim) of the whole redeemed creation. Rather would it have been surprising if there had been no such symbols there. Hence the presence of the "elders" surrounding the throne of God in heaven does not at all support the view that the vision belongs to that future day when the redeemed shall be there *in person*. What the vision shows us in this respect is that, just as God had directed that in His earthly sanctuary there should be the memorials ever before Him ("before Me alway", Ex. 25:30) of His purpose to have a people for His own possession, even so that purpose was ever before Him, suitably symbolized, in His heavenly temple, "the true tabernacle".

This feature of the vision very fitly and beautifully illustrates the truth declared in the first chapter of Ephesians. There we read of what God has eternally "purposed in Himself" concerning those whom He hath chosen in Christ *"before the foundation of the world"*. The language of this passage seems to lift us above the limits of time, and to give us a view of the great plans of God as seen by Him who inhabits eternity, and with whom there is no past or future, but all is simultaneously before His eye. For we are spoken of as having been chosen "before the foundation of the world"; showing that even then we existed in the view of God, and were personally known by Him. Moreover, it is also there stated concerning us that God has already "blessed us with all spiritual blessings in *heavenly places* in Christ Jesus" (Eph. 1:3); and further that He has already "quickened us together with Christ", and "raised us up together, and made us *sit together* in heavenly places in Christ Jesus" (Eph. 2:5, 6). The past tenses in this great passage agree perfectly with what John was given to see in symbolic vision. The correspondence is perfect. Paul declares that we are already quickened together with Christ, raised up (that is, on high) and seated together in heavenly places in Christ. And that is precisely what John sees when given a vision of Christ's ascension to the throne in heaven. Particularly do the words "and made us *sit together* in heavenly places" afford confirmation of John's vision of the elders "sitting" upon their thrones in heaven, for the word "sit" in Ephesians 2:6 means to sit *on a throne*. So there is the closest agreement between the two passages. Each declares that God views all the redeemed as in Christ Jesus, raised from the dead, and ascended into heaven.

The number *twenty-four* is sometimes referred to David's division of the priests into twenty-four classes for their service at Jerusalem. But that was a purely human arrangement for convenience in the division of labor; it has no analogy at all with this scene in heaven, where the redeemed are enthroned, all together (not a few at a time), and where it is their character of kings, not that of priests, that is emphasized. The remark of Zullig, that "the Book hardly ever alludes to anything not Biblical", is true; and attention to it will keep us from straying into the boundless fields of imagination. The right view is given by many of the older (as well as by some of the more modern) commentators. Bousset states it thus:

> "It is the totality of the Old and New Testament saints who are here represented. Those of the Old appeared in the twelve patriarchs and those of the New in the twelve apostles. The same totality of saints is represented afterwards in the twelve gates of the holy city on which were written the names of the twelve tribes, and in the twelve foundations of that city, on which were written the names of the twelve apostles".

With this verse we may profitably compare Isaiah 24:23, where, in a passage that speaks of coming judgment, it is written: "Then the moon shall be confounded, and the sun ashamed, when the Lord of hosts shall reign *in Mount Zion,* and in Jerusalem, and before His ancients *(elders)* gloriously".

4. *The Golden Altar and its Vessels.*

Reference is made in several passages to the golden altar (Rev. 6: 9; 8:3); and we read also of "golden vials full of odors, which are the prayers of saints" (5:8). Again in Chapter 8 we read of an Angel who came and stood at the golden altar just before the beginning of the trumpet judgments, and that to him "there was given much incense, that he should offer it with the prayers of all saints upon the golden altar which was before the throne". Thus in the heavenly sanctuary there was a golden altar, of which that in the earthly sanctuary was a "pattern".

5. The Laver.

John saw before the throne "a sea of glass like unto crystal" (4:6). This answers to the laver in the earthly sanctuary, which, in Solomon's temple. was also termed a "sea" (1 Kings 7:23). The laver of the tabernacle was made of the highly polished copper mirrors of the women (Ex. 38:8). This was an appropriate use for those mirrors; for it is not well for us, while in the mortal bodies of our humiliation, to be occupied with our looks, seeing it is only a sin-disfigured countenance that a mirror can reflect. Furthermore, the laver (with the water it contained) was a constant reminder to the priests and people of their need of cleansing. It is suggestive of the Word of God in its double office of first revealing (as a mirror) the defilement of the person, and then (as by water) removing it.

But the heavenly counterpart is a sea of *glass* like unto crystal. For there is no need there of any water to cleanse God's priests as they approach the place of His Presence. There is no defiling thing there: for we read, "There shall in no wise enter into it anything that defileth" (21:27).

Thus we see that, of the principal appointments of the earthly sanctuary nearly all have corresponding features in the temple of God in heaven. There are, however, several notable exceptions; for there is no *brazen altar* there, and no *vail*. These differences are both appropriate and significant. There is no altar of sacrifice above, for that particular "shadow" of the law pertained to the time of imperfection; and it was for the offering of sacrifices in which God had no pleasure, for the reason that they could "never take away sins". But in heaven is seen "a Lamb as it had been slain" (5:6), the symbol of that "one sacrifice, for sins," whereby Christ accomplished eternal redemption, and at the same time abolished the brazen altar and its defective sacrifices.

There is in heaven no *vail* dividing the sanctuary into two parts, and for the same reason that there is no brazen altar there. The vail in the tabernacle and temple on earth signified that "the way into the holiest of all was *not yet made manifest*" (Heb. 9:8). Moreover, that vail represented the body prepared for the Lord Jesus Christ during "the days of His flesh"; for the Scriptures distinctly speak of the way into the holiest of all, "which He hath consecrated for us, *through the vail,* that is to say, *His flesh*" (Heb. 10:20). For when our Lord died upon the cross, thus putting away sin by the sacrifice of Himself, then the vail was rent in twain from the top to the bottom (signifying that it was God's own act from above); so that God's priests can now come boldly and at all times into His presence, their hearts having been sprinkled from an evil conscience, and their bodies washed with pure water (Heb. 10:19-22).

The groupings of these symbols and celestial beings, with respect to the throne and to Him who sat upon it, should be specially noticed. First there is the "rainbow round about the throne", speaking of mercy to follow judgment, and reminding us that "mercy rejoiceth against judgment".

Then there are the living creatures or cherubim "in the midst of the throne and round about the throne".

Then there are the four and twenty elders seated upon seats (literally *thrones*) forming another circle "round about the throne".

Surrounding these are "many angels" forming a larger circle "round about the throne" (5:11).

And lastly there is a vast circle, the outermost of all, embracing "every creature which is in heaven, and on earth, and under the earth, and such as are in the sea, and all that are in them" (5:13).

From this may be gathered that the event here symbolized is of transcendent interest to the entire universe; and that will help us determine the event itself.

As already noticed, the vision is in two parts. In the first (Chapter IV) the only action is the worship of the four living creatures and the four and twenty elders; and the theme of their worship is *Creation*, as clearly appears by the words of their anthem: "Thou art worthy, O Lord, to receive glory and honour and power; for Thou hast *created* all things, and for Thy pleasure they are (*i. e.,* they exist) and were *created*" (4:11).

This first scene of the vision seems intended to show by symbols what was characteristic of heaven, and of worship in the heavenly sanctuary, before Christ arose

The Vision of the Throne in Heaven

from the dead and sat down upon His Father's throne. It lends impressiveness to that stupendous event, which is symbolically represented in the second scene.

THE SEVEN-SEALED BOOK

In the second scene of this great vision, the attention of the seer was specially directed to a "book", or scroll (for such in those days was the form of books, and of important documents, such as title deeds, royal edicts, and the like). This scroll was "in the right hand of Him that sat on the throne". The book was written on both sides, having been sealed with seven seals.

That book assuredly represents something of the very greatest moment. This is evident from these facts: 1. It was in or at the right hand of God. 2. It was *completely* sealed, as signified by the *seven* seals. 3. The call for one worthy to open it and loose the seals thereof, was uttered by a *strong* angel with a *loud* voice. 4. No one* in heaven, or in earth, or under the earth was found worthy to open it. 5. This caused John great distress, which shows that the finding of one worthy to open the book was a matter of highest consequence. 6. The words spoken by one of the elders, "The Lion of the tribe of Judah, the root of David, hath *prevailed* to open the book, and to loose the seven seals thereof," testify plainly that even the Son of God was not qualified to receive the book until, as the Lion of the tribe of Judah, the Root of David,

---
* The word is "no *one*," not "no *man.*"

He had "prevailed" (or "overcome"), that is, had by His death and resurrection triumphed over all the powers of evil and all the enemies of God. 7. Christ, the One who was found "worthy to take the book and to open the seals thereof" (v. 9) is symbolized by "a Lamb, as it had been slain"; which shows that it was only by His death that even He could qualify to take this book as a matter of right, and open its seven seals. 8. When He has taken the book out of the right hand of Him that sat on the throne, there are transports of joy in heaven, beginning with the living creatures and the elders, then extending to the myriads of angels round about the throne, and finally reaching to "every creature which is in heaven, and on the earth, and under the earth, and such as are in the sea, even all that were in them".

What then is the significance of this book, and of its being given into the hands of the slain and risen Lamb of God, whereby creation from its center to its remotest bounds is so profoundly moved? We believe that by paying attention to the context, and to other pertinent Scriptures, cited below, we shall obtain a clear and satisfactory answer to this question; and it is most needful to have it, for otherwise we could not understand what follows.

The words of the living creatures and elders, "Thou art worthy to *take the book*" (v. 9), in connection with the words of the hosts of angels, "worthy is the Lamb that was slain to *receive power, and riches, and wisdom, and strength, and honour, and glory, and bless-*

ing" (v. 12), show that the delivery of this book into the hands of Jesus Christ carried with it the seven things mentioned by the angels. It was a formal ceremonial act, whereby He was recognized as the Supreme Ruler of the universe, "the blessed and only Potentate, the King of kings, and Lord of lords" (1 Tim. 6:15), and whereby He was invested with royal honors, glories, powers, and dignities. For when He took the book, this regal power, honor and glory, is precisely what the angels declared Him "worthy to *receive".*

Therefore, the passage itself makes it quite clear that this part of the vision presents to our view that supremely important epoch whereof many Scriptures speak, that to which our Lord Himself specially referred when He spake in parable of the nobleman who went into a far country "to *receive* for himself a kingdom" (Lu. 19:12). And, beholding this wondrous vision, we too can say with the writer of Hebrews: "We see not yet all things put under Him; *but we see Jesus,* who was made a little lower than the angels, for the suffering of death, *crowned with glory and honour"* (Heb. 2:8, 9). All the eight features of the vision enumerated above point to the same conclusion. Indeed we have only to reflect upon the matter in the light of all Scripture, in order to realize that there is no event revealed to us that could be made to harmonize with the extraordinary features of this vision, other than the triumphant entrance into heaven of the Victor over sin, death, and the Devil, and the bestowal upon Him of that Kingdom which all the prophets had foretold, which He Himself while on earth had announced as at hand, and which His servants on earth proceeded forthwith to preach to every kindred and tongue and people and nation, with the power of the Holy Ghost sent down from heaven.

We shall find moreover, that the conclusion concerning the seven-sealed book, which we draw from the passage itself, agrees with all the great prophecies of Scripture that had gone before, and also with the events that followed the opening of the several seals.

Psalm II

Turning back to the O. T. prophecies, we naturally go first of all to that great prophecy concerning Christ and His Kingdom given through David in the second Psalm. The first prediction in that prophecy shows us the kings of the earth setting themselves in array, and the rulers taking counsel together, against the LORD and against His Anointed; and this prediction, according to Acts 4:25-28, was fulfilled in the rejection and crucifixion of Jesus Christ. Then follows, in the Psalm, God's response to earth's refusal to accept and submit to His King: "Yet have I set My King upon Zion, the mountain of My holiness"; and this is what is pictured for us in Revelation 5:6, where the Lamb once slain takes His place upon the throne of God. The prophecy would lead us to expect that event to follow immediately after the first. Some, we know, would postpone this prophecy (along with other prophecies concerning the KINGDOM of God) to a time yet future, and would make it mean the setting up again of the Jewish kingdom, with Jesus Christ as the occupant of the throne thereof, on the site of David's palace in the earthly Jerusalem. But, apart from other weighty objections to the entire scheme of futurism, of which the above idea is a part, we point to the fact that in Psalm II God speaks of setting His King upon His Holy *Mountain* (not "hill", as in the A. V.) which of course is the heavenly mount, to which we (the followers of Jesus Christ) "are come" (Heb. 12:22). For a further proof of this we refer to the vision of Revelation 14:1, where John looked, "and lo, a Lamb stood on the *mount Sion*".

Going back to Psalm II, we next hear the voice of Christ, saying, "I will declare the decree: the LORD hath said unto Me, Thou art My Son: this day have I begotten Thee. Ask of Me, and I shall give thee the heathen (or nations) for Thine inheritance, and the uttermost parts of the earth for Thy possession". This we take it, is what is pictured in verse 7 of Revelation V, where Christ takes the book out of the right hand of Him that sat on the throne. For God thus gives Him the "decree", whereby He becomes the sovereign Lord of all the nations of the world, and the Possessor of the uttermost parts of the earth. Thus the things symbolized in the vision of John agree perfectly with the things predicted in the Psalm of David. And with this agrees also the fact that, according to the vision of Revelation V and VI, when Christ proceeds to publish the decree by opening the seals thereof, the effects are seen in happenings on earth.

Psalm CX.

We have also in this vision the fulfilment of Psalm 110, which begins, "The LORD said unto My Lord, Sit Thou *at My right hand,* until I make Thine enemies Thy footstool". Several New Testament Scriptures declare that our Lord, *immediately upon His ascension into heaven, sat "on the right hand" of God* (Mk. 16:19; Ac. 7:56; Rom. 8:34; Heb. 1:3). It is impossible therefore, without setting aside the plainest statements of Scripture, to postpone this session of Christ at God's right hand to a future time. And this settles the question we are considering.

That Christ came to "the right hand" of Him that sat on the throne, is shown in the vision itself. This makes it quite plain that the vision pictures the fulfilment of the great promise of the 110th Psalm, and that the time of the vision is the time of our Lord's ascension into heaven. Thus we are certified that the starting-point for the happening of the events foreshown to John in these visions, the "things which must be hereafter" (4:1), is *the ascension of Christ into heaven.*

Other predictions of Psalm 110 are fulfilled from that time on. Thus the prediction, "The Lord shall send the rod of Thy strength out of Zion: rule Thou in the midst of Thine enemies", was fulfilled when the Holy Spirit was sent down from heaven to be the power of Christ in His Kingdom on earth (Rom.

14:17; 1 Cor. 4:20, 21; note the "rod" in v. 21). He came forth "out of Zion". Christ's people, moreover, are "willing", in this day of His power; for He now reigns in the midst of enemies, and only over a people who *willingly* take His yoke upon them,

Verse 4 of the Psalm says: "The Lord hath sworn and will not repent, Thou art a priest forever after the order of Melchisedek"; and the Epistle to the Hebrews was written particularly to show the fulfilment of this prophecy, and its consequences in abolishing the whole Jewish system of worship;—temple, altar, sacrifices and priesthood—and in transferring the worship of God from the earthly to the heavenly sanctuary, and changing its character from worship by shadows to worship "in spirit and in truth". The concurrent testimony of Psalm 110:4, of the Epistle to the Hebrews, and of the revelation in heaven of the spiritual counterparts of the appointments of the earthly tabernacle, very convincingly proves that the visions we are now beginning to study belong to *this present era of the gospel,* and not to an era that is yet future.

Furthermore, Psalm 110 carries us on, as this vision also does, to the *day of wrath* (Rev. 6:17); for we read in verse 5, "The Lord *at Thy right hand* shall strike through kings in the *day of His wrath*"; and verse 6 speaks further of that day of judgment and wrath.

Daniel VII.

We have already referred to the vision of Daniel VII; but it is appropriate at this point to compare more in detail these two visions, and to observe their striking and significant resemblances.

That part of Daniel's vision which corresponds with the vision of Revelation IV and V, is described in verses 9-14. The subject of the entire vision is the course of earth-rule in the hands of man, which was to pass from one to another of four great empires, pictured as four wild beasts, diverse one from another. Daniel sees those beasts rise successively out of the sea, until the last of the four comes into view, which he describes as "dreadful, and terrible, and strong exceedingly", and as having "great iron teeth", and "ten horns". I reserve our detailed comment on this beast to a more appropriate place, and here would only observe that, in common with practically all evangelical commentators, I take this beast as representing the Roman empire.

But at this point something else comes into view; for Daniel says:

"I beheld till the thrones were cast down (more correctly *were set*) and the Ancient of days did sit, whose garment was white as snow, and the hair of His head like the pure wool: His throne was like the fiery flame, and His wheels as burning fire. A fiery stream issued and came forth from before Him: thousand thousands ministered unto Him, and ten thousand times ten thousand stood before Him: the judgment was set, and the books were opened".

The particulars of resemblance between this scene and that of Revelation IV and V are so plain that I do not stop to point them out. And now comes the culmination of Daniel's vision, which agrees strikingly with that of John, and therefore throws clear light upon it:

"I saw, in the night, visions: and behold, one like a Son of man, came with the clouds of heaven, and came to the Ancient of days, and they brought Him near before Him. And there was *given to Him, dominion* and *glory,* and *a kingdom,* that all people, nations and languages should serve Him. His dominion is an everlasting dominion, and His kingdom that which shall not be destroyed".

It surely is not to be supposed, in the absence of proof, that there could be two distinct events, each of such a momentous character as shown in these two visions, and so much alike in all their revealed features. So we find in this Scripture additional and exceedingly strong confirmation of the view that the delivery of the seven-sealed book to the Lamb that had been slain symbolizes the giving to our risen Lord of that everlasting Kingdom which had been promised Him from of old as Son of man and Son of David.

Finally, as regards the details of this vision, we observe that the "Lamb as it had been slain" is pictured as having *seven horns,* signifying the perfection of kingly power, and *seven eyes,* signifying the perfection of spiritual wisdom. Thus the symbol represents pictorially exactly what the apostle says of "Christ crucified" (the Lamb slain), namely that His is "the power *of God* and the wisdom *of God*" (1 Cor. 1:23, 24).

John's description tells us, moreover, that the seven eyes "are the seven spirits of God, sent forth into all the earth", which reminds us again that all the fullness of the Spirit is His, and declares further that the fullness of the Spirit is now, in this day of grace, "sent forth" to accompany the gospel of Christ, "into all the earth".

In the interpretation of the Book of Revelation as a whole, much depends upon where we locate this vision of the Throne. Therefore I earnestly ask those who have accepted the futurist view to inquire as to what evidence they have for placing this vision at the beginning of the next dispensation, instead of at the beginning of the present dispensation, which is the time when, according to many plain Scriptures, the slain Lamb of God ascended His Father's throne, and assumed His regal powers and glories. My own conclusion, after a painstaking examination of the evidences, and with certainly no prejudice against the futurist system (but rather the reverse), is that there is not a scrap of evidence for postponing this vision; but on the contrary, there is the most abundant and convincing proof that it was gloriously fulfilled when the mighty Conqueror over death and the grave re-entered the courts of heaven.

CHAPTER V

The Opening of the Seals

THE vision is continued in Chapter VI. There we are given to see how the throned Redeemer proceeds to exercise the sovereign authority that has just been placed in His hands. He opens the seals successively, up to and including the sixth, after which the action is interrupted for a description of a distinct vision, (Chapter VII) the subject of which is related to the events of the sixth seal. The opening of the seventh seal is mentioned at the beginning of Chapter VIII.

Keeping in mind the form of the book, namely, a long strip of parchment tightly rolled up and sealed with seven seals, the description before us would give the impression that the Lord breaks the first seal, and thus opens the contents of the book as far as the second seal; then He opens that seal, and further unrolls the scroll; and so on till the book is fully unrolled. Thus He brings to view progressively the theretofore hidden purposes of God, and at the same time exercises His authority in putting those purposes into operation.

For it must ever be remembered that while the risen Son of God is the supreme and absolute Ruler of the whole creation of God, "the blessed and only Potentate", yet His every act is in perfect accord with the will of His Father. God "worketh all things after the counsel of *His own will*" (Eph. 1:11); and "known unto God are all His works, from the beginning of the world" (Ac. 15:18). Christ has indeed all power (or authority) in heaven and in earth (Mat. 28:18), but He "delights" (Ps. 40:8) to exercise that power in carrying out the determined counsels of God the Father. Therefore the unrolling of the book has two effects: *first,* it brings to view the previously hidden purposes of God; and *second,* it starts into operation events whereby those purposes are accomplished.

Some expositors have regarded the book in the right hand of Him who sat upon the throne as the sealed title-deeds to the redeemed creation, whereby the Redeemer was invested with the ownership of what He had purchased at the price of His own blood. This view is supported by the incident of the purchase by Jeremiah, at God's command, of his uncle's field, just before the captivity; for his uncle, by the Word of the Lord, said to him: "Buy my field; . . . for the *right of inheritance* is thine, and *the redemption* is thine". Thereupon Jeremiah bought that field; "And", said he, "I subscribed the evidence and *sealed* it" (Jer. 32: 61-10). Subsequently the Lord further commanded him concerning the matter, saying: "Take these evidences, this evidence of the purchase, both which is *sealed,* and this evidence which is *open,* and put them in an earthen vessel, that they may continue many days" (vi. 14). The earthen vessel is suggestive of the body of flesh which Christ assumed for the work of redemption. And in the Lamb as it had been slain, holding the sealed book in His hands, we have a complete picture of the evidences of redemption, both that which was sealed (the book), and that which was open (the visible marks of His death).

Other expositors have regarded the book or scroll as simply a book of *prophecy,* the opening of which brings to view things to come. That view would make it identical with the Book of the Revelation itself; and indeed some have so explained it. But while the scroll sealed with seven seals is indeed a book of prophecy, it is such only in the sense that, as its seals are successively broken, the purposes of God are manifested by the actions that follow. Thus it is only incidentally that it reveals things that were to come to pass. It is not from the book, but from the vision, that John learns of those future events.

In either view of the matter it is difficult to imagine upon what theory the receiving of it by the slain Lamb, and the opening of the seals thereof, is to be postponed till the close of this dispensation, and is to be located in the brief interval between the taking away of the Lord's people from the earth and the commencement of His millennial reign.

That view seems to be quite arbitrary and fanciful. After much painstaking examination of the writings of those who entertain it, I have found no evidence at all to sustain it. On the contrary, it seems clear that, however the significance of the sealed book may be explained, the delivery thereof to the slain and risen

Redeemer must be located at the time of His exaltation to the throne of God.

The fact that the book is written on both sides suggests the two spheres wherein the risen Christ was given "all power", namely, heaven and earth. It also suggests the two sides of creation, the outside, or physical, and the inside, or spiritual; and that the events following the opening of the seals lie some on the one side and some on the other. Some expositors have overlooked the unseen world, and have failed in their explanations because they have vainly sought some historical event on earth to correspond with every vision, and every symbol. An example which illustrates my meaning will present itself immediately in the case of the events that were seen at the opening of the first four seals.

The Four Horses and Their Riders

As in the case of the preceding chapters, the divisions of Chapter VI are clearly marked. The actions under the first four seals have features in common, which mark them as constituting a distinct group. For at the breaking of each seal one of the living creatures (each in his turn) says in thunderous tones; "Come and see"; and in each case what John sees is *a horse and his rider* going forth.

The vision seen at the opening of the fifth seal is of a wholly different sort (vv. 9-11). And that seen at the opening of the sixth is also quite distinctive (vv.

The Opening of the Seals

12-17), being unlike the group of four, and unlike that of the fifth seal.

THE SIGNIFICANCE OF THE HORSE AS A BIBLE SYMBOL

For a right understanding of this part of the Apocalypse it is needful first of all to learn the significance of *the horse* as a Biblical symbol. This, however, is not a matter of difficulty, for to find the desired meaning it requires only that careful attention be given to what is written concerning that animal. That information must be sought in the Old Testament; for the horse is not mentioned in the New, except in Revelation. In the expositions I have read, little or no consideration has been given to the significance of the horse as a Bible symbol. Attention has been concentrated upon the several riders. And of course, explanations which ignore the most prominent feature could not fail to be defective and unsatisfactory.

Viewing the subject broadly in the light of Scripture, it will be seen that the horse is first of all the symbol of *strength, might,* or *force of a certain kind;* not strength for labor, like the ox, or for the mastery of enemies, like the lion; but of might for *conquest,* and for *progress.* Characterized as he is by strength combined with *speed* and *fearlessness,* the horse fitly symbolizes that form of spiritual vitality and power that sustains, energizes, and carries forward, despite all that opposes, a great spiritual movement, whether good or evil. Especially does it typify strength and courage for *conflict.*

God's own description of the characteristics with which He has endowed the horse should be specially noted. Addressing Job He said: "Hast *thou* given the horse *strength?* hast *thou* clothed his neck *with thunder?* Canst thou make him *afraid* as a grasshopper? The glory of his nostrils is *terrible.* He paweth in the valley and rejoiceth in *his strength.* He goeth on to meet the *armed men.* He *mocketh* at *fear,* and is not *affrighted;* neither turneth he back from *the sword"* (Job. 39:19-23). Here the horse is held up to admiration because of his strength, his utter fearlessness, and his refusal to be turned back by any menace of danger. Further God speaks of his *irresistible determination* and *power to advance in the face of armed resistance:* "He swalloweth the ground with fierceness and rage; neither believeth he that it is the sound of the trumpet". He is at home in the most deadly conflict, and seems to delight in it: "For he saith among the trumpets, Ha, Ha; and he smelleth the battle afar off, the thunder of the captains, and the shouting" (vv. 24, 25).

The symbol of the horse and his rider is as old as Jacob's prophecy, where these words occur: "Dan shall be a serpent by the way, an adder in the path, that biteth the *horse's* heels, so that *his rider* shall fall backward" (Gen. 49:17). And the same figure, in a like sense, occurs in the song of Moses and the children of Israel on the far side of the Red Sea, who said: "I will sing unto the LORD, for He hath triumphed gloriously: the *horse and his rider* hath He thrown

The Opening of the Seals

into the sea" (Ex. 15:1). And that was the refrain of the song, as appears from the response of Miriam and the women (v. 21). From this we get the idea that the horse represents the progress of some great enterprise backed by strong military power. Therefore, anything that is figured as being carried forward by a horse, is a movement that is sustained by mighty power; one that advances into conflict against the opposing forces, but with fearlessness, and with prospects of a successful career.

This will suffice to give us a somewhat definite idea of what is broadly signified in Scripture by the symbol of a horse. But other passages may be examined with profit, as Isaiah 31:1 (note the words, "and trust in horsemen, because they are *very strong*"); Jeremiah 4:13 ("his horses are *swifter* than eagles"); Jeremiah 12:5 ("how canst thou contend with horses?"); Hosea 14:3 ("we will not ride upon horses"); and Psalm 33:17 ("neither shall he deliver any by his *great strength*").

But we come now to something even more specific and more pertinent to our inquiry. For in the prophecy of Zechariah are certain visions in which horses and their riders are conspicuous. Thus we read: "I saw by night, and behold, a man riding upon a *red horse;* . . . and beside him were red horses, speckled (or bay) and white" (Zech. 1:8). We need not for our present purpose seek for the interpretation of this vision. It is only important to note that these horses and riders represented *agencies which the Lord sent forth upon a mission through the earth* (v. 10).

Turning now to Chapter VI of Zechariah's prophecy, we read of a vision in which he saw *four* chariots, in the first of which were *red horses,* in the second black, in the third white, and in the fourth bay (vv. 1-3). So here we have, as in Revelation VI, the earth-number *four,* signifying that the whole world is involved. And again we note the angel's explanation of the symbol of the horses: "These are the *four spirits of the heavens,* which *go forth* from *standing before the Lord of all the earth"* (v. 5). This explanation affords a solid basis for the view that the horses of Revelation VI picture the going forth into the world of certain mighty spiritual energies or agencies. The fact that all four are carried by horses points to a similarity in their general character; while the fact that the horses themselves differ in color shows that specifically they are not alike. What is said concerning their several riders points to other specific differences, as will be noted hereafter.

In the case of the horses and their riders seen by Zechariah, the starting-point is similar to that in the vision of John, *the prosperity and ease of the world,* and the *weakness, oppression* and *distress of the Israel of God.* Hence the suitability at this precise moment of a vision revealing in a large and comprehensive way how God purposes to deal with the entire situation, and the agencies He will employ for the accomplishment of His ends. The showing at this point merely of some bit or fragment of world history, as the historicists interpret the visions of the seals, would not meet the requirements of the case at all.

Taking into consideration the significance of the horse as a Biblical symbol, and viewing the subject in the light of various other facts, I have come to the conclusion that the four horses and their riders present a prophetic picture of the mighty spiritual influences, agencies or powers, which were to arise and *go forth* into the whole world, at the beginning of the "Christian Era", and which were to impart to that great era those special characteristics whereby it is distinguished from all previous periods of the world's history.

That our era *is* clearly marked off from the eras that preceded it, that it *has* various characteristics which are all its own, and that its most distinctive features are due entirely to influences which came into operation *at and immediately after the death and resurrection of Jesus Christ,* are facts which the most prejudiced enemy of Christ would not deny. By common consent this age is known as the *"Christian* Era"; its civilization is commonly termed *"Christian* Civilization"; and throughout the world its system of reckoning time has the (supposed) date of the birth of Jesus Christ for its starting-point. Thus, in various ways, all men throughout the civilized world render involuntary recognition to Jesus Christ. They acknowledge, even though it be most repugnant to them to do so, that His doctrine has been the leading factor in shaping the course of human affairs throughout the age, and that

His coming into the world was the beginning of an *entirely new order of things* among men.

Upon surveying retrospectively the age in which we live, and noting the outstanding features thereof, we cannot fail to observe that the spiritual powers or agencies which have had the chief part in shaping the course of human affairs from the dawn of the era until now, have been *four* in number. Moreover, upon a careful examination of those powers or agencies we find that they correspond respectively, and in the precise order in which they arose, to the symbolical representations of the four horses and their riders; the resemblance being in every case so clear that it is readily seen when pointed out, and that no straining or manipulating of the meaning of the various symbols is required in order to give plausibility to the explanation.

This correspondence between the broad characteristic marks of the christian era and the symbolical pictures shown under the first four seals is strong proof in itself of the correctness of the interpretation; for the agreement is too complete, and it extends to details too numerous, to be attributable to mere chance.

If this reading of the symbols be correct, it follows that expositors of the historical school have missed the mark in attempting to find some definite historical event to fit each of the pictures shown at the opening of the several seals. All who have read attentively even the very best of the historicist expositions must have felt that the respective events cited as fulfilling the several visions bore but a faint, and generally a purely

The Opening of the Seals

imaginary resemblance to their supposed prototypes.

Furthermore, the ordinary historicist interpretations, which refer us back to remote and obscure events of history (as the incidents of the reign of Trajan etc.) for the explanations of these visions, do not only belittle the visions themselves, but also rob them of all interest and value for generations subsequent to those early days. For those interpretations do not give us even the benefit of fulfilments of prophecy as evidences of the inspiration of Scripture; since the supposed fulfilments are too dubious in themselves to serve that useful purpose.

On the other hand, if the visions of these four seals show us the going forth of mighty potencies, which were to shape the course of affairs through the entire age, which were steadily and irresistibly to accomplish *to the very end* the mighty purposes of our God for this dispensation of grace, and especially if they were to reach the very height of their activities in the closing days of this wonderful era, then they are matters of peculiar interest and concern for us, who have so many evidences before our eyes that the end is near, even at the doors.

THE WHITE HORSE

Turning now to the record, we should note with close attention and deepest interest what was the very first use made by the glorified Redeemer of the supreme authority placed in His pierced hands.

"And I saw when the Lamb opened one of the seals; and I heard, as it were the noise of thunder, one of the four living creatures saying, Come and see. And I saw, and behold, a white horse: and he that sat on him had a bow; and a crown was given him: and he went forth conquering and to conquer" (6:1, 2).

The identifying symbols are (1) the color of the horse, *white;* (2) the bow; (3) the crown; (4) the fact that the rider went forth conquering (gaining victories from the start) and ultimately "to conquer" (*i. e.* to triumph finally over all enemies). These marks are amply sufficient for a certain identification (provided one's mind is not shackled by the exigencies of the futurist or other system of interpretation), particularly as there is but one event or epoch in the world's history that fits accurately into the scene we are now viewing. And that is, *the going forth of the gospel of Christ in the power of the Holy Spirit.* Nothing else in the past, and nothing that has been revealed concerning the future, can be made to harmonize with this scene, or with these symbols. But the sending forth of the gospel of Christ, which is the *power* of God *unto salvation,* perfectly fits the scene, and perfectly explains the symbols, just as they are, without any manipulation whatever.

The words by which this vision is described, few though they be, suffice to put before our minds the entire sweep of the gospel from its wondrous beginning to its triumphant end; and this fact serves, as nothing else could, to invest the subject of this vision with the highest possible interest for every generation of the Israel of God, with no abatement, but on the contrary with increasing consolation to the very end. And the indisputable fact is, whatever explanation of the vision one may adopt, that of all the influences that have combined to shape the character of Western civilization, and to control the course of human affairs from the beginning of the age until now, the most potent by far has been, and yet is, THE GOSPEL OF JESUS CHRIST. In fact, the history of the leading nations of the world is practically the history of Christianity; whereas those nations which have been uninfluenced by the gospel are virtually without a history, and without any contributing part in the development of civilization. Their condition has been, at the best, one of age-long stagnation.

Great as is the force of the indisputable fact I have just stated, that force is much augmented by the further fact, equally undeniable, that the other three influences, which have operated effectually in the affairs of men throughout this age, had their rise in the same historical events that occasioned the going forth of the gospel. This will be shown shortly. It makes strongly for the unity of this group of visions.

For Christianity is very far from being a failure, as some like to think it; nor has the energy with which it was launched into the tumultuous sea of the nations been dissipated; for it is energised by the Spirit of God. Nor is there any possibility of failure here; for the white horse rider went forth winning victories everywhere at the beginning, and with the certainty also of a complete triumph at the end—"conquering, and *to conquer.*"

Once we accept the view, for which we believe full proof has been given above, that Chapter V shows us the risen Redeemer ascending the throne and receiving the warrant of His absolute sovereignty over the whole universe, then it follows from the very purpose for which He offered Himself as a Sacrifice (namely, for "the sin of *the world*") that the first exercise of His kingly authority would be the sending forth of the message of salvation into that world which He had died to save.

And with this also agree perfectly His parting words and instructions to His disciples, by whom that message was to be carried into the world: "Thus", He told them, "it is written, and thus it behooved Christ to suffer and to rise from the dead the third day: And" —the very next thing be it noted—"that repentance and remission of sins should be preached in His name *among all nations*". And, furthermore, for this world-wide mission they were shortly to be "endued with POWER FROM ON HIGH" (Lu. 24:46-49).

Much more to the same effect could be cited, but there is no need; for it is beyond controversy that the very next thing after the enthronement of Christ in heaven was the coming down of "power from on high", in the Person of the Holy Spirit, and for the very purpose of energizing the mission of the gospel of Christ, which mission is not yet fully accomplished. Therefore, all we have to do for present purposes is to observe that the foregoing facts concerning the Kingdom of God agree perfectly with the vision of Revelation V, and with the first exercise by the enthroned Redeemer, as pictured in verses 1-3 of Chapter VI, of the sovereign lordship of the universe which was then bestowed upon Him.

The color of the horse, *white,* bears strong testimony to the same effect; for, as we have already pointed out, this color is in every instance throughout the Book (unless this be an exception) used to designate things peculiarly divine; and there is not the slightest imaginable reason for assuming that we have an exception here, and an exception so great as (according to the futurist view) to reverse the meaning of the symbol. Moreover, the evidence in this case is raised from the level of high probability to that of *virtual certainty* by the fact that when Christ issues forth out of heaven to fulfill the words "and to conquer", He comes riding on a *white* horse: "And I *saw heaven opened, and behold, a white horse; and He that sat upon him"* etc. the words italicised being identically the same as those of 6:2 . It is not conceivable that this identity of language could have had any other purpose than to reveal the identity of subject. Could anything be plainer than that the *end* of Christ's war and victory in Chapter 19:11 corresponds with its *beginning* here? Those who make the white horse rider a symbol of the antichrist of the last days, thereby reversing the meaning of the symbol which the Holy Spirit has here employed, realize of course, that the color of the horse contradicts their interpretation. Hence they must needs resort to some expedient to meet the difficulty; and the expedient they have chosen is surely a curious one. They say (though with no proof at all to support it) that antichrist appears on a white horse in *imitation* of Christ. But this, I submit with all respect for those who adopt this explanation, is not dealing either fairly or intelligently with the symbols. For these are not chosen by antichrist or by the Devil, but by the Holy Spirit; and they have in every case a *divine fitness, ascertainable from the Bible itself,* to express pictorially the thing they are intended to represent. If we are permitted to suppose that the deceiver has had a hand in choosing the symbols, we are all at sea. But such a supposition cannot be entertained for a moment. The Apocalypse is written mainly in the sign language, and that sign language is just as much inspired as all the rest of the Bible. Verse 1 of Chapter 1 declares concerning this "Revelation of Jesus Christ" that "He sent and *sign*-i-fied it *(i e.* communicated it *by signs)* to His servant John".

In the one case where a satanic disguise *is* predicted, the fact that it *is* a disguise is made to appear plainly. I refer to the description of the second "beast", of whom it is said, "And he had two horns *like* a lamb" (13:11). Here is an attempt to assume an external resemblance (*homoia*=like to) a lamb. The symbol of antichrist is a "wild beast". It is not conceivable that the Holy Spirit could represent him by the symbol of a lamb, nor that He could represent him as riding upon a *white* horse.

THE BOW

He that sat on the white horse had a bow.

The bow is a familiar weapon of war, its peculiarity being that it can strike at a distance. It is used figuratively for power to make war, whether in a material or a spiritual sense. Thus Jacob prophesies concerning Joseph, saying, "But *his bow* abode in strength" (Gen. 49:24). The bow is employed figuratively as a weapon used by God. Job speaks of "the arrows of the Almighty" (Job. 6:4; see also Dt. 32:23, 42; Lam. 2:4; Ps. 18:14; 45:4; 77:17 etc.). Then we read of "the arrow of the Lord's deliverance" (2 K. 13:17). This is sufficient to show that the bow is a symbol of that which discharges the messages of God towards the mark they are intended to reach. In other words, it symbolizes *the preaching of the gospel in general, and the individual gospel preacher in particular*.

But again in respect to the symbol of the bow, as in the case of the white horse, we have something more definite than general principles to guide us to the right conclusion. For in Habakkuk's prophecy is a highly figurative passage in which the prophet sees a vision, and in describing it he speaks of the Lord as riding upon *horses and chariots of salvation*. In that connection he says: *"Thy bow* was made quite naked, according to the oaths of the tribes, even *Thy Word*. . . .

The sun and moon stood still in their habitation: at the light of *Thine arrows* they went, and at the shining of Thy glittering spear. . . . *Thou wentest forth for the salvation of Thy people, even for salvation with Thine anointed.* Thou woundedst the head out of the house of the wicked" etc. (Hab. 3:8-13; cf. Ps. 110:6). From this Scripture we have ample warrant for regarding the bow as a symbol of God's Word in the day when He goes forth into all the world for the "salvation" of men.*

Another passage that sheds clear light upon the symbol of the bow is Psalm 45, which in Hebrews 1:8 is quoted as applying to Christ. The following is the pertinent portion: "Gird Thy sword upon Thy thigh, O most Mighty, with Thy glory, and Thy majesty. And in Thy majesty ride prosperously because of truth, and meekness, and righteousness; and Thy right hand shall teach Thee terrible things. *Thine arrows are sharp* in the heart of the King's enemies" (vv. 3-5). In this case the mention of the arrows implies that the royal Warrior had a bow, as in the other Scripture the mention of the bow implies the arrows. Moreover, in the Septuagint version, which was that in use in Palestine in those days, and from which our Lord and

---

* In certain expositions which make the white horse rider to be the antichrist of the last days, an attempt is made to build upon the circumstance that, in the brief description given of this rider, there is no mention of arrows. We are asked to assume, first, that this warrior went forth without any arrows for his bow; and second, that the lack of arrows somehow supports the view that he represents antichrist. But we see no warrant for either assumption. That a warrior carrying a bow should have no arrows, particularly if he is to have a conquering career, is surely a strange idea. And in a brief description of such a warrior it would be no more necessary to say that he had arrows for his bow, than in describing a man with a gun it would be necessary to state that he had ammunition for it. That could safely be left to the intelligence of the ordinary reader.

His apostles quoted, verse 4 of the Psalm reads thus: "And in Thy majesty ride, and *bend Thy bow,* and prosper and reign, because of truth", etc. This reading, of course, is not authoritative; for the Hebrew text does not have the words "and bend Thy bow". But the reading of the Septuagint is nevertheless competent evidence to prove how the words of the vision of the white horse and his rider would be understood by believers of apostolic times.

Thus the Scriptures do (figuratively speaking) put a bow and arrows into the hands of Christ and send Him forth on a white horse, in the "day of salvation". Whereas the Scriptures say not a word of any antichrist's going forth on a white horse (or any other), or of his carrying a bow. And inasmuch as we can interpret Scripture only by Scripture, we have in this case no choice but either to be guided by Scripture, and take this passage as referring to Christ in the gospel, or else to abandon Scripture entirely, in which case we are free to assign it to any character we please, whether real or imaginary.

The Crown

It is needless to speak at any length as to the meaning of the clause, "And a crown was given him". Those words agree with the view that in this vision we have Christ, going forth in the gospel. "His goings forth are from of old, from everlasting"; and this one is distinguished from that which led Him to the cross by the fact that now He has *a crown.*

Conquering and to Conquer

If the preceding descriptive items were so dubious as to leave us in uncertainty concerning the identity of the rider of the white horse, the last words of the passage, "And he went forth *conquering, and to conquer*", would surely make the matter perfectly plain. For it needs only a brief reflection thereupon in the light of Scripture to make evident that those words could not refer to any other than Christ, and that they apply to Him only as embracing His entire career of conquest, from beginning to end. We are aware that it is said of the ten-horned beast that "it was given him to make war with the saints, and to *overcome* (same word as here rendered *conquer*) them" (13:7). But it is not said, nor could it be, that the beast went forth conquering *and to conquer*. For those last three words speak in the clearest way of *final* victory; and the beast's career does not end in victory, but in utter and eternal defeat (19:20).

On the other hand, the entire clause is most wonderfully and comprehensively descriptive of the career of Christ in the gospel. *"He went forth conquering"*. These words bring up before our minds the early triumphs of the gospel, from the day it was first preached "with the Holy Ghost sent down from heaven", to the end of the Book of Acts; and all the way from Jerusalem to Rome. Then the last three words, *"and to conquer"*, carry our thoughts onward to "the end", referred to by the apostle Paul in that great passage in which he unfolds the gospel of the Kingdom of Christ, where he says: "Then cometh *the end;* . . . when He shall have put down all rule and all authority and power. For He must reign, till He hath put all enemies under His feet. The last enemy that shall be destroyed is death" (1 Cor. 15:24, 25). It is to this last victory over death and the grave that the words "and to conquer" specially refer; for Chapter 20:14 of Revelation records this final triumph, saying, "And death and hell (Gr. *hades*) were cast into the lake of fire". And, referring to the same event, the apostle Paul in the passage just quoted, says: "Then shall be brought to pass the saying that is written, *Death is swallowed* up in victory. O death, where is thy sting? O grave (Gr. *hades*), where is thy victory?" (1 Cor. 15:54, 55).

Therefore we find in the words, "conquering, and to conquer", strong, indeed conclusive proof, that the passage refers to Christ, not to any antichrist; and further that it particularly symbolizes the going forth of the gospel of Christ into the world, and the career thereof from beginning to end.

THE RED HORSE

"And when He had opened the second seal, I heard the second living creature say, Come and see. And there went out another horse that was red: and (power) was given to him that sat thereon to take peace from the earth, and that they should kill one another, and there was given him a great sword".

These words describe the symbols of another mighty spiritual agency or power that has exerted a potent influence in shaping the developments of this gospel dispensation. The color of the horse (red), the words "to take peace from the earth" and "kill one another", and the symbol of "a great sword", testify quite plainly as to the significance of this feature of the vision. There is general agreement, therefore, that we have here a symbolical prophecy of *war*. But it would be, in my opinion, a great mistake to regard this symbol as meaning only, or even primarily, *physical* wars; for I am convinced that it signifies something much broader than that, namely *strife or variance of every sort;* and moreover I believe that what is here pictured is something spiritual rather than material. Our light as to this comes mainly from the words of our Lord recorded in Matthew 10:34. The occasion was the first sending forth of the twelve apostles to proclaim that the Kingdom of God was at hand; and in that connection occur the significant words, "These twelve Jesus *sent forth*" (v. 5). Their "peace" was to come upon every house they entered that was worthy; but if it were not worthy, their peace was to return to them (v. 13). Then He warned them to "beware of men", foretelling that they should be delivered up to councils, they would be scourged, and brought before kings and governors; and further that brother should deliver up brother to death, and the father the child; and children should rise up against their parents and cause them to be put to death (vv. 17-21). So here we have the Lord's own word, spoken at the *first going forth of the gospel,* that the immediate effect would be antag-

The Opening of the Seals

onism, variance, and deadly strife. We see therefore that the red horse was to follow hard upon the heels of the white horse. And now, to put the whole matter into a single vivid sentence, the Lord draws a word picture which strikingly agrees with this detail of the picture of the rider on the red horse, saying, "Think not that I am come to *send peace* on the earth; I came not to *send peace, but a sword*" (v. 34). When we compare these words with those of the vision, "power was given him *to take peace from the earth*, . . . and there was given him *a great sword*", we are constrained to the conclusion that this striking similarity of language is designed to show us that the prophecy and the vision refer to the same thing. But more than that, our Lord's next words give the explanation of the figurative expression "a sword", those words being: "For I am come to set a man *at variance* against his father, and the daughter against her mother, and the daughter in law against her mother in law. And a man's foes shall be they of his own household" (Mat. 10:35, 36).

The words of our Lord recorded in Luke 12:49-53 throw additional light on the matter. Speaking prophetically and in highly figurative language (vv. 35 ff.) of the period of His absence, He used these words: "I am come to send *fire* on the earth; and what will I if it be already kindled". Now it is clear from what follows that the word "fire" in this saying is descriptive of the same thing as the word "sword" in Matthew 10:34 (and we recall that "fire" and "sword" when used figuratively are commonly joined together). For He goes on to say: "Suppose ye that I am come to *give peace* on the earth? I tell you, Nay; but rather *division*. For *from henceforth*" (He had just referred to His approaching "baptism" of sufferings) "there shall be five in one house divided, three against two, and two against three. The father shall be divided against the son, and the son against the father; the mother against the daughter and the daughter against the mother; the mother in law against her daughter in law, and the daughter in law against her mother in law".

The words of Christ recorded in Matthew 10:35, 36, cited above, are a quotation from Micah, where it is written: "For the son dishonoureth the father, the daughter riseth up against her mother, the daughter in law against her mother in law; a man's enemies are the men of his own house". And it will be remembered that the birth of Christ at Bethlehem is foretold a little earlier in this same prophecy (Mic. 5:2), and His sacrificial death is implied in Chapter 6:6, 7. It is highly interesting and instructive to trace out the connection between the going forth of the gospel and the various forms of strife, including wars, that are sure to follow. Frequently it happens on this wise: The bearers of the gospel message penetrate into regions far beyond the pale of civilization. They encounter opposition from the natives, and often pay for their admission by their lives. But animosity and suspicion are overcome by kindness and gentleness; a hearing is obtained; the gospel begins to do its work; and the community is slowly raised out of the depths of paganism. More over, their confidence in the white man has been gained, so that presently, when the trader arrives on the scene, with an eye to business, he finds a favorable situation whereof he proceeds to take full advantage. The usual developments follow quickly. The natives are shamelessly exploited; and if, as in the case of China, the country be rich in natural resources, one nation after another presses into the opening the missionary has made; competition and rivalry follow; the natives begin to find to their sorrow that men from "Christian countries" are not Christian at all; resentment and hatred of foreigners arise; agitators seize the opportunity to fan the embers of hatred into a blaze; uprisings and other disturbances occur; and presently the whole country is seething, as is China at this hour. Thus the red horse gallops hard after the white horse; and when affairs come to a climax, someone who has the ear of the public will very likely rise up and gravely lay all the evils brought about by a greedy and unscrupulous commercialism at the door of the missionary.

Another instance of the way the outbreak of commercial strife and then actual wars follow the gospel of Christ has just been brought to my notice by a thoughtful article from the pen of an economist ("The Economic Cause of War", by Edward Beach Howell, in *Atlantic Monthly* for July, 1925) who shows that wars have occurred in cycles, and that the eras of great wars have been coincident with those of unusually large increments of gold, the money metal of the world. It works in this way (to take the latest and most impressive instance, the era of the wars between Japan and China, Spain and America, England and the Boers, Japan and Russia, Italy and Turkey, the Balkan States and Turkey, culminating in the "World War") : A new country is opened, as the Rand in South Africa. Gold is discovered. There is the usual rush to that region. Presently there are large additions to the money metal of the world. Prices rise. Trade is stimulated. Commercial rivalry is intensified; "and the commercial phrenzy thereby produced is followed by the phrenzy of war". It is not necessary that we should try to trace out the connection between great increments of the money metal of the world, and the breaking out of wars. But certainly it is a most significant and thought provoking fact that large additions to the world's stores of gold, to which most men look as the source of happiness and prosperity, should in some mysterious way tend invariably to bring upon the human race that greatest of all afflictions, the scourge of war. We shall see more of this in studying the vision of the black horse.

Such then were the various kinds of "wars and fightings" that were to follow the message of the gospel everywhere; and such in truth have followed it from the days of the apostles until now. The gospel has divided families into hostile camps, sundering the very closest ties of nature. Then, its effects widening, it has separated communities into antagonistic parties; and then nations; and finally it has set nation against nation. Sometimes the warfare has been confined to words, feelings and attitudes. But often it has taken the form of physical violence—persecutions, imprisonments, tortures, and where there was resistance (as between Protestants and Catholics in France and elsewhere) civil wars. The "Thirty Years War" ending in 1648, was due entirely to religious antagonism. Indeed the countless wars, fightings, persecutions and martyrdoms, arising out of the political policies of Papal Rome, would never have occurred but for the gospel. In order however to realize fully the important part which the red horse rider has played in shaping the history of Christendom, we should have to take into consideration every instance of strife, variance, hatred, antagonism, and dissension of whatever sort, that has arisen during all these nineteen centuries, because of the preaching of the gospel and of its acceptance by some in a family, a community, or a nation. It is quite safe to say that all other causes of dispute put together have not contributed nearly so much to hostility between human beings as the single cause of religious difference regarding the gospel. How profoundly true then were those few words of Christ: "I came not to send peace, but a sword"! And what marvellous foresight is manifested in them!

I claim then, that the explanation of the meaning of the red horse has been given us by our Lord Himself. And most fitting it is that this explanation should come from His own lips. For here we have what is probably the greatest of the "mysteries" of His Kingdom; and those none other could declare with the same authority. For what could have been more in accord with the natural anticipations of even spiritually minded men than that the setting up of Christ's Kingdom would mean the immediate realization of the angelic anthem, "On earth *peace,* good will toward men"? How needful then that His people should have it clearly from His own lips that it was to be *just the reverse*— "not peace but a sword"!

In the Book of Acts we are given to see clearly the beginning of the career of the red horse rider. Strife began where the gospel began, in Jerusalem, where "a great persecution" arose about Stephen; and thence it *went forth,* following always the course of the gospel. At Antioch in Pisidia, the Jews raised persecution against Paul and Barnabas and expelled them out of their coasts. At Iconium the Jews stirred up the Gentiles against them, so that Paul was stoned and drawn out of the city as dead. At the first appearance of the gospel in Europe, at Philippi, antagonism and persecution were immediately manifested. Next at Thessalonica, all the city was set on an uproar. At Corinth and at Ephesus, it was the same story; and so on to the end. The gospel was making its way against the united opposition of Judaism, Paganism, Greek philosophy, and Roman cynicism (which afterwards changed to fierce persecution), and everywhere causing *strife.* All the way it has been a struggle up stream against the rush of all the surging currents of human tendencies.

It should be observed that there is nothing in the symbols of the second seal that speaks of actual *physical* war. That is seen under the fourth seal, where we find the words "to kill with the sword". Here the words "to take peace from the earth" do not imply war in the ordinary sense. The word "peace" in its Bible significance means *welfare, prosperity, tranquility*. All the world was at that time embraced in the peaceful state known as the *pax Romana*, a state of political tranquility maintained by the iron hand of Imperial Rome. That condition was not to last. The shaking of all things was to begin forthwith. And so it did; and it continues even until now. The present day controversy between "Fundamentalists" and "Modernists", for example, is but one of the ten thousand phases of the "variance", which was to attend, according to the Lord's own prediction, the going forth of His gospel.

Historians describe a remarkable era, in the time of the Roman domination of the world, which they call "The two centuries of peace". That era began with the reign of Augustus Caesar (B. C. 30—A. D. 14) who was at the very height of his wonderful career when Christ was born (Luke 2:1). The reign of Augustus is regarded by secular historians as "the beginning of a new age". Little did the wisest man of those days suspect to what extent, and in what manner, that "new age" was to be shaped by the influence of the Babe of Bethlehem and Man of Galilee. The *pax Romana* was thoroughly established over the whole world in the days of Tiberius Caesar, the successor of Augustus, who ruled the world at the time of our Lord's ministry, and it continued through the reigns of Caligula, Claudius, Nero, Vespasian, Titus, Trajan and Hadrian, to that of Marcus Aurelius. Hence it embraced the period of the visions given to John on Patmos, except for one outbreak in the days of Domitian, which was probably the occasion of John's exile. With this fact in mind, we see peculiar significance in the words spoken concerning the red horse rider, that it was "given him to *take peace from the earth*". That was done effectually and permanently, insomuch that strife, wars and fightings have not ceased till now, nor will to the end. Manifestly, those words would not apply to the last days of our era, for there will then be no "peace" to be taken away from the earth.

It is a remarkable fact indeed that the gospel of Christ was not to bring peace into the parts of the earth to which it was about to come, but on the contrary, conflict. A strange prediction truly; one that it would never have occurred to a mere man to make. But how marvelously it has been fulfilled! For throughout these nineteen centuries the gospel has been the cause of strife wherever it has gone. It has aroused antagonism, hatred and discord everywhere. In other words, the white horse rider with his bow has been closely followed, even to the ends of the earth, by the red horse rider with the "great sword".

It would have been indeed most natural for those who knew the purpose and the power of the gospel of Christ to expect that all men everywhere would be not only ready, but even eager, to accept the grace and salvation it offers freely to all; that they would gladly receive the forgiveness of their sins and the free gift of eternal life; and would welcome the gracious call of God to be at peace with Him, and to enter into the blessings that are to be enjoyed in His Kingdom. But it was to be far otherwise. For the proclamation of the love of God was to have the effect of intensifying and evoking outbursts of the hatred that is in the heart of man. Yes, the Kingdom of God must battle upstream all the way. It must advance against all the opposing currents of human desires, plans, ambitions, opinions, philosophies. Every influence and energy under which men act, every cherished notion and convention of human society, every characteristic impulse of the human heart—pride, envy, covetousness, self-love in all its forms—would be united in opposition to it. Therefore, the Lord's foresight, and His love and care for His people, were wonderfully manifested by the fact that, in parable, in symbol, and in plain speech, He made known that His Kingdom, instead of finding ready acceptance, and being at once established throughout the world, was to encounter the most determined and violent resistance from all the powers of earth and hell; that it was to be *war* from start to finish; that His followers must be prepared to endure hardness as good soldiers; that they must take to themselves all the armour of God; that they would need a sword more than a cloak; that there was to be "no discharge in that war", since they must fight to the very end the good fight of faith. But in revealing all this beforehand, our Lord has incidentally furnished convincing proof both of the truth of His words and also of His perfect knowledge of all that was to come, and hence of His own Deity.

That the spiritual warfare He foretold would last for twenty centuries was not and could not have been for a moment supposed by the first disciples. But from *our* place in the course of time, *we* can see, in the light of these visions of the Apocalypse, that so it was to be. Hence we need that light *just now,* and should earnestly seek it. "The mystery of iniquity" is a deep, dark mystery indeed. That after nineteen centuries the powers of evil should still be dominant in the world which Christ bought back at the cost of His own blood, is profoundly mysterious; and therefore all the light upon it that can be had should be diligently sought. In that quest we are now engaged; and we believe it will not be in vain. We know that "the mystery of God will be finished", and that the time thereof is fixed. For the wondrously glorious "Angel" of Chapter X has declared, and with a great oath, by Him who liveth for ever and ever, who created all things, that, from that time, there should be delay no longer, but that "in the days of the voice of the seventh angel, when he should begin to sound, *the mystery of God should be finished,* as He hath declared to His servants the prophets" (Rev. 10:5-7).

It should be most carefully noted and kept in mind that while the influences or potencies represented by the three horses which follow after the white horse, are in their nature evil and hostile to the gospel, they nevertheless are appointed to further the purposes of God in this gospel-dispensation. We may not be able to trace out the ultimate effects of these hostile influences, which are directly under the control of the adversary. Yet the statements of Scripture are abundant and clear to the effect that all the rage, malignancy and opposition of the great enemy, all the forces he directs against the work of the gospel, all the sufferings and afflictions he brings upon the servants of Christ, will be turned ultimately to his own undoing, and to the accomplishment of the purposes of God. To cite but one instance of many, we recall that the opposition which the adversary raised up everywhere against the apostle Paul, and which seemed to be crowned with success in that it compassed his removal from the field of labor and his imprisonment in Rome, had just the opposite effect from that which Satan intended. For Paul, enlightened by the Spirit of God, was enabled to write from his prison, and say, "I would ye should understand, brethren, that the things which happened unto me have fallen out rather *unto the furtherance of the gospel"* (Phil. 1:12). And so it will be with all these bitterly hostile influences. Hence, while recognizing their evil character, we may nevertheless, to the comfort of our hearts, view them as agencies which our God is using, according to His settled plan and perfect wisdom, for the accomplishment of His great designs for this age.

The Black Horse

"And when he had opened the third seal, I heard the third living creature say, Come and see. And I beheld, and lo, a black horse; and he that sat on him had a pair of balances in his hand. And I heard a voice in the midst of the four living creatures say, A measure of wheat for a penny, and three measures of barley for a penny; and see thou hurt not the oil and the wine".

In the commentaries I have read on this vision the authors plainly show that they are but groping blindly after the meaning of the symbols. It is commonly assumed that this vision represents *famine;* and the prices quoted for the wheat and the barley are supposed to afford support to that idea, for it is said that these are "famine prices". But this is not satisfactory. I know of nothing in Scripture to indicate that a man, going forth with a pair of balances and crying the sale of wheat and barley at any prices, is a symbol of famine. Neither has any proof been given that the prices quoted in the text are "famine prices". Nor is it easy to see what the command not to hurt the oil and the wine has to do with famine. That command does not fit into the picture of famine at all (see the Bible symbols of famine in Genesis 41:1-7). The true explanation will give full effect to the Biblical significance of the color of the horse *(black)*, the *balances,* and the things mentioned by the voice from the midst of the cherubim, that is, *wheat, barley, oil,* and *wine*.

Furthermore it should be noted that to the rider on the pale horse (fourth seal) power is given to kill "with hunger". This is quite enough in itself to show that the black horse rider symbolizes something more and other than famine; for that view makes it the mere duplication of one feature of the next scene.

In seeking the explanation of this vision we must first of all look for some potent influence going forth into the world about the same time as the gospel, and following its course, an influence destined to pervade the world, and to exert power in shaping the manner and the course of "Christian" civilization down to the end of the age. Then, in the second place, the influence or spiritual agency for which we seek must answer, and without forcing a resemblance or manipulating the facts to produce one, to the symbolic description of the black horse and his rider, to the balances, and to the words of the voice.

That we have here something directly in contrast with the gospel itself, is clear; for black is just the opposite of white. Furthermore, the gospel freely *gives* the bread of life, while here is something that *sells* the prime necessities,, both for rich and poor, at fixed prices. The gospel brings blessing for all; but here is something that would "hurt" the oil and the wine, if not restrained by divine command.

Keeping all these things in mind, and in view of other matters to be noticed below, I conclude that the black horse and his rider represent the world of Business *(Industrialism* or *Commercialism),* which has been a mighty factor in shaping the history of the christian era, and in determining the character of "christian" civilization. We would ask special attention to the facts and reasons we shall now adduce in support of this conclusion.

Commercialism had its rise with the apostate Jews, who, after the devastation of their land, city, and temple, were dispersed among all the nations of the earth, to be a race of *traders,* to perfect a marvellous, invisible, yet closely knit system of *international finance and commerce,* a system which just now is attaining the full development of its power; which holds tight within its unseen meshes, strong as steel, the destinies of nations, communities and individuals; which fixes the prices of all commodities: which molds public opinion through the press, commanding its service by the power of advertising; which sets and changes the fashions and styles of dress at its pleasure; which controls public amusements; and which dictates the policies of governments.

For it is matter of indisputable historic fact that at the beginning of our era two mighty agencies "went forth" out of Jewry, each with a world-wide and age-long mission to accomplish. These were identified respectively with the two parts into which the people of Israel were divided by the coming of their Messiah. For truly "there was *a division among the people because of Him"* (John 7:43). They that believed on

The Opening of the Seals

Him were the true seed of Abraham; and they therefore "went forth" to be a blessing to all nations, carrying with them and spreading everywhere the free grace and unspeakable benefits of the gospel. On the other hand they that rejected Him "went forth" to be a "curse" to all nations, and bring them into servitude to the god of gold, "the Mammon of unrighteousness". By them were invented all the instruments and mechanism of international trade, such as bills-of-exchange, as well as "interest", discounts, bills of lading, invoices, etc. So marvellous is this system, so smooth in operation, and above all so *invisible,* that the great majority of people are utterly unaware of its existence; though close observers of latter-day world conditions have pointed out again and again, that an all-powerful though invisible world-empire has come into existence, an empire of "Finance", whose capital, until recently in London, was transferred at the time of the great war to New York City. Thus, quoting from a recent issue of the *New York Evening Post:*

"Dominant at London is a new Power, *virtually independent of politics, and owing only the most shadowy allegiance to any Government;* it is *American Finance.* . . . Formerly finance did not lead; it followed. It exerted powerful influence; but it was always kept within fixed political bounds. The 'money barons' of no nation ever before had an opportunity to exert themselves in so nearly an independent manner as American Finance has assumed in the European situation today".

THE BALANCES OF DECEIT

All this is in fulfilment of the voice of prophecy, which speaks very distinctly to the point, and speaks moreover so fully that we must needs limit our citations to a few of the many pertinent passages. We quote first from Hosea:

> "Israel is swallowed up: now shall they be among the Gentiles as a vessel wherein is no pleasure". "My God will cast them away, because they did not hearken unto Him: and they shall be wanderers among the nations". "He (Jacob) is a *merchant, the balances of deceit are in his hand:* he loveth to oppress" (marg. *deceive*) (Hosea 8:8; 9:17; 12:7).

Here we have a clear prophecy of the career of apostate Israel during the gospel dispensation. As a nation it was to be "swallowed up" among the Gentiles. As individuals they were to be "wanderers among the nations". And for occupation, though originally an agricultural and pastoral people, they would not labor in the fields, nor yet in the factories, but would addict themselves to merchandising; and their methods would be *deceitful*.

The passage last quoted above matches perfectly the symbol of the black horse rider, so perfectly that we cannot doubt the former is given us to explain the latter, particularly in view of the fact that in the Word of God no coincidences can be undesigned. The color *black* symbolizes that which is hidden (deceit), as white fitly represents that which is truthful and open; and the balances are plainly declared to be the representation of merchandising, to which Israel was to addict itself.

Here then is something great enough in its influence upon all mankind to be compared with the gospel itself, though of opposite character; a thing that has followed the course of the gospel everywhere, even as the black horse is shown following the white horse; a thing that has powerfully affected the character of Christian civilization. Thus the history of nineteen centuries fully confirms our conclusion, and shows the fulfilment both of the prophecy of Hosea and of the vision of John. And the end is not yet, though there are increasing indications that it is near.

I feel justified therefore in concluding that even as the white horse rider symbolizes the true Israel going forth with the gospel of truth, so the black horse rider symbolizes apostate Israel going forth with "the balances of deceit".

The Ephah

Strong confirmation of this view of the black horse rider is found in the visions of Zechariah. In Chapter IV this prophet of the captivity describes his vision of the golden candlestick, whose seven lamps were fed with golden oil through golden pipes, this being a figure of God's testimony on earth through His churches. I cite this merely as showing the close resemblance, in this part of Zechariah, to the Patmos visions of John; for it is to the latter part of the same vision of Zechariah (Chapter V) that I wish to direct attention. Turning from the contemplation of the golden candlestick, Zechariah saw a flying roll, or scroll, which the angel that talked with him said was *"the curse* that goeth forth over the face of the whole earth". This further tends to show that out of Judea was to come not only "the *blessing* of Abraham" through those who were of "the faith of Abraham", but also "the *curse*" through those who rejected the faith, and refused to submit themselves to the righteousness of God (Rom. 10:3).

Then Zechariah was bidden to lift up his eyes, and upon so doing he saw an ephah going forth, concerning which the angel said, "This is *their* resemblance through all the earth" (5:6). Here is clear light upon our subject. For the ephah, or corn measure, has virtually the same significance as the balances; and the words "this is their resemblance through all the earth", prophesy the very same thing concerning Israel as the words of Hosea, "He is a merchant".

Furthermore the angel said to Zechariah, "This is a woman that sitteth in the midst of the ephah", and further he said, "This is wickedness". Then there came out two women having the wings of a stork, and the wind filled their wings, and they carried forth the ephah. Thereupon Zechariah inquired, "whither do these bear the ephah?" to which the angel replied, "To build it an house in the land of Shinar (*i. e.* Babylon), and it shall be established, and set there upon her own base" (vv. 7-11).

The correspondence between this vision and that of the black horse is remarkable, and all the more so because of the specific differences in detail—in one case a woman, in the other a man; in the one an ephah, in the other a pair of balances; in the one case the going forth being by means of wings, in the other by means of a horse. There is, of course, instruction to be had by noting these specific differences; but our concern at present is with the broad meaning of the vision. So we call attention to one more feature only, namely the destination of the ephah, the land of Shinar, where a house was to be built for it, and where it was to be established upon its own base.

Shinar is, of course, the mystical city Babylon of Revelation XVIII, "that great city", in which the ultimate development of Commercialism is seen, and which is to be so terribly overthrown. There is where the ephah is enshrined, so to speak; that is to say, where the temple of Mammon is built by its devotees. Now the proper business of the true Israelite is, and always has been from the Exodus onward (Ex. 15:2), to build a habitation for Jehovah. Paul is an example of the true Israelite; for the building of the House of God, that which was to be builded "for an habitation of God through the Spirit" (Eph. 2:20-22), was ever his chief concern, as his writings testify. So he said concerning his own labors, "As a wise master-builder I have laid the foundation, and another buildeth thereon"; and he adds, as regards the foundation or supporting "base" of this vast spiritual temple. "For other foundation can no man lay than that is laid, which is JESUS CHRIST" (1 Cor. 3:10, 11).

David also, in his day, was a true Israelite; for he longed to build the house of God (2 Sam. 7:2), he set his affection to it, and he prepared with all his might for it (1 Chr. 29:1-3).

But those Israelites who have refused God's Foundation Stone (Mat. 21:42; 1 Pet. 2:7, 8) are given over to the building of the temple of Mammon, where the ephah is enshrined, and where the woman concerning whom the angel said, "This is wickedness", is worshipped. That building is not placed, of course, on God's enduring foundation, but even as the angel said, "upon *her own* base". Hence its overthrow will be complete, in the day when the word shall go forth, "Babylon is fallen, is fallen", and heaven will ring with Alleluias.

In the recently published English Version of the O. T. issued by the Jewish Publication Society of America (Fifth impression, 1924)* the word "ephah" in Zechariah V is rendered "measure"—("This is *the measure* that goeth forth"), which brings the vision still closer to that of John, who heard a voice in the midst of the four cherubim say, "A *measure* of wheat for a penny, and three *measures* of barley for a penny" (Rev. 6:6). This brings us to the consideration of the significance of the words uttered by that voice.

"Bread by Weight"

To eat "bread by weight" and to "drink water by measure" (Ezek. 4:16) is to be in an evil state. It means a social condition wherein everything that enters

---

* A really excellent Version, containing a number of improved readings, though its excellencies are due to the fact that it follows closely the A. V., except in certain passages, in most of which it follows the readings of the Am. Stand. Ver.

into the life of human beings, down to the very prime necessities of every individual man, woman, and child, has been completely commercialized. The words that characterize the mission of the black horse and rider mention specifically the bread of the rich, "wheat", and the bread of the poor, "barley"; thus declaring in figurative language that the very bread of life of every individual was to be under the control of this system, which has come to pass most literally, in that the prices of wheat and other grain are fixed from day to day, according to market "quotations", which are precise to a fraction of a cent, those prices being settled in secret by potentates who never appear in the public eye, but whose decrees are more absolute than those of Caesar of old.

It is clear enough to anyone who puts his mind to it that an invisible autocracy, which is able thus to place an inflexible price upon the food of men, is really the master of their lives, or "souls". Hence we can clearly see, in the light of the foregoing facts, that the system described in Chapter XVIII, under the symbol of a great commercial city, which is the outcome of the mission of the black horse and rider, has attained to full development in our day. And in that light we can also see clearly the significance of the fact that the list of the merchandise of that great city begins with "gold and silver", and ends with "bodies and souls of men". The list embraces also "wine and oil and fine flour and wheat" (Rev. 18:12, 13).

This complete domination of the necessities of human existence by an invisible system of finance has come about so quietly, and so gradually, that only a few wide-awake ones have realized what was going on: and their voices, when they have sought to cry an alarm, were easily stifled, or drowned out. Yet any one who will give a little attention to the well-known facts of the history of commercialism will be able to realize what a tremendous change has taken place since the era of the steam-engine and the machine, and what it involves for human society at large.

A short time back there were no daily quotations of the prices of grain, nor could there be. There were no quick fortunes made, no victims impoverished, no homes and hopes destroyed in a day, by the operations of mysterious powers, which moved the prices up or down at pleasure, and to whose "quotations" the whole world must submit. For in those days the ordinary family raised its own grain, had it ground at the mill, baked its own bread, spun and wove its own thread and cloth, made its own clothes, and traded off its surplus for the services of the blacksmith, the shoe-maker, the carpenter or other artizan, who served the little community with his strength and skill. Thus every family was a principality, and every community a self-contained and independent commonwealth; and finance had no more dominance over the lives of men than had the phases of the moon. But that state of human society is gone, and gone forever; and since those who now control "the bodies and souls of men", control also the agencies whereby "public opinion" is shaped, the idea has been impressed upon the minds of the masses that, under this new despotism of "things", they are vastly better off than their forefathers, in the totally different conditions of those days. And again, in these times when the docile multitudes accept ready-made opinions just as they wear ready-made clothes, fashioned according to the autocratic decrees of their rulers, they have been taught that economic and industrial conditions are governed by impersonal "laws", like the laws of nature, with the operation of which we are unable to interfere.

But the commercializing process does not limit its operations to the sphere of man's natural bread. It extends its control over his spiritual food also. For the ministry of the Word of God has been commercialized, and that with a view not merely to the profit and advancement of men who, professing to be Christ's ministers and ambassadors in an evil and hostile world, really make themselves the mouth-pieces of the world, and preach a "gospel" that is thoroughly conformed to its principles, but with a view also to the adulteration of the bread of life, to make it both unpalatable and innutritious. Such a state of things has come into existence throughout christendom, and has now developed to full maturity.

The Oil and the Wine

But the voice that issued from the midst of the cherubim, and which was a voice not merely of prophecy but of authority also, added this prohibitive command: "And see thou hurt not the oil and the wine".

The grouping of symbols here suggests, and directs us to, that great creation-psalm, the 104th. In it the psalmist describes in language of great beauty, and by means of appropriate figures of speech, God's arrangement of the earth for man's habitation and his welfare. There we read: "He causeth the grass to grow for the cattle, and herb for the service of man, that he may bring forth food out of the earth; and *wine* that maketh glad the heart of man, and *oil* to make his face to shine, and *bread* which strengtheneth man's heart" (vv. 14, 15). Here we have the same symbols as in Revelation 6:6, *bread, oil* and *wine;* and we are surely warranted by that circumstance alone in reading the one verse in the light of the other. What we gather by so doing is that the power for harm allowed to the rider on the black horse was restricted, even as God set strict limits to Satan's power to afflict Job. The black horse rider was not to be permitted in any part of his career to "hurt the oil and the wine". There is great comfort in this assurance for those who are truly the people of God. It tells them that even in the days of spiritual dearth, when the giving forth of the bread of life was to be as by measure and price, the "oil" of God's Spirit and the "wine" of His joy were not to be injured; so that even to the very end of things down here, His people can always have a heart gladdened by the wine of God, and a face shining with the oil of God.

One more passage may be cited in which these four symbols, the wheat and the barley, the wine and the oil, are mentioned. The reference is to the first chapter of Joel, where these words are found:

"The field is wasted, the land mourneth; for the corn is wasted: the new *wine* is dried up, the *oil* languisheth. Be ye ashamed, O ye husbandmen; howl, O ye vinedressers, for the *wheat* and for the *barley;* because the harvest of the field is perished. The vine is dried up and the fig tree languisheth; . . . because *joy is withered away* from the sons of men" (vv. 10-12).

This important prophetic passage tends further to show how the chief products of the Holy Land are used as the symbols of spiritual realities.

Specially do the words, "the oil and the wine" recall the beautiful gospel parable of the Good Samaritan who came to the man lying stripped and wounded by the wayside, and who bound up his wounds, "pouring in *oil* and *wine*" (Lu. 10:33, 34. Here again these symbols speak most definitely of the consoling and healing influences of the gospel of Christ; and in the light of this well-known passage, the words of the voice which John heard in the midst of the four living creatures gives us to know that the black horse rider was not to be permitted to "hurt" the restoring and healing ministry of the gospel.

The influence of unbelieving Israel throughout the world during this age was to be very great, insomuch that it must needs figure largely in any foreview of our era. But the influence of that scattered yet coherent people was to affect not only the commercial affairs of men (which is what is here symbolized), but their practical and religious concerns also. We should therefore expect to find in other visions, appropriate symbols of their politico-religious influence also. And such we do find, as will be shown in the following pages.

THE PALE HORSE

"And when He had opened the fourth seal, I heard the voice of the fourth living creature say, Come and see. And I looked, and behold a pale horse, and his name that sat on him was Death, and Hell followed with him. And power has given unto them over the fourth part of the earth to kill with sword, and with hunger, and with death, and with the beasts of the earth".

The word rendered "pale" is *chloros*, from which the gas known as "chlorine" is named. It is of a sickly green, a livid, corpse-like color. The word occurs in two other places in Revelation, in both of which it is translated "green" (8:7 and 9:4). The significance of the color of the horse is not so clear as in the other three cases. But we do not need so much help in this case as in the others, for the name of the rider is given, *Death*. Moreover, Death is here joined with *Hell*, that is, Hades, the nether world, as in Chapter 1:18 (see our comments *supra*), and also in Chapter 20:13 and 14. The rider is "Death", and his mission is "to kill"; and "Hades" is pictured as following with him, to gather in, as it were, the victims.

Inasmuch as death has been busy in the world, and every part of it, since the fall of man, it is evident that the passage is highly figurative and symbolical; and that death must here represent some destructive *spiritual* influence that has been specially active in the gospel era. I think it will not be difficult to identify the influence or agency here symbolized.

We start with the fact that the Devil has the power of death (Heb. 2:14); and we learn from the parable of the Tares in the field that *after the sowing of the "good seed" of the gospel,* the enemy was to come and sow tares among the wheat; and in explaining the parable the Lord said that "the enemy", who sowed the tares, "is the Devil" (Mat. 13:24, 25, 38, 39). If then we are right in the view that the four horses represent respectively the four spiritual agencies that have chiefly influenced and determined the character of "christian" civilization, and that the first horse and rider represent the gospel of Christ, then our Lord's teaching would lead us to expect something going forth after the gospel, representative of some special form of satanic activity, and corresponding to the going forth of "the enemy" into the field (and "the field is the world") after the Son of man has sowed the good seed therein. In other words, the pale horse and its dread rider supplies exactly what is needed to make the vision of the four horses a complete picture of the mighty spiritual agencies that have been at work in christendom during this entire dispensation. Hence it strongly confirms the view we have presented of the meaning of the vision (Chapters IV-VI) as a whole.

Manifestly, the going forth into the world of the gospel of Christ necessitated a complete change of tactics on the part of the "enemy". Those devices which had served to keep the nations in the darkness and corruption of paganism would serve no longer. Other means MUST BE adopted; and the course of the gospel MUST BE observed and followed with something specially adapted to counteract its influence and nullify its effects. The effect of the gospel is to impart *life;* but the purpose of the Devil is "to kill". Those who receive Christ in the gospel, by faith, are gathered into the Kingdom of God, where "grace reigns unto eternal *life"*. In contrast with this, Death is accompanied by Hell, or Hades, into which its victims are gathered. The gospel is "the word of *truth"*; hence by contrast, the Devil would employ for his ends, various forms of "the *lie"* (2 Th. 2:12) that is to say, some deceptive form of teaching, some imitation of the gospel, "another gospel", which presents "another Jesus", a gospel which denies or omits the saving truth of the death and resurrection of Jesus Christ. This deadly, soul-destroying "lie", in various forms has followed the track of the gospel in every part of the field, and from the days of the apostles until now. Wherever the white horse and his rider have gone, in every land, the pale horse and his rider, with Hell following after, have been close behind. And the enemy has employed various destructive agencies, not only killing with the sword,* (which I take as representing the direct thrust of some "lie" such as the denial of the Godhead of Christ, or of His atoning sacrifice); but also "with hunger" (dearth of spiritual food); and "with death" (spiritual pestilence, as some popular heresy like "christian science", spreading like a contagious disease); and "with the beasts of the earth" (which represent the human governments, as appears from Chapter XIII, which the Devil has often been able to use with destructive effect in opposition to the gospel).

We have seen the significance of the number *four*, that it has to do with *creation;* and we observe that the four living creatures, who are associated in a special way with the purposes of God in the new creation, are definitely related to the action of the four horses and their riders. This tends further to confirm the view that what God has here revealed to us are the symbols of the four major spiritual agencies, whereby the character of this age, in which the new creation is in process of completion, has been largely determined. And now, in the light of history, we can plainly see that the religious, social, industrial, and political conditions of our era are what they are, and what they have been, because of these four mighty spiritual potencies, which have had free play therein from the beginning of the dispensation until now. Those influences are peculiar to this age; for they arose out of the coming of the

---
* Not the same word as in 6:4, which might mean the sword in a judicial sense; but a sabre, or any like weapon.

Lord Jesus Christ into the world, and out of what He did, and what was done to Him. The first and greatest in its effect is the gospel, in which God is acting upon the world directly through His Word and Spirit. By the other three the effects of Christ's coming into the world act upon it indirectly. For the *strife* and *variance* (the "sword") which He said He would send throughout the earth, were provoked by the gospel, and have always and everywhere followed in its wake; likewise the powerful influence of international *finance* and *commercialism* has resulted from the judgment of God in scattering throughout the civilized world the apostate, Christ-rejecting nation; and finally, the Devil's campaign of venomous lies, murderous heresies, suppression of the Scriptures, and stirring up the hatred of governments, is directed squarely against the truth of the gospel.

We are so familiar with these conditions, as were our forefathers for generations back, that we see nothing unusual in them; and hence we have assumed that so it has always been. They seem to us like a part of the very course of nature. But by a little effort of the mind, and by throwing the clear light of Scripture upon the history of civilization, we can grasp the fact that the conditions in which we live are such as were unknown to antiquity; and that they originated from the time when Jesus Christ died on the cross at the hands of His own people, and when He rose again, ascended the throne of the universe, received from His Father the inscribed warrant of His sovereignty, and proceeded to exercise His supreme authority in heaven and earth by opening the seals thereof. For a *truly stupendous change in the course of human affairs* took place from the occurrence of what was proclaimed by the apostle Peter to men out of every nation under heaven on the day of Pentecost, in these remarkable words: "Therefore, being by the right hand of God exalted, and having received of the Father the promise of the Holy Ghost, He (Jesus Christ) hath shed forth this, which ye now see and hear" (Acts 2:33).

It is a great encouragement to the writer of these pages to realize that the charter of that everlasting Kingdom is even now in His hands. For it means that things are not going at present and have not in the past gone, hap-hazard in the world; and it means also that if the powers of evil have been allowed wide scope, it is by His permission, and because the conditions resulting therefrom are precisely those which best suit His wise and holy purposes during the day of grace, wherein He is visiting the nations of earth to take out from them a people for His Name.

It has been observed that the color scheme of the horses shows a progression downward, ending in darkness and death. This is "according to the course of this world" (Eph. 2:2). But God's order reverses this. He finds us in a state of death and darkness, and brings us into that place where life is abundant as a river, and where there is no need of the sun, neither of the moon; for the glory of God doth lighten it, and the Lamb is the light thereof.

The Fifth Seal

"And when He had opened the fifth seal, I saw under the altar the souls of them that were slain for the word of God, and for the testimony which they held. And they cried with a loud voice, saying, How long, O Lord, holy and true, dost Thou not judge and avenge our blood on them that dwell on the earth? And white robes were given unto every one of them; and it was said unto them, that they should rest yet for a little season, until their fellow servants also and their brethren, that should be killed as they were, should be fulfilled" (6:9-11).

We have seen that the enthronement of Jesus Christ had immediate and far-reaching effects in heaven and on earth. And now we are given to see that it caused a great commotion also in the place where the holy dead await the coming of the day of glory.

Inasmuch as this vision of the fifth seal has not to do with events on the earth, the cherubim retire from the scene.

Evidently these souls under the altar are the prophets of God and the faithful witnesses of Old Testament times, of whom it is recorded that they were stoned, sawn asunder, were tempted, were slain with the sword; who, "having obtained a good report through faith, received not the promise; God having provided some better thing for us, that they without us should not be made perfect" (Heb. 11:37-40). It is implied that the souls under the altar were sharing the expectation of all who at that time were looking for the manifestation of the Kingdom of God in power and glory, who thought the day would *immediately* come (cf. Lu. 19:11) when the wicked will be judged for their evil deeds, and particularly for their persecution and murder of the saints of God. They had in mind such passages as Deuteronomy 32:41-43: "I will render vengeance to Mine enemies, and will reward them that hate Me . . . Rejoice, O ye nations, with His people; for He will avenge the blood of His servants, and will render vengeance to His adversaries". They did not understand God's purposes in grace, and did not know that the day of salvation for all men through the gospel was to intervene between the cross and the resurrection of Christ, and the day of wrath and revelation of the righteous judgment of God. They are now comforted, however, and white robes were given unto every one of them.

Not much is revealed in the Scripture as to the condition and occupation of those who have passed from this scene and are awaiting the resurrection of the just. But it is made known to us that they are in a state of conscious happiness; and from the statement that "white robes were given to every one of them", we understand that they received some immediate benefit from the enthroned Christ. Their position as "under the altar" speaks of the faith they had when on earth, as looking to God's typical sin-offering, appointed by Him in those days of imperfection as a "shadow" of the true Sin-offering.

The Sixth Seal

"And I beheld when He had opened the sixth seal, and lo, there was a great earthquake; and the sun became black as sackcloth of hair, and the moon became as blood; and the stars of heaven fell to the earth, even as a fig tree casteth her untimely figs, when she is shaken of a mighty wind. And the heaven departed as a scroll when it is rolled together: and every mountain and island were moved out of their places.

"And the kings of the earth, and the great men, and the rich men, and the chief captains, and the mighty men, and every bond man, and every free man, hid themselves in the dens and in the rocks of the mountains, and said to the mountains and rocks, Fall on us, and hide us from the face of Him that sitteth on the throne, and from the wrath of the Lamb. For the great day of his wrath is come; and who shall be able to stand?" (6:12-17).

From the fact that the day of wrath comes into view at the opening of the sixth seal it may be properly inferred that no other influences of the same general character as those pictured by the four horses and their riders were to arise and operate in the affairs of men during the long day of "the kingdom and patience of Jesus Christ". It may also be gathered that those four influences were to continue to shape and give character to the course of human history down to the very end. Thus it is seen that the visions of the seals as a group are complete and unitary. Other matters which God might be pleased in His wisdom to foretell, matters differing in character from those of this series, would be properly shown under other groups. They would be out of place here.

The vision of the sixth seal shows that the dawning of the day of judgment would not find the great ones of the earth converted to God, but just the contrary. It is a picture which could have been drawn only by Him Who sees the end from the beginning.

The opening of the sixth seal brings to the view of the seer the conditions of things on earth at the beginning of "the day of wrath and revelation of the righteous judgment of God", a day long foretold, but which, because of the marvellous forbearance and long-suffering of our God (2 Pet. 3:9, 15) is not yet come. The conditions of that awful "day", as seen by John, are those of world-wide disturbance and extreme violence, such as to strike terror to all hearts; such as to cause the great ones of the world, those who have occupied the highest positions therein and enjoyed its richest benefits, to realize that the great day of the wrath of the Lamb is come at last.

Those conditions are described by the seer in terms which, after the manner of prophetic utterances, are highly figurative. Therefore it is particularly important at this point to remind ourselves that the language of the Book we are studying is *symbolical*. Accordingly, events in political and social spheres of human affairs, as well as those in the spiritual realm, are pictured in terms of physical things and happenings.

The symbols employed in this passage are borrowed from the mightiest agencies and powers of nature; and they are crowded close together. First there is "a *great* earthquake", which speaks of some tremendous social upheaval, one of great violence and of wide extent. At the same time the sun becomes black like sackcloth of hair; and the moon becomes like blood. These being the Bible symbols of "the higher powers" which "are ordained of God" (Gen. 1:16-18; 37:9, 10), it is evident that verse 12 puts before us a scene of anarchy. For the supreme governmental authority, represented by the sun, is blotted out of the political heavens. And because of the complete failure of government there is profuse shedding of blood; while repeated shocks and convulsions occur among the peoples of earth, like the tremors of a great earthquake. What most nearly corresponds in history to this awe-inspiring picture is the so-called "reign of terror" at the beginning of the French Revolution. That fearful epoch of anarchy and bloodshed, which prepared the way for the reign of Napoleon Buonaparte, is a foreshadowing, no doubt, of what will happen on a world-wide scale as a prelude to the final period of the reign of the Beast (Chapter XIII).

Verse 13 adds another vivid detail to the picture. It tells of the stars of heaven falling to the earth, as a fig-tree casts its unripe figs to the ground, when shaken by a mighty wind. Thus the storm and tempest of those days will be such as to shake all things, in fulfilment of the prophecy: "Yet once more I shake, not the earth only, but also heaven" (Hag. 2:6); and those in positions of eminence—rulers, great ecclesiastics, and other persons of distinction—will be toppled

The Opening of the Seals

out of their high places, and cast down to the level of common humanity.

In Hebrews 12:26, 27 we have a brief but inspired commentary on the prophecy of Haggai, whereby we learn that the word "Yet once more", signifies *"the removing of those things that are shaken"*; and in agreement with this, John records, "And the heaven departed as a scroll when it is rolled together; and every mountain and island were moved out of their places".

These images are very appropriate to express a complete breaking up and a sweeping away of the whole system of human government, and organized human society, as it has existed from ancient times. They recall Nebuchadnezzar's dream, in which human government as a whole was imaged as a gigantic figure of a man, and its end was described in these words: "Then was the iron, the clay, the brass, the silver and the gold"—materials whereof the image was composed—"broken to pieces together, and became like the chaff of the summer threshingfloors; and the wind carried them away, that no place was found for them" (Dan. 2:35).

There is a passage in Isaiah that is closely related both in thought and language to the one we are now examining. The prophet is speaking of the time when "the indignation of the Lord shall be upon all nations". (Isa. 34:2-4), of which he says: "And all the host of heaven shall be dissolved, and the heavens shall be rolled together as a scroll; and their host shall fall down, as the leaf falleth from off the vine, and as a falling fig from the fig tree".

The apostle Peter likewise, in the passage referred to above, has this same "day" in view, when he says, "But the day of the Lord will so come as a thief in the night; in the which the heavens will pass away with a great noise, and the elements shall melt with fervent heat; the earth also, and the works that are therein, shall be burned up" (2 Pet. 3:10).

In Ezekiel 32:1-15 is a prophecy that throws light upon the vision now before us. The prophet was foretelling the violent overthrow of Egypt at the hands of Nebuchadnezzar; for the figurative language of the prophecy is explained by the words: "For thus saith the Lord God, The sword of the King of Babylon shall come upon thee. By the swords of the mighty will I cause thy multitude to fall; and they shall spoil the pomp of Egypt, and all the multitude thereof shall be destroyed" (vv. 11, 12). In the prophecy this national overthrow is pictured in these terms:

"And when I shall put thee out (or extinguish thee), I will cover the heaven, and make *the stars* thereof dark; I will cover *the sun* with a cloud, and *the moon* shall not give her light. All the bright lights of heaven will I make dark over thee, and set darkness upon thy land, saith the Lord God" (vv. 7, 8).

The same images appear in Isaiah 13:9, 10:—

"Behold, the day of the Lord cometh, cruel both with wrath and fierce anger, to lay the land desolate; and He shall destroy the sinners thereof out of it. For the *stars of heaven*, and the constellations thereof shall not give their light: *the sun* shall be

The Opening of the Seals

darkened in his going forth, and *the moon* shall not cause her light to shine".

Again, in Joel 3:15, 16 we read: —

"*The sun* and *moon* shall be darkened, and *the stars* shall withdraw their shining. The Lord also shall roar out of Zion, and utter His voice from Jerusalem; and the heavens and the earth *shall shake*".

In the foregoing passages it was in each case but the overthrow of a single nation that was predicted; whereas in Revelation 6:12-17 the upheaval and destruction are world-wide. Hence the images are intensified, as in Joel 2:30, 31, "And I will show wonders in the heavens and in the earth, blood, and fire, and pillars of smoke. The *sun shall be turned into darkness, and the moon into blood,* before the great and terrible day of the Lord come".

These passages indicate clearly the meaning of the symbols here employed. They will come again under our notice in connection with the events of the fourth trumpet (8:12).

The tremendous convulsions of human society which the vision presents to our eye affect principally those who occupy the highest social positions, "the kings of the earth", the great financiers, the captains of industry, and the like. These behold the great industrial and social fabric which they helped to rear up, and which seemed so solid and enduring, tumbling down upon their heads; and the sight is so terrifying that they flee—not however to Christ for refuge from the

coming wrath, as they might have done earlier, but—
to the dens and caves of the earth; and it wrings from
their hearts that despairing cry to the mountains and
rocks, "Fall on us, and hide us from the face of Him
that sitteth on the throne, and from the wrath of the
Lamb".

Isaiah describes this feature of that day also; for,
speaking of those who are proud and lofty, he says:
"And they shall go into the holes of the rocks, and
into the caves of the earth, for fear of the Lord, and
for the glory of His majesty, when He ariseth to shake
terribly the earth" (Isa. 2:17-19). And the Lord
Jesus also spoke of the time to come when they should
"begin to say to the mountains, Fall on us, and to the
hills, Cover us" (Lu. 23:30).

The prophecy of James 5:1-6 applies here. It begins with the words: "Go to now, ye rich men, weep
and howl for your miseries that shall come upon you";
and it warns them that they have "heaped treasure
together for *the last days.*"

We are not given to know the precise way in which
these prophecies are to be fulfilled; nor is it needful
for us to understand more than is made plain by the
words of the cry of these great ones of the earth,
namely, that conditions of danger, violence and upheaval have come to pass, such as to fill the heart of
man with the extremest terror and despair, conditions
such that to be buried under rocks and mountains
would be far preferable.

The Opening of the Seals

Specially it should be noted that this part of John's vision reveals the fulfilment of the concluding verses of the Second Psalm. I have already pointed out that the vision of Chapter V, where the Lamb is seen ascending the throne of the universe, shows the fulfilment of the words of verse 6 of that great prophetic Psalm: "Yet have I set *(i. e., anointed)* My King upon Zion, the mountain of My holiness" (Jewish Version); and that the opening of the seals of the book placed in His hands, answers to the words, "I will declare the decree" (Ps. 2:7). Then we have the admonition to the rulers and leaders whose terror is depicted in John's vision, the kings and chief men of the earth: "Be wise now therefore, O ye *kings;* be instructed, ye *judges* (or *leaders*) of the earth. Serve the Lord with fear, and rejoice with trembling. Kiss the Son, lest He be angry, and ye perish from the way, when *His wrath is kindled* but a little" (vv. 10-12).

The words, "And every mountain and island were moved out of their places", further speak of disturbances among the nations and peoples of the earth; for *mountains* in Scripture stand for conspicuous nationalities (Jer. 3:23, 51:25; Zech. 4:1), and islands represent lesser communities (Isa. 42:4; 51:5; 60:9).

This is not indeed the very end of all. But it is *the beginning of the end,* the last days, the time of the end. As says Hengstenberg:

> "If we do not stand here exactly at the final end, yet we stand at the *beginning* of the end. 'The great day of His wrath' is immediately before the door, is as good as come; and

Chapter VII can only come in as an episode between Chapters VI. 17 and VIII. 1, where the dawn of that day is announced".

THE COMPANY OF THE REDEEMED

After the words of the panic-stricken kings and magnates announcing the advent of the great day of wrath, the action is interrupted, and a scene of a very different character is introduced with these words:—

"And after these things I saw four angels standing on the four corners of the earth, holding the four winds of the earth, that the wind should not blow on the earth, nor on the sea, nor on any tree. And I saw another angel ascending from the east, having the seal of the living God; and he cried with a loud voice to the four angels, to whom it was given to hurt the earth and the sea, saying, Hurt not the earth, neither the sea, nor the trees, till we have sealed the servants of our God in their foreheads" (7:1-3).

Why, we would ask, is this particular vision, occupying the whole of Chapter VII, introduced at this precise point? The answer suggests itself when we observe that the preceding visions of this group reveal how things were to go during this age with *men in general*. Therefore what is needed just here is something to show the provision God has made for the protection of His own people on earth; and this is specially called for at the time when the gathering of storm-clouds of exceptional blackness, along with other unusual commotions, announces the advent of the great day of wrath. So here is just the picture that is needed. For it is apparent at a glance that the company of the sealed ones is in direct contrast with that of the panic-stricken ones of the sixth seal. It is the counterpart of that scene.

And here again it is appropriate to reflect upon the wisdom seen in the design of the Book, in that the time of the fulfilment of many of the visions is left in such uncertainty that every generation of believers could appropriate to itself the consolation it conveys. Thus, while the vision of Chapter VII stands in direct connection with the eve of the day of wrath, and will not be actually fulfilled till then, nevertheless the truth it declares and the comfort it imparts are applicable at every period of storm. For whenever the clouds have gathered in the spiritual or in the political skies, the oppressed saints of God have been permitted to hope that this was *the* storm in which their trials will be forever ended, and have sought (and not in vain) the special consolations contained in this wonderful Book, and particularly in visions such as that now opened to our view.

I am writing these lines (in May, 1925) under the strong conviction that the storm-clouds now gathering so darkly, and of which our political and spiritual weather-prophets are giving us daily information, are the very storm foreshown under the sixth seal; and this, of course, invests the present vision with peculiar interest. Yet, while so believing, I am quite aware that I and others who share this view, may be mistaken, as were those in the days of the French Revolution, and so on back to the first century. But, at the same time, neither I, nor they, am or were mistaken in appropriating the comfort of this vision of Chapter VII.

The relation of this vision to that which immediately precedes it is plainly marked. There we have the darkening of the heavens and the "mighty wind". Here we are taken back to a time anterior, when the four angels are holding the winds in check, ready to release them at the word of command. There we have the effects on land and sea, (mountains and islands) and on the great ones of earth; and here we see the wind ready to blow upon the earth, and the sea, and the trees (the latter being a common Bible symbol for eminent persons, as kings, magnates, etc.).

The wind is a symbol of divine visitation in judgment, and the *four* winds denote the universality of such a visitation. Thus in Jeremiah 51:1 we read: "Thus saith the Lord, Behold, I will raise up against Babylon . . . a *destroying wind.*" In Daniel 7:2 the *four winds* are seen striving upon the great sea, that being explained by the context as the divine judgments that were to be executed by the conquerors of the world. In Jeremiah 49:36, the divine judgments rushing in from every side are spoken of as the four winds: "And upon Elam will I bring the *four winds* from the four quarters of heaven." And the passage in Zechariah 6:1-5 is particularly illuminating. For there the revealing angel tells the seer that the four chariots he had seen represent "the *four winds (marg.)* of the heavens". These Scriptures also give a hint that the armies of powerful and ruthless nations may play a leading part in the fearful storm in which the history of this wonderful age of progress, science and invention will end. And it is pertinent to recall in this connection that "the next war", which the ablest observers of current events are constantly discussing, will be, from the sheer necessities of the case, unprecedentedly destructive, and unprecedentedly merciless.

The command to hurt not the earth, etc., is given in "a loud voice" by an "angel" who is seen ascending from the east, having the seal of the living God. We take it this "angel" represents Christ; for it is He who seals His servants with the Holy Spirit (2 Cor. 1:21, 22; Eph. 1:12-14; 2 Trin. 2:19), and it is He who comes between the impending wrath of God and all the earth, being in that sense "the Saviour (or Preserver) of all men, *specially* of them that believe" (1 Tim. 4:10). In a similar time of impending judgment on the inhabitants of Jerusalem, Ezekiel saw a vision of the glory of God, and heard a command given to one clothed in linen to go through the city and set a *mark on the foreheads* of those who sighed and cried because of the abominations thereof (Ezek. 9:3, 4). After him others were to follow and "slay utterly old and young", but were to "come not near any man on whom is the mark". The correspondence between the vision of Ezekiel and that of John is striking.

The number of those who were sealed, in John's vision, is given as "an hundred and forty four thousand of all the tribes of the children of Israel". This company is seen again at the beginning of Chapter XIV, where we read: "And I looked, and lo, a Lamb stood on the mount Sion, and with Him an hundred forty and four thousand, having His Father's Name written *in their foreheads*".

What does this company represent?

I take it as representing "the Israel of God" (Gal. 6:16) in its totality; that is to say, the complete and perfect number of God's elect. The numerical and other symbols are suitable to the expression of this thought. That numbers, when they appear in visions, as the *seven* spirits of God, the Lamb having *seven* horns, etc. express *ideas* and not *arithmetical values*, is apparent throughout the Book. Now the number *twelve* is definitely associated in Scripture with the people of God. In this vision the meaning is intensified by the fact that of each tribe the number of sealed ones is given as precisely twelve thousand. Thus, in the total, the number twelve is multiplied by itself, and then by one thousand. That is to say, it is the "square" of twelve, multiplied by the number of enlargement and totally, a thousand. Thus the idea expressed by the numerical symbol as a whole is that of solidity and perfection (the square) and completeness. Therefore we feel warranted in taking the meaning of this symbolical language to be that, ere the storm of the wrath of the Lamb actually breaks upon the world of the ungodly, the entire "Israel of God" (Gal. 6:16), perfect and complete to the very last member, is to be gathered out of the world. We believe we have here the fulfilment of our Lord's own prophecy: "And He shall send His angels with a trumpet and a *great voice (marg.);* and they shall gather together His elect *from the four winds,* from one end of heaven to the other" (Mat. 24:31). Giving to the preposition *ek* its usual significance here, the meaning would be a deliverance *from out of* the path of the world-wide storm (four winds). Thus the passage, in connection with what immediately precedes it (both being under the sixth seal), presents a company which is in striking contrast with that other which cries to the rocks and mountains to fall upon them. There are none of God's people in the first company, and none but His in the second.

Clear light upon this passage may be had from Exodus XXX. What is before us in this vision is the final *numbering* of the Israel of God; and in the Exodus passage we have God's original directions for the numbering of His people. The esssential matter appears in these words: "When thou takest *the sum* of the children of Israel, them that are to be *numbered* (marg.), then shall they give *every man a ransom for his soul unto the Lord, when thou numberest them.* This they shall give, *every one* that passeth among them that are numbered, half a shekel after the shekel of the sanctuary. . . . The rich shall not give more, and the poor shall not give less than half a shekel, when they give an offering to the Lord *to make an atonement for your souls"* (Ex. 30:12-15).

The grand and fundamental truth, to which this passage bears clear testimony, is that *every man,* who is finally *numbered* among the people of God, has been *ransomed;* that none are numbered among them save those for whom an atonement has been made. And another closely related truth appears also, namely, that in the great matter of sin and atonement, *all men* stand upon the same level before God. All require precisely the same ransom; "for there is no difference; for all have sinned".

When the people were numbered by Moses, the numbers came out unequal, ragged, incomplete. "For the law made nothing perfect". But in this final enumeration of those for whom Christ "gave Himself *a ransom for all*" (1 Tim. 2:6), the result is perfect and symmetrical. When Satan tempted David to say, "Go, number Israel" (2 Sam. 24:1; 1 Chr. 21:1), the thing displeased the Lord, and "therefore He smote Israel". For His time had not come for the numbering of Israel; because the ransom had not yet been paid.

In the handwriting on the wall at Belshazzar's feast, the first word (twice repeated) was "Mene", meaning *numbered;* and Daniel explained that this meant, "God hath numbered thy Kingdom and *finished* it" (Dan. 5:26). Thus we learn that what God finally numbers, and takes the sum of, is finished. So here we have the completion of the roll of God's elect.

Further support for the view just stated as to the character of the sealed company of a hundred and forty four thousand, is found in the last vision of the Book, where the City of God, the heavenly Jerusalem, is seen. For there again the symbolical number *twelve* appears as characterizing in a special way the eternal abode of God and His redeemed people. This is clear evidence that the number *twelve* pertains not to the earthly people and *their* city, but to the entire company of the redeemed of all the earth and their eternal home. In that last vision we are shown *"twelve* gates, and at the gates *twelve* angels, and names written thereon, which are the names of *the twelve tribes of the children of Israel"* (21:12). Also we find there *"twelve* foundations, and in them the names of the *twelve* apostles of the Lamb" (v. 14). Also the symbolical number "twelve thousand" and "an hundred and forty four" (the square of twelve) appear in the dimensions of the City (vv. 16, 17). Indeed, this thought is carried, in that last vision into three dimensions, the cube; for it is said that the length and breadth and height of the City are equal.

The following comments by others seem to me to give the right view of the matter:

Hengstenberg: "The sealing refers to the entire duration of the christian era, even to its final completion. Therefore, it has not yet lost its significance. And for the present time in particular it is full of consolation, as the sixth seal is beginning to be realized anew in a manner *never seen before"* (so it seemed to him over seventy years ago. And how much the more today!). "The plagues against which the sealing brings security, threaten alike all who have been redeemed by the blood of Christ out of every kindred, and tongue, and people, and nation; not a word being said as to any separate division of Jewish Christians".

Bossuet: "It is necessary to understand in the numbers of the Apocalypse a certain mystical sense to which the Holy Spirit seeks to draw our attention. The mystery we are to learn here is that the number twelve, sacred both in the synagogue and in the church because of the twelve patriarchs and the twelve apostles, is multiplied by itself in order to make twelve thousand in each tribe, and twelve times twelve thousand in all the tribes together, that we might perceive the faith of patriarchs and apostles multiplied in their successors; and in the solidity of a number *so perfectly square* might see the eternal immutability of the truth of God".

The list of the tribes as given in Chapter VII presents a striking peculiarity. Although the company is said to be "of *all* the tribes of the children of Israel", yet in the list that follows, the tribes of Dan and Ephraim are omitted altogether, and the number twelve is made up by including Joseph (along with Manasses his son) and Levi. This peculiarity is enough in itself to indicate clearly that we have here a symbolical and not a historical "Israel". For while it might be possible, though not easy, to suggest a reason why *Joseph* and Manasses should be named instead of *Ephraim* and Manasses (who are never separated in any other enumeration of the tribes), it is not possible, on the theory that this is the literal Israel, to account for the complete omission of the tribe of Dan. All attempts to do so have conspicuously failed.

But if we regard this vision as being, like all the others, composed of *symbols,* then we may hopefully look for an explanation of the peculiarity referred to. My suggestion is that the desired explanation will be found in *the meanings of the names* of Jacob's twelve sons.

The family of Jacob occupies a unique position in the Scriptures. It is a marvellous type of the family of God. This has been clearly recognized, and the significance of the type has been pointed out, by gifted teachers. Each of Jacob's sons receives a name that expresses some characteristic of the people of God, or some truth pertaining to them. This too has been often pointed out; so that we need not enlarge upon it. All that is needed for our purpose is to note the grouping of the names in this enumeration of them (for though they are named a number of times in the Bible, in no two lists is the order exactly the same); and to observe how the meanings of the names apply in this, the last presentation of the "good olive tree", the Israel of God, as it here stands before us in the symmetry and completeness of its final perfection.

The name Israel, a *Prince with God,* was passed on, as we know, from Jacob, to whom it was first given, to the family and nation of which he was the progenitor, and from them to the heavenly people (Gal. 6:16). Like the associated names, *Zion* and *Jerusalem,* the name *Israel* always belonged to that which is heavenly and eternal (Heb. 12:22). It was bestowed only temporarily upon the earthly counterpart. Of the twelve names of Jacob's sons, that of *Judah* obtained special prominence (though he was not the first-born), insomuch that for long periods it shared with *Israel* the distinction of being the generic designation of God's people. Judah means *Praise.* This name *(Jew)* also passed on to the true people of God, as appears from

Romans 2:28, 29: "For he is not a *Jew* who is one outwardly; neither is that 'circumcision' which is outward in the flesh; but he is a *Jew* who is one inwardly, and circumcision is that of the heart, in the spirit and not in the letter; whose *praise* is not of men, but of God". Obviously this last clause would be out of harmony with the rest of the passage but for the fact that *Jew* means *Praise*. Having that fact in mind, we see in it a declaration of the truth that the real *Jew* is one not by natural generation ("of men") but by spiritual generation ("of God").

1. It is most appropriate therefore that in the setting forth of the completed and perfected Israel of God the name *Judah* should lead off. For here we see "the whole family" (Eph. 3:15) whom God had chosen in Christ before the foundation of the world, "to the *praise* of the glory of His grace" (Eph. 1:4-6). In Jacob's blessing of his sons, he says: "Judah, thou art he whom thy brethren shall *praise*" (Gen. 49:8).

2. *Reuben*, the firstborn, comes next in this vision (Rev. 7:5). The meaning of his name is *Behold a Son* (Gen. 29:32). This name appropriately follows the name Judah, since every one of this company is a son of God.

3. The name of *Gad* is next, though he was seventh in the order of birth. His name signifies a *Troop, i. e.* a *great company*, such as is here presented to view. Thus we understand that we have here a vision of the "Many Sons" whom Christ is "bringing unto glory" (Heb. 2:10).

4. Next comes *Asher,* meaning *Happy,* or *Blessed,* this being the company of the "blessed" ones. It belongs to every one of this great *troop* of *sons.*

5. *Nephthalim* follows. This name signifies *Wrestlings.* At his birth Rachel said, "With great *wrestlings* have I wrestled with my sister, and have prevailed" (Gen. 30:8). As one of the designations of the people of God it reminds us of the fact that they by grace have overcome, or prevailed over, their adversaries. They are all *overcomers.*

6. The next is *Manasses,* one of the sons of Joseph, born to him in captivity. The record concerning this son is: "And Joseph called the name of the first-born *Manasseh, (i. e. Forgetting).* For God, said he, hath made me *forget* all my toil, and all my father's house" (Gen. 41:51). The appropriateness of this name as applied to the children of God is obvious. In Psalm 45:10 the bride is addressed in these words: "Hearken, O daughter, and consider, and incline thine ear; *forget* also thine own people, and *thy father's* house". All the redeemed have *forgotten* their connection with the house of their natural father, Adam.

7. *Simeon,* Jacob's second son, comes next. His name means *Hearing.* It was given him because, as his mother said, "the Lord hath *heard* that I was hated" (Gen. 29:33). Every one of the household of faith is entitled to this name also, for "faith cometh by *hearing*". Each one has been given the hearing ear of faith to receive the word of the truth of the gospel.

8. Then follows *Levi*, meaning *Joined*, reminding us of the great truth that every one of the redeemed is *"Joined unto the Lord"* (1 Cor. 6:17).

9. *Issachar* is next on the list. His name signifies "A Hire" (Gen. 30:18), that is, something for which *a price was paid*. So this too is an appropriate name for those to whom it is said, "Ye are not your own; for ye are *bought with a price*" (1 Cor. 6:19, 20).

10. Then follows *Zabulon*, whose name means *Dwelling;* "for Leah said, Now will my husband *dwell* with me" (Gen. 30:20). This prophetic utterance applies also to the redeemed people of God. For they are "builded together for an habitation of God" (Eph. 2:20), even as God had said, "I will *dwell in them*" (2 Cor. 6:16); and even as, in the last of the visions of the Apocalypse, John hears a great voice out of heaven, saying, "Behold, the tabernacle of God is with men, and He will *dwell* with them" (Rev. 21:3).

11. *Joseph* comes next. His name, which means *Adding*, has been variously applied. One thought prominently involved in it is that of *growth and fruitfulness*. This thought comes out clearly in the blessing of Jacob: "Joseph is a *fruitful bough*, even a fruitful bough by a well, whose branches run over the wall" (Gen. 49:22). This description clearly applies to the children of God, of whom it is said, "But now ye have *your fruit* unto holiness" (Rom. 6:22), and of whom Christ Himself said: "I AM the vine, ye are the

branches. He that abideth in Me, and I in him, the same bringeth forth *much fruit"* (John 15:5). Jacob's words, "Whose branches run over the wall", have their fulfilment historically in the fact that the gospel passed beyond that "wall of partition" which formerly separated Jews and Gentiles, but which was "broken down" by the death and resurrection of Christ (Eph. 2:14); so that Gentiles too were "added" to the great household of faith. The same thought is expressed in the name of Joseph's second son, *Ephraim* (who is omitted from the list) so named because, as stated in Joseph's own words "God hath caused me to be *fruitful* in the land of my affliction" (Gen. 41:52). Now inasmuch as Ephraim was, next to Judah, the most important of the tribes of the natural Israel, it would be impossible to account for the omission of Ephraim from this list if it were to be taken literally and as a prophecy to be fulfilled in the earthly people. But if the vision be symbolical, and if the meanings of these names, so carefully recorded and explained in the Book of Genesis, were to be fully revealed in the last Book of the Bible, and in connection with the great antitype of Jacob's wonderful family, then it is easy to be seen that the name *Ephraim* is dispensed with *for the reason that its meaning is embraced in the name Joseph.* The fulfilment of the meaning of Joseph's name begins early in the history of the Kingdom of God as recorded in Acts. For there we read that, from the day of

Pentecost and onward, "The Lord *added* to them daily such as were being saved" (Ac. 2:47).

12. *Benjamin* comes last. His mother named him *Benoni,* meaning the *Son of my Sorrow;* but his father called him *Benjamin,* that is the *Son of the Right Hand* (Gen. 35:18). This two-fold name of Jacob's last son foreshadows the Lord Jesus Christ in a remarkable way. For He was, as it were, the last-born of Jacob, and He came forth of Israel when, like Rachel, Israel was approaching the period of "hard labour", and was at the point of death. Benjamin was born when "there was but a little way to come to Ephrath", which was to be the birth-place of Christ (Gen. 35:16, 17). Moreover, Jesus Christ was both the Son of His mother's *sorrow* (for we recall Simeon's words to Mary, "Yea, a sword shall pierce through thine own soul also", Lu. 2:35), and was also the Son of God's *right hand,* where, and whereby, He is now exalted (Ac. 2:33; 1 Pet. 3:22). But the two-fold name of Jacob's youngest son is appropriate also as the final designation of the entire Israel of God. For they too are both the sons of Christ's sorrow, the fruit of the travail of His soul, and also the sons of the right hand of His power, whereby He has saved them from all their enemies, has lifted them out of the horrible pit into which sin had plunged them, and has raised them up to where He himself is enthroned in the heavenly places.

The Innumerable Company

"After this I beheld, and, lo, a great multitude, which no man could number, of all nations, and kindreds, and peoples, and tongues, stood before the throne, and before the Lamb, clothed with white robes, and palms in their hands; and cried with a loud voice, saying, Salvation to our God which sitteth upon the throne, and unto the Lamb" (Rev. 7:9, 10).

This vision I regard as another pictorial representation of the whole company of the redeemed, supplementing that which immediately precedes it, and showing details that could not be introduced into the preceding vision. Indeed, what is given in verses 4-8 is not strictly a "vision" at all. Those verses only record what John "heard" concerning "the number of them which were sealed". But now he is given to *see* them; and lo, it is an innumerable company gathered out of all nations, kindreds, peoples, and tongues of the earth. Thus the former part of the passage reminds us that the election of God's grace was complete in His mind from eternity past, every one of them having been chosen in Christ before the foundation of the world (Eph. 1:1-6); and it further reminds us that the day of grace cannot end until the *very last* of those chosen ones shall have been saved and *"sealed* with that Holy Spirit of promise" (Eph. 1:13, 14). The latter part of the passage brings to view that the company of the elect, "the whole family" of God (Eph. 3:15), is a vast number, taken out of *all* the nations and tribes of earth. It is what is expressed by the olive-tree in its final form (Rom. 11:17-25).

This vision puts before our eyes the fulfilment of the words of Christ spoken on the occasion of the first manifestation of faith in Himself by a Gentile: "Verily I say unto you, I have not found so great faith, no not in Israel. And I say unto you, That *many* shall come from the east and west and sit down with Abraham, Isaac and Jacob in the kingdom of heaven" (Mat. 8: 10, 11). And here John sees them, an innumerable company, incorporated into the Israel of God.

The latter part of the passage also shows us the position of the elect of God. They stand "before the throne, and before the Lamb"; and it shows that they are clothed in *white robes*, the garb of the redeemed; and also that they have palms in their hands, which proclaims them as sharers of Christ's victory over all His and their enemies. It also gives us the words of their song, the first word being "Salvation".

The words, "of all nations, and kindreds, and peoples, and tongues" identify this company with that which sings the new song of Chapter 5:9 to the Lamb, saying, "For Thou wast slain, and hast redeemed us to God by Thy blood, out of every kindred, and tongue, and people, and nation".

This is evidently that great "salvation" whereof the apostle Peter says, "which things the angels desire to look into" (1 Pet. 1:9-12); for the next words of our passage are: *"And all the angels* stood round about the throne, and about the elders, and the four living creatures, and fell down before the throne on their faces, and worshipped God, saying, Amen: Blessing, and glory, and wisdom, and thanksgiving, and honour, and power and might, be unto our God for ever and ever, Amen". Upon comparing this seven-fold doxology with that of Chapter 5:12, it will be seen that they are identical as to six of the seven terms (for "strength" in 5:12 is the same in the original as "might" in 7:12), the only difference being that in the later song the term "thanksgiving" takes the place of "riches" in the earlier.

Then follows the explanation brought out by a two-fold question addressed to John by one of the elders: "What are these which are arrayed in white robes? and whence come they?" John confesses his inability to answer by saying, "Sir, thou knowest". Whereupon the elder replies: "These are they which *are coming* out of great tribulation, and have washed their robes and made them white in the blood of the Lamb" (Rev. 7:13, 14). We give the correct rendering, "are coming", instead of the incorrect and misleading "came" of our A. V., because the tense is exceedingly important. Some modern expositors take this "great tribulation" to be the same as that whereof our Lord prophesied in Matthew 24:21, and make it a period yet future, a period that is to be immediately *after* the return of the Lord to raise the dead and change the living saints. Indeed it is a leading feature of the futurist system that there is to be a "great tribulation" after the rapture of the saints, and that those who are saved in that period will not be a part of the church, the body of Christ. According to that system of interpretation these white-robed, palm-bearing ones are "tribulation saints", who will occupy a different and a lower place in the glory from that of the redeemed of this present dispensation of grace. But there are various and serious objections to that view:

1. The elder expressly said of those whom John saw in that vision that they were *then,* at that very time, *coming* out of great tribulation. This alone forbids postponing that tribulation to a future dispensation.

2. Those white-robed ones have the very same "salvation" that is now proclaimed to all men, for it is said of them that "they have washed their robes and made them white in the blood of the Lamb" (cf. 1:5, 5:9; 1 Pet. 1:18, 19).

3. The blessedness which is theirs, as described in verses 15-17 of our passage, is *the same as that of all the redeemed,* as described in Chapter 21:1-4.

4. The term "robes" in verse 13 properly designates *marriage robes,* and the definite article precedes this word, and also the important word "white". This gives peculiar force to the entire phrase, the full significance of which might be expressed thus: "Who are these who are arrayed in the richest marriage-robes of purest and most radiant whiteness?" The statement of verse 14, that they have *"washed* their robes and made them white *in the blood* of the Lamb", clearly identifies them as belonging to the company of the redeemed. (Compare the words of Ch. 1:5, "Who loved us, and washed us from our sins *in His own*

blood", and those of Chap. 5:9, "For Thou was slain, and hast redeemed us to God *by Thy blood"*).

5. The Scripture gives us no warrant whatever for preaching or teaching any salvation other than that which the gospel now offers to all alike; or any salvation after the ending of this present day of grace. This modern doctrine of another hope, and of another day of salvation, salvation of another sort than that of the gospel of Christ, has no support in the Scripture that I can discover.

We conclude therefore, that in the vision of Chapter VII we are given two views of the entire company of the redeemed, the two together presenting a complete showing forth, symbolically, of the truth with respect to them.

THE SEVENTH SEAL

"And when he had opened the seventh seal there was silence in heaven about the space of half an hour" (8:1).

This one sentence is all that is recorded of what happened at the opening of the seventh seal. As an ending to the seals series it is remarkable, and not a little mystifying. What is the significance of this silence *in heaven?* (for nothing is here said of anything happening on earth). It surely must have some deep significance, and it will be well worth while to make diligent search for it.

In the first place then, we notice that this *silence* in heaven for a measured period at the opening of the last of the seals (which completely opens the seven-sealed book), is in marked, and doubtless intentional contrast with the *rejoicings* in heaven at the beginning of this series of visions, when the glorified Redeemer "came and took the book out of the right hand of Him that sat upon the throne" (5:7).

Rejecting all speculations, conjectures and surmises, and taking the Scripture as our only guide, let us then seek the meaning of this silence in heaven.

The first clue given us is that the next time we hear the voices of those in heaven, including those of the four and twenty elders, is immediately after the sounding of the seventh trumpet, when again there is an outburst of joy from "great voices in heaven", accompanied by the worship of the elders who, *in this place only,* are seen to fall upon their faces before God, giving Him thanks "because", in their own words, "Thou hast *taken to Thee Thy great power and hast reigned*", these words being in agreement with what the "great voices" had just proclaimed, namely: "The kingdoms of this world are become the kingdoms of our Lord, and of His Christ, and He shall reign for ever and ever" (11:15-17). It is therefore the consummation of the eternal purpose of God, that for which heaven and earth have long waited, which calls forth rejoicings and songs of loudest praises in heaven. Keeping this in mind, I would recall, as has been noted already, that the sixth seal brought us to the eve of the great day of the wrath of the Lamb, that is to say, to "the days of the voice of the seventh angel", in which

The Opening of the Seals

"days" the mystery of God, according to the glad tidings declared to His prophets, is to be *finished* (10:7). Putting these passages together we may gather that the solemn and ominous "silence in heaven", which marked the opening of the seventh seal, was the appropriate prelude, on the heavenly side of things, to the stupendous events of the days of the seventh trumpet, in which the judgments of God upon the earth reach their climax, and the government is wrested finally from the hands of men.

Other Scriptures will help us to fix definitely the meaning of this silence in heaven, touching which it seems to have been the custom of so many expositors to surrender themselves to mere conjecture. The principal passage is Habakkuk 2:10: "The Lord is in His holy temple; let all the earth *keep silence* before Him". These words were spoken in connection with the going forth of the Almighty in Judgment. Hence, when He is about to issue forth for His *final* judgments upon the world, in the great day of His wrath, nothing could be more fitting than that all heaven should stand in breathless silence, awaiting the peal of the last trump.

Then in Zephaniah 1:7, in a passage that contains threatenings of the consuming judgments of God, are the words, *"Hold thy peace* at the presence of the Lord God; *for the day of the Lord is at hand"*, the word "hold thy peace" being identically the same as that rendered "keep silence" in Habakkuk 2:20.

Finally in Zechariah 2:13, upon a similar occasion, are the words: *"Be silent,* O all flesh, before the Lord; for He is raised up out of His holy habitation"; that is, raised up for the purpose of executing judgment.

In the light of these Scriptures it may be clearly seen that the silence in heaven brings the group of seals visions to a most appropriate and most impressive ending.

CHAPTER VI

The Trumpet Series

THE trumpet series occupies a clearly marked division of the Apocalypse. It extends from Chapter 8:1 to 11:18.

What are the special characteristics of this section? and wherein do they differ from those of other sections? It is most important that we should have answers to these questions; for if we proceed without them we are sure to lose our way.

The first thing given for our guidance is that each series of visions is grouped under a distinctive symbol, and the several symbols—candlesticks, seals, trumpets and vials—are very different, both in their appearance and in their significance, from each other. This would lead to the conclusion that the visions of each group have a common character, and also that the general character of the visions of each group differs from that of every other group. This conclusion, if sound, overthrows the historicist system of interpretation. For that system ignores the distinction between seals, trumpets and vials. It looks for a succession of historical events or epochs corresponding to the seals; then for a second series of *like character* (following the first in chronological order) corresponding to the trumpets; and then for a final series of like events (historical) answering to the vials. It makes the difference between the several series merely one of *time;* whereas the symbols plainly direct us to look for differences of *character.* But we search in vain for a series of historical events at the beginning of our era, all of the same general character and answering to the significance of the opening of a seal; then for a series later in date, of a different character, answering to the significance of the sounding of a trumpet; and lastly for another distinct series, answering to the significance of the pouring out of the contents of a bowl. Hence the historicist system does not, in this important respect at least, answer to the symbolical language of the Book.

The trumpet series *stands by itself, separate and complete.* Commotions, distresses and "woes" mark every stage. The sphere is *political* or more exactly *politico-religious,* as will be made evident further on; and the entire series eventuates and culminates in what has ever been the joyful prospect of the people of God, namely, "the kingdoms of this world are become the Kingdoms of our Lord and of His Christ".

Our first inquiry upon arriving at this division of the Book should be as to the meaning of the trumpet as a Bible symbol. In Scripture trumpets are used because of their loud, piercing, and far-reaching sound. The purpose of a trumpet-blast is to demand the attention of all men in view of a matter of urgent importance. It is used when there is need to arouse the people, regardless of the character of what is about to happen, whether joyful or otherwise, whether to announce a season of high public festivity, or to summon the people to resist an approaching enemy. In any case the blowing of trumpets is a call to the congregation in respect to some transaction of unusual importance and significance, the character whereof will be shown by the context. The blast of trumpets may be used to announce a joyful event, a great triumph, as the fall of Jericho; or it may be used to give notice of a time of great distress, as in Joel 2:1, where the day of the Lord is announced by the blowing of trumpets: "Blow ye the trumpet in Zion, and sound an alarm in My holy mountain: let all the inhabitants of the land tremble; for the day of the LORD cometh, for it is nigh at hand".

All the events of the trumpet series are of a punitive nature. They have the definite character of warnings to the inhabitants of the earth, easily understood by all who give any heed whatever to the Word of God. And the main purpose would seem to be to call men to repentance. In this connection notice should be taken of the words: "Yet they repented not" (9:20, 21), and "The remnant were affrighted and gave glory to the God of heaven" (11:13).

The O. T. presents a second case (besides that of the taking of Jericho, hereafter referred to more particularly) of the combination of the blowing of trumpets with the numerical symbol *seven*. For it was ordained in the Mosaic law that after *seven times seven years,* there should be a year of jubilee, which was to be proclaimed by *the blowing of trumpets* in the *seventh* month (Lev. 25:8, 9). This was the year in which the Lord announced His proprietorship of the land ("For the land is Mine", v. 23). It was to be a year of "liberty throughout all the land into all the inhabitants thereof" a "jubilee", a time of the restoration of every one of the people of God to his possessions, a time when there should be no toil of any kind (vv. 10-13). It is easy to see how in this feast, with which the blowing of trumpets was specially associated, there is a foreshowing of that in which the trumpet series of the Apocalypse finally eventuates. And there is a similar foreshadowing in the "memorial of blowing of trumpets in the *seventh* month" (Lev. 23:24, 25), when all servile work was to cease.

The high importance of the trumpet series is further indicated by the statement that the trumpets were given to "the seven angels which *stood before God*". The honor of a constant standing before God belongs only to those of highest rank. That Christ's little ones are in the care of angels who are *always* before the presence of God, is given as a warning against despising any of them (Mat. 18:10). Christ exhorts His disciples to watch and pray always, that they may be accounted worthy to escape the evils He foretold, and "to *stand before* the Son of man" (Lu. 21:36; cf. Dan. 1:5). That will be a high dignity and honor.

THE MEDIATING ANGEL

Again the special character of each division of the Apocalypse is indicated by the particular way the Lord

Jesus Christ Himself is presented therein. For we should ever keep in mind that the Book we are seeking to elucidate is "the revelation of *Jesus Christ*". In Chapter I-III He appears as the glorified "Son of man"; and as such He is robed in a garment down to the foot, is girt about the breasts with a golden girdle, holds the seven stars in His right hand, and walks in the midst of the seven candlesticks.

In Chapters V, VI He is seen as the enthroned Redeemer to whom supreme authority is given over the whole creation. Here He is represented by the symbol of a Lamb that had been slain.

But now, in the section before us, He is presented twice, both times in the character of *Mediator between God and men*. As such He is appropriately presented in the guise of an angel; for the angels are ministering spirits (Psa. 103: 20, 21; Heb. 1:14). The first time, He is seen ministering at the golden altar, where He adds His own merits to the prayers of His people (8:3, 4). The second time, He brings from heaven a little book relating to future events concerning many peoples, nations and kings, in regard to whom John is commanded to prophesy (10:1-11). This "little book" apparently contains the sweet-bitter prophecy of "the days of the voice of the seventh angel" (Chapters XIII-XX).

These visions of the Lord in His office of the One Mediator between God and men (1 Tim. 2:5) afford valuable indications as to the general character of this section of the Book. In Chapter 8:3, 4 He is seen engaged in His great work of making intercession for His people, whereby He saves to the uttermost them that come to God by Him (Rom. 8:34; Heb. 7:25, 26). Because of the strokes that are about to fall upon the inhabitants of the earth, with whom His own people are commingled, He stands at the golden altar, as the mediating High Priest, and adds "much incense" to "the prayers of all the saints".

The reference to the incense takes us back to Exodus 30:34-38. The incense (or perfume) that Moses was commanded to make was a most hallowed thing. It was to be "holy for the Lord". Anyone who should presume to make the like was to be "cut off from his people". Its four ingredients typify severally and collectively the merits and virtues of Christ.

That this "angel" is Christ is hardly open to doubt. For none other than He could receive the prayers of all saints and present them to God, and none other could add anything thereto to make them acceptable to God. Therefore I regard the vision of Revelation 8:3, 4 as representing to the eye the ministry appointed to Christ and His people for this dispensation, as specified in the words of the apostle: "I will therefore that, first of all, supplications, prayers, intercessions and giving of thanks be made for all men, for kings, and for all that are in authority"—(etc. 1 Tim. 2:1 to v. 8 incl.). It represents also what is declared in Hebrews 7:25 concerning Christ as our great High Priest, serving in the power of an endless life, and able therefore to save them to the uttermost who come unto God by Him.

THE DIVISIONS OF THE TRUMPET SERIES

As in the case of the seals, the trumpet series is divided into two parts; first a group of four, and then a group of three. For after the sounding of the fourth trumpet (8:12) the action is interrupted, and John sees an angel (or, as the best manuscripts have it, an *eagle*) flying through the midst of heaven, saying with a loud voice, *"Woe, woe, woe,* to the inhabiters of the earth, by reason of the other voices of the trumpet of the three angels which are yet to sound".

Again, as in the case of the seals, there is a further interruption after the sixth trumpet, where another complete vision is introduced (that of Chapter 10:1-11:13) corresponding in its place in the trumpet series to the vision of Chapter VII, which comes between the 6th and 7th seals.

That the trumpets severally mark distinct events or eras of time in the history of the world is indicated by the words of the mighty Angel that *"in the days* of the voice of the seventh angel, when he shall begin to sound, the mystery of God shall be finished" (10:7). This tells us that the seventh trumpet marks off a definite period of time ("the days"), and also that something of *capital importance* is to occur at the *beginning* of that period. These words, and those of the great voices in heaven (11:15-18), aid materially in the location of the eras of the trumpets; for it is clearly seen thereby that the seventh trumpet brings us to the eve of the great day of the wrath of the Lamb, revealed at the opening of the sixth seal. This appears by the words "and the nations were angry, and *Thy wrath is come*" (11:18). Having thus located the seventh trumpet with relation to the *sixth* seal, of which the fulfilment is clearly yet in the future, we have the assurance that all the events figured in the other six trumpets *precede the day of wrath. Where then do we now stand with respect to the stream of prophetic events here pictured to our minds?* Is it possible to determine this even approximately? An attempt at an answer will be found in the last chapter of this volume.

The description of the events which follow the sounding of the first four trumpets is very brief. It is given, morover, in broad and general terms. This brevity and vagueness are in marked contrast with the description of what follows at the sounding of each of the last three trumpets, where the terms are comparatively definite and many details are given. The explanation of this difference I take to be that the happenings of the first group of four trumpets are the subject of other prophecies of Scripture, so that, for the accomplishment of the design of the Book, it was necessary to present at this place only a brief summary thereof, in order to connect those predictions properly in series with other important events which, together with them, constitute the entire group of trumpet happenings.

The symbology of the trumpet series recalls the siege of Jericho, to which a casual allusion has been already made. There were *seven* trumpets in action during the *seven* days of that siege. Moreover, apart from the stirring sound of the trumpets themselves, which could be plainly heard by all the inhabitants of the doomed city, there was nothing of special moment after the preliminary investment of the city, until the *seventh* day. Its affairs went on in the usual way; and presumably the warning note of the trumpets, though repeated every day, came to be regarded with indifference. Thus it is with the inhabitants of this present world, whose ruinous overthrow is so strikingly foreshadowed by the fall of Jericho. Warning after warning is sounded; but no heed is given. The thought in the minds of men is just what was foretold by the apostle Peter. For in effect they are saying, "where is the promise of His coming (in judgment)? for since the fathers fell asleep, all things continue as they were from the beginning of the creation" (2 Pet. 3:4). This view of the indefinite continuance of all things in an interminable process of orderly progression, is one of the cardinal points of the creed of the modern man. It rests for its support upon the delusive dogma of "evolution".

But on the *seventh* day of the siege of Jericho, there was *seven*-fold activity. For the city was encircled *seven* times; and at the *seventh* round of trumpet-blowing the city fell and was captured and destroyed. In marked correspondence with this is the revelation that in the days of the voice of the *seventh* angel, the resistance of the rebel world will be at last overcome, and the kingdoms thereof will fall into the hands of Christ (11:15).

In the trumpet series then, we have a prophecy of events that affect the *whole world,* and that carry us on to the *very end* of the christian era; and the events of the entire series are of the same general character, answering to the significance of trumpets as a Biblical symbol. They are events of a *politico-religious* nature.

The matters stated above also point to the conclusion that the fulfilment of the visions of the first group of four trumpets should be sought for in events which happened near the beginning of our era, but which were of a nature such as to have *lasting effects.*

Further to guide us, we have the character in which Christ is presented in this division of the Book. For just as the explanation of the visions of the seals was controlled by the revelation, in that part of the Book, of Jesus Christ in His office of enthroned Redeemer and sovereign Lord of the universe, so the explanation of the trumpet visions will be found in events that are related to Christ in His office of High Priest and Mediator of the new covenant, in which office He intercedes for and is "the Saviour (or Preserver) of all men, specially of those that believe" (1 Tim. 4:10).

In verse 5 we read: "And the angel took the censer and filled it with fire of the altar, and cast it into (or upon, *marg.*) the earth: and there were voices, and thunderings, and lightnings, and an earthquake".

The Trumpet Series

These are the figures of threatenings and warnings of judgments soon to come. Throughout the Bible *fire* is the symbol of the consuming wrath of God. This is the element that the Angel casts upon the earth, with the accompaniment of voices (messages of God), thunderings (intimations of approaching judgments, and manifestations of God's mighty power, Ps. 29:3, 4; Job 37:1-5), lightnings (sharp and sudden strokes of judgment), and an earthquake (a great social upheaval).

The fire that was cast upon the earth was taken from the altar, reminding us that fire has a two-fold office. It both consumes the sacrifice, thus bearing up to God the memorial thereof in the smoke that ascends from the altar; and it also consumes the enemies of God, and all that is contrary to His truth and holiness.

Bengel thus comments on the passage:

"Frankincense and prayer draw a great deal after it; it is acceptable; it will be heard. God then causes His righteous judgments to go forth for a terror to the world, for the discomfiture of His enemies, and for the advancement of His kingdom".

And Hengstenberg comments thus:

"The internal connection between the fiery prayer, and the fiery indignation which is to consume the adversaries (Heb. 10:27), is shadowed forth by the circumstance that, of the same fire of the altar with which the frankincense was kindled, there was taken and thrown upon the earth. By the first use of the fire in kindling the frankincense it was in a manner consecrated for the second. Fire is here, as usual in the Apocalypse, the symbol of the holy wrath and judgment of God. The fire, the voices, etc. have here only a *prophetical* character. The fulfilment of what they prophesy begins with the first trumpet and closes with the last. Likewise in Chapter IV. 5 the voices, lightnings and thunders are not the judgment itself, but the symbolical announcement of it".

What was immediately introduced by the scene described in verses 3-5 is, in my opinion, the season of God's special visitation of the Jewish nation in His wrath and fiery indignation as foretold in many prophecies both of the Old Testament and the New. For the time was come, as the apostle Peter declared, "that judgment must begin at the house of God" (1 Pet. 4:17). Thus for example, in Deuteronomy 28:45-47 and 32:22, God plainly foretold what was to befall that people "at their latter end", saying: "For a *fire* is kindled in Mine anger, and shall burn unto the lowest hell, and shall consume *the earth* with her increase, and set *on fire* the foundations of the mountains" (Deut. 32:22). The resemblances in these old prophecies to the passage we are now studying are remarkable. We shall have occasion to return to them.

An incident that illustrates what is now before us, and which doubtless is in view in this passage, is recorded in the 9th and 10th Chapters of Leviticus. Aaron and his sons had just been consecrated as priests unto God; and it is recorded that when they for the first time discharged the duties of that office, and presented a sin offering, first for the high priest himself (9:7-11), and then for the people (15-22), *"there came fire out from before the Lord,* and consumed upon the altar the burnt offering and the fat" (24). Here we have the first use of the fire from God. But immediately thereafter, when Nadab and Abihu, sons of Aaron, offered strange fire before the Lord, *"there went out fire from the Lord and devoured them"* (10:1, 2). This seems to be the typical illustration of the vision we are now considering. For Israel as a nation had been brought nigh to God, and had been sanctified for Himself; and what He said concerning those sons of Aaron applied also to them: "I will be sanctified in them that come nigh Me, and before all the people I will be glorified" (10:3). Then Moses commanded that the bodies of those upon whom the fire of God's wrath had fallen be carried outside the camp; and he commanded that the whole house of Israel "bewail *the burning* which the Lord *hath kindled"* (v. 6). This incident may be, with profit to the reader, compared with that of Aananias and Sapphira, which tallies with it, even to the carrying out of the bodies (Ac. 5:1-10).

The Lord Jesus doubtless had in mind the incident of Nadab and Abihu, and also the season of wrath that was about to come upon Israel, when He said: "I am come to send *fire on the earth;* and what will I if it be *already kindled?"* (Lu. 12:47). The words "send (or cast) fire on the earth" are identically the same as those used of the angel in Revelation 8:5.

It should be noted that the word rendered "earth" in these passages also means "land", and is often so rendered. So it may be that these Scriptures speak of the fire which was to consume the land of Israel.

The apostle Paul likewise spoke distinctly of the fiery wrath of God that was soon to fall upon the apostate nation which had rejected first the Lord Jesus Christ Himself, and then His gospel, when preached to them by His servants with the Holy Ghost sent down from heaven. For he summed up their wickedness by saying: "Who both killed the Lord Jesus and their own prophets, and have persecuted us (the apostles of Christ); and they please not God, and are contrary to all men; forbidding us to speak to the Gentiles, that they might be saved, to fill up their sins alway"; because of which, as he goes on to say, *"the wrath is come upon them to the uttermost"* (1 Th. 2:15, 16). The meaning and force of this important passage seem to have been generally overlooked by expositors, though the words are quite plain, and though the event whereof the apostle spoke, *"the wrath upon them to the uttermost"*, came to pass in a few years from the time they were written. Those words certify that the wickedness of the Jewish nation had reached its predicted climax; that the measure of their iniquity had been *filled up* (see Gen. 15:16; Mat. 23:32); and that therefore the limit of God's forbearance had been reached, and His wrath had come upon them "to the uttermost". This plain declaration forbids the idea, often met with in writings of futurists, that there is to be a yet more severe out-pouring of the wrath of God upon the Jews, when they shall have been regathered in Palestine, and their national existence renewed. If that view be correct, then the Jews did not "fill up" their national sins in the days of Christ and His apostles, as both the Lord Himself (Mat. 23:32) and His servant Paul (1 Th. 2:16) plainly declared. Nor, if that view be correct, did God's wrath come upon them at that time "to the uttermost", as the apostle said, who, in so saying, was but repeating the words of Christ Himself, in foretelling the approaching destruction of Jerusalem, when He plainly stated that at that time there should be "great distress *in the land,* and *wrath* upon *this people"*; that they should "fall by the edge of the sword, and be led away captive into all nations"; and that Jerusalem should be "trodden down of the Gentiles, until the times of the Gentiles be fulfilled" (Lu. 21:23, 24).

In the light of all the Scriptures that bear upon the subject now before us (and they are many), it is clear that the Jewish dispensation was to end in an outpouring of the wrath of God upon that people; that they were to be nationally exterminated, and the survivors scattered all over the earth; and that their land was to become a desolation, and their city and temple were to be utterly destroyed. All this was to come upon them because, though they had "received the law by the dispensation of angels", they had *"not kept it"* (Ac. 7:53; Rom. 2:17-23). By the light of other Scriptures it is equally plain that there is to be, at the end of this Christian dispensation, a *world-wide* outpouring of the wrath of God, which will fall upon the nations to whom *the gospel of God* has come, but who have *not* obeyed it. To this the apostle Peter seems to be referring when he says, "For the time is come that *judgment must begin at the house of God;* and if it first *begin at us*"—the Jewish nation—"what shall the end be of them that *obey not the gospel?*" (1 Pet. 4:12-17). He was speaking, in that passage, of "the *fiery trial*" that was about to try them; for in the period of wrath which was then close at hand, Christ's own people were to be exposed to dangers and sufferings (Mat. 24:20-22; Lu. 21:20-23). In view thereof the Lord had specially commanded His people to "pray" at that particular time (Mat. 24:20); and the prayers that were offered in obedience to that command were doubtless among those which He presented to God when ministering at the golden altar.

There is much light to be had also from the words our Lord spake to the women who followed Him with their lamentations while He was on His way to the cross. For, thinking not of the sufferings He Himself was about to endure, but of the wrath that was to be poured out ere long upon that blinded people, He said: "Weep not for Me, but weep for yourselves, and for your children"; and then He went on to speak of the days of wrath and distress that were soon to come upon them, concerning which days He said, "Then shall they begin to say to the mountains, Fall upon us; and to the hills, Cover us" (Lu. 23:27-30). These words of our Lord refer to the prophecy of Hosea, who spoke of Israel as "the empty vine", and foretold

The Trumpet Series

the coming of a time when, because of their sin, their high places were to be destroyed, and they should "say to the mountains, Cover us; and to the hills, Fall on us" (Hos. 10:8). That prophecy, by the Lord's plain declaration to the wailing women, was to be fulfilled at the then approaching destruction of Jerusalem. And from Revelation 6:16 we learn that the fearful destruction of Jerusalem in those theretofore unparalleled "days of vengeance", was but a type of the *universal* destruction which is to take place at the end of this gospel-dispensation; for the same cry to the mountains and the hills will in that day be upon the lips of "the kings of the earth, and the great men, and the rich men, and the chief captains, and the mighty men, and every bondman, and every free man".

With such clear prophecies as these already written in the Word of God concerning the era of judgments on the Jewish nation, it is easy to see why but a condensed summary thereof is given in the passage we are now studying.

Further help in arriving at the true explanation of this passage (Rev. 8:5) may be had by recalling that the Scriptures make known to us two, and *only two,* great eras of God's "wrath"; *first,* the era which occurred at the close of the dispensation of the law, which was limited to the Jewish people (for to them alone the law of God had been given); and *second,* that which is yet to come at the close of the dispensation of grace, and which will involve the nations that have rejected the grace of God offered to them in the gospel. Paul, who speaks so definitely of the one period as coming upon the Jews in his own time, speaks in the same Epistle, and with the same definiteness, of the other, as a day that shall come *suddenly,* like a thief; in which connection, however, he gives a most comforting assurance to the people of God, telling them that "God hath not appointed *us* unto *wrath,* but to obtain salvation by our Lord Jesus Christ" (1 Th. 5:1-7). Moreover, in another passage he speaks of that coming period of *wrath* as the time when "the Lord Jesus shall be revealed from heaven with His mighty angels, in flaming fire, taking vengeance upon them that know not God, and that *obey not the gospel of our Lord Jesus Christ"* (2 Th. 1:7, 8). The parallel between God's dealings on the one hand with those who obeyed not the law (the Jewish nation) and on the other hand with those that have not obeyed the gospel (the christianized nations) is very exact.

Having these things in mind, it is clear that, inasmuch as the scene just preceding the *first* trumpet is manifestly not the introduction to the yet future day of wrath upon all the nations, for that is expressly placed in the days of the *seventh* trumpet (Rev. 11:18), and is, moreover, introduced by a very different scene (Chap. X), we *must needs* apply Revelation 8:5 to the wrath that came upon Israel in the days of Vespasian and Titus, A. D. 63-70; for there is no other period of *wrath* to which it *could* apply. And even if we were to ignore Bible indications altogether, and allow ourselves, as the manner of some is, to roam at large through secular history in quest of something that could be cited as a possible fulfilment of this prophecy, we should yet be unable to find an epoch that could be taken to be a *day of wrath,* or that answers in other particulars to the symbols here used. Furthermore, I expect to show that the verses which follow lend strong support to what has been suggested above.

The First Trumpet

"The first angel sounded, and there followed hail and fire mingled with blood, and they were cast upon the earth: and the third part of the trees was burnt up, and all green grass was burnt up" (8:7).

The symbols of destruction found here are hail, fire and blood. These form a combination of destructive forces quite outside the domain of nature. Hail commingled with fire constituted the seventh of the plagues of Egypt (Ex. 9:23-25). But here we have an additional element, *blood,* which makes it plain that these natural agencies are to be taken in a figurative sense.

It has been pointed out that "hail speaks of a sharp, swift judgment coming directly from God". This is seen in Exodus 9:23, cited above. In Isaiah 28:2, 17, where the threatened invasion of Judea by the armies of Assyria was the subject of the prophecy, it was said that the Lord had "a mighty and a strong one", who would come "as a tempest *of hail,* and as a destroying storm". In Job 28:22, 23, the Lord Himself speaks of "the treasures of *hail",* which He has reserved "against the time of trouble, against the time of battle and war". The same expression "time of trouble" is found in Daniel 12:1, where it is used (as I understand the application of the phrase) in reference to the period of the destruction of the Jewish nation by the armies of Rome.

We recall also the words of David who, speaking of the manifestation of the anger of the Lord, said: "The LORD also thundered in the heavens, and the Highest gave His voice; *hail stones* and coals of *fire*" (Ps. 18:13).

Therefore, fire and hail as symbols would be most suitable to represent the destructive agencies employed during the invasion and desolation of Judea by the armies of imperial Rome; and the third symbol, *blood*, speaks of the stupendous loss of life at that dreadful time. As Mede has put it: "John has mingled blood (with the other symbols) contrary to nature, that he might indicate how the whole of this image points to slaughter".

Trees are a familiar figure in Scripture for human greatness, for persons of eminence (Judg. 8:9-13; Jer. 7:20; 17:8; Ezek. 31:3; Dan. 4:20-22). The burning up of "a third part of the trees" would therefore signify that a large proportion of the leading men in the nation were to be consumed. The words "and all the green grass was burnt up" would point to the complete destruction of national or earthly prosperity, the sweeping away of the entire population of the land.

Thus the symbols would all be fitly used to picture what happened in the day of the outpouring of God's wrath upon the people of Israel, and their land and city. And I know of no other event or epoch to which they would more aptly apply. In this connection it is to be noted that the word here rendered "earth" also means "land", and specifically the land of Judea.

It is further to be recalled that the hurting of the earth, sea and trees, was restrained, by special command of God, until His servants should be sealed in their foreheads (7:1-3). Corresponding to this is the fact that the judgments following the crucifixion of Christ, and which began and centered in Judea, were delayed between thirty and forty years, during which time the work of the gospel was prosecuted energetically among the Jews.

The phrase, "a third part", which occurs repeatedly in the description of the events of this group of four trumpets, is the signature of their partial character. The time of final and complete judgment and wrath comes later.

The Second Trumpet

"And the second angel sounded, and as it were a great mountain burning with fire was cast into the sea: and the third part of the sea became blood. And the third part of the creatures that were in the sea, and had life, died; and the third part of the ships were destroyed" (vv. 8, 9).

The waters or *seas* represent nations in general. This explanation of the symbol is given in Revelation

17:15. Likewise in Jeremiah 51:13 the prophet addresses Babylon, saying: "O thou that dwellest upon many waters".

A *mountain* is the Bible symbol for a nation. Thus Babylon is called a "destroying mountain" (Jer. 51:25). Daniel speaks of Jerusalem as "the holy mountain of God" (Dan. 9:20). In Zechariah 4:7 the "great mountain" before Zerubbabel was the Persian Kingdom, which had set itself against the building of the temple. In Isaiah 13:2, "the high mountain" whereof the prophet speaks is Babylon. What then is represented by this picture of the casting of a nation, burning with the fire of God's wrath, into the midst of the other nations and peoples of the earth, and with unhappy consequences to them? Only once in the history of mankind has such a thing happened. That was at the beginning of our era, when *the whole Jewish nation was cast out of its own country into the midst of the other nations of the world.*

Moreover, that event was one of exceedingly great importance in the eyes of God. This appears from the many references to it in the prophecies of Scripture, and particularly from the grief of the Lord Jesus Christ when He had occasion to speak of it (Lu. 19:41).

Further light is thrown upon this passage by the words of Christ spoken at the time of the withering of the fig-tree, on which He had found nought but leaves. For when His disciples expressed astonishment that it was so quickly withered away at His word, He said to them: "If ye have faith and doubt not, ye shall not only do this which is done to the fig tree, but also, if ye shall say to *this mountain,* Be thou removed, and be thou *cast into the sea,* it shall be done" (Mat. 21: 21). The symbology of *a mountain cast into the sea* is so remarkable and so unusual that we are fully warranted in assuming a connection between these two occurrences of it. The fig-tree was a literal fig-tree, and the mountain on which it grew was a literal mountain (the mount of Olives). But commentators, and Bible readers as well, see in that fig-tree a symbol of Israel, in one aspect thereof. Why then may not the *mountain* be likewise a figure of Israel in another aspect? Certainly the figure is most suitable; and certainly also the historical facts correspond remarkably well. For He who said to the fig-tree "Let no fruit grow on thee henceforward forever", was soon to say to that mountain "Be thou removed, and be thou cast into the sea".

The mountain of Revelation 8:8 was a *"great* mountain", and it was "burning with fire". The nation of Babylon, when visited by the fire of God's wrath, was to become "a *burnt* mountain" (Jer. 51:25). But in this case the mountain was *"burning* with fire" when cast into the sea; that is to say, the wrath of God was resting upon it *at the time;* and this agrees perfectly with the facts concerning the overthrow and dispersion of the Jewish nation. Babylon, when overthrown, was indeed a "burnt mountain", for as a nation it ceased to exist. But Israel has been like the bush in the desert, *"burning"* but not consumed.

As regards the effects of the casting of this great mountain into the sea, there is close agreement between the picture before us and what is stated in several Scriptures concerning God's purpose to use the people of Israel for the chastisement of the nations. We have already seen that the going forth of the *ephah*, representing the rejected nation, is spoken of as the going forth of the "curse", and of "wickedness" (Zech. 5: 6-8). But even clearer are the words of the Lord by Jeremiah, in which, addressing Jacob, he said:

"Thou art my battle axe and weapons of war: for with thee will I break in pieces the nations, and with thee will I destroy kingdoms; and with thee will I break in pieces the horse and his rider; and with thee will I break in pieces the chariot and his rider. With thee also will I break in pieces man and woman; and with thee will I break in pieces old and young; and with thee will I break in pieces the young man and the maid. I will also break in pieces with thee the shepherd and his flock; and with thee will I break in pieces the husbandman and his yoke of oxen; and with thee will I break in pieces captains and rulers".

These words declare plainly what was to be the mission of apostate Israel throughout the Gentile world in the present dispensation. That mission is not yet accomplished; but considering the hold the Jews have now secured upon the finances of the world; and considering also their dominance in the spheres of commerce and politics in all the leading nations, and their virtual control of public amusements and the public press; and considering also what has happened in Russia within the past decade; there surely is abundant reason for believing that the complete fulfilment of this passage, and of others like it (as Isaiah 41:15, 16) is close at hand.

It will be easily seen that the great event so briefly summarized under the second trumpet follows both historically and also *logically* the events of the first trumpet. For the outpouring of God's desolating judgments "upon the earth" (*i. e. the land* of Judea) was followed immediately by the casting of the nation while yet "burning with the fire" of God's anger, into the "sea" of peoples. This correspondence confirms the view here taken of the trumpet series; and what follows will be found to add further confirmation. Indeed the single fact that the trumpet series has to do throughout with the affairs of the nations of the world, as is quite plain (see 8:13; 10:11; 11:15, 18 etc.), will, if kept in view, prevent us from going far astray as to the explanation of these symbols. And it is certain to begin with, that no other event of human history has had such an effect upon the political affairs of the nations of the world, from the very beginning down to our own times, as the dispersion among them of the Jewish people, with their unique racial characteristics, their traditional purpose to gain the domination of the Gentiles (a purpose based upon the misinterpretation of the prophets) and the amazing tenacity with which they have held on to that purpose. Nothing therefore, can possibly be found to stand in the place to which this group of trumpets belongs, which historically is in the right era, and which in character corresponds to what these symbols call for, except the overthrow and dispersion of the Jewish nation.

Moreover, the fact noted above will serve also to guide us in our quest for the explanation of the three "woe" trumpets; for that also must be sought in happenings of a politico-religious character, happenings which, moreover, had a wide and lasting effect. Nothing else would be appropriate to stand in this trumpet series. To this general subject we shall return when we come to the detached group of the three "woe" trumpets.

The Third Trumpet

"And the third angel sounded, and there fell a great star from heaven, burning as it were a lamp, and it fell upon the third part of the rivers, and upon the fountains of waters; and the name of the star is called Wormwood; and the third part of the waters became wormwood; and many men died of the waters, because they were made bitter" (vv. 10, 11).

A "star" is a notable person, angel or man; and the "heaven" may be either the political heavens, or the spiritual heavens.

Here we have a *great* star, one "burning as a lamp"; and a third part of the rivers and fountains of waters are affected by its fall. Historicists have sought for some great personage in the political sphere who could be regarded as fulfilling this remarkable symbol. But history tells of none that is "great" enough. At the sounding of the fifth trumpet another star falls from heaven, not a "great" one, however, and historicists are agreed that this star symbolizes Mohammed. Certainly there was no political personage prior to Mohammed (or since) that had a greater power and influence for evil than he; or that more successfully opposed the Kingdom of God. So it appears that here again the historicist system fails to explain the symbols.

My opinion is that this "great star" represents the devil himself. His name, "Lucifer", means *light bearer,* so that the words, "How art thou fallen from heaven, O Lucifer, son of the morning?" (Isa. 14:12) agree in meaning with Revelation 8:10. So also do the Lord's words, "I beheld Satan *as lightning* fall from heaven" (Lu. 10:17). Then again we have the words of the Lord in John 12:31-33, which fix the time of the casting out of Satan from heaven: *"Now* is the judgment of this world: *now* shall the prince of this world be cast out. And I, if I be lifted up from the earth will draw all men unto Me. This He said signifying what death He should die". Here we have the most authoritative evidence that one of the immediate results of the cross *("now", "now")* would be the casting out of Satan. The judgment of this world was the sentence passed upon it at the cross. "The Cross is the condemnation of all who reject it" (Plummer). Christ was about to meet the principalities and powers of darkness at Calvary, and to "make a show of them openly, triumphing over them in His cross" (Col. 2:15). He was soon by His own death to "destroy him that had the power of death, that is the devil" (Heb. 2:14).

Moreover, in Revelation 12:1-9 it is shown that at the time of Christ's ascension there was war in heaven between Michael and his angels, and the dragon and his angels; and that the dragon and his angels prevailed not, *"neither was their place found any more in heaven. And the great dragon was cast out, that old serpent, called the Devil and Satan, which deceiveth the whole world: he was cast out into the earth"*. When we come to that chapter, further reasons will be given in support of the conclusion that this war in heaven and the consequent casting out of Satan, was at the time of, and indeed was provoked by Christ's ascension into heaven. This conclusion is fully warranted by the single fact that the war in heaven, mentioned in Chapter 12, follows immediately upon the catching up of the Man child into heaven.

Furthermore, by taking the "great star" as picturing a great spirit being, rather than a great historical personage, we are in accord with the explanation of the Book itself, which tells us that the stars represent angels (1:20).

The name of this great star is called "Wormwood", and his mission is to make a third part of the rivers deadly bitter. This symbology agrees with what the Scriptures tell us concerning the work of Satan. It would not fit at all the career of a mere political personage, however great. For running water (rivers and fountains) in this Book, and in other parts of the Bible as well, figure the life-imparting truth of the Word of God (Rev. 22:1, 17; Ps. 36:9; Jer. 2:13; Jn. 4:14). To poison those waters would be to introduce denials of the vital elements of the gospel, as the Deity of Christ, His atoning death, and His bodily resurrection. An incident in Exodus 15 will illustrate this. We read that when the Israelites came to Marah, "they could not drink of the waters of Marah, for they were *bitter*"; and that when Moses cried to the Lord, He "showed him *a tree,* which, when he had cast into the waters, the waters were made sweet" (Ex. 15:23-25). Taking that "tree" to represent the cross, we have here an illustration of the truth that when the cross is omitted from the preaching of Christ, it is "another gospel", one that spreads *death* instead of *life.*

Therefore, it may be gathered that the symbols of the verses now before us point to the activities of Satan, working in the early days of our era, mainly through unbelieving Jews, in poisoning the streams of truth and the wells of salvation by means of certain great heresies, as the Socinian and Arian, which denied the Deity of our Lord and the saving efficicay of His death.

We note, however, that the efforts of this "star" to poison the fountains of truth and wells of salvation were to have but a partial success. Only "a third part" were to be affected. And with this the facts of history agree.

Moses, in his last words to the people of Israel, warned them against the influence of the idolatries and the religious customs of the nations with whom they were to dwell, saying, "Lest there should be among you man, or woman, or family, or tribe, whose heart turneth away from the LORD our God, to go and serve the gods of these nations; lest there should be among you a root that beareth gall (a poisonous plant) and *wormwood*" (Dt. 29:18). The words "among you", twice repeated, show that the evil referred to is one to be expected not from without, but from within. So likewise in the New Testament, the exhortation is given to the Israel of God to be ever looking diligently "lest any *root of bitterness* springing up trouble you, and thereby many be defiled" (Heb. 12:15). The enemy of truth sows his poisonous seeds where the true *"word of the kingdom"* has been previously sown (Mat. 13:25); and this has been his method from the beginning. His success has been great indeed, but only partial. "A *third part* of the waters became wormwood, and *many* died of the waters, because they were made bitter". This, of course, is spiritual death; for a literal fulfilment of these words is not to be thought of. This fallen star is still here, and is still actively engaged in his deadly work of poisoning the well-springs of truth and eternal life. Thus we see that, in these trumpet visions, we have not to do with some musty and forgotten incidents of long past history, but with events that have a most important bearing upon our own times.

THE FOURTH TRUMPET

"And the fourth angel sounded, and the third part of the sun was smitten, and the third part of the moon, and the third part of the stars; so as the third part of them was darkened, and the day shone not for the third part of it, and the night likewise" (v. 12).

The work of the fourth day of Genesis I was the appointment of the sun, moon, and stars to their offices with respect to the earth; the sun to rule the day and the moon to rule the night, "and the stars also". Thus the fourth day is associated with *government;* and the sun, moon and stars have ever been the symbols of governmental powers and authorities. This appears as early in Bible history as the days of Joseph. For his brethren understood at once the significance of his dream concerning the sun and the moon and the eleven stars (Gen. 37:9, 10). Hence these symbols collectively represent *the whole governmental system of the earth, or that of some nation or part thereof which the particular Scripture has specially in view.*

In prophetic descriptions of coming visitations of God, whether upon a single people only, or in the final judgment upon all men, it is common to refer to the sun, moon and stars as being darkened or otherwise affected, it being evident in all such cases that the language is poetical and figurative, and that disturbances of government and the weakening or obliteration of governmental powers, are what is signified thereby. Thus, in Isaiah XIII, Ezekiel XXX and Joel II, to which reference was made in commenting upon the sixth seal (6:13), where the judgments of God upon various nations are foretold, there is in each case the prediction of the darkening of sun, moon, and stars, it being evident that what is thus foretold in figurative and poetical language is the failure, partial or complete, of the governmental system to fulfil its proper offices for the benefit and protection of the people who are under it, thus leading either to the destruction of the nation, or to revolution, or to anarchy.

The prophecy of Joel II, however, which is directed against Israel, and foretells the invasion of the land by the Assyrians ("the northern army") speaking of it as "a day of darkness and gloominess" (2:2), goes on to predict also the restoration of the people of Israel to their land (2:20-27), and then to foretell this present dispensation of the holy Spirit in the famous passage quoted by Peter on the day of Pentecost. In it the prophet tells of the coming of "the great and terrible day of the Lord", at the end of this dispensation; and in that connection occurs the following: "And I will show wonders in the heavens and in earth, blood, and fire, and pillars of smoke. *The sun* shall be turned into darkness, and *the moon* into blood, before the great and terrible day of the LORD come" (2:28-31). Clearly, if the language of the other passages is figurative, this must be figurative also, and must be understood as referring to the spiritual and political heavens and powers. For it must be remembered that "the powers that be are ordained of God", and are maintained by Him; for which cause His people are to show respect to them and to pray for them. God has set them in the political heavens, and has assigned their offices to them; just as He has set the sun, moon and stars in the physical heavens, and appointed them their several offices.

Therefore, consistency requires that we should take the words of the Lord Jesus Christ in His prophetic discourse on Mt. Olivet, where He foretells the darkening of sun and moon, and the falling of stars from heaven (Mat. 24:29) in a figurative sense. The words "and the powers of the heavens shall be shaken" lend support to this view, especially when we consider them in the light of Hebrews 12:25-29. In that passage the kingdom of God, which *"we"* have received, is spoken of as "a kingdom which *cannot be shaken*". Hence the words, "Yet once more *I shake,* not the earth only, but also heaven", must refer to all dominions and authorities that are in opposition to God.

There is a marked resemblance between the Lord's Olivet prophecy and what is pictured by the imagery of the first four trumpets. The Lord spoke of the great distress that was to be in the land, and the wrath that was to come upon the people of Judea (Lu. 21: 23); which agrees with the symbols of hail, fire, and blood cast upon the earth (or land) at the sounding of the first trumpet. Then He told of the leading forth of the survivors into captivity "into all nations", and of the concurrent treading down of Jerusalem by the Gentiles (v. 24); which agrees with the symbol of the casting of the great mountain burning with fire into the sea. And then He said: "And there shall be signs in *the sun,* and in *the moon,* and in *the stars"* (v. 25), using precisely the same symbols as in Revelation 8:12 (fourth trumpet); "and upon the earth distress of nations with perplexity, men's hearts failing them for fear and for looking after those things which are coming on the earth; for the *powers of heaven shall be shaken";* which words indicate a state of things similar to that pictured in Revelation 8:10, 11 (third trumpet).

The prophet Amos uses similar figurative language in speaking of the day of wrath that was soon to come upon the Kingdom of Israel (the ten tribes), saying, "and it shall come to pass in that day, saith the Lord, that I will cause *the sun to go down at noon,* and I will darken the earth (or land) in the clear day". Micah also, foretelling the same event, says: "Therefore *night* shall be unto you, that ye shall not have a vision; and it shall *be dark* unto you that ye shall not divine; and *the sun shall go down over the prophets,* and the day shall be *dark* over them" (Mic. 3:6).

Therefore, in the light of all these Scriptures, I feel bound to take the symbols of the fourth trumpet as picturing an era of disturbed governmental conditions, an era of the weakening of authority in both the spiritual and political spheres of human affairs; and especially an era of *the darkening of the minds of men through agencies and influences that obscure the truth* (2 Cor. 4:4).

A similar, but far worse, state of affairs is to come at the very end of the christian dispensation. At the era of the fourth trumpet the disturbances and the darkening of the skies were but partial, for only "the third part" of the sun, and of the moon, and of the stars was darkened; whereas at the coming of the great and final day of wrath the sun will become "black as sackcloth of hair", the moon will become *as blood,* and the stars will fall from heaven as unripe figs from a fig-tree when it is shaken by a mighty wind. Conversely, the prophet Isaiah, prophesying of the coming of the Lord for the deliverance of His people, speaks of the augmentation, instead of the diminishing, of the light of the heavenly luminaries, saying: "Moreover, the light of the moon shall be as the light of the sun, and the light of the sun shall be seven fold, as the light of seven days, in the day that the LORD bindeth up the breach of His people, and healeth the stroke of their wound" (Isa. 30:26).

In Isaiah 60:19, 20 and again in Revelation 21:23, the meaning of these symbols is carried out to the full. In the former, where the glory of the heavenly city is in view, "The city of the LORD, the Zion of the Holy One of Israel" (Isa. 60:14), the prophet says: *"The sun* shall be no more thy light by day; neither for brightness shall *the moon* give light unto thee; but the LORD shall be unto thee an everlasting light, and thy God thy glory. *Thy sun* shall no more go down; neither shall *thy moon* withdraw itself: for the LORD shall be thine everlasting light, and the days of thy mourning shall be ended". This speaks in poetical and figurative language of the time when Christ shall have put down all rule and all authority and power, and the Kingdom shall be the Lord's alone. The words of Revelation 21:23 are of like import: "And the city had no need of *the sun*, neither of *the moon* to shine in it: for the glory of God did lighten it, and the Lamb is the light thereof".

When therefore these trumpet symbols are read in the light of Scripture, which is certainly the proper rule of interpretation, they are found to correspond more closely with those momentous and far-reaching happenings that marked the early days of the christian era and have influenced its character throughout, than with any other historical events.

Furthermore, the happenings to which they have been applied in the foregoing pages are directly related to the history of the Kingdom of God on earth, which is the prominent subject of the prophetic Word. On the other hand, the events to which they are commonly referred by historicists (the successive invasions of the territory of Imperial Rome by Goths, Lombards, and Huns) have but a remote bearing upon that subject. Those irruptions did, of course, have some influence in the breaking down of the Roman Empire, and thus they contributed in a measure to the darkening of the political skies; but they were minor factors, the prominent agency being the overthrow and dispersion of the Jewish nation.

As for the futurist interpretations of the passage, they lie beyond the reach of investigation. Hence it is not possible to examine or discuss them intelligently or to any purpose or profit. It would seem, moreover, as if those who adopt the futurist system of interpretation lose sight of the fact that one great purpose of prophecy is that those to whom it is given may know, by the event, whether it be the word of the Lord or not (Deut. 18:22). So likewise the Lord said, "Now I tell you before it come, that, when it is come to pass, ye may believe that I am He" (John 13:19). If this be the purpose of the prophecy of the Apocalypse, it would be defeated completely by the futurist system, which postpones it *en masse* to another dispensation, subsequent to the resurrection and rapture of the saints.

Finally as to this part of the Book, I call attention again to the fact that the first four trumpets constitute a distinct group, whose members are closely connected together. This confirms the view given above, according to which these four visions had their fulfilment in those great and far reaching events which attended the break up of the Jewish nation.

THE THREE GREAT ADVERSARIES OF THE KINGDOM OF GOD

We have now arrived at a point in our exposition where it will be advantageous to take a broad survey of the history of the Kingdom of God during the nineteen centuries that have elapsed since the first proclamation thereof on the day of Pentecost, in order to mark the principal adversaries that have risen up to oppose it. For if the view adopted in this exposition as to the subject of the trumpet-series is the right one, then the visions seen in the course of that series will reveal, by appropriate symbols, the chief of those adversaries.

In making this survey let us have clearly in mind that the very essence of the gospel of God is that to Jesus Christ of the seed of David, raised from the dead, *all authority has been given;* that God has exalted Him to be a Prince and a Saviour; and that it is He Who will judge the living and the dead at His appearing and His kingdom. The gospel is preached for the obedience of faith among all nations on behalf of His Name (Rom. 1:5; 16:26). It calls upon all men everywhere to submit in loyal obedience to Him as sovereign Lord and King. This is the main purpose of the preaching of the gospel. True, the eternal salvation of those who render to Him the obedience of faith is assured; but that is secondary. For God's *highest* purpose is *the glory of His Son* (John 5:21-23; Phil. 2:9-11); and it is for His own glory chiefly that He is become "the Author of eternal salvation to all them that *obey* Him" (Heb. 5:8), that is to say, to those, and those only, who willingly own Him as "Lord", and render to Him the obedience of loyal and loving hearts. For it cannot be too strongly emphasized that the supreme purpose of God in this dispensation is to establish the rule of Jesus Christ in the *hearts* of men, His agencies for the accomplishment of that purpose being the Word of God (the gospel), and the Spirit of God.

Now the absolute sovereignty of Jesus Christ, and His Lordship over men, is being proclaimed by the gospel in the very territory over which the Devil has held sway since sin and death entered into the world. Hence the age-long conflict with the prince of this world, and with all the principalities and powers of darkness, and hosts of spiritual wickedness, that are confederated with him. What is in dispute is *the allegiance of the children of men*. We must not lose sight of that fact; for it is the key to the whole situation. The Evil One is striving desperately to keep his captives from availing themselves of the door of escape opened by the death and resurrection of Christ, and from joining themselves to Him. And to this object he bends all his energies, puts into action all the forces at his disposal, and employs all his subtleties and powers of deception.

Let us remember then that the true explanation of the whole course of human history lies in the region of the unseen; and that it is only by a divine revelation, such as has been given us in this Book, that the hidden causes of the great historical movements and epochs of the world of men can be known. And particularly let us bear in mind that all the disorders, conflicts, restlessness and miseries of the world, proceed from the resistance that the Devil has offered, and still offers, to the establishment of the sovereignty of Jesus Christ over the hearts of men. For once that authority is acknowledged, peace comes to the heart.

Now, in the light of these facts of Scripture, it is of the deepest significance that there have appeared during all the centuries of the Christian era just THREE great systems, having a *religious character* and a *political aim,* which have set themselves in direct opposition to the declared purpose of God, that purpose being to bring everything under the rule, dominion, and sovereignty of Christ. Those three systems are satanically energized, and with the one object of frustrating the purpose of God. For this world was the strong man's palace; and he was keeping his goods (human souls) in peace, until the Stronger than he appeared upon the scene, and stripped him of his armour wherein he trusted (Lu. 11:21, 22). Christ's coming into the world was for the one purpose, which He caused to be proclaimed in the most public way, of setting up a Kingdom—the Kingdom of God. This was a direct challenge to "the prince of this world", who has never ceased, from that time until now, to resist the attempt to "spoil him of his goods".

The first system that offered organized and satanically inspired opposition to the Kingdom of God was the Jewish nation, the leaders of which were declared by Christ Himself to be the children of the Devil (John 8:44). That nation has miraculously maintained its national existence and its traditional religion ("the traditions of the elders") through all the centuries, of our era; and it is, of course, as bitterly opposed as ever to the faith of Jesus Christ. For Judaism has not improved or changed its nature during the nineteen centuries of its existence in "this present evil world". Its aim still is supremacy over the Gentiles, and its religious attitude is as uncompromisingly anti-christian as it ever was. Satan, who inspired and directed its activities at the beginning, is still its spiritual leader and energizer. Apostate Judaism has neither quit the field of conflict, nor has it changed sides. Let us make no mistake about that. Its character and career as an opponent of Christianity is pictured in the first group of four trumpets.

The second of the three great systems, religious in character, but having for its political aim the domination of the world, is Mohammedanism. As we are about to view, under the vision of the fifth trumpet, this stupendous marvel of history, the empire established by the false prophet, I will not describe it here. For our immediate purpose it is necessary only to call attention to the remarkable fact that in Islam we have a movement energized by prodigious spiritual powers of evil, a satanic caricature of the Kingdom of God, being led by a *false* prophet and based upon a *false* Bible (the Koran) and seeking (almost with success) to gain the sovereignty of the world.

The third and last of these adversaries of Christianity is Romanism. Here again we have identically the same distinguishing features that characterized the other two, and marked them plainly as the adversaries of the Kingdom of God: that is to say, this system also is *religious* in character, binding its adherents together by that which has ever been the strongest of all ties—

religion,—but its aim is *political,* the same precisely as that of the other two, namely to gain supreme authority over the nations of the earth. Judaism bases its claim to supremacy over the nations upon its misinterpretation of the prophets. Mohammedanism also claims a God-given right to rule the world, basing its claim upon the Koran and the pretensions of the false prophet. Romanism is, in this respect, the most subtle and deceptive of all, for its claim to supreme governmental authority is based upon the blasphemous pretension that its head, the pope, is the "vicar of Christ".

Such being the general state of things during this Christian era, it is certain that, if the design of the trumpet series of visions was to reveal to the servants of Christ the great adversaries that were to arise in direct opposition to the purpose of God in this age, then we shall find therein the symbolic representations of just three, no more and no less, great and mighty systems religious in character, and having each the single political aim of subjugating the world. And on the other hand, if upon careful study of the symbols of the trumpet series we find them such as may be clearly explained by reference to the three systems that have contested the field of the world (Matt. 13:38) with the soldiers of the cross, then we are fully warranted in concluding that it was the design of those visions to reveal the rise, the development and end of those great adversaries of the Kingdom of God.

One difference between the last of these systems (Romanism) and the other two calls for special notice.

Both Judaism and Mohammedanism have been from the very first the *open* enemies of Christianity. Therefore they are shown in the trumpet visions as openly opposed to God and His saints. But Romanism arose not from without but from within the pale of professed Christianity. It has set itself forth not as the adversary of the Kingdom of God, but on the contrary as being the true realization and embodiment thereof. Hence it is not displayed openly in its real character as the enemy of God and the opposer of His purposes, but is unveiled as a "mystery" in the days of the seventh trumpet, where it is shown by a special vision as developing out of, and in close political association with the Roman Empire, the political frame-work of which was perpetuated and subordinated to its purposes. But this can best be considered when we come to Chapter XIII. For the gradual transformation of Imperial Rome into Papal Rome has been a marvel of history greater and more mysterious even than the rise and career of Mohammedanism.

It is a matter of deep significance that each of these three great systems has manifested unwonted activity in and subsequent to the great war of 1914-1918. For while the political doings of the Jews in connection with the finances of the great nations are studiously concealed, so far as possible, nevertheless the "invisible hand" does sometimes show itself on the surface of affairs; and moreover, the vitality of Zionism, and the progress made in a very brief time towards converting Palestine into a national home for the Jews, are among the most significant of the happenings of these days. Students of prophecy are watching these developments with intense interest, some with expectations (such as that the Temple will be rebuilt, animal sacrifices resumed, etc.) which to my mind are without support in the Scriptures. But there is in the Word of God the clear promise that "all Israel shall be saved" (Rom. 11:26); and that those words refer to the natural, not to the spiritual Israel, appears from the context, where reference is made to the power of God to "graff them in again into their own olive tree" (vv. 23, 24).

Mohammedanism too has had a wonderful recrudescence, notwithstanding the seeming death-wound to the Ottoman Empire in the great war. The marvellous recovery under the régime of the Young Turks, the stirrings in India, Egypt and elsewhere, and the dread possibilities of concerted action by the dark-skinned races against the nations of western Europe ("the Christian nations", so called) are not the least among the anxieties of the heads of governments in these perplexing times. (See the last chapter of this book.)

Finally, as to the activities and gains of the Papacy, in the field of world-politics, as well as in that of religion (where it is taking full advantage of the disintegration of the Protestant denominations under the canker of *Modernism*) it is needless to speak. And indeed it would require a volume to tell the full story. Enough that the anointed eye can see that these three mighty systems of evil, the agencies of the mighty prince of this world, are all ready for instant action when the blast of the seventh trumpet shall announce the hour for the last fatal conflict; in which, nevertheless, all that opposes the kingdom of our God and the power of His Christ shall be finally and completely overthrown.

I venture to suggest, in this connection, that it may turn out to be a very significant fact that, in the little country of Judea, these three great systems are even now in touch with one another, and with results that hint at the most serious consequences. For the Mohammedan Arabs are violently opposed to the re-occupation of Palestine by the Jews; and the Papacy has uttered its protest against the "desecration of the holy places" by Jewish occupancy. So here is a situation that is pregnant with great possibilities. For out of it may easily spring events that will set those mighty forces into operation, whereby the mystery of God shall be finished, His enemies be overwhelmed, and the kingdoms of this world shall become the kingdoms of our Lord and of His Christ.

THE FIFTH TRUMPET

There is a pause after the sounding of the fourth trumpet and the action is interrupted at that point by the vision of an angel (or, as the best manuscripts have it, an *eagle*) flying through the midst of heaven, saying with a loud voice, "Woe, woe, woe, to the inhabiters of earth, by reason of the other voices of the trumpet of the three angels, which are yet to sound!" (Rev. 8:13).

This vision of the flying eagle serves not only to prepare us for events of a yet more calamitous nature than those previously revealed, but also to set off the first four trumpets in a distinct group from the rest; and this tends further to confirm the view that the events pictured in that group are both closely related to each other, and are also separated by a substantial interval of time, possibly quite a long one, from the events now to be pictured at "the voices of the trumpet of the three angels that are yet to sound".

"And the fifth angel sounded, and I saw a star fall from heaven unto the earth: and to him was given the key of the bottomless pit. And he opened the bottomless pit; and there arose a smoke out of the pit, as the smoke of a great furnace; and the sun and the air were darkened by reason of the smoke of the pit. And there came out of the smoke locusts upon the earth: and to them was given power, as the scorpions of the earth have power. And it was commanded them that they should not hurt the grass of the earth, neither any green thing, neither any tree; but only those men which have not the seal of God in their foreheads. And to them it was given that they should not kill them, but that they should be tormented five months: and their torment was as the torment of a scorpion, when he striketh a man. And in those days shall men seek death and shall not find it; and shall desire to die, and death shall flee from them. And the shapes of the locusts were like unto horses prepared unto battle; and on their heads were as it were crowns of gold, and their faces were as the faces of men. And they had hair as the hair of women, and their teeth were as the teeth of lions. And they had breastplates as it were breastplates of iron; and the sound of their wings was as the sound of chariots of many horses running to battle. And they

had tails like unto scorpions, and there were stings in their tails: and their power was to hurt men five months. And they had a king over them, which is the angel of the bottomless pit, whose name in the Hebrew tongue is Abaddon, but in the Greek tongue hath his name, Apollyon" (9:1-11).

The era of the fifth trumpet is manifestly one of relatively great importance for the purposes of the Book we are studying. This appears from the space given to it, and from the character of the symbols. It seems also that the era here foretold ("those days" v. 6) is one of considerable length; for it is described as a period of torment to last, as time is measured in this Book, for a period of "five months" (vv. 5, 10), *five* being a number of incompleteness, showing, as did the phrase "a third part" under the preceding trumpets, that the plague, though great and prolonged, was not complete and final. It required *twice five* plagues to complete God's judgment upon Egypt.

The first action that immediately follows the sounding of the trumpet is the fall of a star from heaven to earth. That this star represents a mighty spirit-being is clear from what has been already explained; and this is confirmed by the next words: "And *to him*"—evidently a *person*—"was given the key of the bottomless pit. And *he* opened the bottomless pit". None but a mighty spirit could do that.

This spirit-being is, however, of lesser dignity than the one that fell from heaven at the sounding of the third trumpet; for that one is described as "a *great* star, burning as a lamp".

Out of the pit arose dense smoke, as the smoke of a great furnace. This recalls one of the signs that are to precede the great and terrible day of the Lord, namely, "pillars (or columns) of smoke" (Joel 2:30). Clearly this smoke is spiritual. It affects "the sun" (the power of government) and "the air" (the spiritual realm). And there came out of the smoke locusts; and to them was given power, as the scorpions of the earth have power. All these and other symbols and figures supply us with clues to the meaning of the vision. One other feature will be noted at this preliminary stage of our inquiry. It is found in the last statement in the passage, namely, that these "locusts" have *a king* over them, which is the angel of the bottomless pit, whose name in Hebrew and in Greek signifies "Destroyer". Thus it is plainly stated that this great host of locusts is ruled by an invisible king, a mighty one among the evil spirits.

In Joel the armies of Assyria which were to overrun the land of Israel were figured as locusts; and there too, as in the passage before us, it was said, "The appearance of them is as the appearance of *horsemen*" (Joel 2:4). So it is plain that the locusts are conquering armies, sweeping over the earth in dense ranks. Furthermore, from Daniel 10:13, 20, it appears that the great empires of earth have each a *presiding angel* over them; so that we have warrant for the view that the vision we are studying pictures the coming upon the scene of a mighty nation, which was to have a supernatural origin, rising up mysteriously out of some obscure region, and which was to pursue a career of conquest, pouring over the earth in dense armies, composed largely of horsemen; a nation that was to have over them a spiritual head whose name signifies "a destroyer".

But this conquering people was to be unlike the Assyrians, the "locusts" of Joel's vision, in that it was to have *spiritual* power, as well as, and more prominently than, *physical* power. The repeated reference to "scorpions" (vv. 3, 5, 10) emphasizes this. Moreover, the statement of verse 10 is illuminating: "And they had tails like unto scorpions, and there were stings in their tails". This may be read in the light of Isaiah 9:15 as indicating the deadly power of *false prophecy,* or some special form of destructive falsehood. For according to that Scripture *"the prophet that teacheth lies, he is the tail"*.

Briefly then, the various symbols here presented to our view all point, and in no uncertain way, to that marvel of history, the empire founded by the false prophet, Mohammed, an empire of vast dimensions that was established and extended through an unprecedented combination of stupendous military forces and mighty spiritual energies; in which latter was the secret of its amazing potency.

For Islam is a mystery of the darkest character. It defies explanation on any natural basis. Its origin is so utterly unlike that of all the other empires as to leave no alternative but the view that it originated supernaturally; and its career is just as difficult to explain upon natural grounds as its origin. It is manifestly a designed counterpart of Christianity; for its visible source was in a *personal leader,* who claims to be the sole representative and prophet of God, and in *a book,* that is venerated by its adherents as the word of God. It has, moreover, the supernatural power to inspire multitudes, even of stern, fierce and bloodthirsty men, with a most extraordinary degree of religious fanaticism, rising at times to the pitch of frenzy. In this particular it is without any parallel in the history of mankind.

The foregoing facts are matters of common knowledge. Keeping them in mind while studying the visions of Chapter 9, two conclusions force themselves upon me: *first,* that the symbols of that chapter correspond with remarkable exactness to the outstanding features of Islamism; and *second,* that there is nothing else in the whole range of human observation that in anywise answers to those symbols. Indeed the history of Islam is so unique, so manifestly supernatural, and corresponds, moreover, so exactly with the symbols of these visions (fifth and six trumpets) that able expositors of the futurist school fully admit the close agreement between them; and some of them go so far as to suggest that, in Mohammedanism, these visions have a "germinant", or anticipatory, fulfilment. Thus it is stated by one of the ablest of that school that:

"Mohammedanism has a superman and a book. It is a satanic imitation of Christianity. It has spread over a great part of the christianized world. At this time it embraces in its

The Trumpet Series 315

curse over 200 millions of souls. Its founder was, without doubt, devil inspired. Mohammed, the fallen star*, opened the pit and let loose the darkening power of Satan; and he flooded the eastern part of the christianized earth, and considerable portions of the western also, with doctrines which can justly be termed hellish in their nature and effects".

In other words, the facts of Islamism agree exactly with the meaning of the symbols shown in these visions. What conclusion then must we draw? The fulfilment of a prophecy is proved, and the divine character of the latter is established, by *the coming to pass of the thing prophesied.* What then is the position of those who, like the writer just quoted, recognize and admit that the things here prophesied have manifestly come to pass, yet refuse to accept them as the fulfilment of the prophecy?

One extraordinary fact in the history of Islam calls for special notice because, to my mind, it lends strong support to the view herein adopted. That fact is that its career has been in *two distinct stages.* Its rise was in the Saracenic form, and is dated from the "Hegira" (the flight of Mahomet) in A. D. 622. The Caliph Omar led his conquering armies of Saracens into Syria in 632; the Roman armies were annihilated; and in 637 Jerusalem was captured. But the spread of Mohammedanism was arrested by Charles Martel at the Battle of Tours, A. D. 732, after which ensued a long period of stagnation. But it had a marvellous recrudescence, under the ferocious Ottoman Turks.

---
* I think it more accurate to say he was energized by the evil spirit, Abaddon, whom the fallen star symbolizes.

These, strangely enough, were not Mohammedans at all, but began their conquering career *against* the Mohammedans. Later, however, for political advantage, they formally embraced Mohammedanism, much as the emperor Constantine had formally embraced Christianity, and in A. D. 1076, Jerusalem was captured by the Turks, and an era of cruel oppression was begun, "which filled all Christendom with sorrow and indignation" (Green's Church History). This led to the Crusades.

In marked agreement with this division of the career of Islam is the two-fold picture presented by the fifth and sixth trumpet visions, which are connected closely together, while being separated from the preceding group of four trumpets, and also from the seventh which stands by itself.

Turning now to the details of the vision of the fifth trumpet, enough has been said concerning the star, the darkening of the sun and air by the dense smoke from the pit, and the locusts with their scorpion-like tails. But further concerning the abyss, or bottomless pit, it may be remarked that the abyss appears in the N. T. as the abode of the demons, the source of the evil spiritual agencies that exercise their influence upon men. This is made evident, for example, by the desire of the wicked spirits whom the Lord cast out of the man dwelling in the tombs, that He should not command them to depart into the abyss (Luke 8:31).

From verse 4 of Revelation 9 we learn that protection was to be given, during the time of this plague, to the true people of God; for it was to fall only upon "those men who have not the seal of God upon their foreheads". Here again is seen the efficacy of the prayers of the saints, sent up to the throne of God by Christ as the Minister of the heavenly sanctuary.

Verse 7 states that the shapes of the locusts were like "horses prepared unto battle". In Judges 6:5 we read that the children of the east came up like *locusts* (not *"grasshoppers"*) for multitude; and in Jeremiah 46: 23, God speaks of the armies that were to overwhelm Egypt, saying that "they are more than the locusts, and are innumerable". Thus we learn that the term *locusts* signifies armies of immense numbers. The words "horses prepared unto battle" point to the readiness, fearlessness, and swiftness of those armies in making war. That they wore crowns marks them as a *sovereign people,* distinguishing them from the mercenary armies of Rome. Further it is said they had faces like those *of men,* and hair as the hair *of women.* Thus they represent a virile people, notwithstanding the long hair, which in Bible times was the mark of a barbaric people (see 1 Cor. 11:14, 15). The breastplate (or coats of mail) speak of their preparedness for battle, and the reference to "horses" again in verse 9, testifies anew of their eagerness to engage therein.

In regard to the long hair, Hengstenberg's comment is also illuminating: "One who permits anything on his body to grow as it will, virtually makes himself known as one who gives free scope to his lusts and passions, who will allow no hindrance to his natural desires".

This seems to point clearly to one of the most conspicuous features of the Mohammedan religion, that which allowed in this life unrestrained indulgence of the animal passions of men (to the great degradation of womankind), and which promised in paradise the most unlimited delights of sensuousness. It was in order to subdue *men,* that appeal was made to what is basest in the nature of *man.* This is grossly demoniacal.

Verse 12 reads: "One woe is past; and behold there come two woes more hereafter". This puts a definite end to the spread of this plague, corresponding with which is the fact that Mohammedanism in its Saracenic form was definitely arrested at the Battle of Tours, and turned back; and this abatement lasted for a period of centuries.

This verse also recalls the thrice-repeated "Woe" of 8:13, reminding us of the specially calamitous nature of the scourges that are symbolized under the last three trumpets.

Grattan Guinness remarks that "Mohammedanism is one of those great movements which have impressed a *new* and *lasting* character upon a vast number of the nations of the world. No power known to history has ever wielded the sceptre over a wider sphere than this has done". And the historian Gibbon *(Decline and Fall of the Roman Empire)* remarks concerning the successors of Mahomet:—

"They reigned by right of conquest over the nations of the East, to whom the name of liberty was unknown, and who were accustomed to applaud in their tyrants the acts of violence and severity that were performed at their own expense. Under the last of the Ommiades the Arabian empire extended two hundred days' journey from east to west, from the confines of Tartary and India, to the shores of the Atlantic Ocean".

It is not, however, because of the amazing spread of Islam in so short a time, or because of the absolute and tyrannical character of its rule, that place is given it in these visions of God. Rather is it because by it the judgment of God was executed upon those parts of the earth which had been illuminated by the gospel from its beginning, but which had turned that heavenly light into a darkness worse than that of Paganism, and of which it might well be exclaimed in the words of Christ, "How great is *that* darkness!" (Mat. 6:23). For, in the words of Dr. Green, "It is needful to remember the character of that 'Christianity' which called Mahomet and his followers to arms"; thereof he quotes the following description by Isaac Taylor:—

"What Mahomet and his caliphs found in all directions whither their scimitars cut a path for them, was a superstition so abject, an idolatry so gross and shameless, church doctrines so arrogant, church practices so dissolute and so puerile, that the strong-minded Arabians felt themselves inspired as God's messengers to reprove the errors of the world, and authorized as God's avengers to punish apostate Christendom".

For it must be remembered that God's judgment upon those who have not received the love of the truth, when it has been presented to them in the gospel of His grace, is first of all to give them over to a "strong delusion, that they should believe *the lie*" (2 Thess.

2:10, 11; see also Rom. 1:25-28). And this, I believe, is what is just now coming to pass in our own day in these who, having "received not the love of the truth that they might be saved", although they have all their lives been within the reach and influence thereof, are now being given over to the "strong delusion" of the evolutionary theory, whereof the foul and degrading doctrine of the ape-ancestry of man is the central feature.

The Sixth Trumpet

"And the sixth angel sounded, and I heard a voice from the four horns of the golden altar which is before God, saying to the sixth angel which had the trumpet, Loose the four angels which are bound in the great river Euphrates. And the four angels were loosed, which were prepared for an hour, and a day, and a month, and a year, for to slay the third part of men. And the number of the army of the horsemen were two hundred thousand thousand: and I heard the number of them. And thus I saw the horses in the vision, and them that sat on them, having breastplates of fire, and of jacinth, and brimstone: and the heads of the horses were as the heads of lions: and out of their mouths issued fire and smoke and brimstone. By these three was the third part of men killed, by the fire, and by smoke, and by the brimstone, which issued out of their mouths. For their power is in their mouth, and in their tails: for their tails were like unto serpents, and had heads, and with them they do hurt. And the rest of the men which were not killed by these plagues, yet repented not of the works of their hands, that they should not worship devils, and idols of gold, and silver, and brass, and stone, and of wood; which neither can see, nor hear, nor walk: neither repented they of their murders, nor of their sorceries, nor of their fornication, nor of their thefts" (9:13-21).

The origin of this "woe" was in the region beyond

the great river Euphrates". It was from that quarter of the world that the Turks made their appearance, and even until now there is a mystery as to the precise part of the East from which they came.

I have already referred, as corresponding to this vision, to the astonishing revival of Islamism after centuries of stagnation, resulting in the Ottoman Empire, which has continued to our own time to be the inveterate foe of the gospel, and a curse to all the nations that have been blessed, in the character of their civilization, from the gospel's beneficent influences.

Briefly, the important facts concerning the Ottoman Empire are these:

"The Ottoman Turks came originally from the region of the Altai mountains in Central Asia. . . . In the 13th century they appeared as the allies of the Seljukian Turks against the Mongols, and for their aid received a grant of lands from the sultan of Iconium, in Asia Minor. Their leader, Othman, became the most powerful Emir in Western Asia. In the year 1300 he proclaimed himself Sultan. Thus was founded the Empire of the Osman or Ottoman Turks in Asia. Osman's successors, princes of great courage and enterprise, who were animated moreover by religious fanaticism, and a passion for military glory, raised it to the rank of the first military power in both Europe and Asia (1300-1566). In the reign of Soliman II, the Magnificent, 1519-1566, the Ottoman Empire reached the highest pitch of power and splendor. From his time the race of Osman degenerated, and the power of the Porte has declined" *(The Standard Dictionary of Facts).*

To this I would add that Constantinople was taken by the Turks in 1453, which date is marked in history as the last end of the old Roman Empire.

The Patmos Visions

Returning now to our chapter, from verse 15 it appears that the destroying angels had been already in preparation for a certain period of time, but were held in restraint. This is according to the revealed ways of God. His judgment upon the Amorites was delayed for four generations, because their iniquity was "not yet full" (Gen. 15:16). And so to the end; for even now He is holding back the day of Judgment (though men scoff at His warnings) because "the long suffering of our God is salvation", and because He is "not willing that any should perish, but that all should come to repentance" (2 Pet. 3:3, 4, 9, 15). Concerning the specified period of preparation, "an hour, and a day and a month, and a year", Bossuet remarks that, "The time being so exactly marked by the prophet, lets us see how exactly God determines the periods".

The number of the armies was myriads of myriads, a number so great that it could not have been computed. John says, "And I *heard* the number of them," else he could not have known it.

The description of verses 17-19 puts before us the conquering power of *lions,* the swiftness and fearlessness of *horses,* the destructive agencies of *fire, smoke,* and *brimstone* (whereby "the third part of men" were killed), and the poison of *serpents* in their *tails.* This is so largely a repetition of the symbols of the fifth trumpet as to assure us that the same people are again brought to view, but with differences which indicate that the identity is not complete. This judgment was not to be final, for it was to affect fatally only "a third part". Bengel aptly remarks upon this removal of a third part by death:

> "In the present day also there is a great corruption among unbelievers and nominal christians, in all parts of Christendom, and in all conditions of men; but if we could see what in former times has been taken away, we should find that God has continually saved out of the corrupt mass a good portion to remain for seed. Those portions that have been extirpated have been for the most part a bad commodity. . . . It is therefore necessary for the holy angels to blow with their trumpets, that men may learn to fear the Lord, and not be forever contending against Him".

Verses, 20, 21 show that this woe had a remedial object, that it was a call to repentance to "the rest of the men that were not killed by these plagues". But they profited not by the warning; for it is twice stated that they "repented not". And to this agrees the voice of history, which shows that the nations which suffered under the Saracenic and Ottoman scourges did not repent of their evil works, their idolatries and their worse than Pagan practices. We may well compare with this the hardness of heart manifested by Pharaoh and the Egyptians of old; and recall the words of the prophet: "For the people turneth not unto Him that smiteth them, neither do they seek the Lord of hosts" (Isa. 9:13).

CHAPTER VII

The Mighty Angel With the Little Book

"And I saw another mighty angel come down from heaven, clothed with a cloud: and a rainbow was upon his head. And his face was as it were the sun, and his feet as pillars of fire: and he had in his hand a little book open: and he set his right foot upon the sea, and his left foot on the earth, and cried with a loud voice, as when a lion roareth: and when he had cried, seven thunders uttered their voices. And when the seven thunders had uttered their voices, I was about to write: and I heard a voice from heaven saying unto me, Seal up those things which the seven thunders uttered, and write them not. And the angel which I saw stand upon the sea and upon the earth lifted up his hand to heaven, and sware by Him that liveth for ever and ever, who created heaven, and the things that therein are, and the earth, and the things that therein are, and the sea, and the things which are therein, that there should be time no longer: but in the days of the voice of the seventh angel, when he shall begin to sound, the mystery of God should be finished, as he hath declared to His servants the prophets" (10:1-17).

THIS vision belongs to the period of the sixth trumpet, as appears by two facts: (1) the ending of the period of the sixth trumpet is plainly marked by the words of Chapter 11:14, "The second woe is past; behold, the third woe cometh quickly"; (2) the Angel of this vision speaks of "the days of the voice of the *seventh* angel when he shall begin to sound", as being future at that time, which makes it certain that this vision was in the era of the *sixth* trumpet. It is important to note this.

This mighty Angel is a symbolical representation of Christ Himself. For everything that is said to characterize this Angel pertains only to Deity. Furthermore, the actions of the Angel belong only to Christ. "The planting of the right foot on the sea, and the other on the earth, as certainly belongs to Christ alone, as it is to Him and not to any angel that God has put in subjection the world to come (Heb. 2:5)". So comments Dr. Hengstenberg; and Vitringa asks: "Does the hope of God's people rest on the oath of a created angel? Is it the part of a created angel to swear that the words of prophecy and promise shall be fulfilled? Surely if their hope is to stand unmoved, it can be sustained only by the faithfulness and oath of that very Person to whose nature failure is not an incident. Wherefore, God swears by Himself, when His purpose is to show to the heirs of the promise, the immutability of His counsel" (Heb. 6:7)

The appearance of this Angel, the stand that He takes, and particularly the words of the oath that He swears, testify impressively to the transcendent importance of what is to happen in the days of the voice of the seventh angel.

In His hand was a *"little* book *open"*. These words suggest a comparison with the (relatively great) book of Chapter 5:1, which was completely *sealed;* and they lead to the conclusion that the "little book" contains some special part of the counsel of God, which Christ, the One who is invested with supreme authority, is responsible to carry into effect. In agreement with this idea are two facts that are declared in the immediate context; (1) John, having eaten the little book, is told that he must prophesy *again:* and (2) there now comes into view another sphere, different from that of the preceding visions, namely, the sphere that is symbolized by "the temple of God". The other scenes had to do with the world and the nations at large; and in viewing them, the question would arise in our minds, how does it fare in those times with the people of God? This question finds an answer in Chapter 11:1-13; and it will be clearly seen, upon comparison of the concluding verses of Chapter 9 ("and the rest of the men repented not") with verses 13 of Chapter 11, ("and the rest were affrighted and gave glory to the God of heaven"), that the two scenes are parallel as to time, differing, however, as to the theaters in which they severally take place.

This arrangement, moreover, is the same as that of the seals. For there also, after the vision of the sixth seal, the action along the line of happenings in the world at large is arrested, in order that it may be seen, by a separate vision (Chapter VII), how it fares with the Israel of God in the era of the preceding visions. Correspondences of this sort, of which there are many, bear witness to the methodical plan upon which the Book as a whole is constructed.

The first item of description of this mighty Angel is that He is "clothed with a cloud", and this indicates the character of the mission on which He is come. For as Bengel remarks: "In such appearances we must keep the *attire,* and the *word spoken,* in connection with each other. Thus the attire of Christ in Chapter I, and what He at that time caused John to write to the churches, throw light mutually upon each other". The cloud, then, conveys a threat against some whom this vision concerns; and the seven thunders mentioned in verse 3 tend to give it the character of a thunder-cloud. But the very next descriptive item is such as to remove all fear from the hearts of those who are truly His. For we read, "and a *rainbow* upon His head", which is the faithful witness of covenant mercy and protection to His own in the business He is about to undertake. That business, as clearly appears from Chapter XI, is that of the *separation* of those who are really His own from the mass of professed disciples.

The planting of the feet, which are likened to pillars of fire, one on the sea (the masses of peoples and nations in general), and one on the earth (the more stable parts of the world), signifies the world-wide scope of His present business, and also the immovable steadfastness of His purpose to accomplish it. So this is a matter of great and peculiar interest to all who share the writer's opinion that we are just on the eve of the sounding of the seventh trumpet.

It is further said of the Angel that He "cried with a loud voice, as when a lion roareth"; and that "when He had cried, seven thunders uttered their voices". This recalls Hosea 11:10, where it is prophesied that the Lord shall "roar like a lion" on behalf of His own people against their enemies. Also Joel 3:16, where, in foretelling the great day of wrath, the prophet says: "The Lord also shall roar out of Zion, and utter His voice from Jerusalem; and the heavens and the earth shall shake; but *the Lord shall be the hope* (lit. *a place of refuge*) for His people". The loud voice, as a lion's, declares the importance of that which is about to happen, and the certainty that it will take place without further delay.

The note of threatening in the loud voice is taken up and emphasized by the seven thunders that immediately uttered their voices. The number *seven* is the signature of the completeness of the threats uttered by the thunders. John, however, was commanded by a voice from heaven to "seal up those things which the thunders uttered, and write them not". This tells us that, however interesting the matters uttered by those voices, they must not be permitted to divert our attention from what *the Angel Himself is about to do and say.* That is the supremely important matter. For, with a sublime gesture, extending His hand heavenward, He swore "by Him that liveth for ever and ever, who created heaven and the things that therein are, and the earth and the things that therein are, and the sea and the things which are therein, that there should be time *(i. e., delay)* no longer; but in the days of the voice of the seventh angel, when he shall begin to sound, the mystery of God should be finished, as He hath declared (lit. *preached the glad tidings*) to His servants the prophets". No words of man could add to the impressiveness of this utterance, whereby, from the lips of the Lord Himself, backed by the force of a tremendous oath, *the greatest of all events yet to happen in the universe of God is announced.*

"The mystery of God" in this case is the mystery of His long delay to exercise His sovereign rights and authority against the principalities and powers of darkness, and against the rebel governments of this world, who have spurned the advice given in the Second Psalm to the kings and rulers of the earth to "Kiss the Son lest He be angry, and ye perish from the way, when suddenly His wrath is kindled" (Jewish Ver.). The day of wrath is in view for them, but the rainbow clearly appears in the next words of the Psalm, "Blessed are all they that put their trust in Him". The nature of this "mystery of God" comes clearly into view in the vision of the beast that came up out of the sea, which received a death-stroke and yet lived and triumphed thereafter over the saints of God.

The words uttered by the great voices in heaven at the blowing of the seventh trumpet (11:15), and those of the elders (11:17), also help to make it clear that it is the mystery of the Kingdom of God mentioned above that is referred to in the oath of the mighty Angel.

This closes the incident of the Angel's announcement. And now John hears again the voice from heaven that had bidden him seal up the things uttered by the seven thunders, the command being, "Go and take the little book which is open in the hand of the Angel which standeth upon the sea and upon the earth". The record continues:

"And I went unto the Angel and said unto him, Give me the little book. And He said unto me, Take it, and eat it up; and it shall make thy belly bitter, but it shall be in thy mouth sweet as honey. And I took the little book out of the Angel's hand and ate it up; and it was in my mouth sweet as honey; and as soon as I had eaten it, my belly was bitter. And He said unto me, Thou must prophesy again before (or *as to,* lit. *upon)* peoples, and nations, and tongues, and kings many" (Bagster's Interlinear Ver.).

The general significance of this incident may be learned from the like event described in Ezekiel. The prophet was commanded to carry a message to the rebellious house of Israel; and in that connection he heard the words, "Open thy mouth and eat that I give thee" (Ezek. 2:8). Thereupon he looked and saw a hand extended toward him, and in it the roll of a book, wherein were written "lamentations, and mourning, and woe". Then he heard the command, "Eat this roll and go speak to the house of Israel". And the prophet says, "Then I did eat it; and it was in my mouth as honey for sweetness". Ezekiel was to speak against Jerusalem and the temple; and the fact that in John's vision the city and temple appear (as symbols, of course) connects the two visions closely together.

John, in order to qualify him for the commission now given him, must take the words of God into his inmost being (cf. Jer. 15:16). Upon so doing he found them, because of their nature, to be bitter and distressing. Nevertheless, to the true servant of God every word of His is sweet to the taste. Upon this Hengstenberg says:

"What is here said to the prophet is in substance applicable to all believers, and especially to those who teach the Word. Their place in the Kingdom of God will be measured by their fidelity in complying with this admonition. We too must eat and even swallow it; not some choice portion of it, *but the whole;* not that alone which is agreeable to ourselves, like those who separate the gospel from the law, but that also which may occasion us the deepest pain".

The reason for John's inward pain upon apprehending the purport of what was in the little book, may be learned from what immediately follows in Chapter 11: 1-12, where the symbols declare how John carried out the command given him to prophesy upon (or concerning) peoples, and nations and tongues and many kings. For the vision involves all who, in the last days, are connected with what is figured by the temple of God, whether really, or merely nominally. For I take it the leading thought in the first part of Chapter XI is *the final separation in Christendom of the real from the unreal.* This will appear in what follows; and that it is a matter of the highest consequence to ourselves, is manifest.

The Measuring of the Temple

"And there was given me a reed like unto a rod: and the angel stood, saying, Rise, and measure the temple of God, and the altar, and them that worship therein. But the court which is without the temple leave out, and measure it not; for it is given unto the Gentiles; and the holy city shall they tread under foot forty and two months. And I will give power unto My two witnesses, and they shall prophesy a thousand two hundred and threescore days, clothed in sackcloth. These are the two olive trees, and the two candlesticks standing before the God of the earth. And if any man will hurt them, fire proceedeth out of their mouth, and devoureth their enemies: and if any man will hurt them, he must in this manner be killed. These have power to shut heaven, that it rain not in the days of their prophecy: and have power over waters to turn them to blood, and to smite the earth with all plagues, as often as they will" (11:1-6).

The portion of the Old Testament to which this vision specially relates, and by which it is to be interpreted, is Zechariah, Chapter II, where the prophet saw a man with a measuring-line, who, when asked, "Whither goes thou?" replied, "To measure Jerusalem, to see what is the breadth thereof, and what is the length thereof". The significance of this, according to the verses that follow, was that Jerusalem was to be *inhabited again with a great multitude;* that the Lord Himself would be to her a protecting wall of fire round about her, and be the glory in the midst of her; that His people *(Zion)* should be separated from all that were not His *(Babylon);* that He would "dwell in the midst" of her, and would "inherit Judah His portion in the holy land", and would "choose Jerusalem again".

From this it is clear that the vision of Revelation XI looks forward to the great consummation of all God's work in redemption, as pictured in the vision of the New Jerusalem, Chapters XXI, XXII, whose length, and breadth, and height are given; the city that is lightened by the glory of God's presence, and where He dwells in the midst of His redeemed people. This is what comes finally into view after all that is opposed to God (great Babylon) shall have been destroyed.

The correspondence between the two visions is very close. For where in Zechariah it is said, "And *many nations* shall be joined to the Lord in that day, and shall be My people", we have the corresponding statement in Revelation 21:24, "And *the nations* of them which are saved shall walk in the light of it; and the kings of the earth do bring their glory and honour into it".

Further in explanation of Zechariah's vision we have the words of the Lord recorded in Chapter 1:16, "I am *returned to Jerusalem with mercies,* My house shall be built in it, and a line shall be stretched forth upon Jerusalem". This word of the Lord came in answer to the cry, "O Lord of hosts, how long wilt thou not have mercy on Jerusalem?" (v. 12).

Answering to this in Revelation we have the oath of the Angel that there should be delay no longer; while the rainbow encircling His head is the beautiful pledge that He is returned to His people (Jerusalem) "with mercies", notwithstanding that He comes mantled with the threatening cloud of judgment, and with the awe-inspiring voices of the seven thunders.

This will suffice to show clearly the general purport of the vision now before us; and particularly it tells us that when something is symbolically *measured*, we are to understand that it is being made ready for *God's occupation and use.*

This is confirmed by the vision of Ezekiel 40:2, where the prophet was given to see the frame of a city, and a man with a measuring reed, with which he proceeded to measure the breadth and height of the building. This vision the seer was commanded to declare to the house of Israel (v. 4).

What corresponds to the subject of this vision in the New Testament is most fully set forth in the Epistle to the Ephesians, where we read that all who are saved by faith in Jesus Christ, whether by nature they were Jews or Gentiles, constitute one "household of faith", and are being "built upon the foundation of the apostles and prophets, Jesus Christ Himself being the chief corner stone; in whom *the whole building, fitly framed together, groweth unto* AN HOLY TEMPLE *in the* Lord: *in whom ye also are* (being) *builded together for an habitation of God through the Spirit*" (Eph. 2:19-22). It is with regard to this dwelling-place of God, this holy temple now being builded by the Holy Spirit, that the apostle prays for us all who have part and place therein, that we might "be able to comprehend, with all saints, *what is the breadth,*

The Mighty Angel With the Little Book

and length, and depth, and height" thereof (3:18). And it should be observed that in the context we have "the commonwealth of Israel" and "the covenants of promise" (2:12), into which the saved from among the Gentiles are now being brought, they being "no more strangers and foreigners, but fellow citizens with the saints, and of the household of God" (2:19). This relationship of perfect equality between saved Jews and saved Gentiles is termed in the next chapter "the *mystery* of Christ", which had not been made known in times past, as God has now revealed it "unto His holy apostles and prophets by the Spirit", namely, "That the Gentiles should be fellow heirs, and of the same body, and partakers of His promise in Christ by (means of) the gospel" (3:4-6)*. This participation by the saved of the Gentiles in the full benefits of Christ's redemption was intimated by what was said in the prophecy of Zechariah concerning the "many nations" (Gentiles), and is confirmed by the like statement in Revelation 21:24. It is presented vividly in Romans XI by the figure of the olive tree, into which the branches of the wild olive tree (Gentiles) are graffed, "contrary to nature", so to speak (Rom. 11: 24). Here again the temporary blindness of the natural Israel and the bringing in of "the fulness of the Gentiles" is spoken of as "this mystery". So here we have further light on the words of the Angel, declaring that in the days of the voice of the seventh angel

---
* As expressed in the Greek, the threefold recurrence of the prefix *sun* (=*joint*) is very forceful: "that the Gentiles should be *joint-heirs*, and a *joint-body*, and *joint-partakers* of His promise in Christ, through the glad-tidings".

"the mystery of God shall be finished". For this process of building the temple of God, though it seems long ("how long"!) to us, *will be "finished" at the appointed time;* and then Christ shall "present it to (or *with*) Himself, a *church of glory,* not having spot, or wrinkle, or any such thing; but that it should be *holy,* and without blemish" (Eph. 5:27). This is what is pictured to us in the dazzling perfections of "the *holy* city, the new Jerusalem" (Rev. XXI).

But the perfection of the Church (for here we have the true meaning of that much-abused word) involves a process of cleansing, for the removal of every "spot" and "wrinkle" and "blemish". In order to "sanctify" it (*i. e.,* to make it *holy*), Christ must needs "cleanse it with the washing of water by the word" (Eph. 5:26). He must not only bring into it every thing necessary to make it complete in all its dimensions— breadth, length, depth, and height—but He must *remove from it* all that is foreign to it. So here is where the work of separation comes into view; and that work includes operations that are painful, though necessary. For God is very exact in all that He does. He finishes His work to the minutest detail, and at the precise moment planned by Him. He works "by weight and measure".

This is what is involved in the symbol of measuring a building. For thereby its limits are *fixed in every direction.* All that belongs to it is included; and whatever does not belong to it is rigidly excluded. As has been pointed out in connection with the vision of Chapter VII, that which is numbered or measured by God's command is what He sets apart, or sanctifies as His own.

In the light of the foregoing Scriptures it is easy to understand the command given to John by the mighty Angel, "Rise, and measure *the temple* of God, and the altar, and them that worship therein". It tells us that the time is come for the complete and eternal separation to God of all that is His, from association and contact with what is not His. The "foundation" of the "great house" has always stood "sure" throughout the centuries; and it has been at all times true that "the Lord knoweth them that are His" (2 Tim. 2:19, 20). Nevertheless, there have ever been those, like Hymenaeus and Philetus (v. 17), who, while not properly belonging to the house, have associated themselves with it. But in the last days, God was to put into operation divine processes of various sorts whereby the separation of these incongruous elements should be effected. First of all is the *call* to separation, a call which is heard to the very end; for the last call of the Bible to the people of God is that which is heard at the eve of the destruction of Babylon, "Come out of her, My people" (Rev. 18:4). And this is the very same call, though now uttered more imperatively, that had been sounded in the ears of Zechariah: "Deliver thyself, O Zion, that dwellest with the daughter of Babylon" (Zech. 2:7). And to the same effect are the words of Paul in the passage cited above: "And let every one that nameth the Name of Christ depart from iniquity" (2 Tim. 2:19).

This work is, I believe, in active progress in our day, and has been for some time past. Evidences of it are seen in every effort by individuals and companies, to withdraw from all that is not according to the revealed truth of God, and to adhere to "the apostles' doctrine" and to the pattern of primitive christianity in all matters of faith and practice. In the present cleavage between "Fundamentalists" and "Modernists" may be seen one phase of this work of separation.

In the passage we are studying, the temple represents the true "building of God" in all its proper parts. It is measured for *preservation*. "But the court, which is *without the temple*," John was commanded to "cast out" *(marg.)* "and measure it not; for it is *given to the Gentiles*". The word "cast out" (not *leave* out, as in the text of the A. V.) is very forceful; for forcible means will be used at the very last. Note also that in this Book the word "Jews" is used in its highest sense, as the proper designation of the true people of God, those who are *within*. Hence "Gentiles" means those who are *without*. This appears quite clearly from Chapter XXII. There the building of God, the eternal abode of God and the Lamb and of His redeemed people, stands revealed, complete and perfect in all its vast dimensions. And there it is said that *"without* are dogs" (22:15) that being the name applied to Gentiles, in contradistinction to Jews, dogs being ceremonially unclean animals (see comments at 22:15).

Thus we have before us in Chapter XI a picture of a real sanctuary, "the temple of God", an altar, and true worshippers (see Heb. 10:19-22 and 13:10,15); but there is appended to it a "court", which is thronged with "Gentiles". Such has been the state of things since the days of the Protestant Reformation. But the court is to be cast out, and given over entirely "to the Gentiles", and they are to trample it under foot for forty and two months. This indicates that the forces of pseudo-christianity, the "liberals", are to have control of the nominal "church", with all its vast possessions, machinery, etc. Such is virtually the present state of things; though some of God's true people are contending for the possession of the outer "court". In the light of this prophecy their efforts are vain. But the true sanctuary with its altar will remain to them. Well for them if they would betake themselves to it without further delay.

In the first chapter of Isaiah, God addresses those who were nominally His people, but whom He repudiated and whose worship He rejected, saying, "To what purpose is the multitude of your sacrifices" etc. "When ye come to appear before Me, who hath required this at your hand, to *trample* My courts" (R. V. and Jewish V.). This passage also throws light on that which we are studying.

The figurative measure of time specified in Revelation 11:2, forty and two months, is the same as the

1260 days of verse 3, and of Chapter 12:6; and the same also as the "time, times, and half a time" of 12:14. It is found again in the oath of the Angel recorded in Daniel 12:7. Being half a week (of years) it speaks of a shortened period of time, a broken seven. It is, of course, a spiritual measure; and how to translate it into the equivalent in natural time is not given to us—at least so far as I am aware. In this Book we are taken back and forth, from the natural realm to the spiritual, from the earthly to the heavenly; and in the spiritual realm we find conditions with which we are quite unfamiliar. Particularly difficult is it for us to comprehend the scales of measurement of time and space that are used by those that dwell in eternity. But further light as to this may come.

THE TWO WITNESSES

During this period of preparatory separation, God gives power to His two witnesses, who are to prophesy in sackcloth for a period that is exactly the same as that during which the court of the temple is given over to be trampled under foot by the Gentiles. By this we know that His testimony to the world will be continued in divine power until His people are taken away from the earth. So we have two things of great importance assured to us for this last period of trial and sifting; *first,* that the true sanctuary, altar, and worshippers shall abide; and *second,* that there shall be a continuance of the testimony of the true gospel of Jesus Christ. And *these two things are one;* for those who worship

The Mighty Angel With the Little Book

inside the true sanctuary, are the same to whom power is given to bear witness outside. For we are not to look for just two divinely endowed persons, as Moses and Elijah, to appear upon the scene, as some suppose. The number *two,* like other numbers in this Book, has a symbolical meaning. Two is the number of *divine sufficiency in testimony.* Out of the mouth of at least *two* witnesses was every word to be established (Deut. 17:6; 19:15; Mat. 18:16). "The true witness", says Hengstenberg, "never stands isolated. He always finds some to whom he can join, hand to hand and heart to heart". And as another has said, "In the midst of all tribulation it is an encouraging thing if a witness has at least one help, who stands side by side with him. Our Lord always sent forth His disciples by two together; and in earlier times there were Moses and Aaron, Joshua and Caleb, Zerubbabel and Joshua, Haggai and Zechariah; as on the opposite side Jannes and Jambres". Likewise Paul had with him on his missionary journeys a Barnabas, a Silas, or a Timothy. For "two is better than one"; and where there are two thus joined for testimony and labor in the Lord, the Holy Spirit with them, the Divine Witness (John 15:26; Acts 5:32) constitutes the *"three*fold cord that is not quickly broken" (Eccl. 4:9, 12).

The two witnesses then are ideal persons; and they have the characteristics of Moses and Elijah, who were pattern witnesses. For, according to verse 6, they have, like the latter, power "to shut heaven that it rain not in the days of their prophecy", and power, like the former, "over waters to turn them to blood, and to smite the earth with all plagues as often as they will". It is not said, as would be if these were an individual Moses and an individual Elijah, that one had the one power, and the other the other. What is said is that the two collectively have the power to do *both*. This enabling is the gift of Christ, "I will *give* My two witnesses *power*", bestowed with special reference to the need of the time. It recalls His words just before His ascension, "Ye shall receive *power*, and ye shall be *witnesses* unto Me" (Acts 1:8).

These witnesses of the end-time are to prophesy "clothed in sack-cloth". This points to the circumstances in which their testimony is to be given. Christ's witnesses will not be clad in ecclesiastical regalia, they will not be personages of rank and title among men, but will be of lowly station, and like Christ's first witnesses will be regarded "as the filth of the world and the offscouring of all things". For their testimony will be not of progress and world-betterment, not of peace and safety, not of the triumphs of science, nor of anything that the world loves to hear when it "goes to church". But they must testify of death and judgment, of the day of wrath and perdition of ungodly men, of the coming of the rejected Lord Jesus Christ in flaming fire, taking vengeance on them—whosoever they may be and howsoever exalted their station—who know not God, and who obey not the gospel of our Lord Jesus Christ, who shall be punished with everlasting destruction from the presence of the Lord and from the glory of His power (2 Thess. 1:7-9).

It is further stated concerning these two witnesses that they are "the two olive trees, and the two candlesticks, standing before the God of the earth". The significance of the candlestick, as representing a witness-bearer, has been fully pointed out in connection with the vision of Chapter I. That these witnesses stand "before the God of the earth" declares that, in the spiritual realm, they have positions of high honor and dignity, though on earth they prophesy in sackcloth. This is in accordance with the principle that "the last" (here) "shall be first" (there). The reference to the two olive trees and two candlesticks takes us again to Zechariah, where in Chapter 4 is described the vision of a golden candlestick and two olive trees, one on the right side and the other on the left (vv. 2, 3); and it is explained that "these are the two anointed ones (lit. *sons of oil*) that stand by the Lord of the whole earth" (v. 13). This shows that God's witnesses are furnished continuously for their ministry with the power and graces of the Holy Spirit as typified by the continuous flow of the "golden oil" through the "golden pipes".

Moreover, by verse 5 we are to understand that God arms His servants against their enemies; and though the weapons of their warfare be not carnal, yet are they "mighty through God". For "where the oil is, there also is *fire*. It is the strength of one and the same Spirit, which manifests itself in the testimony of salvation for those who will have it, and in vengeance on the wicked. The Lord has put His word in their mouth, which is like a fire, and like a hammer that breaks the rock into pieces" (Hengstenberg). Thus the Lord said to Jeremiah in his loneliness and feebleness: "Behold, I will make My words in thy mouth *fire,* and this people wood, and it shall devour them" (Jer. 5:14). This, of course, is not to be understood literally. It meant that all the words of God spoken by Jeremiah would be fulfilled against those who withstood him. And such is the meaning here: "If any man will hurt them, he must in this manner be killed".

"And when they shall have *finished their testimony;* the beast that ascendeth out of the bottomless pit, shall make war against them, and kill them" (v.7).

The reference to the beast that ascendeth out of the abyss is a link with what follows (17:8). It shows that the vision leads on to the era of the last days of beast-government. According to the symbolical language of this Book, we are to understand that the testimony of God's witnesses will be suppressed by governmental authority, which then will be fully in the hands of Satan; but that will not be permitted "until they shall have *finished* their testimony".

The scene of this overcoming of the witnesses is "the street of the *great city,* which spiritually is called Sodom and Egypt, where also our Lord was crucified" (v. 8). In Chapter 18, in the lament over the downfall of the world (there pictured as "Babylon"), are the words, "Alas! alas! that *great city*" (v. 16). Here we have the designations *Sodom* and *Egypt,* which speak respectively, the former of the moral corruption, and the latter of the spiritual darkness of the world, out of which God is about to take His people by an act of power. The words, "where also our Lord was crucified", signify that the guilt of His crucifixion is to be laid upon all those in the whole world who have rejected the mercy that flows from the cross. It is to be according to the word of His betrayers and murderers: "Then answered all the people and said, His blood be on us, and on our children" (Mat. 27:25).

"And they of the people, and kindreds, and tongues and nations, shall see their dead bodies three days and a half, and shall not suffer their dead bodies to be put in graves. And they that dwell upon the earth shall rejoice over them, and make merry, and shall send gifts one to another, because these two prophets tormented them that dwelt on the earth" (vv. 9, 10).

From this we see that the testimony of these witnesses is world-wide, not a mere local affair, as the witness of two individuals would necessarily be. All the peoples and nations of earth are involved in the matter.

And why, it will be asked, do they rejoice over the suppression of the testimony of the witnesses? This is explained by the statement that the word of those prophets was a *torment* to them that dwelt on the earth. And so indeed it is. For notwithstanding that the servants of Christ are but a feeble few; notwithstanding that they are of lowly station, and have no other weapon than the word of their testimony; yet that word is the truth of God, and the hearts and consciences of men bear witness to this even while they scoff at it.

"And after three days and a half the Spirit of life from God entered into them, and they stood upon their feet; and great fear fell upon them which saw them. And they heard a great voice from Heaven saying unto them, Come up hither. And they ascended up to heaven in a cloud; and their enemies beheld them" (vv. 11, 12).

The rejoicing of the enemies of the truth was very brief. For a mighty outpouring of the Spirit is indicated by the words of verse 11, bringing a revival of the testimony. The witnesses spring to life and stand upon their feet. Nor is this last testimony of God's people without avail; for great fear fell on them that saw them. Moreover, verse 13 records that in that same hour there was a great earthquake, and a tenth part of the city fell, and in the earthquake were slain of men seven thousand (a number of completeness) and that *"the remnant were affrighted and gave glory to the God of heaven"*.

What verse 12 describes is the ending of the testimony of the people of God on earth; and the description agrees so closely with that given by the apostle Paul in 1 Thessalonians 4:13-17 that I see no room for doubt that both passages refer to the same event. For here we have "the voice" saying "Come up hither", and the statement that they ascended up to heaven *in a cloud*. Is not this the next predicted event to be looked for?

The Mighty Angel With the Little Book

This catching away of the witnesses is placed *immediately before the sounding of the seventh trumpet,* and the announcement of the coming of God's wrath (v. 18). And this also agrees with the passage in 1 Thessalonians, in which the apostle after describing the descent of the Lord from heaven with a shout, with the voice of the archangel, and the trump of God, and the catching away of both the living and the resurrected saints "in the clouds", goes on to say that "God hath not appointed us *to wrath,* but to obtain salvation by our Lord Jesus Christ" (1 Th. 5:7).

The question will naturally arise as to time indicated by the loud voice of the mighty Angel and the seven thunders. As this is a vision of something that happened on the heavenly side of things, it is not possible to say with certainty just what manifestation of it was given on the earthly and visible side. I may venture the suggestion, however, that what marked this event outwardly was the Protestant Reformation (This is not a new suggestion, though it occurred to me independently). That great event took place at the time the waning of the Turkish power began. It was a world-shaking event. It was the dawn of a new era, the beginning of those great movements that were to usher in the days of the seventh trumpet. Moreover, it was of a nature corresponding to the voice and actions of Christ in the guise of the mighty Angel of Chapter X. Very likely, therefore, there began at that time (sixteenth century) the era of the prophesying anew concerning peoples and nations and tongues and many kings (for certainly it was a new era of the preaching of the Word of God); the separation of the true from the untrue in the house of God; and the final testimony of God, by His two witnesses clothed in sackcloth. At that time also there was a great and wonderful revival of learning. The invention of printing by means of movable type, which invention gave us the printing press, with all, both of good and evil, that has resulted therefrom, coincided with the translation of the Holy Scriptures out of the original languages, Hebrew and Greek, into the vernacular, English and German, with results that have been incalculably great. From that day to the present, the diffusion of the knowledge of the Bible has continued. Even within recent years and months translations have been made into tongues and dialects used by millions of peoples. It is true, indeed, that the prince of darkness has been mightily served by the printing press, and that literature of an antichristian character is increasing at an enormous rate. But both ways it is working toward the accomplishment of the purposes of God, to gather out of all the nations a people for His Name, and to separate them from those who are not His. Most certainly therefore, the era of the Reformation was one of the greatest of the entire dispensation, and hence well deserving of a place in this prophecy. Moreover, the work of that era has the two outstanding features emphasized in the vision of Chapters X and XI, namely, (1) prophesying again over peoples, nations, tongues and kings, and (2) separating to God that which is truly His.

CONCERNING THE FUTURE OF THE EARTHLY ISRAEL

Many of those who adopt the futurist system of interpretation regard prophecies which speak of the temple of God, such as that of Revelation 11:1, 2, as referring to a future rebuilding of the Jewish temple in Jerusalem, and the resumption of animal sacrifices. It will be appropriate at this point to present a brief discussion of this idea.

One of the great and eternal results of the sacrifice of Christ, a result upon which the Scriptures lay the fullest stress, is that it swept away forever the entire system of Jewish ceremonial—temple, priesthood, and especially those sacrifices in which God had "no pleasure", because they could "never take away sins" (Heb. 10:1-12). Another of the results of the cross is that thereby the Lord Jesus abolished that "middle wall of partition" which of old separated Gentiles from Jews (Eph. 2:14-22). These Scriptures make it impossible that God should ever again recognize an "Israel after the flesh", or re-establish the abolished Jewish ritual, or any part thereof. All that system of worship was one of "shadows"; and like the "old covenant", of which it was an integral part, it is done away forever. Moreover, and this is the serious part of the matter, the doctrine of the restoration of the Jewish nation, with its temple, priesthood and sacrifices, is a denial of what the Scriptures point to as one of the most important consequences of the sacrifice of Jesus Chirst. This whole doctrine, and all that goes with it, rests upon the very same mistaken and utterly carnal system of interpretation of the O. T. prophecies that caused the Jews to reject and crucify Christ (Ac. 13:27). For the Zion of prophecy is the spiritual Zion; the Jerusalem of prophecy which God promised to build up, is the heavenly Jerusalem; the Israel of prophecy is "the Israel of God"; and the temple of prophecy is the "spiritual house" of 1 Peter 2:5, and Ephesians 2: 20-22.

The death and resurrection of Christ abolished all national distinctions, so that now we know "no man after the flesh" (2 Cor. 5:16). Most certainly, if the future of Israel is revealed anywhere in the N. T. it would be found in Romans XI and in the Apocalypse. And sure enough we find it in the former, which foretells, not that Israel after the flesh will be re-established as a nation on earth, but that all Israel will be saved by being graffed into that very "olive tree", a figure of spiritual Israel, into which believing Gentiles are now being graffed. And as for the Apocalypse, we search it in vain for any hint of the restoration of the earthly Israel. On the contrary, its predictions leave no room for anything but the spiritual Israel, and the heavenly city and temple; and most certainly no room for any sacrifice but that of the Lamb that was slain. Therefore the doctrine of the restoration of the Jewish nation and the earthly Jerusalem is a baseless dream. Speaking on the subject of "the temple of God" of Chapter XI, Hengstenberg says:

The Mighty Angel With the Little Book 351

"No trace whatever is to be found here of Jerusalem and the temple being in ruins at the time of the vision; nor any trace of a rebuilding to take place in the future, either here or in any other part of the Book. . . . This literal method of exposition belongs to an entire chain of representations in regard to the Kingdom of God, which has recently indeed obtained extensive support, especially in England, where in particular the *Society for the Conversion of the Jews* is pervaded by it. But we cannot regard it as agreeable to the Scriptures. It is a kind of revival of the Jewish-Christian tendency of the ancient church. It nourishes in the unconverted that natural pride, the extirpation of which should be one of the first objects of a true spiritual activity. Let us then look back to the soundness of the older church, and cease to change Jewish Christians into Christian Jews".

Vitringa also discusses this distinction between Jews and Gentiles in the flesh, saying:

"This distinction is entirely taken away under the new economy. For as the heathen, who were converted to Christ, were graffed into the Jewish olive tree; so the Jews, who in the latter days shall be converted to Christ, shall become incorporated with the mystical and spiritual 'Jews,' and shall possess along with them, without any difference, the same condition in the Kingdom of Christ. All are one in Christ."

Speaking of the declarations of the Epistle to the Romans, Hengstenberg remarks:

"They speak much of the blessing which the conversion of the Jews shall bring to the church of the future; but nothing whatever of a new church of the Jews, of the restoration of Jerusalem, the rebuilding of the temple, or generally of a reviving of the old beggarly elements, which have been completely swept away by Christ and His blood, placing all nations on a footing. The question is thus thrown entirely back upon the Old Testament. If anyone is ready to conclude that, whenever Israel is there spoken of, the Jews are meant, he can certainly prove much; but little good will be done by such a light and superficial mode of expounding the Old Testament Scriptures. What the Spirit has said must be spiritually understood. . . . An olive tree, a people of God, *stands from first to last;* an 'Israel', out of which the false seed is excluded, and into which believers from among the Gentiles are adopted". . . .

"He who is truly 'in Christ' can no longer know anyone after the flesh. He to whom Christ is what He was to John, the Alpha and Omega, the first and last, the Prince of the kings of the earth, the One who has loved us and washed us from our sins in His blood, and has made us kings and priests to God and His Father, is raised entirely above the territory of mere Jewish sympathies".

"We maintain therefore, that Revelation knows of no prerogatives belonging peculiarly to the Jews in the Kingdom of God. Gentile Christians have perfectly equal rights imputed to them with the Jewish brethren; so much so that the seer makes no account of any distinction between Jewish and Gentile believers". . . .

"But there is also another line of argument by which we reach the same result. We perceive that everywhere else the things of Judaism serve only as the forms and symbols under which the Book represents things christian; and all these analogies lead to the conclusion that by *the temple* here cannot possibly be meant the temple at Jerusalem. That by 'Israel' the author does not denote those he thought worthy of the name because of their natural descent from Jacob, but the entire body of true Christians, we have already shown. In like manner he holds no other to be 'Jews' but true Christians, for 'Jew' in this book denotes one who is circumcised in heart (2:9). Bold as it may seem, he must also deny to the temple at Jerusalem the name 'temple'. The 'priests' of Revelation, who must of course have a *temple* corresponding to them, are not the sons of Aaron, but are all Christ's people (1:6; 5:10; 20:6). Nay, the temple itself also occurs elsewhere in the Revelation in a spiritual sense. And this is the more decisive in that in each passage the discourse is not of *a* temple, but precisely of *the* temple of God. Even in the first group it is said, 'Him that overcomes will I make a pillar in *the temple of My God,* and he shall go no more out' (3:12) . . .

"Further, it has now again to be pointed out how that (as from the first is felt by a simple faith in the written word) we have here *holy ground,* on which no patriotic imaginations, and no products of common and impure human feeling are to be found."

THE HOPE OF ISRAEL

The Scriptures of the N. T. declare with no uncertain sound that, just as there is but "one faith" for all mankind, Jew and Gentile, even so there is but "one hope" (Eph. 4:4-6). That is "the hope laid up in heaven", "the hope of the gospel" (Col. 1:5, 23). It was for preaching this "one hope" to both Jews and Gentiles that Paul was accused by the leaders of his own people, and sent in chains to Rome. To this he himself testified to the Jews at Rome, saying: "For this cause therefore have I called for you, to see you, and to speak with you; because that *for the hope of Israel* I am bound with this chain" (Ac. 28:20). What *he* had preached as "the hope of Israel" was *the resurrection* (Ac. 23:6; 24:15 &c). He had declared that this was *"the hope of the promise* made of God to our fathers; unto which *our twelve tribes,* instantly serving God day and night, *hope* to come". And he added: "For *which hope's* sake, King Agrippa, I am accused of the Jews" (Ac. 26:6, 7). Furthermore he declared that what he preached was not a departure from the teaching of the O. T., but on the contrary he had witnessed to "none other things than those which the prophets and Moses did say should come" (Ac. 26:22).

The apostle Peter likewise affirms with emphasis that those who preached the gospel, (the apostles of Christ) announced the very same salvation that the prophets had foretold (1 Pet. 2:10-12).

It appears to be quite a modern doctrine that there is to be a special salvation, after the end of the gospel dispensation, for a section of the human family (the natural descendants of Jacob). But whether a modern doctrine or an ancient one, it is directly contrary to the teaching of the N. T. (and hence to that of the O. T. also) which declares in many passages that the cross of Christ has forever removed the ancient wall of partition between Jew and Gentile, has abolished all national distinctions and has swept away the old covenant and all that was connected with it. The N. T. also declares in the plainest way that the day of salvation *for the whole world* will end with the coming of Christ. Therefore, to preach another chance, whether for all (according to Russellism) or for the Jews only, as a specially privileged class, is subversive of foundation truth.

This is a large subject, which cannot be fully treated here. But there is no need of an exhaustive discussion of it. The Lord Himself has declared that when He shall come again in His glory, and all the holy angels with Him, then "before Him shall be gathered *all nations*"; and He will divide them into two companies, to one of which He will say, "Come ye blessed of My Father, inherit the Kingdom prepared for you from the foundation of the world"; and to the other, "Depart from Me, ye cursed into everlasting fire prepared for the devil and His angels" (Mat. 25:31-46). This Scripture makes it certain that none who are unsaved at the time of His second advent will find any mercy thereafter. And to put the matter beyond all doubt, the words of the King make it plain that the difference between the two companies is due to what they did and were *before* His advent. For in one class were those who had manifested by their actions that they had the righteousness of God which the gospel offers, and in the other those whose actions showed they were destitute of it.

Such passages as 2 Thessalonians 1:5-10; 2:7-12, and Revelation 19:11-21, also exclude the possibility of anything but judgment upon those who have rejected the gospel, when Christ shall come again.

We shall presently see that the truth of the one "olive tree", the one and only "Israel", which stands from first to last, has much to do with the right understanding of Chapter XII.

The Seventh Trumpet

"The second woe is past: and, behold, the third woe cometh quickly. And the seventh angel sounded: and there were great voices in heaven, saying, The kingdoms of this world are become the kingdoms of our Lord, and of His Christ; and He shall reign for ever and ever. And the four and twenty elders, which sat before God on their seats, fell upon their faces, and worshipped God, saying, We give Thee thanks, O Lord God almighty, which art, and wast, and art to come; because Thou hast taken to Thee Thy great power, and hast reigned. And the nations were angry, and Thy wrath is come, and the time of the dead that they should be judged, and that Thou shouldest give reward unto Thy servants the prophets, and to the saints, and them that fear Thy name, small and great: and shouldest destroy them which destroy the earth" (11:14-18).

We learn the nature of the great events of the seventh trumpet not from any vision seen by John, but from the announcement made by the great voices in heaven, and by the theme of the praises offered by the elders who, in the intensity of their joy and thankfulness, leave their thrones and fall upon their faces before God. The words that proceed from those two sources give a brief summary of the transcendently important events of that era, ignoring all details, and giving no account at all of the steps whereby this supreme purpose of God is accomplished. This information is supplied by later visions. But for the moment, the realization of what is about to take place fills the heart and mind to overflowing, leaving no room for details. As Bengel discerningly remarks: "As soon as the seventh angel sounds, the kingdom of the world becomes the Lord's and His Christ's forever. It is only in

The Mighty Angel With the Little Book

heaven, however, that this takes place so immediately; and in heaven alone is it celebrated with joy; for dreadful things are still to intervene on earth".

It has been already observed that the vision of the *sixth seal* brought us to the time of the end, as was fully realized by the kings, magnates and plutocrats of the world. But at that point the progress of the revealing of events is arrested, and the action of the day of wrath is held in suspense for the revelation of another line of things, parallel to the visions of the seals; and it is only when we reach the seventh trumpet that we find ourselves at the same point at which we had arrived when, at the opening of the seventh seal, there was an ominous silence in heaven.

The next action noted as taking place on earth is that mentioned in verse 19.

"And the temple of God was opened in heaven, and there was seen in His Temple the ark of His testament (or covenant): and there were lightnings, and voices, and thunderings, and an earthquake, and great hail".

The first statement of this verse connects with the first verse of the chapter concerning the measuring of the temple. *Now* the temple of God is seen *"in heaven"*, indicating its completion. Moreover it is *opened*, and there is seen in it the ark of His covenant, the earthly counterpart whereof had not been seen or heard of since the destruction of the first temple by Nebuchadnezzar. This is the symbol of God's eternal relations with His people. It comes into view most appropriately at the moment of the accomplishment of what He had pledged Himself to do by the terms of the everlasting covenant. The basis of this work of God is the atonement, symbolized by the mercy seat, which was an integral part (the cover) of the ark. As remarked by Hengstenberg:

> "The indispensable condition of God's connection with men, the foundation of His dwelling among them, is the *atoning divine compassion*. This was symbolized by the capporeth (the covering mercy seat). As externally the capporeth covered the ark with its testimony, so spiritually did the divine compassion the sins of the people".

The ark of God's covenant brings to mind His eternal purpose in the creation of man, as declared in Genesis 1:26. That purpose was to be accomplished, of course, through redemption. Therefore, the appearance of the ark is an appropriate introduction to the panoramic vision of Chapter XII, in which the various stages of its accomplishment are traced.

But in remembering His holy covenant, God also brings to mind the long-delayed time for the final judgments upon the wicked. That that dreadful time is now come is signalized by the five symbols of judgments, lightnings, voices, thunderings, an earthquake, and great hail. (See comments on Chapter 8:5).

In the account of the taking of Jericho (Josh. VI), to which these trumpet visions evidently refer, the ark of the covenant of the Lord has a very prominent place (vv. 4, 6, 7, 8, 9, 11, 13). The priests bearing the seven trumpets went before the ark of the Lord (v. 6). And Joshua commanded the people, saying, "Ye shall

The Mighty Angel With the Little Book

not shout nor make any noise with your voice, neither shall any word proceed out of your mouth, until the day I bid you shout: then shall ye shout" (v. 10). But when the priests blew with the trumpets the seventh time, then Joshua said unto the people, "Shout, for the Lord hath given you the city" (v. 16). So likewise here, the seven trumpets precede the appearing of the ark, during all of which time it seems there was "silence in heaven" (Rev. 8:1). But at the sounding of the seventh trumpet, the silence is broken; and there is, so to speak, a mighty shout proceeding from "great voices in heaven", which announce the downfall of the rebel kingdoms of this world.

CHAPTER VIII
The Two Signs in Heaven

"And there appeared a great wonder in heaven: a woman clothed with the sun, and the moon under her feet, and upon her head a crown of twelve stars: and she being with child cried, travailing in birth, and pained to be delivered. And there appeared another wonder in heaven; and behold a great red dragon, having seven heads and ten horns and seven crowns upon his heads" (12:1-3).

THERE is evidently another interruption and the beginning of another new group of visions at this point. It is a group that has its culmination in the era of the seventh trumpet, and its design (I think quite plainly) is to give a panoramic view of the chief events in the history of the conflict that reaches its climax and end in the days of the seventh trumpet. Here are two "wonders" (or more properly "signs", as in the margin) seen in heaven, signs as different in character as it would be possible to conceive. The first is that of a woman, with whom are associated in a striking and impressive way the symbols of governmental authority—sun, moon, and stars. The other is that of a horrible monster, a great red dragon, who is set with one fell purpose, namely to devour the child which the woman is about to bring forth. We are left in no uncertainty as to the symbol of the dragon, for in verse 9 it is stated that it represents "that old serpent, called the Devil and Satan, which deceiveth the whole world". With this information, and with the light of Scripture as to other symbols used in the vision, its meaning can be deciphered with all necessary fullness. The symbols of sun, moon and stars show that what is in controversy in the stupendous conflict here to be pictured, is *the supreme dominion of the world;* and the Devil is shown as the great adversary who dares to resist God's purpose in regard thereto.

That the "Manchild who was to rule all nations with a rod of iron" is Jesus Christ is not reasonably open to dispute. Psalm 2:9 is decisive as to this; and in the light of all Scripture that prophecy applies to Him, and to Him only. He takes it to Himself in Chapter 2:27, as that which He had received from His Father. Certain weak attempts that have been made to give another meaning to verse 5, in order to make a future event of the catching up of the Manchild to God and to His throne, find no support in the Scriptures.

The Sun Clothed Woman

This gives the clue to the meaning of the sun-clothed woman, in whom many, probably most expositors, see *Israel*. And this conclusion is in accord with all the facts, only that the vision takes us back to the very beginning of the Bible, to a time *before Israel was*. Yet Israel existed in the purpose of God before the creation of the world; not of course, the natural Israel, but the spiritual. For while in the order of happening in the world, "that is not first which is spiritual, but that which is natural", it is not so in the mind and view of God. What is displayed therefore, in this "great sign" of verse 1, with its marvellous grouping of the symbols of celestial power and glory, is *God's purpose in the creation of man, a purpose that was to be accomplished, not in the first man Adam, but in the second Man Jesus Christ, the woman's "Seed"*. The proof of this is ample, as I will now seek to show; though I believe those of clear spiritual vision will "see" it, without the piling of proof upon proof.

God's purpose in the creation of man is declared by Him in Genesis 1:26: "Let Us make man, in Our image, after Our likeness; and let them HAVE DOMINION . . . OVER ALL THE EARTH". The symbols of rule over the earth had been described in verse 16: "The greater light to rule the day, and the lesser light to rule the night; the stars also". The great sign displayed in Revelation 12:1 is a woman clothed with the symbol of supreme authority, the *sun*, and having the symbol of lesser authority, *the moon*, in the place of subordination, "under her feet". Moreover, she is crowned with twelve *stars*, stars being princes or rulers, and twelve being the signature of governmental completeness, as has been already shown. Thus, the symbols agree so perfectly with the meaning here assigned to them that further proof is not needed in order to establish the matter. But there is more.

God made man "male and female", so that either might properly serve as a symbol of mankind as a race. The circumstances must determine the choice; and for the purpose of what is symbolized by this vision, the woman is obviously the appropriate figure. This pro-

The Two Signs in Heaven

ceeds from the fact that it is concerning the Seed of *the woman* (*"her"* Seed") that the great promise in Eden was given (Gen. 3:15). This is decisive. But furthermore, in all prophecies and other passages where figurative language is used, God, when speaking of His people collectively, refers to them as a woman, as in Isaiah LIV for example, where He speaks of the true Israel as "a woman forsaken and grieved in spirit" and refers to Himself as her "Husband" and her "Redeemer".

This declared purpose of God in the creation of man was seemingly frustrated by the Devil through his successful temptation of man, whereby his entire race was brought under the "dominion" of sin and death (Rom. 5:12-6:14). But God re-affirmed His purpose, speaking directly to the serpent, and saying: "I will put enmity between thee and the woman, and between thy seed and her seed; it shall *bruise thy head,* and thou shalt bruise his heel". Thus the accomplishment of God's purpose involved the overthrow of the devil; and therefore it became the supreme purpose of the great enemy's heart to "devour" the woman's Seed as soon as He should be born. This is vividly pictured in the vision, where the hideous dragon is represented as standing before the woman, with intent to devour her child as soon as it was born (v. 4). The designation "that *old* serpent" takes us back to Eden, as do also the words "who deceiveth the whole world". For the Devil is as "old" as creation. It was in Eden that he appeared in the guise of a "serpent"; and there he began his career of "deceiver" of mankind. These correspondences make the interpretation thus far quite plain. But more than that, the words of the Lord God to the serpent: "I will put enmity between thee and the woman", are in the closest agreement with the attitude in which the dragon stands with relation to the woman.

Thus we are able to determine with certainty the beginning of the train of events pictured in Chapter XII (and continued in Chapter XIII); and the context tells us that the end thereof is the accomplishment of God's eternal purpose in vesting the sovereignty of the world in the woman's Seed. Knowing then the beginning and the ending of this train of events, it is not a difficult matter to interpret the intermediate scenes thereof. These are outlined with brevity, the object evidently being to lead us to the final scenes of the age-long conflict (shown in subsequent chapters) by a path which will prepare us the better to understand those supremely important visions.

Let us now look more closely at the details of the vision.

Between verses 1 and 2 a great change has taken place in the state of the woman. In verse 1 she appears in serene and lofty majesty, adorned with all the insignia of celestial glory. In verse 2, she is crying with anguish, travailing in birth-pangs, and pained to be delivered. Between the two verses occurs the fall; and in this second scene we plainly beheld the fulfil-

The Two Signs in Heaven

ment of the sentence of Judgment, "In sorrow thou shalt bring forth children" (Gen. 3:16).

According to various Scriptures, the heavy afflictions upon Israel that preceded the birth of the Saviour are represented by the figure of severe birth-pains coming upon Zion. Among those Scriptures are the following: "I have heard a voice as of a woman in travail, the anguish as of her that bringeth forth her first child; the voice of the daughter of Zion that bewaileth herself" (Jer. 4:31). "And thou, O tower of the flock, the stronghold of the daughter of Zion, unto thee shall it come, *even the first dominion; the kingdom shall come to the daughter of Jerusalem.* Now why dost thou cry out aloud? is there *no king* in thee? for pangs have taken thee as a *woman in travail*" (Mic. 4:8, 9). And a few verses further on is the well known prophecy of the birth of Jesus in Bethlehem of Judah (Mic. 5:2).

Commenting upon the picture shown in verses 2 and 3, Vitringa says:

> "Nothing is omitted that might set forth the greatness and severity of the woman's conflict in the most lively colors. She was in the pains of labor seized with the most violent pangs of child-birth, and in this state appears to be supported only by the hope of the male offspring she had so greatly desired. But she sees a frightful dragon, ready to devour her child so soon as it should be born".

And Hartwig, in his work on the Apocalypse, observes with excellent discrimination,

"That in this whole representation there are such unmistakable allusions to the true history of the child Jesus, His mother, and the tyranny of Herod, as related in the second chapter of Matthew, that this chapter receives from it a new confirmation".

The Dragon

The dragon is pictured as fiery red in color, suggesting his cruelty and his bloody career as a murderer from the beginning. This especial word "red" occurs here and in Chapter 6:10 (the red horse) and nowhere else in Scripture. But most significant are the *seven* heads, expressive of the completeness of his dominion, the *ten* horns, symbolizing the world-wide character of his rule, and the *seven* crowns, telling of the fullness of royalty. The significance of these symbols lies in the fact that they tend further, and most impressively to show that it is *the kingdom,* which Satan had so long held in his hands, and purposes not to surrender without the most desperate struggle, that is the subject of this scene, and of what follows. And it is most true, as Hengstenberg remarks, that "Prophecy and history concerning the Kingdom of God come upon the main point only when *the conflict between Christ and Satan comes into view*".

"And his tail drew the third part of the stars of heaven and did cast them to the earth: and the dragon stood before the woman which was ready to be delivered, for to devour her child as soon as it was born. And she brought forth a man child, who was to rule all nations with a rod of iron: and her child was caught up unto God, and to His throne" (vv. 4, 5).

The third part of the stars which the dragon drew after him represent the fallen angels. We have al-

The Two Signs in Heaven

ready had Christ's explanation that *stars* in this Book represent angels; and here we may perceive the consistency of the Book. In agreement with this, we find in verse 7, "and the dragon fought and *his angels*", these being evidently the "stars" of verse 4. In Isaiah 9:15 it is written that "the prophet that speaketh lies, he is *the tail*". Putting this with the statement of the text that the dragon's "tail drew the third part of the stars of heaven", and remembering that "he is a liar, and the father of it" (the lie), we get the thought that it was through some falsehood that the Devil drew these angels after him into rebellion against God, even as by a lie he seduced the woman at the beginning. The ground of this revolt of the angels may be inferred from Hebrews 1:10, where it is recorded of God the Father that, "when He bringeth the First begotten into the world, He saith, And let all the angels of God worship Him". Here were some who refused to submit to Him; and the number was great. Not that the phrase, "a third part", means a mathematical third; for that phrase is of frequent occurrence in the Book, having evidently the meaning of incompleteness—a substantial number, but considerably less than the whole.

Speaking of the action of the dragon in placing himself before the woman with the design of devouring her child, Hengstenberg makes these illuminating comments:

"The same wickedness nad been practiced by him in ancient times. The life of Moses, on whom the hopes of the people of God hung during the fearful oppression exercised over them by the enemy, was brought into extreme peril by him at the very first. At the coming of Christ, whose appearance threatened far greater danger to his dominion upon earth, who was to withdraw from him not only the people of God but the heathen also, who should attack him in his own territory, he set his instruments anew in motion, as is recorded in Matthew 2:1-12, to which allusion is here manifestly made. Herod, the servant of the dragon, as soon as he heard of the birth of Christ, takes measures to have the new born child slain, and kills all the children in Bethlehem under two years old, that he might make sure of destroying the one hated child. He has been manifesting the same wickedness also since, as often as Christ is born anew in the Spirit. What he did through Herod is, because history, also a symbol, a prophecy in action".

What happened between the birth of Christ and His ascension into heaven is fully told in the Gospels. Hence it is all passed over here; and the next thing mentioned is that He was "caught up to God and His throne". This event, therefore, is that which has specially to do with the war in heaven, mentioned in verse 7. But meanwhile we have this statement about the woman:

"And the woman fled into the wilderness, where she hath a place prepared of God, that they should feed her there a thousand two hundred and threescore days" (v. 6).

The next stage in the history of the woman, her sojourn in the wilderness, is here briefly stated by way of anticipation, that it may be placed in direct contrast with that of her child. The thread of the woman's history is taken up again at verse 14. For *her* the world is now a wilderness wide, a place where there are no natural sources of nourishment or of satisfaction for the heart. Yet God's care of her is pledged; for even there a place is "prepared" for her, and nourishment is to be provided for the mystical period of 1260 days. The thought conveyed by this verse is the preservation of God's Israel through all the long period of her earthly sojourn, in spite of all persecutions and assaults of the enemy. And, of course, to us in our day it is easy to see the wisdom of God in concealing the actual length of the woman's stay in the wilderness, while making it clear that it is of *measured length,* not to be exceeded by a single day. This wilderness experience is a necessary one, not only for the people of God collectively, but for each individual. It answers the same purpose as the sojourn of the Israelites for forty years before they were permitted to occupy the promised land. Moreover, the flight of the typical mother of Christ has a parallel in that of the real mother of the child Jesus into Egypt.

We have an illustration of God's care for His people during their wilderness experience in the case of Hagar in the wilderness of Beersheba, where God made special provision for her and her child (Gen. 21: 14-20).

And now we come to a matter of transcendent importance.

The War in Heaven

"And there was war in heaven: Michael and his angels fought against the dragon; and the dragon fought and his angels, and prevailed not; neither was their place found any more in heaven. And the great dragon was cast out, that old serpent, called the Devil, and Satan, which deceiveth the whole world: he was cast out into the earth, and his angels were cast out with him" (vv. 7-9).

The fact that the ascension of Christ to the throne of God is that event in His history which is singled out for mention in this vision, gives an indication both as to the time, and also as to the cause of this war in heaven. For surely, nothing we know or can conceive of could be more provocative to the Devil and his hosts than the exaltation to the throne of God of Him who had just gained by His cross the victory over the powers of death and hell. It is recorded that, when Jesus Christ went into heaven, and took His place at the right hand of God, "angels, and authorities, and powers" were *"made subject unto Him"* (1 Pet. 3:22). That was the moment, therefore, for the revolt of the angels, seeing that the Devil and his associated powers and principalities refused to be "made subject unto Him". But we have something better than inference to fix the time, and to reveal the cause of that terrific war in heaven, which resulted in the Devil's being cast out into the earth, and his angels with him. The words of the Lord Jesus, recorded in John 12:31-33, put the matter beyond all doubt in my opinion, especially when all the circumstances—the frenzy of the excited multitudes gathering to Jerusalem for the Passover; the general expectation caused by the miracle of the raising of Lazarus, that Christ was about to proclaim Himself their King, and set up a kingdom answering to their carnal thoughts; and the desire of the Greeks to see Him who was the cause of all the frantic enthusiasm—are taken into consideration. These are the words, recorded in John 12:31-33:

> "Now is the judgment of this world: now shall the prince of this world be cast out. And I, if I be lifted up from the earth, will draw all men unto Me".

Three things the Lord here mentions as being "now" about to happen, namely (1) the judgment of this world, (2) the casting out of the prince of this world, (3) the drawing of all men (i. e., men of all nations and classes) to Himself, as a result of His being lifted up to die on the cross. This fixes the time when Satan is "cast out" of heaven; for it is here expressly declared to be contemporaneous with the era when Christ is drawing to Himself men out of all nations and classes. The word "now" must mean the same in both clauses.

The title here given to the Devil, that is, "the prince of this world", is highly significant, for it agrees with the symbol of the seven crowned heads (signifying the complete sovereignty) of the dragon seen by John (who also recorded these words of Christ). Hence the words, "Now shall the prince of this world be cast out"; serve to locate the time of the war in heaven, as the result of which the great dragon was "cast out". The title given him in Revelation 12:9 is fourfold: the *Dragon*, the *Serpent*, the *Devil* and *Satan*; the *four* being the numerical symbol of the entire compass of the world. So the words, "which deceiveth the *whole* earth", are in perfect agreement. To my mind this Scripture (John 12:31-33), in connection with what has been already cited, affords ample proof that the war in heaven, which eventuated in Satan's being "cast out", took place soon after the ascension of the Lord Jesus Christ into heaven. But, as will appear later on, there is further proof to be offered by way of corroboration; whereas, on the other hand, I know of nothing to support the idea that the event here described is yet future. The expression "a short time", which occurs in verse 12, is not opposed to the view we are advancing; for that expression is applicable to this present age, during which the coming again of the Lord Jesus has been always viewed as imminent. Now history records the "great fury" of Satan against the people of God, and his bloody persecutions in the early days, which agrees perfectly with what is stated in verses 12 and 13, and affords further proof that the war in heaven and the casting out of the Devil took place at the beginning of our era. But as the age lengthened itself out, and as it became evident that persecutions did but promote the extension of the Kingdom of God, the Devil changed his tactics, and resorted to other and more subtle methods. This change of procedure on the part of the Adversary is

The Two Signs in Heaven

clearly foreshown in this Scripture, as will be pointed out when we reach verses 15, 16.

From the closely related prophecy of Daniel 12:7 we learn that Michael is *"the great prince that standeth up* for the people of Israel". So it is quite in keeping with what had been revealed to Daniel that we should here find Michael standing up for the Israel of God against her adversary. In Jude 9 is another illuminating statement. Speaking of those who despise dominion and speak evil of dignities, the apostle says: "Yet Michael the archangel, when, contending with the Devil, he disputed about the body of Moses, durst not bring against him a railing accusation, but said, The Lord rebuke thee". This tells us that Michael is "the archangel", the only angelic being of that exalted rank; and it also shows that the Devil is even higher in dignity than he, though a rebel against God. It is impossible, I think, in view of this Scripture to maintain, as some excellent commentators seek to do, that "Michael" is one of the names of the Lord Jesus Christ. The passage tells us also that it was no new thing for Michael to contend with the Devil, though in the case of the body of Moses it was a *verbal* dispute only, the word rendered "disputed" meaning to argue, or reason, or dispute in words. Further it tells us that the Devil, who has "the power of death" (Heb. 2:14), jealously keeps the bodies of the dead. The Lord had need of the body of Moses (and his bodily appearance on the mount of Transfiguration along with Elijah, who had been taken *bodily* to heaven, may explain the reason); and therefore to Michael, the archangel, was entrusted the mission of bringing it from the grave. And this is in keeping with the only other passage where the archangel is mentioned, 1 Thessalonians 4:16. For there, when all the dead in Christ are to be brought out of their graves, "the voice of *the archangel*" is heard, along with "the trump of God".

Zechariah 3:1-5 gives further light as to the subject of the great controversy between God and Satan. It is in regard to the sinfulness of those whom God would save out of the Devil's kingdom; for sin is what gives the Devil his claim to the possession of man. In this vision, Joshua is a type of every saved person. He stands before the Lord clad in filthy garments; and the command is given to those that stood before Him, "Take away the filthy garments from him"; while to Joshua himself he says, "I have caused thine iniquity to pass from thee, and I will clothe thee with change of raiment". The work of the cross is clearly implied in this scene, where one by nature a sinner, though by rank the high priest, is divested of his filthy garments of mere human righteousness, and is clothed with the garments of God's righteousness and salvation. But the main feaure of this scene is that Satan stands at the right hand of the angel of the Lord to resist him, *i. e.* "to be his adversary" (marg.). So here is plainly shown the ground of Satan's opposition to God; and from it we may clearly understand the nature of Christ's victory over Satan at the cross, since thereby

He silenced the accusations of the Adversary against every one who takes shelter under His cross. It is very significant that in this passage again the words are spoken (this time by the Lord Himself), "The Lord rebuke thee, O Satan".

The Result of the War in Heaven

This brings us to a matter of prime importance; namely, the immediate result of the war in heaven. As stated in the text: "And the dragon fought, and his angels, and prevailed not; neither was their place found any more in heaven. And the great dragon . . . was cast out into the earth, and his angels were cast out with him". It was a crushing defeat, which nothing but the cross could have inflicted upon the prince of this world. "Its (the world's) power", says Lucke, "is immediately judged, condemned, and broken *in its head*"; in proof whereof he cites the words of Christ, spoken in direct connection with His approaching death on the cross, "Now is the *judgment* of this world, now shall the prince of this world be *cast out*". The Old Testament shows us (Job. 1:6; 2:1; Zech. 3:1) that in those days before the cross, Satan had free access to the courts of heaven. But how could it be so after the work of atonement was finished? How could the accuser, that old serpent, raise his head, and open his mouth, or even present himself before the slain Lamb upon the throne? "Who shall *now* lay *anything* to the charge of God's elect?" The apostle asks this challenging question in a passage that is exuberant with the triumph of the cross. Where have we in the New Testament a word to support the idea (apparently a product of very modern theology) that Satan still appears before the throne of God, as the accuser of the brethren? The New Testament Scriptures place him *on earth*. "Your adversary the devil, as a roaring lion, walketh about, seeking whom he may *devour*" (1 Pet. 5:8). And that is in perfect agreement with the vision before us, in which the Devil and his hosts are "cast out into the earth", and he goes to make war with the remnant of the woman's seed, who keep the commandments of God, and have the testimony of Jesus Christ (v. 17). This certainly is the state of things in this present dispensation. It is a great and serious error to refer it to a future day.

Furthermore, the crushing defeat inflicted upon the great dragon, and his expulsion from heaven, means that his power is broken, though his "wrath" (v. 12) and his will to do evil remain. For Christ took part of flesh and blood "that through death He might *destroy him that had the power of death, that is the devil*" (Heb. 2:14). This breaking of the Devil's power was by *the death* of Christ. Not without serious harm to the truth can it be deferred to a future day. For by the the cross of Christ, "forgiveness of sin has been obtained, and thus Satan's most formidable weapon has been wrenched out of his hands" (Hengstenberg). Therefore, in the New Testament, we are not only plainly told that Satan is already a conquered foe, "cast out", of heaven, that is, deprived of his authority over those whose citizenship is in heaven (see verse 12), but are also told to "resist the devil, and he will flee from you" (Jam. 4:7). This could not be apart from Christ's victory on Calvary; but now that the victory has been won, it could not otherwise.

In keeping with this are the words of 1 Corinthians 15:56-58, which is part of a passage wherein the fruits of Christ's death and resurrection are set forth. We recall the words: "The sting of death is sin: and the strength of sin is the law", which righteously demanded the death of the sinner. "BUT thanks be to God, who giveth us *the victory* through our Lord Jesus Christ". Here is victory for us *now* over the power of sin, and deliverance from the condemnation of the law "through our Lord Jesus Christ". That victory became available for the people of God from the time of the resurrection of Jesus Christ, and because thereof; for God *"giveth"* it (present tense); and simple faith can claim it *now*. Let us therefore shun all teaching that defers to a future day the casting out of Satan from his place of high authority in heaven.

Finally as to this important matter, I would again call attention to that grand passage, Romans 8:31, which begins with the significant question, "If God be for us, who can be *against us?*" What adversary can stand against, or prevail over us? The express ground of the apostle's assurance is that He who spared not His own Son, but delivered Him up for us all, will with

Him also freely give us all things (v. 32). And that the Devil is specially in view is evident from the question, "Who shall lay anything to the charge of God's elect?" (v. 33), and also from the reference to angels, principalities and powers (v. 38). The question has the force of a strong assertion that none can bring any accusation against the elect of God, and this for the express reason that "It is God that justifieth" (v. 33). But more than this, we are further reminded that "It is Christ that died, yea rather that is risen again, who is *even at the right hand of God, who also maketh intercession for us*" (v. 34); and this effectually excludes Satan from the presence of God. What then are the immediate consequences of all this to us, even in the greatest "tribulation, or distress, or persecution" (vv. 35, 36) that the Devil can bring upon us? The answer is that "in all these things we are *more than conquerors, through Him that loved us*". These Scriptures, therefore, declare in the strongest terms that Satan no longer has the upper hand; that he is cast out of his former place of authority; and that, through the knowledge of this great truth, the feeblest saint can be *more* than a conqueror over all the principalities, powers, and hosts of wickedness. I say, "through the knowledge of this truth"; for obviously we must *know* the effect of the cross in nullifying the power of Satan, else we cannot by faith avail ourselves of the benefits thereof.

The Loud Voice in Heaven

"And I heard a loud voice saying in heaven, Now is come salvation, and strength, and the kingdom of our God, and the power of His Christ; for the accuser of our brethren is cast down, which accused them before our God day and night. And they overcame him by the blood of the Lamb, and by the word of their testimony; and they loved not their lives unto the death. Therefore rejoice, ye heavens, and ye that dwell in them. Woe to the inhabiters of the earth, and of the sea! for the devil is come down unto you, having great wrath, because he knoweth that he hath but a short time" (vv. 10-12).

The statements made by this loud voice in heaven should be noted with care, for thereby further and very clear light is given as to the time when the war in heaven and the casting out of Satan took place. From these statements we learn that those important events took place when "salvation" came (and there can be no doubt as to when *that* was), and "strength" from heaven ("ye shall receive power"), and "the kingdom of our God", which Peter proclaimed at Pentecost, when he used the "keys" thereof to open it to those who received the gospel; and "the power of His Christ", which was after His resurrection, when all power was given Him in heaven and on earth (Mat. 28:18). Then it was that the accuser of the brethren was cast down, who previously had accused them before our God day and night. And specially clear are the next words, which declare the ground and the means of victory over the great Adversary, namely, "the blood of the Lamb, and the word of their testimony". When once it is perceived that the casting out of Satan here recorded was coincident with the era wherein the people of God have overcome by the blood of the Lamb, and by the word of their testimony, all question as to the time of that event is removed. In full agreement with this is the word of this same John, "I write unto you, young men, because ye have *overcome the wicked one*. . . . I have written unto you, young men, because ye are strong, and the word of God abideth in you, and ye have *overcome the wicked one*" (1 J. 2:13, 14). The blood of the Lamb is what gives the victory; and the word of testimony, which is the confession of faith in the risen Christ of God upon His throne, is the weapon that the individual saint uses, and all he needs, in his conflict with the conquered foe. "Resist the Devil" with that weapon, and he will not stay to fight; "he will flee from you".

Verse 12 contains a call to rejoice, addressed to the heavens and them that dwell in them. This is grounded on what precedes, as shown by the connecting word, "therefore". The expression "they that dwell (or tabernacle in them" (the heavens) is not to be referred to the angels, or to the holy dead; for according to the New Testament way of speaking, the people of God are viewed as even now dwelling in heaven, their citizenship being there, and they being taught to regard themselves as "strangers and pilgrims on earth". It is said of them that they are raised up and seated together in heavenly places in Christ Jesus (Eph. 2:6), and that already they "are come to Mount Zion, and to the city of the living God, the heavenly Jerusalem"

The Two Signs in Heaven

(Heb. 12:22). Therefore, those here spoken of as they that dwell in the heavens are a class that is in contrast with the other class designated as "the inhabiters of the earth and of the sea", upon whom a woe is pronounced, because the Devil is come down *unto them,* having great wrath, because he knoweth that he hath but a short time".

The Dragon Persecuting the Woman

The scene now shifts back again to the earth; for at verse 13 we read:

"And when the dragon saw that he was cast unto the earth, he persecuted the woman which brought forth the Man child".

Here again is a statement which confirms the view that we have in this chapter a prophetic picture of the present dispensation; for it agrees perfectly with what history records of the activities of the Devil in the early part of the Christian era, and from time to time since. The story of the Israel of God from the beginning, and for long stretches of time, has been one of persecution; first from the Jews, then from imperial Rome, and lastly from Papal Rome, all those persecuting agencies being, of course, the instruments of the Devil. The object of all this malignant and bloody persecution was "the woman which brought forth the Man child"; and this goes to show the continuity of the company of God's people from century to century. It goes to show also that "the reproach of Christ" (which was known even in the days of Moses, Heb. 11:26) is ever the outcome of Satan's animosity.

Persecution, as an experience of the saints of God, dates from the early days of the Christian era. The Jews had been *oppressed* from time to time—not however because of faithfulness to the Lord, but the reverse—but there had been nothing in their history that could be described as "persecution". But soon after Christ ascended into heaven, the persecution of His people began. Saul of Tarsus was a leader in it, as he says in several places, "I persecuted the church of God" (1 Cor. 15:9). This again helps establish the time of this part of the vision.

Apparently the persecutions of the enemy have ceased in our day, and indeed for some centuries prior thereto. But it must not be supposed that the Devil's animosity towards the people of God is in anywise abated. He has learned, however, that persecutions do not accomplish the purpose of blotting out the testimony of the gospel, but rather the reverse. Therefore, he has wisely changed his tactics, and adopted other methods. This too was foreshown in the vision we are now studying, as will be seen shortly.

The Woman in the Wilderness
Revelation 12:14

"And to the woman were given two wings of a great eagle, that she might fly into the wilderness, into her place, where she is nourished for a time, and times, and half a time, from the face of the serpent" (v. 14).

Verse 14 resumes the course of the narrative where

it was interrupted at verse 6. For this vision embraces both sides of creation, showing events that were to take place simultaneously, some on the heavenly and some on the earthly side of things.

What is now added to the statement of verse 6 is that to the woman there were given two wings of a great eagle, that thereby she might *fly* into the place prepared for her in the wilderness. This speaks of divine help given the people of God to escape from their enemies, Satan's persecuting agents; and also of divine provision made for them during their sojourn in the enemy's country. There is much comfort in this, of which, however, if the passage be referred to a future dispensation, we lose the benefit. The significance of the eagle's wings becomes evident in the light of two passages in the Old Testament. The first is in Exodus 19:4, where God, speaking to the Israelites through Moses, says: "Ye have seen what I did unto the Egyptians, and how I bare you *on eagles' wings,* and brought you unto Myself". This was said of the people whose experiences were the Divinely ordained types and foreshadowing of the experiences of God's New Covenant people. Hence we should expect Divine interventions on behalf of the latter of just the sort which answer to the figurative expressions of Revelation 12:14.

The second is the following beautiful passage in Deuteronomy 32:10, 11:

"He found him (Jacob) in the desert land and in the waste howling wilderness. He led him about; He instructed him; He kept him as the apple of His eye. *As an eagle* stirreth up her nest, fluttereth over her young, spreadeth abroad *her wings,* taketh them, beareth them *on her wings;* so the Lord alone did lead him".

Also from Isaiah 40:31 we get the thought that the eagle's wings are the symbol of soaring strength and swiftness.

Particularly at the time of the destruction of Jerusalem and the desolation of Judea, the company of believers was furnished, so to speak, with the wings of a great eagle, whereby they were enabled to fly for safety far and wide "into the wilderness" of this world.

Other instances of this sort are recorded in the long and eventful history of the Kingdom of God; but it will suffice for our present purpose to recall that, in comparatively recent times, when the fires of persecution waxed hot in Europe, God provided a refuge where His people might be nourished from the face of the serpent in the "wilderness" of the Western Hemisphere, and that He supplied them with means to escape thither (eagles' wings).

A Change of Tactics

The next verse (15) indicates that, when the Dragon failed to accomplish his purpose of destroying the people of God and their testimony through violence, he adopted another method of attack. The verse reads:

"And the serpent cast out of his mouth water as a flood after the woman, that he might cause her to be carried away of the flood".

This picture is very significant. The figure of a flood is used in the Scriptures to represent overwhelming powers of destruction poured forth (Psa. 90:5; Dan. 9:26; Psa. 124:4, 5; Jer. 47:2). It is a most suitable figure, therefore, to picture the stupendous efforts put forth by the enemy to sweep away the people of God and their testimony by pouring forth a "flood" of heresies and false doctrines, such as gnosticism, pagan philosophy, and corrupted Judaism, in the early centuries, and Russellism, Spiritism, Christian Science, Modernism, Higher Criticism, and the like, in recent times. The statement that this "flood" was poured out of the mouth of the dragon clearly indicates that the figure symbolizes an eruption of false doctrines. For as the doctrine of Christ proceeds out of His mouth (Mat. 5:2) so it would be appropriate to represent Satanic doctrines as proceeding out of the dragon's mouth.

Such is the present method of Satanic attack; for there have been no violent or bloody persecutions of the saints of God for several centuries, but on the other hand these days are marked by a great outpouring of false teachings, and by the distressing fact that errors which, not long ago, were recognized by all as being antichristian, now flourish unrebuked within groups and circles once professedly sound and orthodox. So disastrous is the effect of this recent change within the various denominational bodies of Protestant Christendom, that the work of the gospel in pagan lands is well nigh paralyzed. To the intelligent heathen, like the Chinese, Japanese, and Mohammedans, "Christianity" is synonymous with western civilization. But to them western civilization is the breeder of ruinous wars, the parent of grasping commercialism, or rapacious covetousness, and of the very worst species of vice and debauchery. "Christian" England debauches the Chinese in the interest of the opium trade, and "Christian" America sells liquor to the Mohammedans, thus giving ground for the bitter gibe recently uttered by a Turkish statesman, who said, "America sends us spiritual and spiritous commodities, which we do not want". With pain it must be acknowledged the true Christianity is almost submerged in a "flood" of doctrines, which are essentially antichristian and spurious—far worse, indeed, than paganism.

But we are not to suppose that the enemy has permanently abandoned the ancient method of violence and persecution; for there may be another outbreak of that sort at any time. God has no doubt suppressed violent and bloody opposition to the gospel during the past century to the end that the various nations of earth might be evangelized, according to His plan (Mat. 24:14; Acts 1:8). Meanwhile the Devil's lust for blood finds ample gratification in the wars which "Christian" nations wage against each other; and he has reason to exult exceedingly in the part which "Christian" churches and "Christian" ministers take therein.

The next verse (16) says: "And the earth helped the woman, and the earth opened her mouth, and swallowed up the flood which the dragon cast out of his mouth". We regard this as a reference to the disappearance of many of those heresies (such as those against which Paul wrote in Colossians) which in the early days flooded the countries where the gospel was first preached. They have been swallowed up, so to speak, as if buried in the earth. Here again we must recognize a Divine intervention to prevent the testimoney of His few and feeble people from being completely submerged and swept away. Just what will be the result of the present outpourings of false teachings, destructive heresies, doctrines of demons, and the like, we cannot say definitely. But we have the assurance that God will be with His people, and will afford them all needful help and protection, until the moment comes for them to be taken out of the world (1 Thess. 4:14-17).

WAR WITH THE REMNANT OF THE WOMAN'S SEED

We come now to the last verse of the chapter. It speaks of another change of tactics on the part of the enemy. The verse reads:

"And the dragon was wroth with the woman, and went to make war with the remnant of her seed, which keep the commandments of God, and have the testimony of Jesus Christ" (Rev. 12:17).

The "enmity" decreed in Genesis 3:15 was to be between the serpent and the woman, and between its seed and her seed. It might seem that in the sense of the verse last quoted we could not make a distinction between the woman and her seed. But the meaning can be readily understood in the light of the fact that the Scriptures of the prophets frequently speak of Israel or Zion as a woman, and of individual Israelites as the "children" of Israel, or Zion (see Isa. 54:13). So here we take the woman to represent, throughout the chapter, the "holy nation", the Israel of God, composed of all the saints on earth at any one time, and "the remnant of her seed" to be the comparatively few individual believers who are left to bear testimony to the truth in the last days.

For the chapter gives a very rapid survey of the progress of the Divinely decreed "enmity" between the serpent and the woman; and the last verse indicates that the Adversary, having failed to extinguish the light of Christianity by means of his "flood" of satanic heresies and doctrines of demons (1 Tim. 4:1), now puts forth his mighty powers for a last supreme effort against the purpose of God.

The main design of the vision of Chapter XII is seemingly to conduct us rapidly to the very last stage of the great conflict, which is presented by the vision of the two wild beasts of Chapter XIII, supplemented as to important details by subsequent visions. For whereas each scene in Chapter XII is described with greatest brevity, and long eras of time are compressed into a few sentences, when we come to Chapter XIII, the description becomes detailed and specific. This shows that what went before was simply leading up to this scene, and was given in order that this picture of the last phase of satanic opposition to God's purpose with respect to the Kingdoms of this world, might be set before us in its true relation to all the great events of human history from the very beginning of time.

The last verse defines the Lord's people as those who "keep the commandments of God, and have the testimony of Jesus Christ". The first part of this definition is very significant, as showing what God expects in His redeemed people, and what should distinguish them in the last days, which are specially to be characterized by lawlessness (11:3). Those who "obey the gospel" are the "children of obedience"; that is to say, they obey from the heart that pattern of doctrine which has been delivered to them in the N. T. Scriptures, and they serve God in a new and willing spirit (Rom. 6:17; 7:6). This is not to be taken in the strictest sense, as if there were any, even among the most devoted servants of God, in whom He saw no faults. But on the other hand, it is certain that among the changes wrought in those who receive the new birth, there comes the spirit of obedience, taking the form of a desire to do the will of Him who has called them unto His eternal kingdom and glory.

CHAPTER IX

The Vision of the Two Wild Beasts

"And I stood upon the sand of the sea, and saw a beast rise up out of the sea, having seven heads and ten horns, and upon his horns ten crowns, and upon his heads the name of blasphemy. And the beast which I saw was like unto a leopard, and his feet were as the feet of a bear, and his mouth as the mouth of a lion: and the dragon gave him his power, and his seat, and great authority".

LET it be remembered that what is now to be shown us are the various phases of the *last stage* of the conflict between God and Satan, whereof the outcome was announced in the words of the great voices in heaven: "The kingdoms of this world are become the kingdoms of our Lord and of His Christ" (11:15). We have already had pictured to us one of the actors in that final scene, the great red dragon. The chapter to which we are now come brings two other prominent actors into view, the ten-horned beast that arose out of the sea (v. 1) and the two-horned beast that arose out of the earth (v. 11). The first of these beasts appears again in Chapter XVII, where a woman arrayed in purple and scarlet, and lavishly adorned with gold and jewels, is seen seated upon it. (Note the contrast between this woman and the woman clothed with the sun of Chapter 12:7). The beast is mentioned again in Chapter XIX, in association with "the false prophet", which the text clearly identifies with the second or two-horned beast. These are here associated also with "the kings of the earth and their armies", who are gathered together for the last battle against Christ and the armies of heaven, the outcome of which is that both the beast and the false prophet are taken, and are cast alive into a lake of fire, burning with brimstone (19:19-21). From this it is clear that the history of these two beasts, as pictured in the visions of the Apocalypse, extends to the nineteenth chapter; and that at the end of that chapter is given the picture of the *very last* struggle in the long conflict, whereof the issue was announced by the great voices in heaven. These preliminary remarks will inform the reader of the general subject of these chapters, and prepare his mind for an examination of their contents in detail.

In the light of Scripture, particularly that of the fundamental prophecy of Daniel VII, wild beasts are the symbols of great world empires, or rather, of the *governmental systems* thereof. These may differ among themselves, much as wild beasts differ from one another in minor respects, though they are all of the same nature. The appropriateness of this symbol lies not in any "beastliness" inherent in the chief governments of the world; but in characteristics of quite a different sort, as strength, courage, ferocity, agility, crushing power, and the like. The wild beasts of Daniel's prophecy, as well as those of the one now before us, were the lion, the bear, the leopard (or panther), and a fourth beast of nondescript character, not found in the realm of nature. The three that are named are beasts whose character is noble rather than despicable. But what most prominently characterizes all the beasts of the earth, as distinguished from men outwardly, is their *downward look,* suggesting a mind that is wholly engrossed by the things of earth. Such are characteristically "the kingdoms of this world".

The first beast seen by John is a composite symbol, for it combines in the one creature the features of the four beasts which came *successively* into view in Daniel's vision. This quite plainly indicates that it symbolizes *the ungodly governmental power of the world in general.* It presents in one figure a summary view of *the whole of beast government* in its main stages, from the beginning of Gentile history down to the end of time. It is important that this be kept in mind in the study of these last visions.

Hengstenberg puts the matter clearly, saying:

"The arrangement of the section before us is the following: We are presented first (Chap. 13:1, 2) with a full delineation of the enemy, in which his *past, present* and *future* history are brought together precisely as in the case of the first enemy (the dragon). Respect is had to the past, *in order to set the present in its true light.* The prophet sees a beast with seven heads and ten horns rise out of the sea, to which the dragon gives his strength, and his throne, and great power. Under this symbol is represented the God-opposing power of this world in its seven phases, the seven being again subdivided". He also refers to the fact that whereas in the prophecy of Daniel VII "the plurality of the world powers is exhibited by a *succession* of different beasts, here only *one beast* appears on the scene, combining the properties of all the beasts of Daniel".

Attention should be given to the statement that the dragon gave to this beast his power, and his seat (throne), and great authority. That is to say, this beast receives from Satan what Christ refused to accept from him, when the tempter offered Him all the kingdoms of this world, and the glory of them (Mat. 4:8-10).

These beast governments serve a useful, indeed an indispensable, purpose to society in general; for without a system of government, strong enough to command respect both at home and abroad, the condition of the people would be one of intolerable misery. It would be a state of anarchy. On the other hand, they accomplish the purposes of God in the chastisement of the nations that have refused obedience to His anointed King. This purpose of God is seen in such passages as Jeremiah 5:6, where, in warning the people of Israel of the punishments He would bring upon them, He said: "Wherefore a *lion* out of the forest shall slay them, and a *wolf* of the deserts shall spoil them, a *leopard* shall watch over their cities; . . . because their transgressions are many and their backslidings are increased". This punishment came speedily upon them; for they were soon thereafter delivered over to the Babylonian Empire, which is pictured in Daniel's prophecy as a *lion;* and now they are under the various forms of beast government that exist in the world.

As regards the circumstance that this first beast arose out of the sea (whereas the other arose out of the earth) I would recall that the sea is a symbol of the restless nations in general (17:15). It suggests "the restless, stirring agitation that characterizes all that are out of God's kingdom" (Havernick). The symbol conveys the idea of the *multitudinous* nations of earth ("peoples and *multitudes*") and also their perpetual *unrest*. For "there is no peace to the wicked"; they are like "the *troubled* sea when it cannot rest" (Isa. 57:20).

For the purpose of viewing this new scene, John is placed in a new position: "And I stood upon the sand of the sea". Another reading, equally well supported as that of the A. V., has *"he* (the dragon) stood". But I conclude with Hengstenberg that "the internal grounds are in favor of John's being the subject of the discourse". There is no question but that the verb "saw" has John for its subject. Therefore, there must have been a change of position on the part of the seer. This view has also the support of the analogous vision of Daniel, who says, "And I saw in a vision, and I was by the river Ulai" (8:2); and again, "I was by the side of the great river, . . . then I lifted up mine eyes and looked" (10:4).

The phrase "sand of the sea" is not used in Scripture to describe the *shore* of the sea, but to convey the idea of an enormous multitude of people (Gen. 22:17; 41:49; Judg. 7:12; 1 K. 4:20; Job 29:18; Ps. 78:27; Jer. 33:22; Heb. 11:12, etc., etc.). "The sand is specified here because it suggests the thought of the innumerable multitude of the inhabitants of the earth over whom the beast was to exert an influence" (Hengstenberg).

The prophecy of Isaiah 27:1 has a direct application here: "In that day the Lord, with His sore and great and strong sword, will punish *leviathan* the slant *serpent,* and leviathan the tortuous *serpent;* and He will slay *the dragon that is in the sea*" (Jewish V.). It is "that day" of the punishment of this leviathan of the sea, who is here also identified with the *serpent,* and the *dragon,* to which this present vision brings us. We must be careful to observe, however, that, as the manner of the Book is, we are first *taken back to the time past,* and are shown the origin of Gentile world-government, even as Daniel saw it in his day, arising out of the sea, figuratively speaking; and from that point are led rapidly to the last scene of all in the history of the beast, which it is the main purpose of the vision to reveal. Hengstenberg puts the matter clearly when he says:

"What in reality has existed already for a long time, may be seen in vision rising into existence as it were anew, if the object is to give *a summary view of the whole manifestation.* Thus, the first of the four beasts which Daniel saw in the act of rising out of the sea, denotes a kingdom (the Chaldean) which had in fact *for a long time already occupied a place upon the stage of history.* True it is that the past as such is not the subject of what is testified in the Revelation; but that it may nevertheless be drawn into the sphere embraced by the vision, on account of its connection with the present and the future, is abundantly plain from Chapter XII".

The purpose of the visions of this present group clearly is to exhibit the *final form* and the *very end* of "the mystery of iniquity", which here is presented in the completeness of its embodiment in that trinity of evil, the dragon, the beast out of the sea, and the beast out of the earth. But the apostle Paul in his day made it known that the mystery of iniquity was already working, and that it would continue to work until a time when "that Wicked one" should be revealed, "whom the Lord shall consume with the spirit of His mouth, and shall destroy with the brightness of His coming" (2 Thess. 2:7, 8; cf. Rev. 19:15, 20, 21).

In John's vision the beasts forming the composite symbol are named in the reverse order to that in which they successively appeared to Daniel. To the latter the ten-horned monster (Rome) was the last of the four. But in John's vision it is the first; and then is named the leopard (Greece), then the bear (Medo-Persia), and lastly the lion (Babylon), which in Daniel's vision was the first. A simple explanation of this reversal of the order of the beasts suggests itself in the fact that whereas Daniel viewed the picture of world-government from the time of the dominion of *the lion,* in which he lived, and thence as stretching off into the future, John on the contrary viewed it in the period of the *fourth beast,* and thence as stretching backward in time to the days of Babylon. Thus Daniel's fourth beast, which to him was in the distant future, has now, in John's day, come into the foreground;

The Vision of the Two Wild Beasts

and the dominion of Babylon, present in Daniel's day, has receded into the distant past. In other words, the beast that was nearest to Daniel was furthest from John, and *vice versa*.

The Heads and the Horns. The first feature of this beast to which attention is directed is that it had seven heads and ten horns. The heads represent the successive phases assumed by the Gentile world-government from the beginning of history to the end. That is to say, the succession of world governments, which was represented in Daniel's vision by *four beasts* that appeared one after the other, is here represented by the *seven heads*. The proof of this will be shown presently; but it is desirable that first the thought be clearly grasped. The succession of world empires, one following and displacing another, could not be shown by a succession of beasts in this vision, for Gentile world government *as a whole* is here pictured by a *single* beast of composite character. But that fact of succession is too important to be omitted, and therefore other symbols must be used to express it. And not only so, but whereas Daniel's vision was concerned with only the *four* Gentile powers that were to have dominion successively over his people (the Jews), the design of the present vision is to show the totality of Gentile government; and hence the *seven* heads, seven being the signature of completeness.

An analogy is presented by the vision of the colossal metallic figure described in Daniel II. There the four empires which were to figure in the history of Israel from that day on to its overthrow as a nation, were all represented in a single image, as here in a single beast. So that, as the eye traversed the image from head to foot, it surveyed the several empires that were to follow one another in the years to come; and so likewise in John's vision, as the eye passes from one of the seven heads to another, it surveys Gentile world dominion from its beginning to its end.

Two points are to be noted ere we pass on: *First,* we are not to think of the beast as having seven heads *all at the same time;* for while they are *seen* all at once, even as the several parts of Nebuchadnezzar's image were seen all at once, the kingdoms which they severally represent succeeded each other in history. *Second,* it follows that the ten horns all appertain to the last head; for *they* do all exist at the same time, as appears from Chapter 17:12, 16.

Now for the meaning of the seven heads, we turn to Chapter 17:9-11, which reads as follows:

"And here is the mind which hath wisdom. The seven heads are seven mountains, on which the woman sitteth. And there are seven kings: five are fallen, and one is, and the other is not yet come; and when he cometh, he must continue a short space. And the beast that was, and is not, even he is the eighth, and is of the seven, and goeth into perdition" (vv. 9-11).

The matter here presented is one calling for the exercise of spiritual discernment, as is evident from the words, "Here is the mind that hath wisdom". Then follows the statement, "The seven heads are seven mountains"; and this explains what is symbolized by

The Vision of the Two Wild Beasts

the seven heads; for as we have already shown, mountains in Scripture symbolize great nations. Moreover, two of the nations that are represented in the O. T. as mountains, are identified as Babylon and Medo-Persia; and this makes it easy for us to identify the other five. For verse 10 informs us that in John's day five of those kings (or kingdoms) had already fallen, one (the sixth) was then in existence ("one is"), and the other (the seventh and last) was "not yet come". Here is information that we should fix clearly in our minds, namely, (1) that the Roman Empire, under which John was living when he wrote this description, was the sixth in the succession of seven Gentile world kingdoms; and (2) that another was to follow, which should be the last, and which should have but a short term of existence. This last of the seven is an object of special interest in our present study; for it is that kingdom which comes into collision with Christ and the armies of heaven in the final conflict (19: 11-21).

Verse 11 is somewhat enigmatical. It states concerning the beast itself that "even he is the (or rather *an*) eighth, and is of the seven, and goeth into perdition". I have seen various attempts at explaining this verse; but to my mind they left the subject even more obscure than they found it. But the explanation given by Dr. Hengstenberg is simple and satisfactory. Strictly speaking, the beast could not exist apart from one of its seven heads, and hence, when the seventh head is destroyed, it being the last, the beast itself would cease to exist. Yet in representing the totality of Gentile world-rule pictorially, we have to view the beast as having an *ideal* existence *apart from its heads;* and therefore, in order to express the idea that not only does the seventh head, the last world power, go into perdition, but that *human world government in its entirety* is to be finally disposed of; it is stated also that the beast itself likewise "goeth into perdition". The beast itself is obviously "of the seven", for it has been at one time identified with each; and it is also "an eighth", in that it shares the fate of the seven heads.

Having identified the Roman Empire as the sixth head, it is easy to identify the five that preceded it. Daniel (Chapters VII and VIII) shows that three of them (counting backwards) were Greece, Persia, and Babylon; and other passages of the O. T. make it plain that the other two were (still counting backwards) Assyria and Egypt. For the Israel of God, in its total life history from the days of Abraham, Isaac and Jacob, has up to now come into contact with, and, has been in subjection to, these six powers successively, Egypt, Assyria, Babylon, Persia, Greece, and Rome; leaving *but one more,* the seventh, to make that history of oppression and subjection full and complete. For the establishing of this last statement it will suffice to refer to the following Scriptures: "For thus saith the Lord of hosts, My people went down aforetime into *Egypt,* and the *Assyrian* oppressed them without cause" (Isa. 52:4). This was a divine summary of the nations that had oppressed Israel up to that time, and it was spoken in view of the *then approaching Babylonian oppression* (see also Isa. 10:24-26; and 27:13; Hos. 9:3, and 11:11). In Zechariah 10:10, 11, Egypt and Assyria are used as types of the oppressors of the latter times.

The Ten Horns. We have seen that a horn represents power, and especially a kingdom, not necessarily an empire or world power, but usually a minor nation. But here again the explanation is given us; for in Chapter 17:12 is the statement: "And the ten horns which thou sawest are ten kings, which have received no kingdom as yet". The latter clause shows that those kingdoms had not come into being in John's day; and what follows places their existence in the very time of the end: "But receive power as kings one hour *with the beast* . . . These shall *make war with the Lamb, and the Lamb shall overcome them*" (vv. 12-14). They are mentioned again in association with the beast on the eve of the final battle (19:19). This is a matter of peculiar interest to ourselves at the present moment, when the events of world politics are rapidly assuming a form, and taking a direction, that make the last embodiment of world empire, the seventh head, with its associated kingdoms, a possibility of the very near future.

THE HEAD THAT RECEIVED THE DEADLY WOUND

"And I saw one of his heads, as it were wounded to death; and his deadly wound was healed: and all the world wondered after the beast. And they worshipped the dragon which gave power unto the beast: and they worshipped the beast, saying,

Who is like unto the beast? who is able to make war with him?" (13:3, 4).

Close examination of the text leads to the conclusion that the wound was a thing of the past when the beast came into John's view. The parallel expression is "a Lamb as it had been slain" (5:6). The beast had already received the death-stroke, and yet lived again, when John first saw it. Much is made of this matter; for in verses 12 and 14, reference is made to "the beast which had the wound with the sword and did live"; and it should be noted that what is said in verse 3 of "one of its heads" is said in verses 12 and 14 of *the beast itself*, showing that the beast is identified with *one head at a time*.

This important event in the career of the beast comes to view again in Chapter 17:8, in the words, "was, and is not, and shall ascend out of the bottomless pit, and go into perdition". Thus the stroke is regarded as having put the beast to death; and its revival is viewed as a coming up again out of the abyss. Further the importance of this episode is emphasized by the threefold repetition of the words, "was, and is not, and yet is" (vv. 8 and 11). These verses show also that it was the sixth head that received the death stroke.

To what then does this refer? Considering the great importance given to this death wound of the beast, the fact that it was something that had already taken place when John saw the vision, and the further fact especially that the dragon and the beasts are so closely identified as to be virtually one (v. 2), it is clear that the death stroke referred to could have been nothing else than that which befell the dragon and all that is associated with him through the death of Jesus Christ. It is another pictorial representation of the truth that our Lord *by death* destroyed him that had the power of death (Heb. 2:14); or as another Scripture that speaks of Christ and the cross puts it, "having *slain* the enmity thereby" (Eph. 2:16). This latter passage is seen to be specially pertinent when it is observed that the phrase "as wounded to death" in Revelation 13:3, is literally "as *slain* to death" (see margin). According to the words of the Lord, recorded by this same John, the cross was the stroke of judgment upon the prince of this world. It is most fitting then that this vision should display conspicuously the effect of the cross of Christ upon the Devil *in his character of world ruler*.

Let us dwell a little upon this matter; for not only is the truth involved therein of supreme importance, but moreover it is needful, for the proper understanding of the vision as a whole, that we should be quite clear as to what that death stroke was, from which the beast so miraculously revived.

In the early days of imperial Rome (the beginning of the stage of the sixth head of the beast) Jesus, God's Christ and King, to Whom the sceptre of the world is promised, was born. He proclaimed to the Jews the coming of the long-promised Kingdom of God, and testified that it was at hand. But He was rejected, was delivered up to the power of the beast, and was put to death; both Jews and Gentiles taking part in that deed. Thus was fulfilled, as the Scripture itself declares (Acts 4:25-28), the first part of the prophecy of the second Psalm: "The kings of the earth set themselves (in array), and the rulers take counsel together, against the Lord, and against His Anointed". And thereupon His body was laid in a tomb, the mouth of which was closed with a great stone, and which was sealed and guarded. But He burst the tomb. He triumphed over principalities and powers; He made a show of them *openly;* He was enthroned in heaven far above them; they were one and all "made subject to Him". Now the Scriptures represent this triumph of Christ as being a *death blow* to the governmental authority or lordship of Satan, the one who has "the power of death" (Heb. 2:14, 15). Here we have the bruising of his *head* (Gen. 3:15), a subject which properly follows in the line of events pictured in Chapter XII. Here also is fulfilled the prophecy of Hosea 13:10-14: "I will be *thy King,* where is there any other that can *save thee?* I will ransom thee from the power of the grave. I will redeem thee from death".

Why then was not the beast government brought to an immediate end? It would be natural to expect that, after a victory so complete, the great dragon enemy would be at once stripped of all authority and put where he could do no further harm. Such was the expectation of the disciples, when the Lord came back to them a Victor over death and the grave; for they

The Vision of the Two Wild Beasts

asked Him, "Lord, wilt thou at this time restore again the kingdom to Israel?" (Ac. 1:6). And we cannot wonder that they should have asked that question, and should have expected an affirmative answer. For as yet the Holy Spirit had not come upon them and enlightened them as to the truth of the Kingdom of God. They were still ignorant of "the mystery of Christ; . . . that the Gentiles were to be fellow heirs, and of the same body, and partakers of God's promise in Christ by means of the gospel" (Eph. 3:4-6). They did not know that, according to "the mystery of godliness", Christ must be not only "manifested in the flesh, justified in the Spirit and seen of angels", but must also be "preached unto *the Gentiles* and believed on *in the world*" (1 Tim. 3:16). They were as yet "ignorant of this mystery, that blindness in part was happened to Israel", and was to last "until the fulness of *the Gentiles be come in*" (Rom. 11:25). So likewise were they ignorant of "the mystery of iniquity", that the Devil was to be permitted to sow his tares in every part of the field where the good seed of the gospel should be sown; and that the beast government would survive the deadly wound, as by a miracle, and would continue in control of the world for many centuries. This long interval of "mystery" between the victory of the cross and the overthrow of the beast that received the death-stroke, that long period of waiting and suffering on the part of Christ's true people, is the era of "the Kingdom and *patience* of Jesus Christ" (Rev. 1:9). This is recalled at 13:10, by the words,

"Here is the patience and the faith of the saints"; and again at 14:12 by the words: "Here is the patience of the saints".

Commenting on the passage we are now studying Hengstenberg says:

> "Whatever destroys the power of the dragon must also be fatal to the beast. But the victory of Christ affected the ungodly power of Rome not as such, but only as a part of the ungodly power of the world in general. All other discomfitures save this one only bore but a partial character; they could but affect a single head of the beast, and not the beast as a whole. This however, is the one event in the world's history by which the whole beast was smitten in the one head; for in former times the overthrow of one head was immediately followed by the rising up of another. From what has been said, the beast must already have existed at the time of our Lord's death. For, by means of the atonement then effected, one of his heads was wounded to death. This alone serves to refute those who would understand by the beast a power that did not arise until a much later period—the Papacy".

If then the prince of this world was crushingly defeated, and the governmental system to which he had given "his power and his throne and great authority", received a mortal wound by the cross, what a marvel that it should have lived again, and waxed mighty, and have even been enabled "to make war with the saints and to overcome them", and to exercise power "over all kindreds, and tongues, and nations"! (v. 7). It is not surprising that "all the world wondered after the beast, and worshipped the dragon that gave power to the beast". "The wondering astonishment with which the earth follows the beast comes not merely in spite of the *death,* but also *on account of the healing"* (Hengstenberg). "Nothing", says Zullig, "awoke more astonishment and greater faith in respect to the Messiah, than His resurrection after He had been killed. And it was not otherwise in the case of the beast, the earthly power of heathendom". Not that the masses of people realized what they were doing, or rendered this worship to the dragon and the beast consciously. For, as remarked by Bengel:

"Those who regarded the beast as worthy of admiration, at the same time worshipped the dragon without being themselves conscious of it. This was very agreeable to the dragon. Those who despise the Son of God despise also the Father, though they be not aware of it. And there is the same connection on the other side in regard to the beast and the dragon".

A parallel case is noted in 1 Corinthians 10:19, 20, where the apostle says that the Gentiles who offer sacrifices to idols, "sacrifice to devils"; though, of course, they are unaware of what they are doing.

Those who worshipped the beast did homage to him by saying, *"who is like unto the beast? Who is able to make war with him"?* Now the property of being incomparable belongs to God only. Hence the first question is a blasphemous application to the beast of the question that God asks, "To whom then will ye liken Me?" (Isa. 40:25). In the second question we see a mocking reference to the war in heaven of the preceding chapter. For just as there was a great shout of rejoicing in heaven when Michael and his angels prevailed over the dragon and his hosts, so now there is a jubilant cry on earth because of the invincibility attributed to the beast, to whom it was given "to make war with the saints and to overcome them" (v. 7). This refers, of course, to the fierce and bloody persecutions of the people of God by Imperial Rome. History records ten such persecutions, beginning with that in Nero's reign (A. D. 64-68), the last being under Diocletian (303-313). That trial was to be so severe that all save those whose names were written in the Lamb's book of life would yield to the pressure and worship the beast; and inasmuch as the worship of the Roman Emperors was made compulsory in those days, and was enforced under penalty of torture and death, there is little room for doubt as to the manner and time of the fulfilment of this prophecy. On this Hengstenberg remarks:

"Since the book of life is unreservedly ascribed to the Lamb that was slain, all salvation, not excepting that of the saints of the Old Testament, is thus represented as depending on the one sacrifice of Christ".

That the matter here presented is of high consequence is evident from verses 9 and 10, and specially from the words, "If any man have an ear, let him hear". Those words also imply that the truth which is here presented is a hard one to receive. It would seem as if the beast were indeed invincible, and were to continue indefinitely carrying everything before him. So God at this point introduces a strong and definite assurance as to the final outcome. *"He that leadeth into captivity, shall go into captivity"*. This is fulfilled

The Vision of the Two Wild Beasts

at Chapter 20:1-3, where Satan is bound in the bottomless pit for a thousand years. *"He that killeth with the sword, must be killed with the sword"*. This is fulfilled at Chapter 19:15-21, where Christ appears and smites the enemy with the sword that proceedeth out of His mouth. The words, *"Here is the patience and the faith of the saints"*, are equivalent to saying that God's saints will receive these assurances in *faith,* and will gain therefrom power to *endure,* whatever afflictions may fall to their lot.

"And there was given unto him a mouth speaking great things and blasphemies; and power was given unto him to continue forty and two months. And he opened his mouth in blasphemy against God, to blaspheme his name, and his tabernacle, and them that dwell in heaven" (vv. 5, 6).

There is comfort in the fact that the power given to the beast is not of unlimited, nor of indefinite duration. The length thereof is definitely fixed; though here again we have to realize and confess our ignorance concerning spiritual measurements of time and space. The words "it was *given* unto him", which occur three times in verses 5-7, also convey the comforting assurance that the beast can do nothing but what is permitted him to do. God holds the situation in hand at all times. Indeed He has declared in advance both the limit of the beast's power, and the length of time he is to exercise it. As to the mouth speaking great things and blasphemies, history abounds in instances of the promulgation, by the ungodly world power, particularly in the stage of the 6th head (the

Roman Empire) of laws and decrees adverse to God and His people. All such are in themselves "great things", and in their moral character, as being contrary to God, "blasphemies".

THE SECOND BEAST

Thus far the career of the first beast alone. But now a companion beast appears upon the scene, of which the following is the description:

> "And I beheld another beast coming up out of the earth; and he had two horns like a lamb, and he spake as a dragon. And he exerciseth all the power of the first beast before him, and causeth the earth and them which dwell therein to worship the first beast, whose deadly wound was healed" (vv. 11, 12).

The fact that the first beast represents a system of world-government gives strong reason for taking the second beast to represent something of like nature; for the symbol being the same, the thing symbolized must be the same. This second beast has identifying marks of a very striking character. In the first place, it comes into the closest association with the first beast, and continues along with it to the end, when both perish together (19:20). We should therefore inquire whether there has been anything in the nature of a political system that arose "out of the earth" (the ordered part of the world) during the continuance of the Roman Empire; that came into intimate union therewith; and that has continued in that intimacy until now? And if such there be, then we should inquire further, does it correspond with the identifying marks here given for our enlightenment? To these questions, every one who has the slightest acquaintance with history will say, there *has* been such a system; for beyond a doubt, *Romanism* did arise during the course of existence of the Roman Empire; it is a system of religious character and political aim; and it has been, from the very beginning, closely identified with the nations composing the Roman Empire. Moreover, it corresponds with what is said in the text concerning the second beast.

In commenting upon the preceding visions of the trumpet series, I mentioned the fact that in this gospel dispensation the Israel of God has been opposed by three great systems, that have arisen at different times, and under divers circumstances, each of which was of a definitely, not to say fanatically, religious character, each of which was animated by the very same political ambition, namely, to possess the dominion of the earth, and each severally claiming the authority of Almighty God in support of their pretensions. The first two, Judaism and Islamism, have been considered. And now we come to the last and most formidable, Romanism. It is a fact of immense significance that what these three great systems have in common, namely, the purpose to seize the dominion of the world, is precisely the aim of the Devil himself. From this it may be certainly deduced that each of them is but an instrument of the great Adversary. Now it has been made abundantly evident that the visions of the trumpet series have to do with the age-long conflict concerning the kingdom of this world; and such being the case, those visions must be occupied mainly with the hostile doings of the three great Satanic systems. This view receives strong confirmation in the fact that the symbols of the first group of four trumpets correspond closely with Judaism, and those of the next group of two with Mohammedanism. From this it would be a well-nigh inevitable conclusion that the symbols of the seventh trumpet should reveal the career and end of Romanism. Indeed, the view herein presented of the trumpet series, which is divinely divided into just three groups, so clearly explains that series in its entirety, in its several groups, and in its individual visions, as to be practically self-authenticating; even as the correct solution of an intricate problem proves itself, seeing that none but the right one could explain every detail.

It is a matter of moment that Romanism arose in a manner *essentially different from the other two systems of evil;* for whereas they appeared in open antagonism to the faith of Jesus Christ, it presented itself as the embodiment, and as the only embodiment, of true christianity, as the veritable and only kingdom of God. Here we have "the depths of Satan" (2:24). The bearing of this fact upon the question of interpretation is most important. For if the design of the trumpet series was indeed to exhibit the whole conflict between the people of God and the three politico-religious systems that have disputed the ground with them, then the vision that shows the rise of Romanism will present a marked difference from the other visions corresponding to this difference of origin. How very important then is the fact that precisely such a characteristic difference appears in the vision of the second beast! For how could the remarkably peculiar manner in which Romanism came into existence (in close alliance from the very start with the Roman Empire), be more appropriately symbolized than by the picture of a beast *coming up out of the earth, in guise like a lamb, but speaking as a dragon, and exercising all the power of the first beast before him?*

The first descriptive item is the phrase, "coming up out of *the earth*", this being in manifestly intentional contrast with the statement that the first beast arose "out of *the sea*" (v. 7). And what are the historical facts? The Roman Empire itself arose out of the tumultuous and restless sea of the multitudinous nations; whereas the Papacy, as a political system, arose out of the stabilized part of the world, in fact, in the very heart of the Roman Empire itself. So closely have they been identified from the beginning, that the capital city of the Empire has been also the seat of the Papacy.

The root of that system of mystery can easily be traced to the emperor Constantine who, in 323, after professing conversion to christianity, and giving as the cause thereof a pretended vision of a cross suspended above the sun with the legend surrounding it "In this sign conquer", made christianity the state religion, even compelling his pagan soldiers to be baptized, whole regiments at a time. Dr. Greene sums up the situation (speaking of the state of the Roman Empire at the death of Licinius in 323) in these words: "For good or for evil, Constantine now held undisputed sovereignty over that mighty realm, which his word of command was soon to transform into a nominal *Christendom*" (*Handbook of Church History*, pg.93). Here the Kingdom of God came first into favor, and then into alliance, with the beast-government of the world; and the result was disastrous alike to both faith and morals. But our present concern is solely with the rise and development of Romanism as a *political* system. Another stage therein was reached when the western half of the Roman Empire fell to Odoacer, A. D. 475, whereby the influence of the Bishop of Rome was incidentally augmented. That influence continued to increase slowly until, in the hands of Gregory, surnamed "the Great" (590-604), it became well-nigh supreme throughout Christendom in ecclesiastical matters. The claim to temporal dominion, however, was not advanced until several centuries later. It first took concrete shape in the days of Hildebrand (latter part of the eleventh century). The manner in which it was first asserted appears in the following extract from a letter which Pope Gregory VII (Hildebrand) addressed to William I of England (William the Conqueror):

"Like the two great luminaries fixed by the Creator in the firmament of the heaven to give light to His creatures, so also hath He ordained two great powers on earth, by which all are to be governed and preserved from error. Those powers are

The Vision of the Two Wild Beasts 415

the *pontifical* and the *royal;* but the former is the *greater,* the latter the *lesser* light. Yet under both, the religion of Christ is so ordered that, by God's assistance, the *apostolical power* shall govern *the royal;* and Scripture teacheth that the apostolical and pontifical dignity is ordained to be responsible for all Christian Kings, nay for all men, before the divine tribunal". And on these grounds the Pontiff demanded of King William "upon the peril of his soul", to render to him "unconditional obedience" (Henderson's *Select Historical Documents of the Middle Ages.* Bohn's ed. 1896).

The reference by the Pope to the two great luminaries is remarkable indeed, in that he uses the very imagery of Revelation 12:1 in presenting his arrogant demand, attempting, so to speak, to occupy the place of the sun-clothed woman, to clothe *himself* with the sun, and to put the moon under his own feet. It will be observed that at the date of that letter the Pope still distinguished the royal power from the pontifical, claiming for himself only the latter. King William curtly "refused to do fealty"; and King Philip of France simply ignored the claim of the Pope to a power superior to the royal. But successive popes persisted in the claim, taking advantage of every turn in the political affairs of Europe to strengthen themselves in the assertion of it, until in 1198 Innocent III designated himself, as none of his predecessors had presumed to do, "the representative of God on earth". The claims of the Papacy were carried to their extremest limit by Boniface VIII (1294-1303). As to the doings of that pontiff, Dr. Green's History contains the following (p. 468):

"At his inauguration two kings held his stirrups. He proclaimed a Jubilee for the year 1300. . . . It is credibly reported that in the course of the proceedings, he appeared before the multitude on one day in his pontificals, on another with sword, crown and sceptre, exclaiming, '*I am Caesar! I am Emperor!*' This same Boniface issued a famous Bull *(Unam Sanctam)* in which with marvellous exegesis, he quoted the words of the disciples regarding the 'two swords' (Lu. 22:38), saying: 'Both swords, the spiritual and the temporal are in the power of the Church'. That Bull further explicitly declares that 'there is one holy catholic and apostolic Church, outside of which there is no salvation or remission of sins. We declare, announce and define, that it is *altogether necessary to salvation for every human creature to be subject to the Roman pontiff*' ".

This is not only the most blasphemous pretension a mortal man could make, but (and this is more to the purpose of our present study) it is an audacious attempt to make the salvation of God, which He has freely proclaimed to all men upon the simple condition of faith in Jesus Christ, the means of advancing the claim of the Papacy to supreme earthly dominion. At this date (about 1300) the Papacy was at its height.

Coming back now to the text, it will be easily seen that the words, "he had two horns like a lamb, and he spake as a dragon", fitly summarize the great outstanding facts concerning the Papacy: (1) that the occupant of the papal chair assumed the guise of a representative of Jesus Christ, which is the basis of his entire pretensions; (2) that inwardly as shown by the voice, which proceeds from within, his purpose is identically that of the dragon himself, namely, to seize and hold the dominion of the earth. The fundamental

Scripture on which this reference is based is Matthew 7:15, where we have the warning of Christ, "Beware of *false prophets*"— and this beast is called in Chapter 16:3, and 19:20, *the* false prophet—"which come to you *in sheep's clothing*", that is to say, outwardly like a lamb, "but INWARDLY they are ravening wolves".

Verse 12 states that "he exerciseth all the power of the first beast before him"; and surely it would be exceedingly difficult in any other sentence of equal brevity to set forth so clearly the historical fact that all the powers of the state were exercised by the Papacy, *while the kings and their ministers of state continued to exist, and nominally to discharge their official duties.* The last part of the verse is appropriately to be referred to the worship demanded by the popes and their personal representatives (papal legates). Bengel remarks: "What the first beast has power to do, this other does in his name, since the first can no longer take the business in hand, although his power in itself still continues".

In the vision of Daniel VII, which tallies closely with this one, the appearance of another power during the era of the fourth beast (which by practically all commentators is taken as symbolizing the Roman Empire) is plainly indicated by the words:

"I considered the horns, and behold, there came up among them *another little horn,* before whom were three of the first horns plucked up by the roots; and behold, in this horn were eyes, like the eyes of a man, and a mouth speaking great things" (Dan. 7:8).

In the explanation of the vision given by the revealing angel, this occurs:

> "And the ten horns out of this kingdom are ten kings that shall arise: and another shall arise after them; and he shall be diverse from the first, and shall subdue three kings. And he shall speak great words against the Most High, and wear out the saints of the Most High; and they shall be given into his hand until a time, and times, and the dividing of time" (vv. 24, 25).

I do not undertake to explain the details of this prophecy. Its close resemblance to that of Revelation XIII is seen at a glance. I wish only to remark that most Protestant commentators see in this "little horn" a prophecy of the papacy, and that I find no reason for disagreeing with them.

> "And he doeth great wonders, so that he maketh fire come down from heaven on the earth in the sight of men. And deceiveth them that dwell on the earth by the means of those miracles which he had power to do in the sight of the beast; saying to them that dwell on the earth, that they should make an image of the beast, which had the wound by a sword, and did live. And he had power to give life unto the image of the beast, that the image of the beast should both speak, and cause that as many as would not worship the image of the beast should be killed" (vv. 13-15).

It is characteristic of all pretenders to work miracles; sometimes real ones by satanic agency, sometimes spurious ones. The Lord said, "For there shall arise false Christs, and false prophets, and shall show *great signs and wonders;* insomuch that, if it were possible, they shall deceive the very elect" (Mat. 24:24). The alleged miracles of papal Rome are legion; and

The Vision of the Two Wild Beasts

innumerable multitudes have been duped thereby. Not that I count the miracles of Rome as being all spurious; for the Scripture, from the days of Moses in Egypt onward, makes many references to the working of signs and wonders through the agency of the supernatural powers of evil.

"Sooth-saying and witchcraft are rejected in Scripture, not on the ground of their nothingness, but because they are an abomination to the Lord (Dt. 18:9). Though signs should here and there rise above what is common, they still remain widely different from true signs and wonders *through their aim,* and by their mixture with common frauds. Besides, as the signs of the Egyptian wise men were occasioned by those of Moses, so the signs of the false prophet here are occasioned by those of Christ. It is unnecessary to adduce any historical quotation to show that, in the conflict of heathendom with Christianity, wonders and signs played an important part. Every church history supplies the proof" (Hengstenberg).

It is particularly stated that "he maketh fire come down from heaven on the earth in the sight of men". Bearing in mind that fire from heaven is, in this Book, the figure of judgments falling upon men, I take this as referring to the terrific papal anathemas often carrying with them the sentence of death by sword, or by the flames, which have been a common incident of the rule of the Papacy.

Again it is said that the second Beast will cause an image to be made to the first Beast, and that he will give life, or literally "breath" thereto. Taking into account the figurative language of this prophecy, this may mean that the second Beast will supply, for the furtherance of the ends in view, a religious organization, or system of worship. The word "image" *(eikon)* is used in Heb. 10:1 in this very sense. Further it is said that he had power to give breath *(pneuma)* to the image, giving it, as it were, a voice, and power also to slay all who will not bow down to this eikon.

Hengstenberg, after referring to the great image which king Nebuchadnezzar set up, and which he required all the nations of his dominion to worship, comments as follows:

"The setting up of the likeness of the emperor was one of the most effectual means which heathen despotism could employ to place itself in the center of the world. By means of this image the beast was rendered in a manner omnipresent. Its *living* representative, the Roman emperor, was confined to no particular place. In this way the choice was set before Christians between martyrdom and apostasy".

We do not have to suppose, therefore, a literal image of metal or other material, supernaturally endowed with life and power of speech. An *ideal* set before people's minds as standing for the supreme authority to which they are to bow in adoring homage, would as well, or better, answer to what is stated concerning the image of the beast. As to this it is well said by Hengstenberg that the "life" *(breath* or *spirit)*

"which, according to verse 15, belongs to the image of the beast, is not properly residing in him, but flowing out of him along with the *speech* given to him by the wisdom of this world. It can only, therefore, be an apparent *life* that is spoken of. The spirit is first given to the image of the beast in this way, that *men's minds are filled with exalted representations of the beast himself, and of his almighty power,* in contrast to the supposed impotence of his opponent".

"And he causeth all, both small and great, rich and poor, free and bond, to receive a mark in their right hand, or in their foreheads: And that no man might buy or sell, save he that had the mark, or the name of the beast, or the number of his name" (vv. 16, 17).

Hengstenberg points out that "the named here are seven, the *all* first, and then the three pairs". This points to the completeness of the authority of the beast, in that all classes of society are subject to it. Buying and selling is one of the commonest of the avocations of life. This may be a figurative way of expressing the abject servitude of the masses of people to the beast. But it may also, and in my opinion does, point to the development in the last days of this dispensation of a *vast business organization,* having its ramifications throughout the world, a monster "combine", or "trust", in such complete control of commerce and industry that none can, without its license, engage in any business—"buy or sell". That we are fast heading towards such a system is apparent upon the face of current events. But, in order that its control may be as absolute as here indicated, it must be vested with *super-governmental powers;* and that too has been envisaged by the forward looking minds of our day. Moreover, we saw in the recent world-war a brand new development, in that all the factories and industries of the land were mobilized and placed under governmental control. Thus the way was prepared for the final heading up of all the national resources in one gigantic system. But again there will be needed a superlative *binding agent,* to cement and hold together the divers part of such a titanic affair. And this is where the *religious element* comes in. For nothing else than a common religious bond would serve this purpose, and there is but one religion of world-wide extent, entering into the national life of all the civilized nations, having uniform ceremonies (the mass etc.), a common language (Latin), an iron-bound hierarchy, and a single head; and that, of course is Romanism.

Behold, then, the three great actors in the last drama of earth's history: (1) the dragon, the real potency behind it all, though invisible; (2) the beast, the Roman Empire, still existing in its iron framework of civil government, and now in process of assuming its final ten-horned form; and (3) the Papacy, with its vast organization, its millions of blinded and superstitious devotees, and its steadfast political aim!

Returning to the vision, it is to be noted that the privilege of buying and selling is to be enjoyed only by such as have the mark of the beast on their right hand, or on their forehead. In order to translate this into common language, we have first to remember that a brand, or mark, upon one's person is a badge of the complete ownership of the one so marked by him whose mark he bears. It was common practice to brand slaves, as well as sheep and cattle, with the mark of their

The Vision of the Two Wild Beasts

owner. Therefore, to bear the mark of the beast is to be his servant. The *right* hand is the instrument of action and of strength. Hence to bear the mark of the beast on that hand signifies that the one so marked serves the beast in all his actions, and with all his powers. The forehead is the most exposed and most conspicuous part of the body; hence, to have the mark there is equivalent to an open acknowledgment of the beast's ownership. These thoughts in connection with the hand and forehead appear in Scripture in a passage in which God teaches the respect to be paid to His Word by the people who had professed to give themselves wholly into His service, saying: "And these words, which I command thee this day, shall be in thine heart. And thou shalt teach them diligently to thy children, . . . And thou shalt bind them for a sign upon thine *hand,* and they shall be as frontlets *between thine eyes*" (Deut. 6:6-8).

We come now to the last verse of the chapter, and of the vision:

"Here is wisdom. Let him that hath understanding count the number of the beast: for it is the number of a man; and his number is six hundred threescore and six" (v. 18).

At the end of what was revealed concerning the first beast it was said, "Here is the patience and the faith of the saints"; and now at the end of what is revealed concerning the second beast is the parallel expression, "Here is wisdom". In the former case the situation was one that demanded patience and faith to endure. Here it is a problem requiring "wisdom" and "understanding" to solve. Nature supplies none of these things; nor can human efforts attain unto them. But as faith and patience are God's gifts, freely bestowed upon them that seek Him, so likewise are wisdom and understanding, "For the Lord *giveth wisdom:* out of His mouth cometh knowledge and *understanding*" (Prov. 2:6). Therefore, "If any of you lack *wisdom,* let him ask of God, who *giveth* liberally, and upbraideth not" (Jam. 1:5).

Yet the problem here presented to us demands wisdom in no ordinary measure; as is evident from the fact that various and contradictory explanations have been offered by men not lacking in spiritual discernment, men too who would not have failed to ask of God the needed wisdom ere attempting the solution. So let us approach the matter cautiously, and with "no confidence in the flesh".

My own thought about it, as given in a former book *(The Number of Man,* published about 1908) is that the clue to the meaning lies in the words, "for it is the number of (a) man", that is to say the *sum total of all human achievement.* That "number of man" is *six,* repeated again and yet again, but still remaining, no matter how often repeated, the number of incompleteness and imperfection, never attaining to the complete *seven.* Solomon, in his book of human wisdom, seems to be expressing the same thought when he says: "This have I found, *counting one by one* to find out the account, . . . Lo, this only have I found, that God hath made man upright; but they have sought out many inventions" (Eccl. 7:27, 29). And now the vision before us brings us to the end of man's efforts, to the summing up of his "account", to the full fruition of his "many inventions". And what is the total sum of his six thousand years of ceaseless activities? Has he reached a *sabbath* at last? has he achieved a state of rest and satisfaction? has he attained a *seven?* Alas! no. He is as far from it as ever. The world, as man has made it by *his* six days of toil, and *his* "many inventions", is a place of hideous *un*rest, a place of ever-increasing turmoil, corruption and violence. He never gets beyond the number *six,* and never could. What a contrast between man's work and God's! When *God's* sixth day came, its sun went down upon a *finished* creation. The work was complete and perfect. "And God saw everything that He had made, and behold it was VERY GOOD. And the evening and the morning were the *sixth* day" (Gen. 1:31). But God's "account" does not stop at six. It goes on to completeness. For the next words are: "Thus the heavens and the earth were *finished,* and all the host of them. And on the *seventh* day, God *ended* His work which He had made; and He *rested* on the *seventh* day from all His work which He had made. And God blessed the seventh day and sanctified it, because that in it He had rested from all His work which God created and made" (Gen. 2:1-3).

There is indeed a day of rest to come, a millennium of blessedness, as this Book of the Revelation of Jesus Christ shows us. But that *seventh* thousand years of heavenly rest will not be the fruit of *man's* efforts, for his best works are but "dead works". They eventuate in no sabbath day, but, on the contrary are works such as call for "repentance"; and his conscience needs to be purged from them by the blood of Christ (Heb. 6:1; 9:14). So God must step in. He must settle man's long account. He must bring every work into judgment. He must blot out all the vain works of man. And then, when the earth shall have been purged from them all by the outpouring of the seven vials of His scorching wrath ("for in them is *filled* up the wrath of God", 15:1), and when the two beasts shall have been cast into the lake of fire, and "the dragon, that old serpent, which is the Devil and Satan", shall have been bound for a thousand years, and shut up in the bottomless pit till the thousand years be fulfilled, *then* will dawn that day of "sabbath rest which remaineth unto the people of God" (Heb. 4:9).

Such was the writer's thought concerning this passage seventeen years ago, and such is his thought about it still; and therefore it has been no small satisfaction to him to find in Hengstenberg's comments on the passage the following:

"The 666 is, as it were, the swollen, blown up *six;* the six in its highest potency, but still, when swelled up and increased to the uttermost, *no more than six* . . . By the six being carried through units, tens, and hundreds, the number marks the soaring pretensions and might of the beast; while on the other side, the relation of the six to the seven and twelve, implies that in respect to the church he still after all came short".

Hengstenberg also calls attention to the only other passage in the Scripture where this number, 666, is to be found, saying·

"Here we must not wander about after our own imaginations. *The seer of the Apocalypse lives entirely in holy Scripture.* On this territory therefore is the solution of the sacred riddle to be sought. And there also it can be found with certainty. In the whole of the O. T. there is but one instance in which the number 666 occurs in connection with a name. It is written in Ezra 2:13, *The children of Adonikam, six hundred sixty and six"*.

From this he deduces that the name Adonikam must be the number of the beast. It means, *the Lord arises.* As given in Jackson's *Dictionary of Scripture Names* it is, *the Lord of rising up.* And Hengstenberg sees in this a reference to the rising up again of the beast after it had received its death-wound, so to speak. I make a note of this interesting suggestion, that the reader may have the benefit of it; but I do not pass judgment upon it.

As regards the application of the prophecy as a whole, Bengel notes the fact that,

"As old as is the description here given of the papacy, so old also is the testimony to the truth by which this prophecy is applied to the papacy. This was done long ago by the Waldenses, and afterwards by the followers of Wicliff and Huss. Such was the case before Luther's time, and by him the light was more widely diffused".

But Bengel is here referring to the first beast; for with Vitringa he held that, "The beast *from the sea* is the pope; the beast from the earth is that power which supports and defends the pope's authority", instancing the various religious orders, Franciscans, Dominicans, Jesuits, etc. But Hengstenberg points out various and serious objections to this view, saying for instance that,

> "It would be singular if the heathen persecution, which began soon after our Lord's ascension and raged for centuries, under which also John himself had to suffer, should have been entirely unnoticed, and yet a persecution be delineated which did not commence till a thousand years afterwards".

To this I heartily assent; but there is much more to oppose to Bengel's view. For the evidence presented above makes it clear to my mind that the first part of Chapter XIII refers to, and exactly delineates, the Roman Empire, and the persecutions the people of God endured at its hands; and that the second part of the chapter as clearly pictures Papal Rome, exercising "all the power of the first beast before him". Therefore it strikes me as strange indeed that Hengstenberg, who saw so clearly the meaning of the first symbolic beast, should not have recognized the papacy in the second, which he makes out to be "the *wisdom of this world,* lending its support to the God-opposing *power of this world*". This is a very weak invention; for it makes the two beasts to be merely the respective symbols of two attributes of one and the same world-system. But Hengstenberg himself had shown, and most convincingly too, that the first beast represents heathen world-government itself, *in its totality*. Hence the *wisdom* of the world is as much embraced in the symbols that delineate the first beast as is the *power* of the world. Nor would it be possible, by this view of the vision, to explain why the first beast arises out of the sea, and the second, at a later time, out of the earth. For surely the *wisdom* of the world did not have a different origin, and a later one, than the *power* of the world. Neither is it possible by this view to explain the exercising by the second beast of all the power of the first beast "before him"; for we cannot conceive of such an action as the transfer of "all the power" of "the power of the world" to "the wisdom of the world".

I am convinced, therefore, that the explanation of this vision, given in the foregoing pages, is in the main correct, notwithstanding there may be in it manifold imperfections and errors as to details. I was myself very reluctant to part with the long-cherished idea that the second beast represents a personal antichrist to come. That such an one is coming, I do not doubt; but the facts have compelled me to accept the view stated above. Whether they are sufficient or not to support it, is a matter for the reader's individual judgment.

What then is to be the outcome of the great movements of our times? This is not the appropriate point at which to introduce a discussion of that question; so I will only say that my later observations confirm the view presented in the book quoted above *(The Number of Man)* which briefly is this: The movements now in progress in the three great departments of human affairs, the political, the commercial, and the religious, are converging to one end, and will eventuate in a single system, comprehending in its vast embrace all human affairs of every sort and kind. This monstrosity will be a supergovernment, and will be headed, during its brief career, by the "superman", for whom the world is looking. Its religion will be "Humanism", the worship of Man. All the "progressive", "liberal" and "modernistic" forces in the religious field are thoroughly humanistic. The "Church of Man", the "Universal Brotherhood" is already an ideal; and will ere long have at least a formal realization. And while on the surface it may appear that these new religious tendencies are the opposite in many respects to Catholicism, the reverse is the case. For Catholicism too is thoroughly humanistic; and in the person of the pope a mere human being is already worshipped by millions. It will therefore be but the natural outcome of existing tendencies and potencies for all the religious systems and forces, "Christian" in name, which are opposed to the gospel of Christ, to amalgamate under the headship of the pope. As I see it there are but two things requisite for the accomplishment of what is briefly outlined above: *first,* a sufficient *motive,* which must be one that has *a worldwide appeal; second,* an adequate political machine also capable of embracing the whole world. *And these necessary things already exist.* The first is seen in the insistent and universal demand for WORLD-PEACE; and the second in the LEAGUE OF NATIONS. And in estimating the possibilities of the present situation, account must be specially taken of the great expansion of the political influence of the Vatican since the great European War, and of the fact that political leaders are more and more looking in that direction for the salvation of the world, and of civilization. This interesting part of our subject will receive fuller treatment in the last chapter of this volume.

CHAPTER X

Seven Visions of the Time of the End

Rev. 14:1-5

"And I looked, and, lo, a Lamb stood on the mount Sion, and with Him an hundred forty and four thousand, having His Father's name written in their foreheads. And I heard a voice from heaven, as the voice of many waters, and as the voice of a great thunder: and I heard the voice of harpers harping with their harps: And they sung as it were a new song before the throne, and before the four beasts, and the elders: and no man could learn that song but the hundred and forty and four thousand, which were redeemed from the earth. These are they which were not defiled with women; for they are virgins. These are they which follow the Lamb whithersoever He goeth. These were redeemed from among men, being the first fruits unto God, and to the Lamb. And in their mouth was found no guile: for they are without fault before the throne of God".

THE history of the two beasts is interrupted at the end of Chapter XIII, to be resumed and finished in subsequent visions. Chapter XIII shows us the coming into existence of those two beasts, and it pictures their character, and especially their murderous hatred and persecution of the people of God. Their end is shown in Chapter XIX.

Chapter XIV contains a complete program of seven numbers. It is a series within a series; a wheel within a wheel. These are the several parts thereof:—

1. The Lamb and the 144,000 on Mount Sion (verses 1-5 quoted above).

2. The angel with the everlasting gospel (verses 6, 7).

3. Another angel announcing the fall of Babyion (verse 8).

4. The third angel with a special warning against worshipping the beast, or receiving his mark (verses 9-12).

5. The voice crying, "Blessed are the dead who die in the Lord" (verse 13).

6. The harvest of the earth (verses 14-16).

7. The vintage of the earth (verses 17-20).

As in the case of the trumpet series, so here, we get our bearing as to the time of the events revealed in this entire group of visions from the last of the series. For the vintage of the earth is plainly God's final judgment upon the wickedness of man, and His extermination thereof root and branch, in "the great winepress of the wrath of God". It is a summary of "the seven last plagues" (15:1), whereof the details are given in Chapter XVI. So this series of visions conducts us to the very end of the day of wrath. Therefore its starting-point must be sought for at some earlier epoch.

The next to the last of the series shows us "the harvest of the earth". A cloud is seen, of that dazzling *whiteness* so often referred to in this Book, and always applied to that with which the brightness of the glory of God is associated; and upon the cloud is One like unto the Son of man, who forthwith proceeds to reap the harvest of the earth. This vision registers with

Chapter 11:12, where God's witnesses of the last days are caught up to heaven "in a cloud"; and it corresponds with what is described in 1 Thessalonians 4:16, the descending of the Lord from heaven, and the catching away of His people "in the clouds", to meet Him in the air.

At the *fourth* of this series we find ourselves in the period of the reign of the beast; and the *second* presents a time of great activity in the gospel, corresponding to that of the final testimony of God's witnesses (Chapter 11:3-6). Thus we are able to approximate the time of the beginning of this group.

Viewing the chapter as a whole, it shows us the winding up of the affairs of the world in a group of seven successive pictures. It stands related to the days of the seventh *trumpet* in the same manner as Chapter VII, (the sealing of the 144,000) is related to the seventh *seal*.

1. The sight that greets John's eye in this vision is in striking contrast with that of the preceding chapter. Instead of a hideous beast rising out of the sea, he beholds a Lamb standing on Mount Sion, and with Him 144,000. These have His Father's name in their foreheads, in contrast with those of the preceding vision who have the mark of the beast in their foreheads. It may be inferred, therefore, that the design of the vision is to comfort the people of God by showing them, at a time when seemingly all the world is wondering after the beast, that there is nevertheless another company, who "follow the Lamb whithersoever

Seven Visions of the Time of the End 435

He goeth". From various indications it is clear that this 144,000 is a symbolic number, representing the *whole company of the saved,* and not some select portion thereof. What was said concerning the 144,000 of Chapter VII, would lead to that conclusion. The twelve times twelve is the signature of the eternal city, the home of all the redeemed; and the *numerical* identifications in this Book are specially to be heeded.

Furthermore, it is stated that they stand with the Lamb on Mount Sion, and this, in the light of Hebrews 12:22, is decisive; for it is there written to and of those who, one and all, are looking unto Jesus, the crucified One, as the author and finisher of their faith (v. 2), that "ye are come unto Mount Sion, and unto the city of the living God, the heavenly Jerusalem, and to an innumerable company of angels" etc. The vision agrees perfectly with, and clearly illustrates that great passage in Hebrews 12:18-24. It agrees also with the statements of Ephesians 2:4-6, previously referred to, namely, that we are quickened together with Christ, and raised up together, and seated together in heavenly places. These statements apply to all who believe in Jesus Christ. The comfort and encouragement which this vision conveys is the same whereof the apostle wrote, and which was imparted to him by "the Father of mercies and God of all comfort, who comforteth us in all our tribulation", namely, that "this present light affliction, which is but for a moment, worketh for us a far more exceeding and eternal weight of glory; while we look not at the things which are seen, but at the things which are not seen" (2 Cor. 1:3, 4; 4:17, 18). This vision simply lifts the vail, so that those who suffer for the truth's sake from the powers of earth may look away to the things that the natural eye cannot see, but which God has prepared for them that love Him.

While John beholds this sight, he also hears a voice from heaven as that of many waters, and as the voice of a great thunder, and the voice of harpers, singing a new song before the throne. The voice, while of tremendous volume, comparable to that of many waters and of a great thunder, was nevertheless a melodious "song", to the accompaniment of harps. Again in Chapter 19:6, the voice of the multitude in heaven who rejoice over the fall of Babylon is likened to "the voice of many waters and the voice of mighty thunderings". In a previous vision, those who sing the new song, falling down before the Lamb as He takes the throne and the seven-sealed book, have harps; and the words of their song declare them to be the redeemed out of every kindred, and tongue, and people, and nation (5:8, 9). And here again, those who stand with the Lamb on Mount Sion are said to be they who "were redeemed from among men" (v. 4).

The "new song" is here, as in 5:9; represented as being sung by those to whom it relates.

"The new song which no one can learn except the 144,000, corresponds to the new name, which no one knows save him who receives it (2:17). Even now on earth no one but the true believer can learn the songs of Sion. For all others they are too high. How glorious then must that be which entirely transcends all the natural powers of comprehension! How exuberant the joy of these who are there made happy with the name of Christ! The 144,000 are described as those who have been *redeemed from the earth*. The costly price is the blood of Christ (5:9) by virtue whereof they have pressed through everything that would have arrested their progress toward heaven. The phrase 'from the earth' is explained by the 'out of every kindred, and tongue' etc. of 5:9" (Hengstenberg).

The presence of the four living creatures and the four and twenty elders serves further to emphasize the part which the earth takes in this heavenly scene.

The 144,000 are described as those who are "not defiled with women; for they are virgins". This, and what is said of them in verse 5, is a description of what they are as new creatures in Christ Jesus. What is here said is true of all the redeemed. It would be a most carnal interpretation of the passage to make it mean that only such as have led a celibate life on earth are among the 144,000. Even Roman Catholic expositors, with all their desire to exalt celibacy, do not so misread it. *All* believers are viewed as chaste virgins, and as having been presented to Christ *as such* (2 Cor. 11:2). And this results not from the chastity and blamelessness of their own conduct, but solely from the merit of the blood of Jesus Christ, which "cleanseth us from all sin" (1 J. 1:7).

It is further said that "these are they which follow the Lamb whithersoever he goeth"; and this again is what characterizes all of Christ's sheep; for He has said, "My sheep hear My voice, and I know them, and *they follow Me*" (John 10:27).

They are also described as "the first fruits unto God and to the Lamb". This does not mark them off as a separate company, selected out of the general mass of believers. James says of those whom God had begotten with the word of truth, that they were "a kind of firstfruits of His creatures" (Jam. 1:18). The "firstfruits" of the Mosaic economy was simply that which was set apart as God's portion of the produce of the earth. So likewise the "redeemed from among men", as these 144,000 are expressly said to be, are simply God's portion of the children of men. In other words, they are the Israel of God, as it is written, "Israel was holiness unto the Lord, the *firstfruits* of His increase" (Jer. 2:3). The thought is that God gives the "increase" of men, just as He gives that of the fruits of the ground (for "the fruit of the womb is His reward", Ps. 127, 3); and that His portion or "Israel", is so to speak, the firstfruits thereof.

Further it is said of the 144,000 that "in their mouth was found no guile; for they are *without fault* before the throne of God" (v. 5). It is part of what Christ undertakes to do for His people to present them *"faultless* before the presence of His glory with exceeding joy" (Jude 24). It is manifest that this is precisely the *position,* and also the *condition* of this 144,000. It is impossible therefore to make them a special or select company, distinguished from the rest by the exceptional sanctity of their lives while on earth.

2. "And I saw another angel fly in the midst of heaven, having the everlasting gospel to preach unto them that dwell on the earth, and to every nation, and kindred, and tongue, and people; saying with a loud voice, Fear God, and give glory to Him; for the hour of His judgment is come: and worship Him that made heaven, and earth, and the sea, and the fountains of waters".

The second scene of this group of visions is very different in subject from the first. An angel is seen flying in the midst of heaven. He has "the everlasting gospel", and it is for the whole world; for it is preached to (lit. *upon,* or *over*) "every nation, and kindred, and tongue and people". These are terms of the very widest scope. The gospel which this angel has is the one unchangeable gospel, the *everlasting* gospel, that concerning which the apostle said "though we (apostles) or *an angel from heaven* preach any other gospel unto you, than that which we have preached unto you, let him be accursed" (Gal 1:9). It is the gospel whereof in another place he said, "which is come unto you, as it is in *all the world*" (Col. 1:6); that is to say, the one unchangeable gospel that was for the whole world. For, in the words of Christ in His great parable of the harvest-field (to which this chapter has special reference) "the field is *the world*" (Mat. 13:38). The angel is "flying", which speaks of celerity; and inasmuch as the angels are beings which "excel in strength", this picture presents vividly to the mind the thought of *a season of vigorous and rapid evangelization of the tribes of earth.* There is an obvious connection between this vision and the sixth of the series, in which the Son of man comes to gather the harvest of the earth. From the two we may properly infer that a time of special gospel effort, vigorous in character, swift in movement, and universal in scope, was to precede the harvest. And to this agrees the word of the Lord, "And this gospel of the kingdom", which is none other than the *everlasting* gospel, "shall be preached *in all the world* for a witness unto *all nations*. And *then* shall the end come" (Mat. 24:14).

As has been already stated, this scene seems to coincide as to time, with the final testimony of God's witnesses (Chap. 11:3-12). Their testimony reached all the world, as is evident from the reference in verse 9 to "the people, and kindreds, and tongues, and nations". That scene is followed by another in which the witnesses, after having been put to death by the beast, are revived and caught up to heaven "in a cloud". So here the testimony of the angel is followed, *first,* by a reference to the beast (v. 9); then by a proclamation of the blessedness of the dead which die in the Lord from henceforth (v. 13); and then by the appearance of the Son of man coming for His redeemed ones, on a "white cloud".

Those who defer all the visions of this Book after Chapter III to a dispensation subsequent to the gospel era, are compelled by the exigences of their system of interpretation to make "the *everlasting* gospel", *another* gospel, one which brings to those who receive it *another* salvation. But this necessary implication of the futurist system should be enough in itself to expose to all discerning minds its thoroughly unscriptural character. All Scripture bears witness to the great and fundamental truth that there is but *one* gospel, and *one* salvation, but *one* Name given under heaven among men whereby we must be saved, but "one body" of the redeemed, the one church of God, embracing all the saved from Adam, Eve and Abel down to the end of time; but *one* "household of God" embracing "the *whole* family in heaven and earth" (Eph. 3:15), one Lord, one faith, one Spirit, one baptism, one God and Father of *all* (Eph. 4:3-6).

Furthermore the Scriptures also bear the clearest testimony to the fact, as already pointed out, that there will be no salvation for any part of the human race after the close of this gospel dispensation. Hence we are compelled to place the passage we are now considering before the second advent of Christ.

And certainly it is most strange that any should take the words of the angel recorded in verse 7 to be the everlasting gospel. For clearly there is no *gospel* in them at all. They are words of exhortation and warning, addressed to the inhabitants of earth, calling upon them to fear God and give glory to Him, for the reason that "the hour of His judgment is come". Thus likewise Paul in his day impressed upon his hearers the vital importance of giving heed to the gospel of God, because of the coming judgment (Ac. 13:41; 17:31; Rom. 2:16, etc.). But it would be a sad error to mistake the warning of coming judgment for the gospel of God concerning His Son. The call to the inhabitants of the earth to worship Him that made the heaven and earth, the sea and fountains of waters, has obvious reference to the worship of the beast which is to prevail at that time. See Acts 14:15, where Paul, speaking to the heathen, says: "We preach unto you that ye should turn from these vanities to the living God, who *made heaven and earth, and the sea, and all things that are therein*". Now that "the glorious gospel of the blessed God" (1 Tim. 1:11) has been fully revealed and published to the world, and has been "made known to *all nations* for the obedience of faith" (Rom. 16:26), it is certain that there could never be in any subsequent day a *lesser* gospel. There could be no returning to those "days of ignorance" which were before the gospel era began. Much less is it conceivable that there could be, in a later day, a species of salvation different in kind from that which is now preached, and received in some way other than by simple faith in Jesus Christ, the slain Lamb, Who is risen from the dead.

Even in the time of shadows, salvation was by faith in God who quickeneth the dead (Gen. 15:6; Rom. 4:17); and it was based upon blood atonement. The gospel, as preached in Eden to the first sinners of the human race, was the gospel of redemption; and there the blood of innocent creatures was shed to meet their need as sinners. The sin-offering was from the very start the only ground of the sinner's acceptance with God (Heb. 11:4). Yet there be some among the

Seven Visions of the Time of the End 443

most orthodox teachers in our day who teach that, in the next dispensation, after the removal of the people of God from the earth, there will be a company of people saved out of all nations ("tribulation saints", they are pleased to call them), saved by a gospel which has in it no sin-offering, no Saviour, no blood redemption. And not only so, but they even say that that "gospel", which is such as never was from the entrance of sin into the world until now, is *"the everlasting gospel"*. Surely any system of interpretation that involves a doctrine so subversive of the truth of the gospel, and so contrary to the words of the text itself, is condemned by that fact alone.

The words of the angel, "for the hour of His judgment *is come"*, clearly indicate that we have here a scene which immediately precedes the blowing of the seventh trumpet.

3. "And there followed another angel, saying, Babylon is fallen, is fallen, that great city, because she made all nations drink of the wine of the wrath of her fornication".

The third vision of the series is closely linked with the second. For in that was announced the hour of God's judgment; and in this it is announced that Babylon is fallen, that great city; this being the judgment referred to by the preceding angel. For all the doings of men, all their great enterprises, projects and activities, eventuate in that state of godless civilization and worldly grandeur whereof great Babylon of antiquity was the type, and the great Babylon of the Apocalypse is the divine symbol. This announcement looks on to Chapter XVIII. For so important in the eyes of God is this coming event, the destruction of mystical Babylon, that, in addition to several references to it, an entire vision is given to the revealing of the details thereof. Babylon here stands for the entire world-system, in all its grandeur and magnificence, and not specially the religious aspect thereof. The latter in its final phase is pictured separately by the scarlet-clad woman of Chapter XVII, who also bears the name "Babylon", with the qualifying prefix "Mystery" (17:5). The city, Babylon the great, has strong attractions, not for the religiously-minded only, but also for the many who are wholly irreligious. And it is the power of allurement, the fascinating attractiveness of the world, its power to seduce the hearts of men from God, Who has a just claim to their undivided affections, that is emphasized by this vision. This clearly appears by the words, "Because she made all nations drink of the wine of the wrath of her fornication". Many of God's dealings with men, and many passages of Scripture otherwise obscure, become clear in the light of the great truth that *"God is love"*. And herein does man's likeness to God chiefly consist, that he was made *capable of loving,* after the same manner, though not after the same *measure,* as God Himself loves. Therefore, the great commandment of the law is, and needs must be "Thou shalt love *the Lord thy God* with all thy heart, and with all thy soul, and with all thy mind" (Mat. 22:37). Nothing less than this is God's due;

and nothing less can He require of His people. Therefore, there is no greater wrong done to God, and hence no greater sin, than the bestowal upon another object of the affections of the human heart, which are rightfully His. It follows that whatever seduces the affections away from God must needs be the object of His severest condemnation and of His jealous anger. And this is the sin of Babylon, as a type of the world; as it is written: "Ye adulterers and adulteresses, know ye not that the friendship of the world is enmity against God? Whosoever therefore will be a friend of the world is the enemy of God" (Jam. 4:4). The supreme object of the mission of Christ was to restore to God the hearts of His human creatures. This is the result of His cross; for the Spirit of Christ in the prophet, in a passage that vividly pictures His sufferings on the cross, exclaims, *"Then* I restored that which I took not away" (Psa. 69:1-4).

The making of the nations drunk with wine is an image of frequent occurrence in the O. T. The point of the comparison is found in the misery, degradation, helplessness and shamefulness of the condition into which men are brought by indulgence in excess of wine. Jeremiah 51:7 is particularly pertinent because the literal Babylon is there the subject of the prophecy: "Babylon hath been a golden cup in the Lord's hand, *that made all the earth drunken: the nations have drunken of her wine;* therefore the nations are mad". And the next verse announces God's judgment upon her: "Babylon is suddenly fallen, and destroyed".

That the end of the antitypical "Babylon" is to come *suddenly* is emphasized in Chapter XVIII of the Apocalypse. Jeremiah 25:15-28 describes how God will cause the nations of the earth to take the cup of His fury, and to drink of it. See also Hab. 2:15, 16 and Na. 3:11). The repetition of the announcement of Babylon's fall ("is fallen, is fallen"; see also 18:2) —may be understood by reference to Joseph's explanation to Pharaoh of the fact that his dream was doubled: "And for that the dream was doubled unto Pharaoh twice; it is because the thing is *established*, and God will *shortly* bring it to pass" (Gen. 41:32).

4. "And the third angel followed them, saying with a loud voice, If any man worship the beast and his image, and receive his mark in his forehead, or in his hand, the same shall drink of the wine of the wrath of God which is poured out without mixture into the cup of his indignation; and he shall be tormented with fire and brimstone in the presence of the holy angels, and in the presence of the Lamb: and the smoke of their torment ascendeth up for ever and ever: and they have no rest day nor night, who worship the beast and his image, and whosoever receiveth the mark of his name".

Just as the third vision of this series is linked with the second by specifying the judgment there announced in general terms, so likewise the fourth is linked with the third by the warning that they who worship the beast and his image shall drink of *the wine* of the wrath of God. This vision also connects itself with the vision of Chapter XIII, and shows that the three preceding numbers of this series were leading up to this one, which has the place of central importance. Par-

Seven Visions of the Time of the End 447

ticularly do the words of verse 12, "Here is the patience of the saints" etc., refer us back to the like words of Chapter 13:10. It is evidently a danger of the most fearful sort that is here foreseen; for the terms in which the warning is expressed are the strongest that could be used. Every power with which Satan can endow the beast, and every means and deception his cunning can devise, will be brought into play, in that last stage of human affairs, to draw away the affections, devotion and zeal of men, to the beast. Among the emotions that will be aroused and worked up to the highest pitch is that called "patriotism", the blind, fanatical love of some earthly country. It is a matter of deep significance that in our public school system patriotism is now being made virtually a religion. Increasing attention is given to patriotic songs, days, and ceremonies. And the flag, to which our school children are compelled to do homage, is one of the things which become an ideal or "image" of the beast government, and under which men worship it. This danger is very real, and very imminent. Therefore, we should lay these solemn words to heart, and be ever upon our guard against the peril whereof they warn us.

The fearful punishment that awaits those who worship the beast and his image is two-fold: *First,* they shall drink of the wine of the wrath of God; *second,* they shall suffer the punishments of hell. The first judgment falls upon them here, in this world; the second, in the world to come. The passage on which the first of these punishments is based is Psalm 75:8,

"For in the hand of the Lord there is a cup, with foaming wine; it is full of mixture, and He poureth out of the same: Surely the dregs thereof, all the wicked of the earth shall drain them, and drink them" *(Jewish Version)*. Jeremiah XXV is also in view, concerning which Bengel remarks, "Jeremiah must, out of a cup of wine full of wrath from God's hand, pour out to many nations; by which was meant the misery that the king of Babylon was to bring on them". See also Isaiah 51:17, 22; and Jeremiah 49:12.

The reference to the torment of fire and brimstone is based primarily upon the destruction of Sodom and Gomorrah (Gen. 19:24), to which the Lord Himself referred, saying, "But the same day that Lot went out of Sodom, it rained *fire and brimstone* from heaven, and destroyed them all" (Lu. 17:29). On the strength of these and other like passages the fire of brimstone is used in this Book as an image of the torments of hell (Chaps. 19:20; 20:10; 21:8)

5. "And I heard a voice from heaven, saying unto me, Write, Blessed are the dead which die in the Lord from henceforth: Yea, saith the Spirit, that they may rest from their labours; and their works do follow them".

Here is a word of strong consolation. It is most appropriate at this point, for it has reference especially to a time when many will be faced with the dread alternative of death or worship of the beast. There is a wonderful difference, in the light of Scripture, between those who die "in the Lord" ("the dead *in Christ*",

1 Th. 4:16) and those who die *in their sins* (John 8:21).

"The dead who die in the Lord" are blessed *from henceforth*. The word means literally *from now, i. e.* from the *very moment of death*. Its meaning is illustrated by the word of the Lord Jesus to the thief on the cross: "Verily I say unto thee, *today* thou shalt be with Me in paradise" (Lu. 23:43).

Hengstenberg makes this edifying comment:

> "This word *from henceforth* is a precious jewel, an antidote against the cheerless doctrine that would make a long night go before the bright day; such for example, as theirs is, who dream of a sleep of the soul. The real sting of the comfortless character of this doctrine is not in its throwing the full inheritance of salvation so far back; but rather in that the throwing back is so much at variance with the essential nature of faith, that the *matter itself* becomes thereby uncertain. If as our Lord declared, 'he that heareth My word . . . *hath* everlasting life . . . and *is passed* from death into life,' then the soul's life in Christ *can suffer no interruption;* and whenever any interruption is believed to exist, eternal life itself is indirectly denied".

Special force is given to this passage by the word "Yea, saith the Spirit", which puts it among the things the Spirit is now saying to the churches. The words "that they may *rest*", points to a state of conscious enjoyment, as in Genesis 2:1, 2. The words, "and their works do follow them", implies a reward awaiting them *there* for their good works *here*. As Bengel says, "The following of the works indicates that there is to be a reward". To the same effect is the assurance given by the apostle Paul, "For as much as ye know that your labor is not in vain *in the Lord*" (1 Cor. 15:58).

6. "And I looked, and behold a white cloud, and upon the cloud one sat like unto the Son of man, having on His head a golden crown, and in His hand a sharp sickle. And another angel came out of the temple, crying with a loud voice to Him that sat on the cloud, Thrust in Thy sickle, and reap: for the time is come for Thee to reap; for the harvest of the earth is ripe. And He that sat on the cloud thrust in His sickle on the earth; and the earth was reaped".

The meaning of this vision is very plain in the light of the Lord's parable of the tares of the field (Mat. 13:24-30; 36-43). That parable begins with these words: "The Kingdom of heaven is likened (lit. *become like*) unto a man which sowed good seed in his field". This is the Lord's own picture of the kingdom of heaven as it was to be down to "the end of the age" (v. 39). That to which the parable gives prominence is the devil's activity in sowing tares, "the children of the wicked one", among the wheat, "the children of the kingdom"; and that he is allowed to do so without hindrance. But what chiefly concerns us for the moment is the harvest. As to this the Lord said:

"The harvest is the end of the age; and the reapers are the angels. As therefore the tares are gathered and burned in the fire, so shall it be in the end of this age. The *Son of man* (cf. Rev. 14:14) shall send forth His angels, and they shall gather out of His Kingdom all things that offend, and them that do iniquity, and shall cast them into a furnace of fire; there shall be weeping and gnashing of teeth. Then shall the righteous shine forth as the sun in the Kingdom of their Father. Who hath ears to hear, let him hear".

Seven Visions of the Time of the End 451

The vision agrees so closely with this description of the harvest at the end of the gospel age, that it is not necessary to point out the resemblances. The designation of Christ as the "Son of man", which occurs in only one other place in this Book (Rev. 1:13), is intended no doubt to direct attention to the parable. In the Lord's explanation of the parable He tells of the separation of the tares from the wheat *just before the reaping takes place.* We have seen that such a work of separation is indicated as taking place just before the blowing of the seventh trumpet (11:1, 2), the separation being there followed by the catching away of God's witnesses "in a cloud", which corresponds with the reaping of the earth in the vision, and with the gathering of the wheat into the barn in the parable (Mat. 13:30). In Chapter XIV the separation again appears conspicuously, in that the judgment upon the wicked who are left (the tares of the parable, which are bound in bundles ready to be burned) is shown in a separate vision, that of the vintage and winepress, which is the next and last of this series.

That the Son of man, as seen in this vision, has on His head a golden crown indicates clearly that He is come in the character of King. This accords with the parable of the nobleman who was to go into a far country to receive for himself a *kingdom* and to return (Lu. 19:12. See comments on Chap. V). I am at a loss to see on what principles of exegesis this coming of the Son of man to reap the harvest of the earth can be deferred to the close of a *future* dispensation, or made to mean anything but the coming of Christ described in 1 Corinthians 15:52, and 1 Thessalonians 4: 13-17.

7. "And another angel came out of the temple which is in heaven, he also having a sharp sickle. And another angel came out from the altar, which had power over fire; and cried with a loud cry to him that had the sharp sickle, saying, Thrust in thy sharp sickle, and gather the clusters of the vine of the earth; for her grapes are fully ripe. And the angel thrust in his sickle into the earth, and gathered the vine of the earth, and cast it into the great winepress of the wrath of God. And the winepress was trodden without the city, and blood came out of the winepress, even unto the horse bridles, by the space of a thousand and six hundred furlongs".

The angel who executes this judgment comes out from the altar, and he has power over *fire*. This brings to mind the vision of Chapter 8:1-5, which occurs immediately after the opening of the seventh seal. There an angel is seen standing at the altar, who, after offering up the prayers of the saints, adding much incense thereto, takes *fire* from the altar and casts it upon the earth, when, in the voices, thunderings, lightnings and earthquake, there were threatenings of judgments about to fall upon the earth. This plainly registers with the scene now before us, in which the vine of the earth is removed altogether, root and branch, and is cast into the *great winepress* of the wrath of God. The figure represents a work of judgment thorough and complete.

The winepress is said to be trodden *without the city*. This may be understood in the light of Chapter 22:15, where, speaking of the heavenly city, it is said, "*with-*

out are dogs", etc. Nothing that is unclean or defiling is to enter into that city.

Christ is the treader of the winepress of God's wrath (Isa. 63:3, 4); and we are now told that when this *"great"* winepress is trodden, blood flows out of it in a stream of such volume that it rose even to the horse bridles, and for a length of 1600 furlongs. The mention of the horse bridles connects this scene with that of Chapter 19:11-16, where Christ appears mounted upon a white horse, clothed in a vesture dipped in blood; and followed by the armies of heaven, also mounted upon white horses.

This seventh vision gives only the general result. It tells us that the vine of the earth is completely removed, and it conducts us to the series of the vials, in which the details of this great work of judgment are shown.

CHAPTER XI

The Seven Vials

"And I saw another sign in heaven, great and marvellous, seven angels having the seven last plagues; for in them is filled up the wrath of God" (15:1).

THIS is the third and last of the three great *signs in heaven* described by John in this Book. The first is the woman clothed with the sun, having the moon under her feet, and on her head a crown of twelve stars (12:1, the word "wonder" there, and in v. 3, being the same as "sign" in 15:1). That was the sign of God's purpose in the creation of man to invest him with supreme governmental power and glory. It appeared at that point as the proper beginning of the history of Jesus Christ, the Man-child, in whom that purpose was to be accomplished. It is the sign of the mystery of Godliness, *"God manifest in the flesh,* justified in the Spirit, *seen of angels,* preached unto the Gentiles, *received up into glory"* (1 Tim. 3:16).

The second "sign in heaven" (12:3) is the great red dragon, the great opposer of God's purpose, the one who has the power of death, who had succeeded in bringing the whole family of man under that power, and who purposed to resist to the uttermost the accomplishment of God's plan for the government of the earth. It is the sign of "the mystery of iniquity", concerning which the apostle said in his day that "it doth already work"; and which will culminate in "that Wicked one, whom the Lord shall consume with the spirit of His mouth, and shall destroy with the brightness of His coming" (2 Th. 2:7, 8). Between these two, the Man-child and the dragon, the fight for the dominion of the world is to be fought.

The third "sign in heaven" is the vision of the seven angels having the seven last plagues. It is described as "great and marvellous", which refers to what was to be accomplished by those plagues, namely the complete and overwhelming destruction of the opposing forces, the might of the beast and the false prophet aided by all the power of the dragon. This appears from the repetition of the phrase "great and marvellous" in verse 3, in the song of those who have gotten the victory over the beast, who say, "Great and marvellous are *Thy works,* . . . for Thy *judgments* are made manifest". Thus the "sign" of the seven angels declares that events of transcendent importance are about to take place, events having the character of *finality,* and by means of which the eternal purpose of God pictured by the first sign in heaven, and proclaimed by the oath of the mighty Angel of Chapter X, is at last to be accomplished.

What God is now about to do by means of these *last* plagues, is the subject of many prophecies, of which that of Zephaniah 3:8 said:

"Therefore wait ye upon Me, saith the Lord, until *the day that I rise up to the prey;* for My determination is to gather the nations, that I may assemble the kingdoms, to *pour upon*

them Mine indignation, even all My fierce anger: for ALL THE
EARTH SHALL BE DEVOURED WITH THE FIRE OF MY JEALOUSY".

For what is specially emphasized in verse 1 of **Rev. 15**, is that these are the *last* plagues; that by them the purpose of God will be fully accomplished ,"for in them the wrath of God is *filled up*".

"And I saw as it were a sea of glass mingled with fire: and them that had gotten the victory over the beast, and over his image, and over his mark, and over the number of his name, stand on the sea of glass, having the harps of God. And they sing the song of Moses the servant of God, and the song of the Lamb, saying, Great and marvellous are Thy works, Lord God Almighty; just and true are Thy ways, thou King of saints. Who shall not fear Thee, O Lord, and glorify Thy name? for Thou only art holy: for all nations shall come and worship before Thee; for Thy judgments are made manifest" (vv. 2-4).

The vision of the seven angels constitutes the great and marvellous *sign*. And now we have another vision, introduced by the usual words, "And I saw". In this companion vision is seen a sea as it were of glass mingled with fire, upon which stand *"the overcomers of the beast"* (that being the force of the words, as well as the literal rendering thereof) having the harps of God.

This impressive scene connects with the preceding Chapters, XIII and XIV, showing us the great reward of those who refused to worship the beast and his image, and to receive his mark. The symbols used in this passage point distinctly to the passage of the Red Sea by those whom God delivered out of Egypt, where the ungodly world-power, Egypt, was overwhelmed,

The Seven Vials

and upon the shore of which the delivered people sang the song of victory.

The word "plagues", which was not used to designate the trumpet judgments, is evidently a key-word, intended to refer us back to the parallel case of God's deliverance of His afflicted people from Pharaoh, who typifies that whereof the beast is the symbol here. Those were the *first* "plagues", a series of ten, which represents fullness of punitive visitations; these are *the last,* a series of seven, which represents completeness and finality.

The "sea" in this vision is as it were of glass, mingled with fire. The sea was that which overwhelmed Pharaoh and his hosts, God's flood of judgments upon them. But God's people walked safely through it. Here is a greater thing; for now His delivered people are represented as *standing upon* the sea. The *fire,* with which this symbolical sea is mingled, shows that it represents the judgments of God, now fully accomplished. Those who have gained the victory over the beast are represented as being *above,* that is to say, beyond the reach of, the sea of judgments. Their position corresponds with that of Noah and his family whom the ark kept always above the waters. That this symbolical sea is as it were "of glass", may be taken as expressing the transparent purity and the perfect justice of the acts of God, in bringing this flood of annihilating judgments upon the world of the ungodly (cf. 2 Pet. 2:5). The same thought is expressed in the words of the song, *"Just* and *true* are

Thy ways, Thou King of nations. . . . Thy judgments are *made manifest*". (The reading "King of saints" of the A. V. has very slender support, and is, moreover, not in keeping with the sentiment of the passage. The true reading is, "Thou King of the nations", *i. e.* the heathen.) The truth and righteousness of God's judgments appear in that He manifests Himself as the King of the heathen. This is according to the word of the prophet: "Who would not fear Thee, O King of the nations?" (Jer. 10:7).

Those who have "gotten the victory" have gotten it through no valor or might of their own. As declared in Chapter 12:11, "they *overcame*" (same word as here rendered "gotten the victory") "him (the dragon) *by the blood of the Lamb,* and by the word of their testimony". Hence the song they sing is "the song of the Lamb", meaning not a song whereof He is the author, but whereof He is *the theme.* That it is also called "the song of Moses" helps to an understanding of the entire scene. For those few words tell us that what is here put before us is a situation of the same sort as that in which the children of Israel found themselves, when the Lord had "saved Israel out of the hand of the Egyptians, and Israel saw *that great work,* which the Lord did upon the Egyptians"; for "*Then* sang *Moses* and the children of Israel *this song* unto the Lord" (Ex. 14:30; 15:1). It is a song of exultant triumph, ascribing power, glory and salvation to the Lord, whose right hand had become glorious in power, whose right hand had dashed the enemy in pieces.

Another scene follows which, with the two preceding, constitutes the introduction to the vial series.

"And after that I looked, and, behold, the temple of the tabernacle of the testimony in heaven was opened: And the seven angels came out of the temple, having the seven plagues, clothed in pure and white linen, and having their breasts girded with golden girdles. And one of the four beasts gave unto the seven angels seven golden vials, full of the wrath of God, who liveth for ever and ever. And the temple was filled with smoke from the glory of God, and from his power; and no man was able to enter into the temple, till the seven plagues of the seven angels were fulfilled" (vv. 5-8).

The fact that it is not until now that the seven angels receive the seven golden vials, full of the wrath of God, shows that the scenes described in the preceding verses are designed to give a pictorial summary anticipative of what was to follow.

These seven angels issue forth out of the temple, which indicates that they are of high rank and dignity. This further appears by their clothing, which is pure linen of dazzling whiteness—(again we have the now familiar symbol of the glory of God) and by their being girded about their breasts with golden girdles (cf. 1:13). One of the cherubim hands to the angels the seven golden vials full of the wrath of God. The cherubim represent *the earth* and its creatures. So this agency of one of them in this matter is explained by the words of 16:1, "Go your ways, and pour out the vials of the wrath of God *upon the earth*".

The pouring out, or outpouring, is expressive of the *copiousness* and *finality* of this judgment, as may be inferred from several passages of the O. T. Thus we have in Psalm 79:6, *"Pour out Thy wrath* upon the heathen that have not known Thee, and upon the nations that have not called upon Thy Name". This is repeated almost word for word in Jeremiah 10:25. Then in Zephaniah 3:8 we read: "Therefore wait ye upon Me, saith the Lord, until the day that I rise up to the prey: for My determination is to gather the nations, that I may assemble the kingdoms, to *pour upon them Mine indignation,* even *all* My fierce anger. *For all the earth shall be devoured with the fire of My jealousy".* These are some of the prophecies that are to be fulfilled in the pouring out of the seven vials.

The final verse of Chapter XV, which speaks of the temple's being filled with smoke from the glory of God, rests upon Numbers 16:19, where the wrathful glory of God was manifested before the entire congregation; and upon Isaiah 6:4, where are found the words, "And the house was filled with smoke". Exodus 40:34,35 also comes to mind: "Then a cloud covered the tent of the congregation, and the glory of the Lord *filled the tabernacle.* And Moses was not able to enter into the tent of the congregation, because the cloud abode thereon, and the glory of the Lord *filled the tabernacle".*

"And I heard a great voice out of the temple saying to the seven angels, Go your ways, and pour out the vials of the wrath of God upon the earth" (16:1).

The Seven Vials

The command to the seven angels to pour out their vials upon the earth is given by a "great voice", that proceeds out of the temple. This must be the voice of God Himself, seeing that, from the last preceding verse, none other was able to enter the temple at that time. That accords also with Ezekiel 9:1, where the Lord called out "with a loud voice", commanding His servants who were about to execute His vengeance upon the apostate people of Jerusalem, to go through the city and smite. Ezekiel, in interceding with God, speaks of this as the *"pouring out of Thy fury upon Jerusalem"* (v. 8).

This command to the seven angels is executed with speed; for the pouring out of the seven vials, one after the other, proceeds swiftly to the end; and then at the pouring out of the seventh vial, there comes once more "a *great voice* out of the temple of heaven, from the throne, saying, It is done" (v. 17). The phrase, "from the throne", makes it certain that this great voice is the voice of God.

Like the series of the seven seals, and that of the seven trumpets, the vial series is also divided into three groups. For, after the first group of three, there is an interruption caused by the saying of the angel of the waters, and the response from the altar (vv. 5-7); and again after the pouring out of the sixth vial, there is a word evidently spoken by the Lord Jesus Christ (v. 15).

The action of the first vial is upon the earth, that of the second upon the sea, that of the third upon the rivers and fountains of waters. In the second group of three, the fourth vial affects the sun, the fifth the throne of the beast, and the sixth opens the way for the instruments of God's vengeance that are waiting beyond the river Euphrates. The last vial is poured out into the air.

First Vial

"And the first went, and poured out his vial upon the earth; and there fell a noisome and grievous sore upon the men which had the mark of the beast, and upon them which worshipped his image" (v. 2).

The regions that are affected respectively by the several vials are the same in most cases as those that were affected by the corresponding trumpets; for the first trumpet affected the earth, the second the sea, the third the rivers and fountains of waters, the fourth the sun, and the sixth loosed the four angels that were bound in the river Euphrates. This correspondence, however, is but faintly seen between the fifth of the respective series, and not at all in respect to the seventh.

It has been already remarked that the word "plagues", applied to the vial judgments, recalls God's punitive dealings with the Egyptians; and it will be remembered that, in Chapter 11:8, "Egypt" is one of the names that is given to apostate Christendom. The significance of these terms becomes evident when the nature of these vial plagues is observed and the resemblances between them and the plagues of Egypt are noted. These will be pointed out in the comments below.

At the pouring out of the first vial, there fell a noisome and grievous sore, that is to say a botch or eruption that cannot be healed, upon the men which had the mark of the beast, and which worshipped his image. The word "earth" here must be taken in the sense in which it is customarily used in this Book, that is to say, as designating the more settled, ordered, and stabilized part of the earth, as distinguished from the turbulent and restless "sea" of the nations and peoples in general. Roughly speaking, "the earth" would designate the Western or christianized nations, and "the sea" (on which the second vial is poured out) would designate the surrounding peoples and tribes of Asia, Africa, and South America. Hengstenberg's comment expresses practically my understanding of it:

"There must be an *'earth'* upon *the* earth, which was set off as a special region for the first vial. . . . The commentary on the 'earth' is formed by 'the men who have the mark of the beast'. The worshippers of the beast have themselves become beast-like".

Those who are directly under the sovereignty of the beast would be more ready to worship him, than those in the remoter regions of the world.

The grievous sore of the first vial is similar to the sixth of the plagues of Egypt, "a boil breaking forth with blains upon man and beast" (Ex. 9:8-12). The boils there mentioned were of a peculiarly virulent and loathsome kind, for they are the source from which leprosy may break out (Lev. 13:20). In Deuteronomy 28:27 the same disease is spoken of as "the botch of Egypt"; and in verse 35 of the same chapter it is described as "a sore botch that cannot be healed", and as a thing that might appear all over the body, from the sole of the foot to the top of the head. This plague in Egypt was no doubt literal and physical; but here, in keeping with the character of the Apocalypse, it probably represents a distemper or eruption of a moral character, breaking forth upon the surface of human society, something of which a putrid and loathsome ulcer would be an appropriate symbol.

Second Vial

"And the second angel poured out his vial upon the sea; and it became as the blood of a dead man: and every living soul died in the sea" (v. 3).

At the sounding of the second trumpet a great mountain, burning with fire, was cast into the sea, and a third part of the sea became blood. Here the same region is visited, the heathen world in general; but the destruction now is complete. There is a resemblance here to the first of the ten plagues of Egypt, when the waters of the river Nile were turned into blood, and the fish that were in the river died, and the river stank (Ex. 7:20, 21). It is quite evident that the plague in Egypt was literal, whereas that of the second vial is figurative; for the literal ocean would not be the sphere for a punitive visitation. The expression "became as the blood of a dead man", is peculiar and somewhat obscure. It has been variously explained. Literally the phrase is "as the blood of one dead". Having regard to this literal rendering, the words present to our minds the picture of *mortality by violence upon an enormous scale*. For "blood" is the symbol of death by violence; though ofttimes blood flows from wounds that are not mortal. In this case, however, it is the blood of *death-wounds* that is specified, the blood as of one *dead;* and the extent of this blood-shedding is so vast that the whole world of the miscellaneous nations (what is commonly called "the heathen world") is figuratively colored red thereby. This view of the passage is suported by the last clause of the verse, "and every living soul that was in the sea died". Hengstenberg on this passage says:

"That we are not to think here of some general mortality, but of the *shedding of blood in war,* is evident alone from the symbol of the sea, out of which the beast arose. In Chapter 20:13 also, the dead that are in the sea are those who perished by a violent death in political conflicts. The scourge of destroying war is placed before our eyes by a double image; first the changing of the sea into blood, second the dying of the living creatures in the sea. But the two, perhaps, are not simply co-ordinate. The changing of the sea into blood may be referred to those who perish in actual battle; while the dying of all the living creatures in the sea may be understood of the infinitely greater number of those who die in consequence of the war, as by distress, hunger, sorrow and disconsolateness".

One need not exert much power of imagination, when considering the present state of political affairs in Russia, China, North Africa, and elsewhere upon the fringes of civilization, in order to conceive of causes and agencies capable of bringing about the conditions pictured so vividly by the few words in which this vision is described. For such causes and agencies are already at work.

Third Vial

"And the third angel poured out his vial upon the rivers and fountains of waters; and they became blood. And I heard the angel of the waters say, Thou art righteous, O Lord, which art, and wast, and shalt be, because Thou hast judged thus. For they have shed the blood of saints and prophets, and Thou hast given them blood to drink; for they are worthy. And I heard another out of the altar say, Even so, Lord God Almighty, true and righteous are Thy judgments" (vv. 4-7).

The waters of rivers and fountains (or springs) are the sources of abundant, vigorous and fruitful vegetation. Figuratively therefore they stand for whatever is conducive to the welfare and prosperity of the individual or the community. The man whose delight is in the law of the Lord, and who meditates therein day and night, finds the Word of God to be to him like a fountain of water. He is "like a tree planted by the rivers of water, that bringeth forth his fruit in his season; his leaf also shall not wither; and whatsoever he doeth shall prosper" (Psa. 1:1-3; also Jer. 17:7, 8). Thus the highest application of this figure is to the sources of *spiritual* prosperity and fruitfulness, as was pointed out in the comments above on Chapter 8:10, 11. But obviously the figure has a much wider application, wide enough to embrace the sources also of material and worldly prosperity. And that must be what is in view here; for in the days in which this vision will be fulfilled there will be no springs of spiritual waters in the world.

In the days of the third trumpet a third part of the waters became *wormwood;* but here there is a complete turning of the rivers and fountains, not into wormwood, but into *blood.* Now, the agencies of material prosperity are the great industrial plants, the various means of transportation, and all the contributory agencies of manufacture and commerce. If we think of all of these as being converted into factories for the production of engines of destruction, and instrumentalities and agencies, including poison gases, for destroying life and property (a purpose that in our day is always kept in view and carefully provided for in every important industrial plant) and into appliances for transporting these quickly to points where they can do the most deadly work, we will have in mind a condition of affairs which not only could be brought quickly into existence even as things now are, but which also would answer perfectly to the symbols used in the passage before us.

We may clearly see a progression of deadliness and destructiveness in this group of three vials. First there is an eruption of moral or political disorders, causing distresses and painful conditions of various kinds. This affliction visits the more civilized parts of the world. Next comes a state of revolution, civil wars, and uprisings, prevailing throughout the heathen world, and converting it into a sea of blood. And finally we have a further development among the progressive nations, such that all the sources and agencies of their material wealth and prosperity are transformed into instrumentalities of death and destruction. Here is a word-picture painted nearly two thousand years ago. In it, all that I have suggested above is vividly set forth, and in the fewest possible words—(but seventy-seven words in all, in the original). And now, after all these centuries of time, a state of things political and industrial has at last developed throughout the entire world, such that men who never read the Bible and are as ignorant of the visions of the Apocalypse as they are of the statutes of Omri, but who keep a sharp eye on current events, are solemnly and almost daily assuring their fellow mortals that *the precise things here foretold* are close at hand, and will inevitably come upon them, unless averted by the League of Nations, or by a World Court, or by a Disarmament Treaty, or some other miracle-working agency of man's creation (see the last chapter of this volume). The storm whereof these political weather-prophets warn us is *surely coming,* and it is even now at the doors. On the other hand, the things in which they are trusting to avert it are as little likely to happen as that all the wild beasts of the jungle will assemble themselves together for the purpose of mutually extracting one another's teeth and claws.

The words of the angel of the waters challenge our attention. In the first place it is a noteworthy fact that the angels are employed about such matters as the flow of rivers and streams. This is one of the examples of what has been often noted in these pages, namely that we are taken again and again behind the scenes, and are shown the agencies that God uses in carrying on the operations of His physical creation. Hengstenberg's comment is instructive:

"The angel of the waters here represents the whole host of angels whom God employs in this service. He stands in a near relation to the angel who moves the water in John 5:4. We have here a delicate and intimate bond, uniting the Apocalypse with the Gospel".

This angel proclaims what had been previously declared in the song of the conquerors of the beast (vv. 1-4), namely, the righteousness and truth of God's ways in the execution of His judgments. Because they have shed the innocent blood of saints and prophets, God has given them blood to drink. This is strictly in accord with that foundation-principle of divine justice which was laid down at the beginning of the development of human society after the flood, "whoso sheddeth man's blood, by man shall his blood be shed" (Gen. 9:6). Also we have here a fulfilment of Isaiah 49:26, "I will feed them that oppress thee with their own flesh; and they shall be drunken *with their own blood,* as with sweet wine".

Verse 7 gives a response to the words of the angel, which response comes from the altar, "Even so, Lord

God Almighty, true and righteous are Thy judgments". This points back to the cry of the souls from under the altar, "How long, O Lord, holy and true, dost Thou not avenge our blood on them that dwell on the earth?" (6:10). The hour of vengeance long waited for, is come at last.

Fourth Vial

"And the fourth angel poured out his vial upon the sun; and power was given unto him to scorch men with fire. And men were scorched with great heat, and blasphemed the name of God, which hath power over these plagues: and they repented not, to give Him glory".

The first group of three vials kept to the level of the earth. They affected the earth, the sea, and the streams of water. The last group begins with the sun and ends with the air. The fifth touches the throne of the beast, which is the loftiest place in the political realm.

The sun is now turned from a source of supreme blessing to mankind into an agency of fearful torment. This is, of course, symbolical, and is to be taken as signifying that the supreme governmental authority of those days, instead of being a source of good, a preserver of life, a benefaction to the people, will be an instrument of the most cruel oppression. The words "and it was given to him (or *to it*) to scorch men with *fire*", make it plain that the governmental powers of those days are to become instruments for the execution of the wrath of God, of which *fire* is the usual symbol. The effect on the men upon whom this judgment falls shows their hopelessly hardened condition. Instead of humbling themselves under the mighty hand of Him who has power over these plagues, they blaspheme His Name; and they repent not to give Him glory. This brings forcibly to mind the statement of Scripture, that God *gives repentance* (Acts 5:31; 11:18); and it shows that in those awful days the time for repentance will have gone forever. Bengel's comment is appropriate:

"In repentance the most essential thing is to give glory to God. Man must at once shut his mouth, and even lay his hand upon it; but God receives the glory. Where, however, man does not yield, but stands out in a spirit of proud and hardened defiance, there also God does not yield; and in such a conflict man must come far short; he must even be consumed".

Fifth Vial

"And the fifth angel poured out his vial upon the seat of the beast; and his kingdom was full of darkness; and they gnawed their tongues for pain, and blasphemed the God of heaven because of their pains and their sores, and repented not of their deeds" (vv. 10, 11).

The last preceding plague came through the supreme governmental authority of the world; but retribution follows swiftly; for this plague falls upon the throne of the beast. This has now become, in the fullest sense, "the throne of iniquity", concerning which the Psalmist asks: "Shall the throne of iniquity have the fellowship with Thee, which frameth mischief by a law?" (Psa. 94:20). That Psalm begins with an invocation to the God *to whom vengeance belongeth* to show Himself, and to render a reward to *the proud.* And the question is asked, "Lord, how long shall the wicked, how long shall the wicked flourish?" (vv. 1-3). The last verse carries us to the conclusion, "And He shall bring upon them *their own iniquity;* and He will cut them off in their own evil; the Lord our God will cut them off".

The judgment of the fifth vial has this in common with that of the fifth trumpet, namely, that the chief feature of the plague is *darkness.* Under the fifth trumpet the darkness was caused by a dense smoke arising from the bottomless pit, whereby the sun and the air were darkened (9:2). Here the agency whereby the darkness is produced is not specified. It is stated merely that the kingdom of the beast was "full of darkness". In fact there is a notable absence of details in the description of these vial judgments. The writer hurries from one to the next as if in great haste to reach the end of the series.

Under the fourth plague the sun became intensely hot, insomuch that men were scorched with fire. Now it is the other extreme. In the former case we are to understand a time of fierce persecutions and oppressions proceeding from the government itself; and in the latter, a time of weakness and failure of the power of the government. Whatever the details may be, they are such as to produce acute distress; for men gnawed their tongues with pain; but again there is no turning to God, but "they blasphemed the God of heaven because of their pains and their sores, and repented not of their deeds". These words describe a state of extreme hardness and rebellion. For they show that they upon whom this plague falls have some knowledge of God, sufficient at least to realize that He is the Author of these judgments; yet the hardness of their hearts is such that they withstand Him and speak blasphemies against His Name. This plague is like the ninth of the plagues of Egypt, which consisted in "a darkness over all the land, even a darkness which might be felt" (Ex. 10:21).

SIXTH VIAL

"And the sixth angel poured out his vial upon the great river Euphrates; and the water thereof was dried up, that the way of the kings of the east might be prepared. And I saw three unclean spirits like frogs come out of the mouth of the dragon, and out of the mouth of the beast, and out of the mouth of the false prophet. For they are the spirits of devils, working miracles, which go forth unto the kings of the earth and of the whole world, to gather them to the battle of that great day of God Almighty. Behold, I come as a thief. Blessed is he that watcheth, and keepeth his garments, lest he walk naked, and they see his shame. And he gathered them together into a place called in the Hebrew tongue Armageddon" (vv. 12-16).

The description of the last two of the vial judgments is more in detail than that of the others. We are now reaching the end. Forces are released which operate to the gathering together of all the remaining elements of human society. The region East of the Euphrates is that from which conquering hordes were wont to come, the latest in history being that of the Turks. It is therefore most appropriate that the Euphrates should be used to represent a dividing line between the civilized and the uncivilized peoples. The agencies that effect this tremendous gathering are represented as three unclean spirits likened to slimy frogs in their loathsomeness and repulsiveness. In these frogs there is a reminder of the second of the plagues of Egypt. The three evil spirits proceed, one out of the mouth of the dragon, one out of the mouth of the beast, and one out of the mouth of the false prophet. Since *breath* (or *spirit*) and *speech* issue forth from the mouth, we may understand from this that the spirits and evil influences of these three great enemies of God are now unitedly put forth to their uttermost, in a last prodigious effort of resistance to His purpose. The result is a great concentration of the hosts of wickedness at a place which is figuratively called *Armageddon*. For not only "the kings of the East", mentioned in verse 12, are there, but "the kings of the earth, and of the *whole world*" are also present. The meaning of the complete name Armageddon, according to Jackson *(Dict. of Scripture Names)* is "The Hill of Slaughter". The root meaning of the Hebrew original is given as a *place of rendezvous* or *gathering*. Clearly therefore the word has a figurative, not a geographical meaning., The purpose for which the hosts are gathered is stated. They are come together "to the battle of that great day of God Almighty". The description given here carries us no further. We see only the *concentration* of all the powers and hosts of evil. We see no opposing forces, and nothing is said of the battle itself, or of its outcome. But what is lacking here to make a complete description, is given in Chapter 19:11-21; and in this we see again another example of what is common throughout the Book, that is, a turning back to take up a line of events that had been dropped, or to give particulars concerning a matter that had theretofore received only a general mention.

Verse 15 is very striking. The speaker is not named or referred to in any way. But the words are unmistakably those of the Lord Jesus Christ. In the message to Sardis He had said "If therefore thou shalt not watch, I will come on thee *as a thief*"; and He also speaks there of a few "even in Sardis, which have not defiled their garments" (3:3,4). His coming "as a thief", means at a *wholly unexpected moment*. The foundation passage is Matthew 24:43, "But know this, that if the good man of the house had known in what watch the thief would come, he would have watched". *This is a lesson for all the people of God at all times.* It is much too broad to be limited to the second advent of Christ. Nevertheless, to that event it points particularly; for then the unexpectedness of His coming will be specially exemplified. This appears from the words of Peter, who, in warning those that scoff at the promise of His coming, says, "But the day of the Lord will come *as a thief in the night*" (2 Pet. 3:10), that is to say, as an overwhelming surprise. The *day of the Lord,* whereof Peter speaks, is manifestly "that *great day of* God Almighty", of Revelation 16:14. The apostle Paul likewise reminds the Thessalonian saints of what they already knew "perfectly", namely, "that the day of the Lord so cometh *as a thief in the night*" (1 Th. 5:2). He adds however, this comforting assurance, "But ye, brethren, are not in darkness, that *that day* should overtake *you* as a thief" (v. 4). So, when the day actually arrives, there are none of "the children of light" on the earth; for in all the description of the vial period, which is coincident with the seventh trumpet period, there is no indication of the presence on earth of any of the people of God. The *whole earth* is, during that entire period, the theater of the outpouring of the fullness of God's wrath and fiery indignation, from which His faithful promise guarantees them a perfect deliverance. For the Scripture last quoted goes on to say, "For God hath not appointed us *to wrath*" (1 Th. 5:9). They who are truly Christ's give proof thereof by watching and keeping their garments. Hence they are among the "blessed ones" who are "delivered from *the wrath to come*" (1 Th. 1:10); not because of their watchfulness, however, but because *they are His*. Therefore this word of Christ's is put in at this point, I take it, for the benefit of those whom He will "bring with Him" (1 Th. 4:14); as well as to stimulate and encourage all His people at all times to *watch* and to *keep their garments* (their outward behaviour) from the defilements of the world. Bengel aptly says:

"*Watch—garments:* two parts of an admonition that belong together and go together. For when about to go to sleep one lays aside his garments; but when awake he keeps them. Now, if something suddenly happens, such as the arrival of the Lord, one who is asleep does not readily get himself clothed; but he who is in a wakeful attitude is safe also in respect to his clothing".

SEVENTH VIAL

"And the seventh angel poured out his vial into the air; and there came a great voice out of the temple of heaven, from the throne, saying, It is done. And there were voices, and thunders, and lightnings; and there was a great earthquake, such as was not since men were upon the earth, so mighty an earthquake, and so great. And the great city was divided into three parts, and the cities of the nations fell: and great Babylon came in remembrance before God, to give unto her the cup of the wine of the fierceness of His wrath. And every island fled away, and the mountains were not found. And there fell upon men a great hail out of heaven, every stone about the weight of a talent: and men blasphemed God because of the plague of the hail; for the plague thereof was exceeding great" (vv. 17-21).

This last vial is poured out into the air. As the air entirely envelops the earth, the suggestion is that of an all-embracing judgment. But more than that, the air is the abode of hosts of evil powers and spirits (Eph. 2:2; 6:12). Hence this vial seems to have those evil spirits for its principal object. The preceding vial was a comprehensive judgment upon all the enemies of God upon the *earth*. Now the *air* is visited.

In discussing verse one I commented upon the great voice out of the temple, showing that it was the voice of God. His words, "It is done", expressly declare the comprehensiveness and finality of the judgment. There are the usual symbolical manifestations of judgments in the *voices, thunderings, lightnings,* and the *earthquake.* The latter, however, is declared to be such as was not since men were upon earth. This reminds us of the final shaking of all things, foretold in Hebrews 12:26, 27, quoted from Haggai 2:6, which signifies *"the removing* of those things that are shaken". So the impression is given that "all the powers that had withstood God's purpose concerning His kingdom, are now laid in ruins".

One part of the world-system that is singled out here for special mention, as having been struck under this judgment, is "the great city"; and after the brief but sufficient statement, "and the cities of the nations fell" (which means, of course, fell to rise no more), it is said that great Babylon came into remembrance before God, to give unto her the cup of the fierceness of His wrath. This great subject, like that of the battle of Armageddon, is left unfinished, to be taken up in a subsequent vision (Chapter XVIII). Hengstenberg points out that the words *"Babylon the great"* correspond to "the great city" in the preceding part of the verse; and that the *islands* and *mountains* correspond with "the cites of the nations". In any view of the passage, it conveys the idea of the utter prostration of all the strongholds of the enemy, and the destruction of all his possessions.

Finally, special mention is made of the great hail that fell out of heaven, the hailstones being of prodigious size. That this incident is mentioned last is no proof that it was the last to occur; though hail is so uniformly spread out that it is certain when it falls to strike down everything that might survive the other agents of destruction. Seemingly the point which this concluding verse of the passage is intended to emphasize is the continuance to the very end of the blasphemy of these enemies of God. It is as if they blasphemed Him with their last breath. Is not this repeated reference to the hardness of the hearts of these, the last of the civilized and progressive, the cultured and educated nations and races of men, intended as a most solemn and impressive warning to those who refuse the call to repentance in the day when forgiveness is freely offered? Bengel's comment is most appropriate:

"The blaspheming of God had twice already been mentioned under three plagues, and along with that it was said that *they did not repent*. But here, when the blaspheming of God is recorded the third time, no notice is taken of the other point, whether they repented or not; from which we may infer that the men were killed by this hail, as the Amorites in Joshua X. 11. Men could not receive in this case the punishment due to their blasphemy in *time*. Hence we must the more on that account suppose a respect had to the judgment of God *in eternity*. We have here the end of God's judgment on the *earth,* though still not the end of all things".

THE VISION OF MYSTERY BABYLON

Glancing ahead at what yet remains before us, we find a series of detached visions, each complete in itself, but all belonging to the period covered by the series of the seven vials. That is to say, they are visions each of a particular judgment belonging to the events of the general series of vial judgments, "the last plagues".

These are: I. The vision of the judgment of the scarlet-clad woman, Mystery Babylon (Chapter 17: 1-18).

II. The vision of the overthrow of the great city Babylon (Chapter 18).

III. The vision of the battle of the great day of God Almighty (Chapter 19:11-21).

IV. The vision of the chaining of Satan for a thousand years in the bottomless pit (Chapter 20:1-3).

"And there came one of the seven angels which had the seven vials, and talked with me, saying unto me, Come hither: I will show unto thee the judgment of the great whore that sitteth upon many waters: with whom the kings of the earth have committed fornication, and the inhabitants of the earth have been made drunk with the wine of her fornication. So he carried me away in the spirit into the wilderness: and I saw a woman sit upon a scarlet coloured beast, full of names of blasphemy, having seven heads and ten horns. And the woman was arrayed in purple and scarlet colour, and decked with gold and precious stones and pearls, having a golden cup in her hand full of abominations and filthiness of her fornication: and upon her forehead was a name written, MYSTERY, BABYLON THE GREAT, THE MOTHER OF HARLOTS AND ABOMINATIONS OF THE EARTH" (17:1-5).

There is a link between this vision and the series of vial judgments in the circumstance that the angel by whom John was taken to the place where he was to see it, was one of the seven angels that had the seven golden vials. It is connected specially with the third vial by the words which describe the woman as "drunken *with the blood* of the saints, and *with the blood* of the martyrs of Jesus" (v. 6). These visions of judgments subsequent to the pouring out of the vials, afford clear and certain proof that the Book is divided into groups, and that there is a constant returning in later visions to ground that has been already traversed, either for a fresh start, or else to show in detail something of which only a summary had been previously given. For here are several scenes of specific judgments coming into view after "the *last* plagues", those in which were "filled up the wrath of God"; after the voice from the throne had said "It is done", which saying showed that the end of the judgments had absolutely been reached. Yet the vision of Chapter XVII is expressely called *"the judgment* of the great whore"; and in Chapters XVIII, XIX, and XX, are other judgments involving the great city, the beasts and kings of the earth, and finally Satan himself. The only possible explanation of these facts is that at Chapter XVII we have a new beginning, a going back to certain of the judgments of the vial series.

The woman of this vision is *"Mystery Babylon* the great". The vision of the next chapter shows the fall of the *city* "Babylon the great" (18:2); but that is not termed a mystery. There is evidently an internal connection between the woman and the city, in that the same name, "Babylon the great", is given to each. (See also the explicit statement of 17:18). But there is a difference, in that the woman is a "mystery"; that is to say there is that about her which could not be known without further revelation from God. The mystery lay in *the real character of her relations with the kings and inhabitants of the earth,* and in the miserable doom that awaited her at the hands of those she had duped. On the other hand, the character and doom of the spiritual city Babylon were foretold in the type of the literal Babylon (Jer. 51:7, 8, 48, 61-64).

There are several things to guide us to the meaning of the symbol of the gorgeously-attired woman. The statement that she was seen *in the wilderness* puts before us a contrast with that other woman in the wilderness (Chapter XII). And since the latter represented the company of God's true people in the world, the Israel of God, this other woman must represent that which claims to be the company of God's elect, but in reality is in league with the powers of earth. This is confirmed by another comparison and contrast. For the woman of Chapter XII is identified with the bride of the Lamb, and with the heavenly city, the New Jerusalem (21:9-11). Moreover, as here, it is one of the seven angels who had the seven vials, that shows John that vision. The woman of Chapter XVII, on the other hand, is identified with the earthly city, Babylon (vv. 5, 18), and instead of being the immaculate bride of the Lamb, is one with whom the kings of the earth have committed fornication (v. 2). This then is the false "Church", which has had a recognizable existence in the world since the fourth century, and which had had its most conspicuous exemplification in Catholicism. All the symbols and descriptive items

The Seven Vials

confirm this view, some of them in a very striking way, as will be pointed out shortly. It is needful, however, to bear in mind that the vision shows us the *very last development* of that system of falsehood, cruelty, and spiritual harlotry, which this woman represents; and further that the full development is *yet to come*. For here we see the very last stage of beast government, that of the last of the *seven heads,* that of the *ten kingdoms* which will make war with the Lamb, but whom the Lamb shall overcome (v. 14, with 19:19); and here we see the end of this "mother of harlots", for the ten kingdoms whereof she had been for a time the mistress, make her desolate and naked, eat her flesh, and burn her with fire (v. 16).

The reader should recall at this point what was said on Chapter 13:18, as to the ultimate development of the religion of man *(Humanism),* by the amalgamation of the various religious factions, which howevermuch they may differ among themselves, agree in this, that they exalt man, and deny the faith of Jesus Christ. For this woman is not only herself a harlot, but is expressly "the mother of harlots and abominations of the earth", an *abomination* being an idol, or anything that is worshipped and trusted. This *"mother* church" will no doubt gather her daughters to her ample bosom ere the end comes. For, as everything that is of God will be consolidated into one temple (11:1), so everything not of God will be consolidated into one opposing system.

We have seen that the papacy as a political system is represented by the second beast; for as a government it has all the distinguishing characteristics of other world governments. Therefore another symbol was required to set it forth as a religious system, particularly since the elements that make up the one are not wholly the same as those that compose the other. What is emphasized particularly in this vision is the relations of this dissolute woman with "the kings of the earth", and the influence exerted by her over "the inhabitants of the earth". Those relations and that influence are described figuratively by the expressive word "fornication". The love of a harlot is a *feigned* love; and its hatefulness consists largely in the fact that it is put in the place of the true love of a wife. The harlot's aim is to secure favors for herself. To that end she not only prostitutes whatever she may have of womanly charm, but she brings into play all manner of seductive arts, and adorns her person with whatever may increase her attractions in the eyes of men. But specially reprehensible is her *pretended affection* for those she seeks to ensnare in the web of her fascinations and enchantments. Such is the false religion that feigns a deep solicitude for the spiritual good of the great ones of the earth, and exerts a mysterious and intoxicating influence over the inhabitants of the earth, making them, as it were "*drunk* with the wine of her fornication", the religion that conceals the basest of motives behind the mask of pretended affection and fondness. This is the chief feature, according to the figures here used, of the guilt for which this woman is about to be judged.

She is identified as "the great whore that sitteth upon many waters"; and this may be taken to mean greatness in earthly power and glory, as well as greatness in wickedness. The statement concerning the many waters is purely incidental, thrown in apparently as an aid to the identification of the woman. Clearly, from what is said in verse 15, the "many waters" are a symbol for the "peoples and multitudes". The reference here is to Jeremiah 51:13, where the prophet, addressing the literal Babylon, says: "O thou that dwellest *upon many waters, abundant in treasures,* thine end is come, and *the measure of thy covetousness*". These words fit very exactly the case of "Mystery Babylon the Great". The phrase "abundant in treasures", indicates that the "waters" are in this place used, as in many passages, as a symbol of that which causes fruitfulness and prosperity. For Babylon was not situated on the seas, but was an inland city. The application is plain. Papal Rome has enormously enriched herself at the expense of the peoples, multitudes and nations (the "many waters") upon which she has practiced her seductive arts and enchantments. Her "treasures" are fabulous, her revenues enormous, and the aggregate value of her holdings of lands and buildings runs into astronomical figures. There is not to be found in all the world a more flagrant example of disregard of Christ's command, "Lay not up for yourselves *treasures on earth*". But now is come "the end" of this prodigy of wickedness, so "abundant in treasures", and now is come "the measure of her covetousness".

Another identifying mark is given in the description of the woman's attire, which is of *purple and scarlet color,* with adornments of gold and precious stones. The colors, purple and scarlet, are conspicuous in the vestments of the Roman hierarchy, scarlet being specially identified with the cardinals, the "princes of the church"; while the gold and precious stones and pearls figure aptly the earthly gorgeousness and magnificence of the trappings with which this system adorns all its temples, altars, rites and ceremonies. Nothing could be farther than this ornate display from God's mind for His people, as expressed by the apostle Peter, to whom the false "church" accords special veneration: "Whose adorning, *let it not be* that outward adorning of plaiting the hair, and of wearing of gold, or of putting on of apparel; but let it be *the hidden man of the heart,* in that which is not corruptible, even the ornament of a meek and quiet spirit, which is in the sight of God of great price" (1 Pet. 3:3, 4). The true Israel of God, the woman of Chapter XII, during her sojourn in the wilderness of this world, seeks not to please the carnal eye by arts and ornaments which enhance personal attractiveness. Like her Lord she has in the eyes of men "no form nor comeliness", and they see in her no beauty that they should desire her.

A further mark of identification is given in the statement that the woman was seated upon a scarlet-colored beast, full of names of blasphemy, having seven heads and ten horns (v. 3). This symbolizes very aptly the dominance of the religious system which the woman represents over the governing power of the earth. The scarlet color of the beast is a link with the scarlet attire of the woman herself. They are of the same complexion. It is also a link with the great red dragon of Chapter 12:3.

"And I saw the woman drunken with the blood of the saints, and with the blood of the martyrs of Jesus: and when I saw her, I wondered with great admiration. And the angel said unto me, Wherefore didst thou marvel? I will tell thee the mystery of the woman, and of the beast that carrieth her, which hath the seven heads and ten horns. The beast that thou sawest was, and is not; and shall ascend out of the bottomless pit, and go into perdition; and they that dwell on the earth shall wonder, whose names were not written in the book of life from the foundation of the world, when they behold the beast that was, and is not, and yet is. And here is the mind which hath wisdom. The seven heads are seven mountains, on which the woman sitteth. And there are seven kings: five are fallen, and one is, and the other is not yet come; and when he cometh, he must continue a short space. And the beast that was, and is not, even he is the eighth, and is of the seven, and goeth into perdition. And the ten horns which thou sawest are ten kings, which have received no kingdom as yet; but receive power as kings one hour with the beast. These have one mind, and shall give their power and strength unto the beast. These shall make war with the Lamb, and the Lamb shall overcome them: for He is Lord of lords, and King of kings: and they that are with Him are called, and chosen, and faithful. And he saith unto me, The waters which thou sawest, where the whore sitteth, are peoples, and multitudes, and nations, and tongues. And the ten horns which thou sawest upon the beast, these shall hate the whore, and shall make her desolate and naked, and shall eat her flesh, and burn her with fire. For God hath put in their hearts to fulfil His will, and to agree, and give their kingdom unto the beast, until the words of God shall be fulfilled. And the woman which thou sawest is that great city, which reigneth over the kings of the earth" (17:6-18).

A further and final mark of identification is found in verse 6, which points definitely to Rome's bloody record of persecution and slaughter of the saints of God and of the martyrs of Jesus. The word "drunken" expresses forcibly the state of being glutted or surfeited with blood; though in truth it has seemed as if her thirst for the blood of God's saints were insatiable. A distinction is made in this book between God's people in general, His "saints", and the special class of martyrs. The appropriate inference is that, as the day of rewards is in view, God would specially encourage those who have to face death for Jesus Christ's sake, by bringing to mind the great and glorious rewards that await them.

Then follows the angel's explanation to John of the mystery of the woman and of the beast that carried her, a mystery so extraordinary that it had caused John to wonder with a great wonder (v. 6). Sufficient comment has already been made on the explanation concerning the beast (see remarks on 13:1-3). It is well, however, to recall particularly that in John's day the ungodly world-power was in its sixth stage, that of the Roman Empire, corresponding to the sixth head of the beast, and that there was to be yet another stage, as declared by the words: "The other is not yet come; and when he cometh he must continue a short space" (v. 10). On this verse Hengstenberg says:—

"Of the seven kings mentioned, *five* belonged to the period already past; and of the two others, *one* was on the stage of history at the time then present, and *the other* had not yet appeared upon it".

It was in the sixth head that the beast had received the deadly wound, from which he had seemingly revived as by a miracle; though in that head the power of the beast, which he had received from the dragon (13:2), was permanently broken (Heb. 2:14). On this Bengel remarks:

"This one king (the sixth) however impotent he may be, is yet *not off the stage*. Were it otherwise, then the continued existence of the beast, from his ascending out of the sea to his precipitation into the lake of fire, would be thereby interrupted. But the Lord had said, '*I have overcome the world*'; and in that mighty fact lies the foundation of the difference between the 'one' (the sixth king) and the 'five'. When the other (the seventh) comes, then the *sixth* falls. That *is now;* it is the Roman Empire. But from the statement made respecting the *seventh,* that he should abide but a short time, we infer that the one then in being was likely to continue yet a pretty long time".

As to the one that was (and is) yet to come, there are various and cogent reasons for believing, though we may not affirm it with certainty, that it is even now in process of formation, and at a rapid rate, in the political doings, compacts, discussions and alliances between the principal states of Europe (see last chapter of this volume). What is apparently close at hand is a superstate (the League of Nations) which will be the seventh and last stage of beast government, and ten associated kingdoms which will "receive power as kings one hour *with the beast*". Such a system is in such plain sight that the natural eye can see it; and furthermore, the fear of the ruin, which would certainly be the result of another war, is so great, that the statesmen of Europe are sparing no effort to bring it into effective existence. For they see no other way of escape from complete annihilation. It requires however a revelation from God to tell us that the seventh head will have but a brief existence, "one hour" (v. 12), that all the associated powers of earth will make war with the Lamb, and the Lamb shall overcome them (v. 14). That event is the subject of a later vision (Chap. 19:11-21). But before that final overthrow of world-power in the hands of men, the ten kings will completely change their attitude towards the great harlot; their fondness will be turned to extremest enmity; for they will "hate her, and make her desolate and naked, and shall eat her flesh, and burn her with fire" (v. 16). Her end will be like that of Jezebel, who typifies her both in life, and in death (2 K. 9:30-37). As to the similarities between the licentious queen Jezebel and the woman of this chapter, see comments above on 2:20, 21.

The terrible end of this enchantress will appear to proceed from natural causes. It will seem as if the ten kings were simply accomplishing their own mind, and were turned against this monstrous system of duplicity and covetousness by some more than usually arrogant assumption of authority, or usurpation of power. But it is given us to know that *God's* hand will be the active agent in it; that He will "put in their hearts to fulfil *His* will, and to agree, and give their kingdom unto the beast (the League of Nations, or something similar) until the words of God shall be fulfilled" (v. 17).

BABYLON FALLEN

"And after these things I saw another angel come down from heaven, having great power; and the earth was lightened with his glory. And he cried mightily with a strong voice, saying, Babylon the great is fallen, is fallen, and is become the habitation of devils, and the hold of every foul spirit, and a cage of every unclean and hateful bird. For all nations have drunk of the wine of the wrath for her fornication, and the kings of the earth have committed fornication with her, and the merchants of the earth are waxed rich through the abundance of her delicacies" (18:1-3).

The culmination of man's activities along *religious* lines is pictured in the woman, Mystery Babylon, of Chapter XVII. The culmination of his activities along the parallel line of *"business"* is seen in the city, Babylon the Great, of the vision now before us. There yet remains the culmination of human activities along a third parallel line, that of *politics,* which comes into view in the vision of Chapter 19:11-21.

The importance of the subject of this vision is testified by the manner of its introduction. The angel having great power, by whose glory the earth is illuminated, can be none other than Christ. The words "He cried mightily with a strong voice", further indicate the Lord Himself. They recall the statement of Chapter 10:3, "And He cried with a loud voice, as when a lion roareth". He repeats the proclamation of the angel of Chapter 14:8, "Babylon is fallen is fallen". The vision apparently comes under the seventh vial, for there it is recorded that "the great city was divided into three parts", that being the effect of the mighty earthquake, such as had never been since men were upon the earth; and there it is also recorded that "great Babylon came in remembrance before God, to give her the cup of the wine of the fierceness of His wrath" (16:18, 19). The earthquake is not mentioned in Chapter 18 as the agent of the destruction of Babylon; but it is said, "And she shall be utterly burned with fire" (v. 8). Fires always break out in a city that has been visited with a severe earthquake.

That which great Babylon typifies is a thing that is monstrously evil in the sight of God. It represents *the world,* of course; but particularly the world in the aspect of a gigantic system for the pursuit of wealth and pleasure. There is no one word that fully expresses what is here symbolized. I have said it represents *Commercialism,* or *Industrialism;* but neither of those words adequately defines the symbol, though they help to convey the idea embodied in it. The great world of "Business" has been growing bigger and bigger; it has been exerting more and more fascinations upon the hearts and imaginations of men; it has been increasing marvellously in the complexity of its machinery and the magnitude of its operations; it has become virtually a religion to countless millions of people; and its leaders, the captains of industry, are practically the rulers of the world. The *framework* or *body* of Industrialism is tangible and visible. It is seen in the factories, warehouses, power houses, mercantile and business houses, railroads, steamships, motor trucks etc., etc. But the animating *spirit* of it all is that mysterious thing called "Finance". This is the only god that the many know and worship in our day; for a man's god is that to which he consecrates his life, and to which he looks for meeting his needs, satisfying his desires, and overcoming his difficulties. Money, then, is the greatest of all the idols of the present day. It numbers its devotees by the hundreds of millions, and they include the most intelligent and cultivated members of society. It is not an exaggeration to say that Money, of which the financiers are the priests, and "Business" the handmaid, is the greatest rival of God for the affections and devotions of men. This is implied in the teaching of Christ, "Ye cannot serve God and Mammon" (Mat. 6:24). In those words He declares the rivalry of God and Mammon for the service (which as the context shows, involves the *love*) of men. Babylon the great is the Biblical type and symbol of all this; which fully explains the intensity of God's hatred of it, and the great rejoicings of heaven at its overthrow.

The name *Babel* comes into prominence in the Bible soon after the flood. It was given to the city which men attempted to build as a place of safety for themselves, and as a central attraction to unify and hold the race of human beings together (Gen. 11:1-9). It is easy therefore, to glean from that passage the main ideas associated with Babel, or Babylon; namely, the *consolidation* of humanity, and salvation for man through his own works, that is to say, *Humanism*. It is utterly opposed to God and to His purposes for man. Therefore, it is no place for the people of God; and when He sent Israel there it was as a punishment. This explains God's urgency to call His people out of Babylon, and His oft-declared purpose utterly to destroy her.

The call to depart from Babylon is first heard in the prophecy of Isaiah, and is heard seven times in all, the last being in Revelation 18:4. It is a significant fact also that, in each of these seven instances, the city of God, Jerusalem (or Zion) is in the context. Thus the Scriptures remind us repeatedly of the rivalry between the city of man and the city of God. The passages are these:—

1. Isaiah 48:20, *"Go ye forth of Babylon,* flee ye from the Chaldeans, with a voice of singing declare ye, tell this, utter it even to the end of the earth; say ye, the Lord hath redeemed His servant Jacob".

Even in this first passage the note of exultation is heard, as God contemplates the redemption of His people, and their deliverance from Babylon. In the context we read that "He will do His pleasure on Babylon, and His arm shall be on the Chaldeans" (v. 14). Also we find in verse 2 a reference to "the holy city".

2. Isaiah 52:11, *"Depart ye, depart ye, go ye out from thence;* touch no unclean thing; go ye out of the midst of her; be ye clean that bear the vessels of the Lord".

Babylon is not mentioned here by name; but she is the subject of the passage. For in verse 4 God speaks of the sojourn of His people aforetime in Egypt, and of the subsequent oppression by the Assyrian; and then He asks, "Now therefore, what have I *here,* that My people is taken away for nought?" This refers to the coming captivity in Babylon, which is the general subject of this part of the prophecy. Zion is named in verse 8, and Jerusalem in verse 9.

3. Jeremiah 50:8, 9, *"Remove out of the midst of Babylon,* and go forth out of the land of the Chaldeans, and be as the he goats before the flocks. For lo, I will raise, and cause to come up against Babylon, an assembly of great nations from the north country; and they shall set themselves in array against her; from thence she shall be taken".

In verse 3 it is said concerning the people of God, "They shall ask the way to Zion with their faces thitherward". The punishment of Babylon is foretold in verses 13, 15, 18, 23, etc.

4. Jeremiah 51:6, 8, *"Flee out of the midst of Babylon,* and deliver every man his soul; *be not cut off in her iniquity:* for this is the time of the Lord's vengeance; He will render unto her a recompense. Babylon is *suddenly* fallen, and destroyed".

496   *The Patmos Visions*

The call here is very urgent, and the similarity of the language to that of Revelation 18:2-4 will be noted. In verse 10 Zion is named.

5. Zechariah 2:6, 7, *"Ho, ho, come forth and flee from the land of the north,* saith the Lord: for I have spread you abroad as the four winds of the heaven, saith the Lord. Deliver thyself, O Zion, that dwellest with the daughter *of Babylon".*

This is the vision, to which reference has already been made, wherein Jerusalem is being measured with a view to her being inhabited again (vv. 1-4).

6. 2 Corinthians 6:17, 18, "Wherefore, *come out from among them,* and be ye separate, saith the Lord, and touch not the unclean thing; and I will receive you, and will be a Father unto you, and ye shall be My sons and daughters, saith the Lord Almighty".

Babylon is not named in this passage, but it is implied in the confusion and mixture of believers and unbelievers, christianity and paganism, described in verses 14-16. Moreover, the first part of the passage is a direct quotation from Isaiah 52:11, cited above. Neither is the holy city of God mentioned by name; but that too is implied in the words, "And I will receive you, and be a Father unto you". The family relation implies the family home.

7. Rev. 18:4-8, "And I heard another voice from heaven, saying, Come out of her, My people, that ye be not partakers of her sins, and that ye receive not of her plagues. For her sins have reached unto heaven, and God hath remembered her iniquities. Reward her even as she rewarded you, and double unto her double according to her works: in the cup which she hath filled, fill to her double. How much she hath glorified

herself, and lived deliciously, so much torment and sorrow give her; for she saith in her heart, I sit a queen, and am no widow, and shall see no sorrow. Therefore shall her plagues come in one day, death, and mourning, and famine; and she shall be utterly burned with fire: for strong is the Lord God who judgeth her".

This sevenfold call of God to His people to come out of great Babylon is most impressive. The call to come out implies that the way is open for them to depart. And such is the case, for Christ "gave Himself for our sins that He might deliver us out of this present evil world, according to the will of God and our Father" (Gal. 1:4). The door of escape has been set open by Him who openeth and no man shutteth. But it should be remembered that whereas God brought His people out of Egypt in a body, with a strong hand and an outstretched arm, it was otherwise with respect to their deliverance from Babylon; for there He simply opened the way, and only those came out who were minded so to do.

The fascinations of the city of Babylon are of the same sort as those of the woman, "Mystery Babylon"; for it is said by the mighty angel that all the heathen have drunk of her wine. This agrees with Jeremiah 51:7, "the nations have drunken of her wine, therefore the nations are mad". It is further said that "her sins have reached unto heaven"; and this again is in accord with Jeremiah 51:9, "for her judgment reacheth unto heaven, and is lifted up even to the skies". This indicates the highest degree of sin, and sin of the most conspicuous kind. Such was the sin of those before the flood who, in the face of God's solemn warnings and the testimony of Noah, "a preacher of righteousness" (2 Pet. 2:5), continued in their own ways, eating and drinking, marrying and giving in marriage, until the day that Noah entered into the ark, and the flood came, and destroyed them all (Lu. 17:27). *Contemptuous disregard and defiance of the Word of God* is the essence of the sin of Babylon; and in her case, as portrayed in the scene now before us, that sin is carried to its greatest height; "for her sins have reached *unto heaven*". And such is the spirit of the world in these last days. Men to whom the Word of God has come in its fullness, in whose ears His warnings concerning the doom of this world have been plainly spoken, treat them as old wives' fables, and go on with their great projects, planning enterprises on an ever increasing scale of grandeur and magnificence, thus by the whole course of their daily lives making God a liar. The spirit of Babylon is manifested by what "she saith *in her heart*", namely, "I sit a queen", that is, upon a throne, "and am no widow, and shall see no sorrow" (18:7); though God has said directly the contrary. And this is precisely the spirit of the leaders of the affairs of the world today, who are saying in all their actions (which truly speak louder than words), "Where is the promise of His coming? for since the fathers fell asleep, all things continue as they were from the beginning of the creation" (2 Pet. 3:4). This sin of high-handed presumption, of contempt and defiance of the Word of God,

has surely been carried to the greatest height by the
men of our day, "men of *the world,* which have their
portion in *this life"* (Ps. 17:14). How great then is
"the long suffering of our Lord", who still withholds
the threatened judgment, for that He is "not willing
that any should perish, but that all should come to
repentance"! (2 Pet. 3:9).

"And the kings of the earth, who have committed fornication and lived deliciously with her, shall bewail her, and lament for her, when they shall see the smoke of her burning. Standing afar off for the fear of her torment, saying, Alas, alas, that great city Babylon, that mighty city! for in one hour is thy judgment come. And the merchants of the earth shall weep and mourn over her; for no man buyeth their merchandise any more; the merchandise of gold, and silver, and precious stones, and of pearls, and fine linen, and purple, and silk, and scarlet, and all thyine wood, and all manner vessels of ivory, and all manner vessels of most precious wood, and of brass, and iron, and marble. And cinnamon, and odours, and ointments, and frankincense, and wine, and oil, and fine flour, and wheat, and beasts, and sheep, and horses, and chariots, and slaves, and souls of men" (18:9-13).

In this lament over the sudden fall and destruction
of the great city, "the merchants of the earth" are
joined with *"the kings* of the earth". This prophecy
of the uniting of politics and business is of great significance at the present hour, when the leaders of the business affairs of the world stand on an equal footing with
the leaders of its political affairs, and when their interests and concerns are practically identical. It was
not so a generation or two ago. The kings of the
earth will bewail and lament for Babylon, because they

lived luxuriously, or voluptuously, with her; and the merchant princes of the earth shall weep and mourn over her, because the markets for their wares are gone; "for no man buyeth their merchandise any more". In the list of the "merchandise" wherewith men engaged in traffic in the marts of the great city, gold and silver and precious stones come first—earthly treasure which surely has the first place in the affections of men, and which never were so highly prized and so eagerly sought as at the present time. Then come things for show and personal adornment; and then choice articles of rare and precious wood, metal and ivory. Then come perfumes and other luxuries, which speak of the sensuousness of modern living; and then the more substantial commodities, including horses and chariots, which brings to mind the extraordinary development in our day of conveyances for travel and moving about. Most significantly this remarkable list of the wares of great Babylon ends with the "bodies and souls of men" (the word *slaves* in the text being literally *bodies*). For here is where men and women barter their bodies and souls for some trifle, something that at best can afford but a momentary satisfaction. Here is where the multitude of the Esaus of our day exchange their birthright for a mere mess of pottage. How pertinent and how impressive in this connection are the words of the Lord Jesus Christ, "For what is a man profited, if he shall gain the whole world and lose his own soul? For the Son of man shall come in the glory of His Father, with His angels, and then He shall reward every man according to his works" (Mat. 16:26, 27). Those who make the shrewdest bargains in the marts of the great city, who get the greatest return in exchange for their souls, must part forever with what they received, and be losers for eternity, when Christ shall come. But they that lose their lives in this world for His sake, waiting for their wealth, honors and pleasures until He shall return in power and glory, with the angels of His strength, will have enduring riches; they will enter upon pleasures for evermore, and will receive an inheritance which is incorruptible, and undefiled, and that fadeth not away.

"And the fruits that thy soul lusted after are departed from thee, and all things which were dainty and goodly are departed from thee, and thou shalt find them no more at all. The merchants of these things, which were made rich by her, shall stand afar off for the fear of her torment, weeping and wailing; and saying, Alas, alas, that great city, that was clothed in fine linen, and purple, and scarlet, and decked with gold, and precious stones and pearls! For in one hour so great riches is come to nought. And every shipmaster, and all the company in ships, and sailors, and as many as trade by sea, stood afar off, and cried when they saw the smoke of her burning, saying, What city is like unto this great city! And they cast dust on their heads, and cried, weeping and wailing, saying, Alas, alas, that great city, wherein were made rich all that had ships in the sea by reason of her costliness! for in one hour is she made desolate" (18:14-19).

These verses picture most vividly the remorseful sorrows of those whose affections have been set upon the great world-system, and whose expectations have been all from that quarter. They set forth as only the words of the Holy Spirit could portray, the bitterness of the disappointment and the anguish of soul of those who see the source of all their fond hopes and desires extinguished; and who realize that it is a disappointment that must be forever. The repeated cry Alas! Alas! (or *Woe, Woe,* for the word is the same as that of the angel who cried the three *woes* in Chapter 8:13) is like that of Esau's, "a great and exceeding bitter cry" (Gen. 27:34); and the casting of dust upon the head is the act of one who realizes that he has been brought into a condition of extreme humiliation and distress.

The recurrence of the word "woe" *(Alas!* verses 16 and 19) serves as a reminder that all this is in the period of the third and last *woe* (11:14).

"And a mighty angel took up a stone like a great millstone, and cast it into the sea, saying, Thus with violence shall that great city Babylon be thrown down, and shall be found no more at all. And the voice of harpers, and musicians, and of pipers, and trumpeters, shall be heard no more at all in thee; and no craftsman, of whatsoever craft he be, shall be found any more in thee; and the sound of a millstone shall be heard no more at all in thee; and the light of a candle shall shine no more at all in thee; and the voice of the bridegroom and of the bride shall be heard no more at all in thee; for thy merchants were the great men of the earth; for by thy sorceries were all nations deceived. And in her was found the blood of prophets, and of saints, and of all that were slain upon the earth (18:21-24).

The rejoicing of heaven, and of those whose hearts and treasures are there, is set in direct contrast with the lamentations and woes of those who bartered away their bodies and souls in the marts of Babylon the great. Verse 20 is anticipative of what is more fully developed in the first part of the next chapter; so comment thereon will be reserved till we reach that passage.

The symbolic action of the strong angel described in verse 21 is an intensified picture of the act which Jeremiah commanded Seraiah to perform when he should come to Babylon, namely, to read all the words of the prophecy of the utter destruction of Babylon, and then to bind a stone to the book of the prophecy, and cast it into the midst of the Euphates, and say, "Thus shall Babylon sink, and shall not rise from the evil that I shall bring upon her" (Jer. 51:59-64). This makes very clear that the destruction of the literal Babylon, and the prophecies regarding the same, were typical foreshadowings of the destruction of spiritual Babylon.

The angel's words announce most impressively the vanishing forever of all the joys and delights of the great city, the music and the song, the hum of industry, the brightness of its illumination, and above all, the rejoicings of bridegroom and bride, which in the Bible stand for the highest of all human joys. In this connection Jeremiah 25:10 should be recalled. Speaking there of the coming doom of Babylon, God said: "I will take from them the voice of mirth and the voice of gladness, the voice of the bridegroom and the voice of the bride, the sound of the millstones, and the light of the candle".

The concluding words of God's indictment of the spiritual Babylon set her sin in the clearest light. Her merchants were the great ones of the earth, whereas Christ, the lawful King, has no place in this world, and has commanded His followers to take the lowest place in it. By her sorceries all nations have been deceived; and in her was found the blood of prophets, and of saints, and of all that were slain upon the earth.

CHAPTER XII

Rejoicings in Heaven. The Marriage of the Lamb. The Battle of Armageddon.

"And after these things I heard a great voice of much people in heaven, saying, Alleluia; Salvation, and glory, and honour, and power, unto the Lord our God. For true and righteous are His judgments: for He hath judged the great whore, which did corrupt the earth with her fornication, and hath avenged the blood of His servants at her hand. And again they said, Alleluia. And her smoke rose up for ever and ever. And the four and twenty elders and the four beasts fell down and worshipped God that sat on the throne, saying, Amen: Alleluia" (19:1-4).

AT VERSE 20 of the preceding chapter is a call to heaven, and to the holy apostles and prophets of God, to rejoice over the downfall of Babylon, because God has avenged them on her. And here is the response, which comes in "a great voice of much people in heaven". It is, of course, the voice of the redeemed saints of God, with apostles and prophets at their head. These break forth into *Hallelujahs;* and as has been often remarked, these are the only Hallelujahs in the New Testament. It seems as if they had been reserved for this special occasion; and in this we have a further proof of the transcendent importance in God's eyes of what is delineated in the preceding chapter. The Hallelujahs are four in number (three in the verses quoted above, and the fourth in verse 6) which points to God's victory over the powers of earth, of which four is the numerical symbol. The participation of the four and twenty elders and the four living creatures in this celebration is also significant. One of the Hallelujahs is uttered by them, and with it they join an *Amen*. These, being *pure Hebrew words*, serve to mark the connection between the Old Testament and the New, and particularly to show the continuity of God's people, as constituting one body, embracing all the elect of all the dispensations.

The O. T. basis for this wonderful scene is found in Psalm 104:35. It is the Psalm of the earth, describing, in language of surpassing beauty its "foundations" (v. 5), its covering waters, its mountains and valleys and running streams, its verdure and trees, and all the creatures, man included, to whom God has given it for a home. And it ends in these words: "I will sing unto the Lord as long as I live; I will sing praise to my God while I have my being. My meditation of Him shall be sweet; I will be glad in the Lord. *Let the sinners be consumed out of the earth, and let the wicked be no more"*; and in anticipation of this, the psalmist exclaims, "Bless thou the Lord, O my soul. *Hallelujah*"! Thus the thought of the destruction of the wicked out of the earth evokes a *Hallelujah* from one who is in accord with the mind and purposes of God. For just as in this day of salvation, His people rejoice with Him in the *salvation* of sinners, even so, in the coming day of judgment they will rejoice with Him in the *judgment* of the wicked.

The ground of the ascription of praise in Revelation 19:1 and 2, is *the truth and justice of God's judgments,* as exemplified in the judgment of the great whore who had corrupted the earth with her fornication, by which judgment He had avenged the blood of His servants that had been shed by her. (The phrase *at her hand,* is literally, *out of* her hand, as if their blood had flowed from her hand. Thus God spake concerning Jezebel, "that I may avenge the blood of My servants .... *at the hand* of Jezebel", 2 K. 9:7).

The redeemed in glory now know beyond a doubt or misgiving that "Salvation is of the Lord" (Ps. 3:9; Jonah 2:9). Hence they ascribe *"Salvation,* and glory, and honor, and power, unto the Lord our God". Concerning this ascription of praise, Hengstenberg remarks:

"The whole doxology rests upon the doxology of the Lord's prayer in Matthew 6:13, 'For Thine is the kingdom, and the power, and the glory', for the genuineness of which this very passage affords decisive evidence. *There* redemption out of evil is grounded in the power and glory of God, *here* the power and glory are deduced from the redemption out of evil. . . . The realization of the doxology in the Paternoster is there anticipated by faith; here it has in part entered into reality, though the kingdom, the dominion, still awaits its full realization".

He goes on to point out that allusions to the first Gospel pervade the whole Apocalypse, saying:

"An allusion specially to Matthew was the more natural here, as among the first three Gospels, this of the fellow-apostle of John *everywhere occupies the foreground in the Apocalypse,* which is a remarkable fact, and fraught with important results".

THE MARRIAGE OF THE LAMB

"And a voice came out of the throne, saying, Praise our God, all ye His servants, and ye that fear Him, both small and great. And I heard as it were the voice of a great multitude, and as the voice of many waters, and as the voice of mighty thunderings, saying, Alleluia; for the Lord God omnipotent reigneth. Let us be glad and rejoice, and give honour to Him: for the marriage of the Lamb is come, and His wife hath made herself ready. And to her was granted that she should be arrayed in fine linen, clean and white; for the fine linen is the righteousness of saints. And he saith unto me, Write, Blessed are they which are called unto the marriage supper of the Lamb. And he saith unto me, These are the true sayings of God. And I fell at his feet to worship him. And he said unto me, See thou do it not: I am thy fellowservant, and of thy brethren that have the testimony of Jesus: worship God: for the testimony of Jesus is the spirit of prophecy" (19:5-10).

This voice from the throne is, of course, that of God Himself, Who now calls for a universal anthem of praise, from all His servants, and from all who fear Him, both small and great. The response is tremendous; and the expressed reason for this last "Hallelujah" is that *the Lord has taken the kingdom.* Thus is accomplished that which the mighty angel so solemnly announced in Chapter 10:6, 7, and the great voices in heaven of Chapter 11:15 celebrated anticipatively.

The hosts of the redeemed are now made aware of another development about to take place, a further occasion for them to be glad, and rejoice, and give honor to God; for *the marriage of the Lamb* approaches, and His wife has made herself ready.

There is little room for doubt that "the bride of the Lamb" is a symbol for the one body of the redeemed, and not the symbol for a special company selected out of the entire number, nor for the saved of a particular dispensation only. For commonly in the N. T. the one church of Christ (embracing all the saints of God) is represented under the image of a bride. The earliest occurrence of this figure historically is in John 3:29, in the days of the ministry of John the Baptist, where Christ is referred to as "the Bridegroom", and those who were turning to Him are spoken of as "the bride". The passage before us is itself sufficient to exclude the idea that the bride is a select company less than the whole number of God's saints; for in referring to her garments of fine linen, pure and lustrous white, the explanation is introduced that "the fine linen is the righteousness *of the saints*". And since in any view of the word "righteousness", as here used, it pertains equally to *all* the saints; and since all wear the bridal attire, all are included in the symbol of the bride. The phrase "of the Lamb" points in no uncertain way to the same conclusion. For in the word "Lamb" we have another symbol of Christ's relation to His people, a relation that, beyond all dispute, extends to *all* who are redeemed by His precious blood, and whose names were written, from the foundation of the world, in *the Lamb's* book of life. As to what is commonly advanced to support the contrary view, it need only be remarked that it is pressing the details of a figure or symbolic image altogether too far to argue that those invited to the marriage supper of the Lamb must be a different company from those that form the bride.

What verse 8 declares is that the fine linen is the righteousnesses, or righteous *acts,* of the saints. That is to say, it represents "not the *glory* of the saints, but their *excellencies*" (Hengstenberg). In this there is, of course, no contradiction to the doctrine of Scripture that all human righteousness is as filthy rags, and that apart from the grace of God none can do a single meritorious act. For notwithstanding that without Him we can do nothing, God is nevertheless pleased to ascribe excellence and "righteousness" to everything that His people may seek to do in obedience to His will.

The announcement of the approaching marriage of the Lamb is put directly in contrast with that of the preceding chapter concerning Babylon, "And the voice of the bridegroom and of the bride shall be heard no more at all in thee". Joy has now departed from the earth; but it breaks out in its fullness in heaven. For this is the joy of the heavenly Bridegroom, the supreme joy of Christ, Who for *the joy that was set before Him,* endured the cross, and made Himself the sacrificial *Lamb* (Heb. 12:2). Now as the risen and glorified Lamb, He is to "see of the travail of His soul and *be satisfied*" (Isa. 53:11).

That much importance is attached to this announcement of the marriage supper of the Lamb appears from the circumstance that the revealing angel charges John specially to write: "Blessed are they which are called unto the marriage supper of the Lamb", and adds the assurance that "these are the true sayings of God". John himself is so deeply impressed that he falls at the feet of the angel to worship him. There is no need to comment further upon this incident.

This vision takes us only to the announcement of the approaching marriage of the Lamb. The subject is interrupted here, to be resumed at chapter 21:9.

The Battle of Armageddon

"And I saw heaven opened, and behold, a white horse; and He that sat upon him was called Faithful and True, and in righteousness He doth judge and make war. His eyes were as a flame of fire, and on His head were many crowns; and He had a name written, that no man knew but He Himself. And He was clothed with a vesture dipped in blood: and His name is called The Word of God and the armies which were in heaven followed Him upon white horses, clothed in fine linen, white and clean. And out of His mouth goeth a sharp sword, that with it He should smite the nations: and He shall rule them with a rod of iron: and He treadeth the winepress of the fierceness and wrath of Almighty God. And He hath on His vesture and on His thigh a name written, KING OF KINGS, AND LORD OF LORDS" (19:11-16).

Here is another description of Christ in the glory of His Human nature, comparable to that of Chapter I. In two particulars the several descriptions agree; for here again it is said that His eyes were as a flame of fire, and out of His mouth goeth a sharp sword. In all other particulars the present description differs from the earlier one, the differences being such as to express the very different character of the mission upon which He now comes forth. He now comes as "King of kings and Lord of lords", in keeping with which He is not on foot, as when walking in the midst of the golden candlesticks, but is mounted on a white horse. Moreover, He now has upon His head many diadems. He comes at this time to "judge and make war"; and in keeping with this He is clothed with a vesture dipped in blood (see Isa. 63:1-3). In the former vision He stood alone; but now He is accompanied by the armies of heaven.

The white horse upon which Christ is mounted forms a contrast with His last entry into Jerusalem, when He was mounted upon the foal of an ass (Mat. 21:7). It also connects this vision with that of 6:2. There He is seen going forth in the gospel, "conquering"; and now He comes "to conquer". For there can be no doubt as to the issue of the approaching conflict. Psalm XLV is in view. The psalmist is there speaking of things he has made "touching *the King*", of whom he says: "Gird Thy sword upon Thy thigh, O most Mighty, with Thy glory and Thy majesty, and in Thy majesty *ride prosperously*". His Name is here called "The Word of God". What the Word of God is able to accomplish is shown in the first chapter of the Bible; and certainly none can withstand Him who now comes in the might of that Name. On this, Bengel, remarks:

"It is not said here, His Name is called *Jesus;* for here He manifests Himself not as the Saviour of His people, but as the destroyer of His enemies. The Name *Jesus* especially unfolds His grace; and the Name, *the Word of God,* His majesty. How deep must that, which is indicated by this Name, lie in the unsearchable God-head!"

"And I saw an angel standing in the sun; and he cried with a loud voice, saying to all the fowls that fly in the midst of heaven, Come and gather yourselves together unto the supper of the great God; that ye may eat the flesh of kings, and the flesh of captains, and the flesh of mighty men, and the flesh of horses, and of them that sit on them, and the flesh of all men, both free and bond, both small and great" (19:17, 18).

That the issue of the approaching conflict is certain, further appears by this summons to all the fowls of the air to come to the great supper of God (for the adjective *great* belongs to the noun *supper*). The foundation passage in this case is Ezekiel 39:17-32, where God commands the prophet to

"Speak to every feathered fowl and to every beast of the field, Assemble yourselves and come, gather yourselves on every side to My sacrifice that I do sacrifice for you, that ye may eat flesh and drink blood. Ye shall eat the flesh of the mighty, and drink the blood of the princes of the earth".

There is a striking contrast between this great supper of God, to which the fowls of the air are summoned, and that of the preceding chapter, concerning which it is written, "Blessed are they which are called to the *marriage supper* of the Lamb".

"And I saw the beast, and the kings of the earth, and their armies, gathered together to make war against Him that sat on the horse, and against his army. And the beast was taken, and with him the false prophet that wrought miracles before him, with which he deceived them that had received the mark of the beast, and them that worshipped his image. These both were cast alive into a lake of fire burning with brimstone. And the remnant were slain with the sword of him that sat upon the horse, which sword proceeded out of his mouth; and all the fowls were filled with their flesh" (19:20, 21).

The description of this great battle, which decides forever the possession of the kingdoms of this world, is remarkably brief; and this noticeable brevity in describing that upon which such tremendous issues hung, is the more significant because of the comparatively long account given in this same passage of the appearance of Christ. Thus we are reminded again that this Book is the Revelation of *Jesus Christ*.

This concentration of hostile forces includes the beast, and the kings of the earth, and their armies. The false prophet (the second beast) is not named in this enumeration of those whom John saw "gathered together to make war against Him that sat on the horse, and against His army", which would suggest that the second beast did not take the field to engage actively in the battle. But in the next verse it is stated that "the beast was taken (lit. *seized*) and *with him* the false prophet". These *both* were cast alive into a lake of fire, burning with brimstone. There is a close agreement here with what Daniel saw of the end of the fourth beast of his vision, and of the little horn that had a mouth speaking great things: "I beheld then, because of the voice of the great words which the horn spake; I beheld even till the beast was slain, and his body destroyed and given to the burning flame" (Dan. 7:11).

Christ's earthly enemies are now all consumed; for the remnant were slain with the sword of His mouth, "which is a *spiritual* weapon of resistless might" (Bengel). This recalls what He Himself has said: "He that rejecteth Me, and receiveth not My words, hath one that judgeth him; *the word that I have spoken*"—the sword of His mouth—"the same shall judge him *in the last day*" (John 12:48).

The Binding of Satan. The Thousand Years. The Last Judgment

"And I saw an angel come down from heaven, having the key of the bottomless pit and a great chain in his hand. And he laid hold on the dragon, that old serpent, which is the Devil, and Satan, and bound him a thousand years. And cast him into the bottomless pit, and shut him up, and set a seal upon him, that he should deceive the nations no more till the thousand years should be fulfilled: and after that he must be loosed a little season" (20:1-3).

The end of all the earthly enemies of Christ was shown in the visions of the preceding chapter. There remains, therefore, only the arch enemy, the great spiritual adversary; and now he too is dealt with. It is a further proof of the greatness of the Devil that he is not disposed of in summary fashion, as were his instruments, the beast, the false prophet, and the kings of the earth. Satan is dealt with in two distinct stages. For at this stage of affairs he is bound with a great chain, and cast into the bottomless pit, where he is shut up, and a seal set upon him. But his imprisonment there is not for eternity; for after a thousand years he is to be "loosed out of his prison" (v. 8). Then after "a little season" he is to be "cast into the lake of fire and brimstone, where the beast and the false prophet are, and be tormented day and night for ever and ever" (v. 10).

From the fact that the angel of verse 1 *has* the key of the bottomless pit (not that it was *given* him, as in 9:1) it is inferred, and I think rightly, that this angel is Christ. Other considerations point to the same conclusion. Thus, none of the created angels is great enough for this (Jude 9). Again, in Chapter 12:9, where it is said that the dragon, that old serpent, called the Devil and Satan (which four titles are repeated here) was cast out of heaven, the clear implication is that Christ, the Manchild, cast him out, in fulfilment of the prophecy of Genesis 3:15. This affords ground for the belief that, in this further casting down of Satan, Christ Himself is the Actor.

The bottomless pit was opened once before. Then it was to let an evil and destructive thing *out* (9:1-3). Now it is to put the author of all evil and destruction *in*. Moreover, the abyss is now sealed up; and inasmuch as this seal is set upon the mouth of the pit by the hand of God, we have perfect assurance that the pit will not open its mouth to let out any evil thing, until the thousand years be fulfilled. This is the means whereby not only the banishment of the Devil himself is secured, but also the earth is protected from all noxious influences. Parallel to this, but wonderfully in contrast, is the attempt that was made to seal the body of Christ in the tomb; as it is written, "So they went, and made the sepulchre sure, *sealing* the stone, and setting a watch" (Mat. 27:66). But that was as vain as the attempt to keep His soul in hades. For God raised Him up, "having loosed the pains of death, because it *was not possible* that He should be holden of it" (Ac. 2:24). That was a vain attempt to seal up in the nether world the Author of life and blessing. This is the effectual sealing up in the abyss of the author of death and the curse.

And so at last an era of life and blessing comes to the world, over which sin and death have held sway for six thousand years; and the first guaranty of this (and the first condition necessary to secure it) is that the earthly enemies of God are destroyed, that the Devil is cast into the pit, and that its mouth is absolutely stopped for a thousand years.

"And I saw thrones, and they sat upon them, and judgment was given unto them: and I saw the souls of them that were beheaded for the witness of Jesus, and for the word of God, and which had not worshipped the beast, neither his image, neither had received his mark upon their foreheads, or in their hands; and they lived and reigned with Christ a thousand years. But the rest of the dead lived not again until the thousand years were finished. This is the first resurrection. Blessed and holy is he that hath part in the first resurrection: on such the second death hath no power, but they shall be priests of God and of Christ, and shall reign with Him a thousand years" (vv. 4-6).

Another scene here presents itself, very different in character from the last. Thrones are set up, and persons are seated upon them. These are the victors over the beast; and prominent among them are those who had suffered martyrdom for the testimony of Jesus Christ. The description of these reigning ones tallies with that of the company of Chapter 15:2-4, who stand upon the sea of glass and sing the song of Moses and the Lamb. Furthermore, we have in this vision the fulfilment of the song of the four living creatures and the four and twenty elders, those whom Christ had redeemed by His blood, and had made kings and priests unto God (5:9, 10). Particularly does this vision answer to the last words of that redemption song, *"And we shall reign on* (or *over*) *the earth"*. For here it is expressly declared that these are they who have part "in the first resurrection, over whom the second death hath no power, but they shall be *priests* of God and of Christ, and *shall reign* with Him a thousand years" (v. 6). Therefore I see no reason to doubt that these throned ones of v. 4 are those whom Christ has redeemed to God by His blood out of every kindred, and tongue, and people, and nation (5: 9, 10). Moreover, verse 6 of Chapter 20 says of *all* who have part in the first resurrection, that they shall be priests of God, and shall reign with Christ during the thousand years. The description of verse 4 is not to be taken as limited to a particular and select company of the redeemed (martyrs, and such as have gained the victory in some special way over the beast);

for all who are Christ's participate in the victory. The victory is *His;* but He *gives* it to us. This was said with particular reference to overcoming the powers of death and hell (1 Cor. 15:55-57). Furthermore, it is plainly taught that the exaltation of the redeemed of the Lord to the rank and dignity of kings is just as much a matter of grace, as is the forgiveness of their sins. For the very same passage which declares that in Christ Jesus we have "redemption through His blood, the forgiveness of sins, according to *the riches of His grace"*, goes on to say that God "hath quickened us together with Christ *(by grace ye are saved)* and hath *raised us up together,* and made us *sit together* in heavenly places in Christ Jesus"; that is to say, has *exalted us* together and *enthroned us* together, in Christ Jesus; for "raised up" here means exalted to high dignity; and to "sit", is to sit on a throne (Eph. 1:7; 2:5-8). And this exaltation to the throne, be it noted, is as much comprehended in the twice-repeated statement, "by grace ye are saved", as is the forgiveness of sins. It should also be noted that the words of Revelation 20:4, "they *lived* and *reigned* with Christ", agree with the words, *"quickened* us together, and made us *sit* together ... in Christ Jesus". I deem it clear, therefore, that the passage in Ephesians which views "the eternal purpose of God in Christ Jesus" (3:11) as if it were already accomplished, looks forward to this vision of Revelation XX. And we must remember that the things John saw, and which he describes as already past—("they *lived* and *reigned"*)—

were in fact many centuries in the future at the time he saw and described them. Likewise in the passage in Ephesians, past tenses are used in speaking of things not yet accomplished.

As regards the period here given as "a thousand years", we should seek the spiritual and symbolical meaning of the term. What chiefly impresses me is that it conveys the idea of fullness and completeness. That coming period of blessing will be *full measure*. It will not be broken or curtailed. And that satisfies me better than to know the duration of the period, in the measure of years as we now count them. The longest human life fell short of a thousand years (Gen. 5:27); but that period during which the Devil will be incarcerated, and the redeemed of the Lord shall reign with Him, will be fully rounded out and complete. That is one side of the matter.

But nevertheless the millennium is not the eternal state of perfection and blessedness. Hence it will come to an end. It is to be observed that the phrase, *a thousand years,* occurs *six times* in these few verses. This impresses upon our minds the importance in God's eyes of what those words denote; and the subject surely is immensely important. But the *six* is itself significant. It very definitely signifies that the millennium, with all its blessings, nevertheless *comes short of perfection.* It does not reach either to *seven* or *twelve*. It is not the new heaven and the new earth. It is not the eternal dwelling place of God and His children. The Bible would be incomplete if it carried us no further than the millennium. But more is to come. We are to see even "greater things than these".

"And when the thousand years are expired, Satan shall be loosed out of his prison, and shall go out to deceive the nations which are in the four quarters of the earth, Gog and Magog, to gather them together to battle; the number of whom is as the sand of the sea. And they went up on the breadth of the earth, and compassed the camp of the saints about, and the beloved city: and fire came down from God out of heaven, and devoured them. And the devil that deceived them was cast into the lake of fire and brimstone, where the beast and the false prophets are, and shall be tormented day and night for ever and ever" (vv. 7-10).

The facts here stated are of deep interest; but there are no explanations given of the questions to which they give rise. Why is Satan loosed again out of his prison? And who are these nations that are in the four quarers of the earth, Gog and Magog, the number of whom is as the sand of the sea? And whence came they? seeing that the kings of the earth and of the whole world were gathered to the battle of that great day of God Almighty, and were slain with the sword of Him that sat upon the horse? (16:14; 19: 21). God has not given us, so far as I know, the means whereby to obtain answers to these interesting questions; and personally I am not disposed to spend much time upon them. For during the millennium, that is now close at hand, we shall have not only the opportunity, but also the ability, to inquire fully into these matters. Therefore, I shall content myself with but a few suggestions in respect to this passage.

In the first place, the millennium is a period during which the *natural* creation is restored virtually to the state in which it subsisted before the entrance of sin into the world; and moreover, God's plan for the natural creation will then be carried out, in that man will "have dominion over all the earth", and over all living creatures. It is evidently a part of God's plan to give a good long view of His creation as it was, and as it would have continued to be if sin had not brought death and the curse upon it. But it was for some good reason necessary at the beginning, in order that God's purposes might be fully accomplished, that the Devil be permitted to tempt man, and to have opportunity to practice deception upon him. Evidently there exists, in the wisdom of God, a similar need in the *restored* creation. Will a long period of millennial conditions instil into the hearts of natural men the spirit of obedience to God? The Devil is reserved for use in putting that matter to the test; and he is ready and eager to make the attempt, for the "thousand years" in the abyss have not wrought any change of heart *in him*.

Then as to the nations (or *heathen,* for such appears to be the invariable significance of the word in this Book) whom the Devil goes out to deceive, who and whence are they? The statement that they are in the four quarters (corners) of the earth is generally taken to mean that they are people inhabiting remote regions, beyond even the fringes of civilization; and it is thought that some of these might have escaped the judgments of the great day of wrath. This is at least a possibility, since "Babylon" would embrace only those within the limits of christendom; and the battle of Armageddon would involve only the active enemies of Christ. Furthermore, the words "Gog and Magog" (v. 8) can have been introduced into this vision for no other purpose than to direct us to the prophecy of Ezekiel, Chapters XXXVIII, XXXIX. The subject of that prophecy is the *final* conflict of God's people (Israel) with their enemies; final, because the prophecy closes with the promise that God will not hide His face from them ("the *whole* house of Israel") *any more* (39:25, 29). This prophecy follows immediately the vision of the valley of dry bones, which represents (as therein explained) God's purpose to bring "the whole house of Israel" out of their graves, and to bring them into the land of Israel (37:11-14). It is really a part of that prophecy, since Chapter 38 begins with the word "And". So we have here, as in Revelation XX, a scene representing the resurrection of the people of God, followed by an attack upon them of heathen from remote quarters of the earth, led by Gog, the chief prince of the region designated as "Magog". The words, "and ye shall *live*" (Ez. 37:14) are re-echoed in the words, "and they *lived*" (Rev. 20:4). Gog and Magog, with their heathen hordes, were to "ascend and come like a storm"; they were to come up "against My people Israel", said the Lord, "as a cloud to cover the land; it shall be *in the latter days,* and I will bring thee against My land, that the heathen may know Me, when I shall be sanctified in thee, O Gog, before their eyes" (38:9, 16). But Gog and his hosts were to be overthrown:

> "Thou shalt fall upon the mountains of Israel, thou and *all thy bands, and the people that is with thee:* I will give thee unto the ravenous birds of every sort, and to the beasts of the field to be devoured. Thou shalt fall upon the open field; for I have spoken it, saith the Lord God. And I will *send fire* on Magog, and among them that dwell carelessly in the isles; and they shall know that I am the Lord" (39:4-6).

That the matter of this prophecy is of the utmost importance appears from the words that follow:

> "Behold, *it is come, and it is done,* saith the Lord God; *this is the day whereof I have spoken"* (v. 8).

From the above it will be clearly seen that, notwithstanding differences in detail, the prophecy of Ezekiel and that of Revelation resemble each other closely in their general features, the resemblances being sufficiently close to warrant the conclusion that they refer to the same event.

In Revelation 20:11 is God's record of the final disposition to be made of the last and greatest of His enemies, the Devil, who is to be cast into the lake of fire and brimstone, where the other two enemies already are, and where he shall be tormented day and night for ever and ever.

> "And I saw a great white throne, and Him that sat on it, from whose face the earth and the heaven fled away; and there was found no place for them. And I saw the dead, small and great, stand before God; and the books were opened: and an-

Rejoicings in Heaven

other book was opened, which is the book of life; and the dead were judged out of those things which were written in the books, according to their works. And the sea gave up the dead which were in it; and death and hell delivered up the dead which were in them: and they were judged every man according to their works. And death and hell were cast into the lake of fire. This is the second death. And whosoever was not found written in the book of life was cast into the lake of fire" (vv. 11-15).

We come now to the last scene of the old creation, a scene of awful solemnity. John sees a throne, of which but two things are stated; it is *great* and it is *white*. "The throne", says Bengel, "is *white* as an emblem of the glory of the Judge, and *great* as befits His great and infinite majesty"; and to this, Hengstenberg adds, "He who sits on the throne is *God in the undivided unity of His Being*, without respect to the diversity of Persons".

And now is fulfilled the prophecy of Peter; "The heavens shall pass away with a great noise, and the elements shall melt with fervent heat; the earth also, and the works that are therein, shall be burned up" (2 Pet. 3:10). John's brief statement, "from whose face the earth and the heaven fled away; and there was found *no place for them*", declare that now they have ceased to exist.

And who are these that stand before God? They are "the *dead*"; and all are there, both "small and great". These are in contrast with the company of verse 4, of whom it was said that "they *lived*". For these are the spiritually dead; they who have never received God's free gift of eternal life through Jesus Christ; they who are *dead* even while they live (1 Tim. 5:6). For *death* is not extinction of being. On the contrary, it is, like *life,* a *state* of being; a state of existence however, that is in every particular the opposite of life. Christ when on earth declared concerning those who heard His word and believed on Him who had sent Him, that they should not come unto *judgment,* but were passed *out of death into life* (John 5:24). So here we have those who believed not, for they are come into *judgment,* and are in the state of *death.*

This is the day and the scene whereof the apostle Paul wrote in his Epistle to the Romans, "the day when God shall judge the secrets of men" (Rom. 2:6). For the records are all there; and we may be well assured that God's accounts are both complete and exact. And the books are now opened, and *the dead*—not the living, for none of them will come into judgment—are judged out of those things which were written in the books, according to their works. For while all "the dead" share the same condemnation, there are varying degrees of punishments, as of rewards. The Lord will "reward every man according to his works" (Mat. 16:27). Daniel too foresaw this scene, though his vision was not so full as to the details. He merely says, "The judgment was set, and the books were opened" (Dan. 7:9).

But there is "another book" there, *the book of life.* The reason why it is there appears from verse 15. It was there to show that the names of those who are judged are not written therein.

Heaven and earth and sea have now fled away. But the sea gave up the dead that were in it; and death and the nether world gave up the dead that were in them; and they were judged *"every man"* (for not one can escape) "according to their works"; and all whose names were not found written in the book of life were cast into the lake of fire. This is the second death, whereof Christ had already spoken in His message to the church in Smyrna (2:11). It is an eternal state.

Moreover, it is here recorded that "death and hell (*hades,* or the nether world) were cast into the lake of fire". Death is now completely cast out of God's creation, into which it had entered "by sin" (Ro. 5:12). And there being no death, there is no longer any need for a place of the dead; so hades is cast out with it. And thus is fulfilled the apostle's saying: "The last enemy that shall be destroyed is death" (1 Cor. 15:26).

CHAPTER XIII

The New Heaven and New Earth. The Bride. The Holy Jerusalem.

"And I saw a new heaven and a new earth: for the first heaven and the first earth were passed away; and there was no more sea" (21:1).

ETERNITY. The things of time and sense are passed away. The final shaking, not of "the earth only, but also heaven", has taken place, "that those things which cannot be shaken may remain" (Heb. 12:26, 27).

In the passage quoted above, wherein Peter foretells the passing away of "the heavens and the earth which now are", he goes on immediately to say: "Nevertheless we, according to His promise, look for new heavens and a new earth, wherein dwelleth righteousness" (2 Pet. 3:13). And this is what is now shown to John, a new heaven and a new earth, *in which dwelleth righteousness*. As Hengstenberg says:

"Everything is now prepared for the entrance of the *last* phase of the Kingdom of God; for the foundation of the new earth in which righteousness dwells; for the erection upon it of the Kingdom of glory; for the solemnization of the marriage of the Lamb, to the threshold of which we were brought by the song of praise in Chapter 19:6-8. This sacred closing history is the subject of the present group of visions. A church which has such a hope will not faint under tribulations. She beholds the end and is comforted".

The New Heaven and New Earth

"And I John saw the holy city, new Jerusalem, coming down from God out of heaven, prepared as a bride adorned for her husband. And I heard a great voice out of heaven, saying, Behold, the tabernacle of God is with men, and He will dwell with them, and they shall be His people, and God Himself shall be with them, and be their God. And God shall wipe away all tears from their eyes; and there shall be no more death, neither sorrow, nor crying, neither shall there be any more pain: for the former things are passed away. And He that sat upon the throne said, Behold, I make all things new. And He said, unto me, Write; for these words are true and faithful. And He said unto me, It is done. I am Alpha and Omega, the beginning and the end. I will give unto him that is athirst of the fountain of the water of life freely. He that overcometh shall inherit all things; and I will be his God, and he shall be My son. But the fearful, and unbelieving, and the abominable, and murderers, and whoremongers, and sorcerers, and idolaters, and all liars, shall have their part in the lake which burneth with fire and brimstone: which is the second death" (vv. 2-8).

No description is given of the new heaven and earth, beyond the statement that there was no more sea, which probably refers, as elsewhere in this Book, to the turbulent sea of the God-disowning nations, as that view would be in keeping also with the statement that now the tabernacle of God is with men, and He shall dwell with them. John's attention is engaged by the wondrous sight of the holy city, new Jerusalem, coming down out of heaven, as a bride adorned for her husband. Bengel remarks: "It is not the new city of the millennium, but one perfectly new and eternal, as is shown by the series of visions, the magnificence of the description, and the contrast in regard to the second death".

Verse 2 merely announces the subject of the vision. This is taken up with various particulars at verse 9. Meanwhile two voices are heard. One, a great voice out of heaven, proclaims that God will now make His abode with men, and will be their God; and that tears, death, sorrow, crying, and pain shall be no more; for the former things are passed away. The other which is that of God Himself, confirms this, saying: "Behold, I make all things new"; and John is charged specially to write this. Further He declares, speaking directly to John, "It is done". This is the same word that was uttered at the pouring out of the seventh vial (16:17). It signifies the accomplishment of something of the greatest moment. The added words "I AM Alpha and Omega", lend force to the declaration; for they imply the completion at last of some long cherished purpose. The next words indicate that that purpose was the opening again, to this death-ruled world, of the fountain of *the water of life,* so that all might freely drink thereof. This saying points on to Chapter 22:1 and 17. It announces the completion of Christ's salvation, as prophesied in Isaiah 55:1-4. Under the appropriate figure of an ever flowing river, proceeding from an eternal source—the throne of God and the Lamb, it proclaims the fullness and the endlessness of the life of the redeemed. Continuing (and still speaking directly to John) He sums up in a short, comprehensive saying, the wonderful reward about to be given to him that overcometh: "He that overcometh shall *inherit all things;* and I will be his God, and he shall be My son".

The New Heaven and New Earth

So we have, in these introductory verses, a brief summing up of God's great purposes in redemption, now at last fulfilled.

By way of strong contrast verse 8 proclaims the awful doom of the lost. These are comprehended in eight categories arranged in four pairs, four being the symbol of the unredeemed earth.

"And there came unto me one of the seven angels which had the seven vials full of the seven last plagues, and talked with me, saying, Come hither, I will shew thee the bride, the Lamb's wife. And he carried me away in the spirit to a great and high mountain, and shewed me that great city, the holy Jerusalem, descending out of heaven from God, having the glory of God: and her light was like unto a stone most precious, even like a jasper stone, clear as crystal; And had a wall great and high, and had twelve gates, and at the gates twelve angels, and names written thereon, which are the names of the twelve tribes of the children of Israel" (vv. 9-12).

After the introduction, we have the main subject of the vision, the holy Jerusalem, here presented as the bride, the Lamb's wife, her chief adornment being stated in the words, "*Having the glory of God*". This is a distinction and a splendor that cannot be surpassed; and further it is said that her light is like unto the *most precious* of stones, even like a *jasper*, clear as crystal. This recalls the appearance of Him Who sat upon the throne, in John's first vision of heaven, who was like a jasper and a sardius. Thus the glory of the very Person and of the throne of God envelops and adorns the holy City. The same association of ideas, that is the idea of the company of God's redeemed people as being His *bride,* and as being also the glorious *city* of His habitation, is found in Isaiah LIV where it is written, "For thy Maker is *thy Husband;* the Lord of hosts is His name; and thy Redeemer, the Holy One of Israel" (v. 5); and further, "Behold, I will lay thy stones with fair colors, and thy foundations with sapphires. And I will make thy windows of agates, and thy gates of carbuncles, and all thy borders of pleasant stones" (vv. 11, 12). In what follows (in Rev. XXI), mention is made of her walls and gates, of her foundations and measurements, and lastly of her inhabitants. Her gates are twelve in number, every several gate of one pearl (v. 21); and her foundations also are twelve in number, each foundation being of a precious stone different from the others (vv. 19, 20). Again in verse 18 it is stated that the wall of the city is of jasper, that stone of dazzling whiteness; and the city of pure gold, like unto clear glass. This part of the description is also an amplification of a passage in Isaiah, which has for its subject, "The city of the Lord, the Zion of the Holy One of Israel", where it is written:

"Violence shall no more be heard in thy land, wasting nor destruction within thy borders: but thou shalt call *thy walls, Salvation,* and *thy gates, Praise.* The sun shall be no more thy light by day; neither for brightness shall the moon give light unto thee; but the Lord shall be unto thee an everlasting light, and *thy God thy glory.* Thy sun shall no more go down; neither shall thy moon withdraw itself; for the Lord shall be thine everlasting light, and the days of thy mourning shall be ended" (Isa. 60:18-20).

The Psalmist of old also wrote concerning the city of our God, saying, "Beautiful for situation, the joy of the whole earth, is mount Zion, on the sides of the north (or *in the extreme north*), the city of the great King. God is known in her palaces for a refuge." (Ps. 48:2, 3). Surely the psalmist's eyes also must have been lifted up to see afar the city for which Abraham was looking in his day, "the city which hath *the foundations, whose Builder and Maker is God*" (Heb. 11:10); for the language he uses is too glowing for any city of earth. And these words especially should move us as we contemplate the glory and effulgence of our future and eternal home:—"Walk about Zion, and go round about her; tell the towers thereof. Mark ye well her bulwarks, consider her palaces; that ye may tell it to the generation following" (Ps. 48:12,13). The reader should also consult Ezekiel's delineation of the temple and city of God that was to be (which is too long to be discussed here), ending with the words, "And the name of the city from that day shall be, JEHOVAH THEREIN" (Ezek. 48:35).

In order that John might see this wondrous city, he is carried away in the spirit to a great and high mountain (v. 10). That mountain, we must remember, is on the *new* earth. This is the true "Zion", the eternal mountain of God's holiness, whereof the psalmist sang and the prophets spake, whose name was temporarily given to the elevated part of Jerusalem upon which the palace of king David stood. John is brought to that place of vision by one of the seven angels who had the golden vials. This is a link with the preceding visions; for it was one of those seven angels that carried John away in the spirit to the wilderness that he might see the judgment of Mystery Babylon the great. Thus our attention is directed to the parallelism of the two visions, in each of which is a woman, who also is a city.

The wall of the New Jerusalem is "great and high". This speaks, in symbolic language, of the *absolute security* of the inhabitants of that city; for the great purpose of the wall of a city is *protection from enemies;* and therefore a wall is commonly used in Scripture as an image of protection and safety. The same thought is beautifully expressed in the passage quoted above from Isaiah 60, "And thou shalt call thy walls, *Salvation*".

As to the significance of the measuring of the city, enough has been said in connection with Chapter 11: 1,2. The prominent feature here is the frequent occurrence of the significant number *twelve*. In these few verses (12-21) may be noted at least twelve appearances of that number and multiples thereof. Thus, in verse 12 we find the twelve gates, twelve angels and twelve tribes (three occurrences); in verse 14 *two* occurrences; in verse 16 the *three* dimensions of the city (length, breadth and height) *each* twelve thousand furlongs; in verse 17 the wall, 144 (twelve times twelve) furlongs (*one* occurrence); in verses 19 and 20 the twelve foundations *(one);* and in verse 21 the twelve gates and twelve pearls *(two)*. This number, as has been shown, is specially associated with "the

Israel of God" (His special name for His elect people), as exemplified particularly in the twelve tribes of the Old Testament, and the twelve apostles of the New. These two companies of twelves come prominently into notice in the vision of the Eternal City, the former in connection with the gates, the latter in connection with the foundations. And first of all, this close association, in the eternal City, of the twelve tribes and twelve apostles, testifies in the clearest way *the oneness of God's true people,* regardless of dispensational differences, and the continuity of His purpose throughout all the ages and stages of His dealings with mankind.

Gates are for entrance, and that is the first thing that concerns those who are outside. There is but *one way* of entrance into the City whose walls are "Salvation"; and hence the gates are identical, each being of *one pearl;* which may be taken as expressing either the preciousness of God's salvation to those who find it in Jesus Christ, or the preciousness to Him of those who enter in by the one "Door". According to Isaiah the gates of the City were to be called, "Praise", that being the name of the leading tribe, Judah.

Foundations are for support, and it is in laying the foundation that the apostles were specially occupied. For Paul speaks of "the foundation of the apostles and prophets" (Eph. 2:20); and in describing his own work, said, "As a wise masterbuilder I have laid the foundation" (1 Cor. 3:9). Both these passages show that Jesus Christ is *the* Foundation, as all the Scriptures testify. Therefore, just as there is but one Door of entrance, so likewise there is but one Foundation. Christ is the Door, and Christ is the Foundation. But in the language of symbols, and to express another aspect of the truth, the one gate is represented as twelve gates, and the one foundation as twelve foundations; just as, for the like purpose, the One Spirit is represented as seven Spirits. There is no contradiction here, but on the contrary a beautiful harmony when the elements of the language of symbols (which are not difficult) are understood. When, therefore, we come to the foundation laid by the apostles, we find, not the sameness exhibited by the twelve gates, but on the contrary, the greatest variety of dazzling splendor and brilliancy, each of the twelve foundations being a precious stone different from every other. Thus they speak, in literally "glowing" and "sparkling" terms, of the various glories and excellencies of Christ, the One Foundation.

This grouping together of precious stones for the symbolic expression of a great truth is first presented to us in the directions God gave Moses for the fabrication of the breast-plate of Urim and Thummim, that was to be worn by the high priests. It was to have "set in it settings of stones", twelve in number, in four rows, three in each row; and upon them were to be engraved "the names of the children of Israel, twelve, according to their names, like the engravings of a signet" (Ex. 28:15-21). It will be observed (and it is a point of much interest) that here the precious stones

The New Heaven and New Earth 537

are emblems of the twelve tribes, and that, as in the case of the gates of the Eternal City to which the names of the twelve tribes are given, they are arranged in four groups of three each. In the breast-plate of Israel's high priest the precious stones speak plainly to God of the preciousness of His people Israel to Him; as it is elsewhere written, "For the Lord hath chosen Jacob for Himself, and Israel for His *peculiar treasure*" (Ps. 135:4). But here again the symbols speak of Christ; for all the excellencies and beauties that God sees, or ever will see, in us, His people, are the excellencies and beauties of Christ, wrought in us by the power of His Holy Spirit. For the Spirit is given to work the mind and purpose of God in us, whom He did "predestinate to be *conformed to the image of His Son, that He might be the First born among many brethren*" (Rom. 8:26-29; 1 John 3:2; Phil. 3:21). The great truth that can be plainly read in these symbols, in the various uses made of them in the Scriptures, is *God's purpose to glorify His chosen people with His own glories, as seen in their perfection in Christ*. And this is in precise agreement with *His* high-priestly prayer for them, wherein He said, "And the glory which Thou gavest Me, *I have given them*" (John 17:22).

Regarding the dimensions and shape of the City, it is recorded that the length, breadth and height of it are equal. Those who overlook the fact that this Book is written in the sign-language, have produced some curiosities of interpretation (and of architecture as well) by applying these statements in a literal and materialistic way. "The square was regarded among the ancients as that which is complete and perfect" (Hengstenberg). And here the thought is carried into three dimensions, to express more forcibly the idea of absolute perfection, as well as solidity.

Finally, as to the street of the city (the word *street* being obviously used generically for *streets*) which is described as "pure gold, as it were transparent glass" (v. 21), we are not, of course to tax our imagination with the vain effort to conceive of gold that is transparent. What is here emphasized is the absolute *purity* of the gold; and since transparent glass is a Bible symbol of purity, it is here used as a figure of the *purity* of the gold, as if it were said, "The gold is as pure as the most transparent crystal".

"And I saw no temple therein; for the Lord God Almighty and the Lamb are the temple of it. And the city had no need of the sun, neither of the moon, to shine in it: for the glory of God did lighten it, and the Lamb is the light thereof" (vv. 22, 23).

The temple was the chief ornament, and the glory of the earthly Jerusalem; and to dwell in it was the highest aspiration of the spiritually-minded Israelite (Ps. 23:6; 27:4). The foundation thought embodied in the earthly sanctuary was *God's dwelling with His people.* This appears in the first mention of it, "And let them make Me a sanctuary, *that I may dwell among them*" (Ex. 25:8). This great purpose of God has its final and eternal realization, not in a special building located within the confines of the City, but in *the City itself*. The wondrous truth here revealed goes far beyond what the types would have suggested to even the most spiritually-minded of the saints, namely, that God purposes not only to bring His redeemed people into His own house, but to bring them into a vital and perfect union with Himself, such as it is not possible for us now to comprehend. This is what was in view in the words of Christ, following the quotation above concerning the glory He has given His people, "I in them, and Thou in Me, that they may be *made perfect in one*" (John 17:23). When this thought is perceived, even faintly, it is at once seen that a separate temple, distinct from the City itself, would mar the picture, and misrepresent its meaning. For, in meditating upon this symbol of the City, we must not lose sight of the truth that what this City represents is also "the Bride, the Lamb's wife".

As there is no place in this City for a temple, neither is there any need in it for the sun, the light of nature: for the glory of God illumines it, and the Lamb, Who is the Bridegroom and the Redeemer, is the Light thereof. For He is "the True Light" (John 1:9).

"And the nations of them which are saved shall walk in the light of it: and the kings of the earth do bring their glory and honour into it. And the gates of it shall not be shut at all by day: for there shall be no night there. And they shall bring the glory and honour of the nations into it. And there shall in no wise enter into it anything that defileth, neither whatsoever worketh abomination, or maketh a lie: but they which are written in the Lamb's book of life" (vv. 24-27).

In the consideration of these last visions there is special need to remember that what is shown in them must be taken figuratively, else we would be at a loss as to the "nations", and "the kings of the earth" who are mentioned in this passage. This is an entirely *new earth*. Moreover, none but the redeemed from among men now remain of the children of Adam. For all who were not found written in the book of life were cast into the lake of fire. Verse 27 of this very chapter also declares that none enter into the City but "they which are written in the Lamb's book of life".

"The nations are not to be conceived of as *without* the city, but *within;* and being within the city they shall be illuminated by its light. The situations of the several parties here are altogether of an absolute kind. All are either in the New Jerusalem or in the lake of fire (v. 8). There is no third position. The *bringing* belongs only to the symbolic style of the delineation. Again in 22:14 mention is made of all true citizens as entering in through the gates into the city" (Hengstenberg).

This being understood, we need only to remember, for the comprehension of the thought of this passage, that even as among the angels there are distinctions of rank and authority, so it will be among glorified men. To some Christ will give authority over ten cities, to some over five (Luke 19:17, 19). All will partake of the same glory, but as "star *differeth* from star in glory, *so also is the resurrection of the dead*" (1 Cor. 15:41, 42).

"And he shewed me a pure river of water of life, clear as crystal, proceeding out of the throne of God and of the Lamb. In the midst of the street of it, and on either side of the river, was there the tree of life, which bare twelve manner of fruits and yielded her fruit every month: and the leaves of the tree were for the healing of the nations. And there shall be no more curse: but the throne of God and of the Lamb shall be in it; and His servants shall serve Him: and they shall see His face; and His name shall be in their foreheads. And there shall be no night there: and they need no candle, neither light of the sun; for the Lord God giveth them light: and they shall reign for ever and ever" (21:1-5).

The prominent theme of this last chapter of the Bible is LIFE. All that is contrary to God, all that developed in consequence of the coming of sin into the world, ends in the *second death*. All that is saved from the dominion of sin and death enters into the fullness of the abundant *life* of the new creation. The contrast is most impressive. Life is here presented in a threefold way; for we read of the *book* of life, the *water* of life, and the *tree* of life; and each is mentioned twice, the *book* in 21:27 and 22:19, the *water* 22:1 and 17, and the *tree* in 22:2 and 14. The order of these six occurrences forms an *introversion;* the order being the *book,* the *water,* the *tree,* the *tree,* the *water,* the *book.* The Trinity is suggested; for the book is expressly that of the Lamb, the water is an acknowledged emblem of the Holy Spirit (John 7:38, 39), and the tree is associated with the original creation of God "Who created all things by Jesus Christ" (Eph. 3:9). The book contains the names of all the redeemed; the water is a *river;* and the tree bears twelve manner of fruits, and yields her fruit every month. All these figures speak of that *abundant* life, of which Christ Himself spake, and which He came to bring into the very place where death had reigned over all (John 10:10). All the Old Testament promises and types, which relate to fountains and rivers, have here their complete and glorious fulfilment (Ps. 36:8; Joel 3:18; Ezek. 47:1-12; Zech. 14:8). In Genesis II and in Ezekiel XLVII the tree and the river are in close association with each other. The river in Revelation 22:1 proceeds from the highest and holiest place in the universe, the throne of God and of the Lamb. That Christ is here mentioned as the Lamb, emphasizes the truth that the river of life is made available to the redeemed by reason of *His sacrifice of Himself on their behalf*. This verse also pictures the truth of the Trinity; for God and Christ are named, and the Spirit appears under the emblem of the water.

The water figures that which quenches the thirst, that is to say, satisfies the desires, of the redeemed. What the river does under the type of water for the thirsty, the tree does under the type of food for the hungry (v. 2). The one *flows* perennially, and the other *bears* perennially. The order in which these blessings of the Eternal City are presented in these three successive verses (21:28; 22:1, 2) is this: Those whose names are written in the *book* of life, have access to the water of life, and also to the *tree* of life. Moreover, it is said that the leaves of the tree are for the healing of the nations. But as to the form in which the blessings thus figured will be actually enjoyed in the eternal state, we can now form no idea.

The words, "and there shall be no more curse" (v. 3) also take us back to Eden, where the curse was brought in by the eating of the forbidden tree. That can never be again; for the throne of God and of the Lamb shall *be (i. e. permanently)* in it; and His servants shall serve *Him;* they shall never be brought unto bondage to another. Moreover, "they shall see His Face"; and to see the King's face is to enjoy His favor (2 Sa. 14:24, 32). Not only so, but "His Name shall be in their foreheads", which is equivalent to saying that they are sealed and openly acknowledged as His (14:1). And now once more it is stated that "there shall be no night there, and they need no candle, neither light of the sun; for the Lord God giveth them light" (v. 5). The like statements of the preceding chapter (vv. 23, 25) were made in describing the glories of the City; whereas here they appear as part of a description of the blessedness of its inhabitants. That there will be no night there, signifies in this connection that God will never withdraw His favor from them. They will stand forevermore in the light of His countenance. And not only so, but the crowning blessing of all, "they shall reign for ever and ever".

Thus ends the transcendently wonderful description of the holy Jerusalem, the Bride, the Lamb's wife. May some gleams of her divinely-bestowed glories and beauties penetrate into our hearts, and serve to turn all our thoughts and affections from things on earth to things which are above, where Christ sitteth on the right hand of God!

Bengel's comment forms an appropriate ending for this portion of the Book:—

"Thus far the holy city Jerusalem! Would that we may enter therein! Would that we were even now therein! Now it is in our power to attain to a happy portion there, if we but turn our back on a lost world, and renounce the service of its prince. There is need for a good, instant resolution to act, under the impulse of grace. But whosoever hath steadfastly set his face to go toward *this* Jerusalem, shall abide in it and shall never err from the way of life".

"And he said unto me, These sayings are faithful and true: and the Lord God of the holy prophets sent His angel to shew unto His servants the things which must shortly be done. Behold, I come quickly: blessed is he that keepeth the sayings of the prophecy of this book. And I John saw these things, and heard them. And when I had heard and seen, I fell down to worship before the feet of the angel which shewed me these things. Then saith he unto me, See thou do it not: for I am thy fellowservant, and of thy brethren the prophets, and of them which keep the sayings of this book: worship God. And he saith unto me, Seal not the sayings of the prophecy of this book: for the time is at hand. He that is unjust, let him be unjust still: and he which is filthy, let him be filthy still: and he that is righteous, let him be righteous still: and he that is holy, let him be holy still. And behold, I come quickly; and My reward is with me, to give every man according as his work shall be. I am Alpha and Omega, the beginning and the end, the first and the last" (vv. 6-13).

Attention has been called, in the comments on Chapter I, to the correspondence between the beginning of the Book of Revelation and its ending. Therefore a detailed comment upon the remaining verses would be largely a repetition of what has been already pointed out, for which reason my observations on these verses will be brief. What should be principally impressed upon our minds is the stress that is here laid upon *the high importance* of the things that are written in this Book. And the greater is the need that we should seek to do this, because by the many it has been treated with neglect, and by not a few even its authenticity has been called into question. How very significant then that, immediately the description of the Holy City is finished, the angel repeats once more the assurance that, "These sayings are faithful and true". The form in which this assurance is given here and in 21:5 differs from that used in 19:9. There we read, "And he saith unto me, These are the true sayings of God". In these last chapters we have a form of assurance used elsewhere only by Paul in his letters to Timothy and Titus, who, like those to whom John's message is specially sent, were the servants of God. It is first used in connection with Paul's great gospel testimony, "This is a *faithful saying,* and worthy of all acceptation, that Christ Jesus came into the world to *save sinners*" (1 Tim. 1:15). Therefore the very form in which this assurance is given lifts the matters embraced in it to the level of highest importance. In 19:9 the assurance had reference specially to the destruction of Babylon the great, and the marriage of the Lamb. In 21:5 it has reference to the creation of the new heaven and new earth, and the coming down from heaven of the Holy City, the new Jerusalem. And in

22:6 it has reference to the blessings promised to the inhabitants of that City.

The latter part of verse 6 is virtually a repetition of what was declared in Chapter 1:1, that God had sent His angel with this express object, namely, to show to His servants things which must *shortly* be done. Moreover, the word "shortly" is immediately reiterated in verse 7 (there rendered *quickly*), the saying of that verse being evidently uttered by the Lord Jesus Christ Himself. It contains also a repetition of the blessing promised in Chapter 1:3 to those who keep the sayings of the prophecy of *this Book*.

Then John adds again his personal assurance that he saw these things and heard them, an affirmation that should carry great weight and impart strong conviction by reason of its very simplicity. Moreover, again he was so overpowered by the wonder and the greatness of the things which he had seen and heard, that he fell down to do homage before the angel who had showed them to him. No further comment upon this incident is needed.

Further testimony to the great importance of the Book is given in verses 10-12. John is not to seal the sayings of the prophecy of this Book, for the time (of the things threatened as well as of the things promised) is come near. Its message, therefore, is one of urgency for all. The unrighteous and the unclean, if they neglect its warnings and flee not to the Lamb of God for safety, will just as surely experience the judgments it foretells, as the righteous and the holy will enter into its promised blessings. For Christ is coming quickly to give to every man, those in the one class and those in the other, according as his work shall be. This is spoken by Him who here again declares Himself to be "the Alpha and Omega, the beginning and the end, the first and the last".

"Blessed are they that do His commandments, that they may have right to the tree of life, and may enter in through the gates into the city" (v. 14).

This is the last beatitude of the Bible; and surely it is the all-inclusive one; for there can be no real happiness apart from the doing of God's commandments, and it is ever in the doing of them that the very highest blessedness is enjoyed. This beatitude in this place it not so much an encouragement or inducement to men to enter and to continue in the path of obedience (which is the "narrow way" that one enters by the "strait gate" of the new birth), as *a description of the actual state of the redeemed throughout eternity,* whose delight will ever be in the doing of His commandments. Nevertheless, the promise of this verse and the warning of the next, are there for any who will give heed thereto.

This, the last, beatitude of the Bible also brings forcibly to mind that the curse, with all its attendant miseries, was brought upon the world through disobedience to His commandment.

In contrast with those who are within, and who delight in the doing of the will of God, verse 15 names those who are "without". The completeness of this list is testified by the fact that it consists of seven classes of persons. It is headed by "dogs", which in Scripture are representative of the entire class of unclean animals, and hence typify those whose hearts have not been changed by grace, and have not been cleansed by the blood of Christ, through faith in Him (Deut. 23:18; Mat. 15:26; 2 Pet. 2:22). Such are they of whom the people of God are cautioned to "beware" (Phil. 3:2).

"I Jesus have sent Mine angel to testify unto you these things in the churches. I am the root and the offspring of David, and the bright and morning star. And the Spirit and the bride say, Come. And let him that heareth say, Come. And let him that is athirst come: and whosoever will, let him take the water of life freely. For I testify unto every man that heareth the words of the prophecy of this book, If any man shall add unto these things, God shall add unto him the plagues that are written in this book: and if any man shall take away from the words of the book of this prophecy, God shall take away his part out of the book of life, and out of the holy city, and from the things which are written in this book. He which testifieth these things saith, Surely I come quickly; Amen. Even so, come, Lord Jesus. The grace of our Lord Jesus Christ be with you all, Amen" (vv. 16-21).

The "I JESUS" stands in contrast with the "I John" of verse 8. The great things of this Book, its great prophecies, great promises, great judgments, rest not for their acceptance upon the word of a mere man, though he be the best and most truthful of men. For now again at the very end we have the word of "the faithful and true Witness" for every one of "these things". In this verse He steps forward, as it were, and with his "I JESUS" answers every denial, doubt or questioning in regard to these things and all of them. This affirmation He backs up with a surpassingly wonderful revelation of Himself: "I AM the root and the offspring of David, the bright and morning Star". Here is the last of His I AM'S. It sends us back to the word of prophecy:

> "And there shall come forth a rod out of the stem of Jesse, and a Branch shall grow out of his roots: And the Spirit of the Lord shall be upon Him. . . . And in that day there shall be a root of Jesse which shall stand for an ensign of the people; to it shall the Gentiles seek; and His rest shall be *glory*" (Isa. 11:1, 2, 10, *marg.*).

All the purposes of God concerning His everlasting Kingdom, concerning the salvation of the Gentiles, and concerning the glory of His eternal rest, depended upon that Root of David. When the matter of opening the seven-sealed book was standing in doubt in John's mind, causing him acute distress, he was relieved from his anxiety by the assurance that the Lion of the tribe of Judah, the *Root of David,* had prevailed to open the book, and to loose the seven seals thereof (5:5). It is the tremendous weight of *His* authority that is here given to establish the authenticity of this Book. "The race of David is here brought into view in respect to the unconquerable strength and everlasting dominion promised it by God. What *He* testifies, in Whom the race of David culminates, will assuredly go into fulfilment" (Hengstenberg).

The added designation "the bright and morning star", from the connection, is a call to *watchfulness throughout the night*. The first thing that rewards them "that watch for the morning" (Ps. 130:6), is the appearance of the morning star. Speaking of the word of prophecy, made "more sure" by the first coming of Christ, Peter admonishes us to take heed thereto, as unto *a light* that shineth in a dark place, until the day dawn, and *the day star arise* in our hearts (2 Pet. 1:19). And Christ here declares that He Himself will appear as the bright and morning star to those who, believing His testimony concerning the things that are written in this Book, set their hearts to look for His coming. The effect of *futurism* has been to obscure the light of the word of prophecy; but when we remove the lampshade, by putting aside these modern theories, we find that the light thereof shines as brightly as ever; yea, and more so. Thus we may have as our Lord surely intended, both the external light of prophecy upon the whole course of time, and also the inner light of the Morning Star shining in our hearts. "And I will give him the Morning Star. He that hath an ear, let him hear what the Spirit saith unto the churches".

To the voice of the Lord Jesus Christ, saying, "I Jesus have sent Mine angel to testify unto you these things in the churches", is now added that of "the Spirit and the bride" (v. 17). Their message is compressed into the single word, "Come". To whom is it addressed? The joining together of the Spirit and the bride is a new thing in this Book; but it is not a new thing in the Scripture. John the Baptist saw "the bride" in those who were turning to Jesus Christ in his day. Paul applies this figure to believers both collectively (Rom. 7:4) and also individually (2 Cor. 11:2). So the Spirit and the bride are united in their testimony. "He (the Holy Spirit) shall testify of Me; and *ye also* shall bear witness" (John 15:26, 27). "Ye shall receive power, the Holy Ghost coming upon you; and ye shall be *witnesses unto Me*" (Ac. 1:8). "And *we*," said Peter, "are His witnesses of these things; and so is also *the Holy Ghost*" (Ac. 5:32). This recalls to our minds at the very end of the Book what was emphasized at the beginning thereof, namely, that the churches are appointed to be light-bearers; that they are to "shine as lights in the world, holding forth the word of life". And this *is* the word of life, as this very verse declares under the familiar symbol of "the water of life". The Lord Jesus has just said that He had sent His angel to testify these things unto us in the churches. Hence it becomes the responsibility of the churches to testify these things to others. But the Holy Spirit is with them to share that great responsibility. By this present testimony of Christ to His churches, the Word of life is completed, and His witnesses are thereby fully equipped for their calling, "thoroughly furnished unto all good works" (2 Tim. 3:16, 17). And this is most impressively declared in verses 18, 19, where the voice of Christ is heard again. The connecting word "For" shows that, in the words which follow, the reason is given why the churches are to say *"Come"*. The fearful punishments that will fall upon those who add to *these things* (which Christ has now testified to His churches), or who take from them, declare in the most forceful way the supreme importance of "these things"; and they serve also to impress upon His witnesses the greatness of the responsibility that rests upon them in respect thereto.

A little reflection will suffice to make evident that these closing words refer to the *present* use of the Book, and not to future times. It is *now* that the Spirit and the bride say "Come"; it is now that he that heareth is to say, "Come"; it is now that he that is athirst may come and take of the water of life. And again it is only now, in this present age, that any can commit the sin of adding to or taking from the things that are written in this Book. The warning at the end should be placed alongside of the blessing promised at the beginning, to him that readeth, and to them that hear and that keep the things that are written herein; and the result must be a deep conviction in our hearts that "these things" are indeed of supreme importance at this very time. For the establishing of that conviction in us, our Lord gives the weight of a threefold testimony: "I Jesus have sent Mine angel to *testify*" (v. 16); "For I *testify* unto every man" (v. 18); "He which *testifieth* these things" (v. 20).

Another word that is prominent in this closing portion is "come". We have noted its threefold occurrence in verse 17. Then we have the *very* last word of our blessed Lord to His own, "Surely I COME quickly". Finally we are permitted to use His own word, addressing it to Him, as our reply to all this; and may it be the expression of the supreme desire of every heart as we say, "Even so, COME, Lord Jesus"; for it is to that end He has done these things, and testified these things.

"*The grace of our Lord Jesus Christ be with you all. Amen*".

CHAPTER XIV

Conclusion—Where We Now Stand

WHERE do we now stand in the stream of predicted events? is a question that comes often to one's mind as he looks into the word of prophecy. For the answer I turn to Chapter XI; for there, in the days immediately preceding the sounding of the seventh trumpet, I find what seems to me to be the description of the work which the Spirit of God is now doing in the world. That work is presented to us under the figures of (1) the measuring of the temple of God; and (2) the testifying of God's two witnesses, clothed in sackcloth. The measuring of the temple of God signifies, as has been shown, the completion of the work of calling out a people for the Name of the Lord; and the testifying of the two witnesses means the completion of the work begun on the day of Pentecost by the disciples of Christ, to whom He had just previously said, "Ye shall *receive power* . . . and ye shall be *witnesses* unto Me". And here we have the prophecy, "And I will *give power* unto My two *witnesses*". Their testimony is to be "finished" (11:7). And thus Christ's word to His disciples will be fulfilled: "This gospel of the Kingdom *shall be preached* in all the world for a *witness* unto *all nations:* and *then* shall the end come" (Mat. 24:14). His witnesses have no other testimony to give to the nations of the world

Conclusion—Where We Now Stand

than the gospel of the kingdom, for that embraces "all the counsel of God" (Ac. 20:25, 27; 28:31); and when that testimony shall have been given to "all the world", *then shall "the end" come.*

And this is the way the end will come: The beast that ascended out of the bottomless pit "shall make war against them, and shall overcome them, and kill them". The two witnesses are a symbol, representing the testimony itself. So it is not the putting to death of the Lord's people that is here foreshown, but the suppression of their testimony by governmental authority. We are even now under beast-government (Gentile world-power) and who can say how soon a situation may arise such that "the powers that be" may deem it "necessary to the welfare of the state" to suppress the testimony of the Kingdom of God, and the circulation of the Scriptures which declare the certainty of the overthrow of the kingdom of the beast? Whenever that occurs, there will be a brief season of rejoicing (three days and a half) by those to whom the Word of God was a "torment"; then, a sudden reviving of the testimony, and the catching up of the witnesses into heaven in a cloud (11:7-12). This rapture of the witnesses is coincident with the sounding of the seventh trumpet (v. 15), when "the days" begin which the voice of that trumpet ushers in (10:7). That is the beginning of the day of wrath, during which there will be no testimony for God in the world, and the powers of evil will have it all their own way. Let us just observe once more, that we have here the three prominent things of 1 Thessalonians 4:16, 17, the great voice from heaven ("the voice of the archangel"), the trump of God, and the catching up of the witnesses to heaven "in a cloud".

After that event, the course of affairs on earth continues. Developments in the several departments of human affairs will be such as to eventuate in that state of things which has been pictured to us in the vision of the gorgeously arrayed woman (apostate christianity, or organized religion in its ultimate form), who sits upon the ten horned beast.

Therefore the field of observation that now lies before us, is in two great spheres, radically opposed the one to the other: (1) the Kingdom of God, and (2) the kingdom of Satan (Mat. 12:25-29). We look first at—

The Kingdom of God

Measured by its effects upon human society as a whole, as well as upon individual nations and communities, the greatest event of history subsequent to the resurrection of Jesus Christ and the coming of the Holy Spirit into the world, is the Protestant Reformation, at the beginning of the sixteenth century. From that event sprang two divergent movements which were to bring about the heading up of all human affairs, one eventuating in mystical Babylon, the *"mother of harlots and abominations of the earth"*, and the other in the heavenly Jerusalem, "which is the *mother of us all"* (Gal. 4:26). The first of the spiritual movements that

Conclusion—Where We Now Stand

then arose is expending its energy in accomplishing that *one thing* for which the return of Christ must wait, namely the publishing of the glad tidings of His Kingdom among all nations *for a witness*. The other is leading on to the final stage of the kingdom of Satan, that of the seventh head of the beast, with which will be closely allied "the kings of the earth" (ten kingdoms) and the consolidated world-religion, and world-federation of business, symbolized respectively by Babylon the woman, and Babylon the great city. The *final issue is between the two rival kingdoms.* And we know how it will end; for "the kingdoms of this world shall become the kingdoms of our Lord, and of His Christ; and He shall reign for ever and ever" (11:15). The two movements here referred to, answer respectively to the measuring of the temple of God, and the casting out of the court of the Gentiles.

In the sphere we are now viewing (that of the Kingdom of God) what most impresses me is that of all that has resulted from the Reformation of four hundred years ago, by far the greatest thing in its influence upon human affairs has been *the translation of the Bible into the languages now spoken on earth.* It would seem as if the Reformation had been ordained for that very purpose, and that all other results that have flowed from it were incidental and subsidiary. That was a thing *so immensely great* that whatever other event may be thought of as an epoch in history, is dwarfed into insignificance in comparison with it. For the Bible, in "tongues understanded of the people", is God's instrument for the completing of His Church (the measuring of the temple of God) through the broadcasting of the saving truth of the gospel of Christ. This, be it noted, is precisely what was begun on the day of Pentecost. For the outstanding feature thereof was the hearing, by those of the many nations that were represented there, *every man in his own native tongue,* the wonderful works of God, that is to say, the raising up of Jesus Christ from the dead, and the sending forth of the Holy Spirit to bear witness thereto. Therefore it is of the utmost significance that the work begun on the day of Pentecost, accompanied by mighty signs and wonders, a work which was interrupted for more than a thousand years (the dark ages), was resumed, four hundred years ago, amidst world-shaking events, *and has been prosecuted uninterruptedly ever since.* And what increases greatly the significance of this fact is that, even in the present time of spiritual decline, the work of circulating the Scriptures in the languages and dialects of the day, instead of slackening, as might be expected, is advancing at an accelerating speed. As an illustration of this, let me mention that about 18 years ago I was shown, in a Bible distributing agency in Switzerland, a little book containing John 3:16 in about 400 different tongues. This little book had been compiled in order to exhibit the wide extent of the publication of the Scriptures in the common languages of the nations; and it impressed me greatly. But the expansion since that date has been at a rate far more rapid than in the years prior thereto.

For today, the Bible (or essential parts thereof) is giving forth its soul-saving message in about 800 tongues and dialects. Within a month of the day on which I am writing these lines, my attention was called to the fact that the translation of the Bible into Annamese had just been completed, thereby bringing its vital truth within the reach of another group of peoples, numbering about sixteen millions, who heretofore have not had the written word in their own tongues. Thus the work begun at Pentecost is spreading at an amazing rate in our day, insomuch that the reaching of the remotest confines of the inhabited earth is now a matter of but a very brief time. Indeed, when we consider the number of missionary societies and other agencies that are prosecuting this work independently of each other, we are warranted in saying that "the end" whereof our Lord spake (Mat. 24:14) may "come" any day. Rightly viewed, this work is the combination and enlargement of the great miracle of Pentecost, which consisted in this, that the truth of the resurrection of Jesus Christ from the dead, and of the coming of the Holy Ghost from heaven, and the significance of that truth for all mankind, even to those that were "afar off" (Ac. 2:39), *was proclaimed in the languages of the heathen world.*

This work—the finishing of the miracle of Pentecost—is a thing that is little noticed, because it does not lie upon the surface of affairs; and notwithstanding that the great issue of the kingdom of this world depends mainly upon it, even the people of God give but slight attention to it. Therefore I lay the more stress upon it.

The Kingdom of Satan

Turning now to the other sphere, and viewing the mighty forces that are operating, and the movements now going on, in the three great departments of human society, it seems that here also the most notable phenomenon of the present hour is the amazing *celerity* at which everything connected with the life of individuals and of nations is rushing ahead. Nobody knows where he is going; but all are in a tremendous hurry to get there. And the speed is not only great, but it is *accelerating*. In fact, among the social phenomena of the day, *acceleration* is the most distinctive feature; and this has been specially noticeable since the era of the world-war of 1914-18. That cataclysm seems to have infused diabolical energies into all the agencies and instrumentalities of evil. The straining after higher speed in autos and airplanes is but a sign of what is taking place in all departments of life. Everybody and everything is rushing ahead at breathless speed. The whole world is now acting as if it were aware that, like its prince, it "hath but a short time".

This field of observation is so broad, the actors and factors therein are so numerous, and the movements are so complex, that no one could possibly comprehend in detail a thousandth part of what is going on. Yet it is quite possible to discern the main drift of things, and to determine the direction and probable outcome of the more important of the movements that are now in progress. To a few of these I will briefly refer, taking the three great departments of human affairs in this order: 1. Things Industrial; 2. Things Religious; 3. Things Political.

1. Things Industrial

In the great field of business (industry and commerce) the two-fold tendency towards *expansion* and *consolidation* continues with unabated energy. There has been a marked change of late in the policy of the government towards "trusts" and "combines". Instead of strong opposition, there is now benevolent approbation. The consolidation of railroads and of other business enterprises is now favored, instead of being resisted. The principal governments of the world themselves went into business, and on a very large scale, during the great war; and that seems to have made a marvellous difference. It has served to bring business and politics quite close together. Furthermore, business is taking on more and more an international character. The growing importance of oil as a source of power for transportation purposes, and for military and naval uses in particular, has had much to do with this; for but few of the leading nations have within their own borders sufficient supplies of that indispensable commodity for even current uses. Especially is *Finance* assuming a thoroughly cosmopolitan character. "International Finance" is now an established institution. The supremacy of Mammon, and the universality of its empire, are clearly recognized. And so the building up of Babylon, that great city, keeps pace with the building up of the temple of God; each in its own sphere, and upon its "own base". The development of things in this line will continue until *the end* of the days of the voice of the seventh angel. It is not necessary therefore that there should be any striking developments in this department of human affairs before those days *begin*.

2. Things Religious

In this field there is intense activity. The movements are many and various; but they have a common trend and converge to a common point. Rome continues unswervingly in the pursuit of her single aim, to sit in the seat of supreme authority over the nations— in other words, to ride upon the great beast. That her political influence is increasing is apparent to all. For proof, it is sufficient to point to the fact that, for the first time since the Reformation, England has entered into diplomatic relations with the Vatican; and that the attitude of Italy and of France towards the claims of the papacy has undergone a marked change, in the direction of amity and concord, within a few years. In order to the fulfilment of prophecy it is not necessary that any alteration should take place in either the policy or the organization of that ancient system of deception and error. But the visions we have been studying would lead us to expect *the combining of all* the religious elements of christendom that are hostile

Conclusion—Where We Now Stand 563

to the faith of Jesus Christ; and this is going on at a rapid rate among various Protestant bodies, notwithstanding the collapse of the famous "Inter-Church Movement" of a few years ago. This too, I think, is the tendency of the present-day movements classed as *liberalistic* or *modernistic*. The basic principle of all these, no matter how diverse their form, is *Humanism,* the exaltation of *man* to the place of *God;* whereof the cardinal doctrine is the inherent nobility and goodness of man, his progressiveness, and his sufficiency, by means of his own efforts and devices, to save himself and regenerate the world.

The notion of "evolution", which has such a prominent place just now in public discussions, has ceased to be a scientific theory, and has become strictly a *religious dogma*. That is why men are ready to fight for it. No one ever gets hot over a question of scientific truth. Even those classed as "scientists" (who are not different from other men) when they profess faith in evolution, and contend for it, do so not as scientists, but as religionists. Evolution therefore is not irreligious. On the contrary, it is essentially and intensely religious. It is the basic doctrine of the religion of Humanism; the design of its author being thereby to displace God the Creator and Sustainer of the universe, and to enthrone Man as the supreme being in nature, who is accountable to no one for his conduct

At the present moment Romanism and Modernism are to all appearances, directly opposed to each other. But while the former is stable, the latter is in a state of flux; so that the now existing differences may be readily composed. Rome cares little what men believe, provided only they conform outwardly to the system and acknowledge the authority of the hierarchy. In my unconverted days I was told on good authority that I could become a member of the "Church" without discarding or modifying my pantheistic and evolutionary beliefs. The essential matter is that the basic principle of Humanism, that is to say, the salvation of man *by his own works,* is common to both, and is the central doctrine of both. Therefore, it needs only the continued working of the same forces, in the same general direction, to bring about the unification of all the apostate systems of christendom; for the thought of "one Church", "one Brotherhood", is more and more taking hold of the imaginations of men. Moreover, that consummation may be, and very likely will be, precipitated by some crisis or convulsion of such a sort as, in the present state of human affairs might happen any day.

Therefore, just as we are able to foresee the full development of "Babylon, that great city", as an event of the near future, even so can we also foresee the early manifestation of that mother of harlots and abominations of the earth, "Mystery Babylon the great".

3. THINGS POLITICAL

Here is where the energies in operation are the greatest, the movements the swiftest, and the signs the

Conclusion—Where We Now Stand 565

clearest. There is no need of unusual discernment or of close observation to make one aware of the real state and drift of things in the field of world-politics. For those who are thoroughly conversant with the affairs of the nations, and who take leading parts therein, are themselves proclaiming, loudly and unceasingly, the near approach of a catastrophe which, they tell us, will be of world-wide extent and of unparalleled magnitude; a catastrophe of such sort and such scope as (if sufficient measures be not taken seasonably to avert it) will plunge the whole of human society, the whole of christian civilization, and of mankind itself, into utter and irretrievable ruin.

Such being the prospect that immediately confronts the world, what measures will the leaders of the world adopt in order to avert it? what measures *can* be devised that would avail to save the world from its impending fate? Compacts among the nations are but ropes of sand, mere "scraps of paper"; and no one understands this better than the political leaders themselves. What then? Human wisdom and statescrift can suggest but one expedient, in this desperate situation, a *Super-state*. Nothing else is in view. And indeed the nations that live most in dread of another war *have already committed themselves definitely to that plan*. For the "League of Nations" is no longer an experiment, but an established institution. Let us then open our eyes wide to the startling fact that *the final embodiment of world government has already appeared upon the scene*. Thus the prophecies of the end are being fulfilled in a most unmistakable way before our eyes at this very moment.

One thing we often hear by way of dissatisfaction with the League as it now exists, is that it lacks "teeth"; that is to say, it is without means to enforce its decrees, and to deal punitively with the nations who would resist them. But *teeth* belong to maturity, and the League is yet in its infancy. Measures are being taken to supply this deficiency, and they will be effectual; for Daniel, in beholding this beast, was specially impressed by the fact that "it had *great iron teeth*" (Dan. 7:7). That the lack of "teeth" will be met, is further indicated by that part of the prophecy which shows that men will come to regard the beast as invincible, saying, "Who is like unto the beast? Who can make war with him?" (Rev. 13:4). So let us realize that the framework of the super-governmental system of John's visions already exists; and that a compelling motive for investing it with supreme authority and with irresistible military power also exists in the recognition, on the part of all the statesmen of Europe, of the *absolute necessity* of maintaining "world-peace", the alternative being utter ruin.

Such is the political situation as it actually exists at the present moment; and inasmuch as we are now considering nothing that is in the least speculative, nothing but what is recognized as the plainest of plain facts by all who are acquainted with that situation, I would urge every reader to make whatever mental effort may be necessary in order to the comprehension of it. What follows will, I hope, be found helpful to that end.

The Inevitableness of the Predicted Outcome

One thing that forcibly impresses me as I reflect upon the present political situation, and the current political development, is the *inevitablesness* of the outcome. Usually when a danger is clearly foreseen it can be averted by the concerting of timely and effective measures of prevention. But here is a frightful danger looming up, and rapidly approaching, of such a peculiar character that the only conceivable measures for preventing it do but make it *the more certain to happen,* and *the more ruinous when it does happen.* This is the apotheosis of paradoxes; but however paradoxical, it is true. For in view of the threat of another war, which will be waged with new and truly diabolical appliances, the nations are under the strongest compulsion to "preparedness"; and yet, as Lord Gray and other authorities have pointed out again and again, it was the principle of "preparedness" that *brought on the last world-war,* and gave it its character of unparalleled destructiveness; and as the authorities have also pointed out, it is the same principle, and the devotion of the nations thereto, that makes the next war a moral certainty, and insures to it such a potency for barbarity, destruction and ruin, as nothing human and mortal could possibly survive. Therefore, we have here a situation such, that the more earnestly and thoroughly the various nations prosecute the *only conceivable plan of warding off the threatened catastrophe, the more certain do they thereby make the happening of that catastrophe, and the more horrible its consequences.*

Let me give a concrete illustration of this important point. Among the developments and achievements of our times there is nothing that is viewed with greater admiration, or upon which the modern man more often prides himself, than the progress of aviation. And truly it is a marvel. What a commentary then upon human nature! what a revelation have we of what human nature really is, in the fact that *the greater and more marvellous the achievements of man, the more he has to fear from them!* Speaking on the subject of the frightful menace of the airplane, in connection with other recent developments in methods and appliances of destruction, a prominent English journal remarks:

> "It has been noticed for a long time that we moderns have immensely increased the physical applicances at our command, and especially our means of hurting one another, without any corresponding improvement in our characters. And now an ironical fate would seem to have put a climax to this kind of evolution by giving nations an unthought-of freedom to murder other nations, and taking away from them most of their former power to keep murderers at a distance from themselves".

England is the most influential of the nations that are directly involved in world-politics; and England more than any other has reason to fear, and *does* fear, this new "terror of the air". Heretofore the command of *the seas* was all that was needed to protect Great Britain, in her insular position, from the attacks of her enemies, and to keep open the lines of communication with her colonies, upon which she depends for food-supplies. But a new situation has arisen; for prospective enemies have now at their disposal weapons which could make the centers of population and industry of the entire country a desolation and a series of charnel-houses in the course of a few days, *and against which no means of defense exists, or can be imagined.* The Chief of the British Air Staff, Sir Hugh Trenchard, has lately called public attention to

"The terrible extent to which the means of air *attack* have outdistanced the means of air *defence* since combatant flying began". He believes that "more bombs could now be dropped on London *in one day* than were dropped upon it in the four years of the great war. They would, too, be bombs of a far more lethal and generally destructive character". And he also believes that "however strong we may be in the air, we could not prevent this visitation".

What then must be the plan of action of a nation so situated, in the event of an outbreak of war? (And let us remember that what is true of England in this respect, is true also to a greater or less extent of all nations). Manifestly, and as the English journal quoted above points out,

"With effectual defense so far past hope, any future war between the Great Powers must take the form of an *immediate and enormous competition in the destruction of civilian life and property,* each state trying desperately to quell and numb the enemy nation's will by the approach of extermination, before a similar process of depopulation has broken the spirit of its own. Any available air-forces, it is held, would so obviously go farther in *offense* than in *defense,* that defense would scarcely be attempted".

From the foregoing illustration may be clearly seen the *inevitableness,* in view of conditions already existing, of a line of political developments that must lead to the fulfilment of the prophecies of Revelation concerning the ending of human history, and of "the kingdoms of this world". The dread of the next war is upon all the nations. The horrible character thereof, and the utter havoc it would work, are clearly foreseen. This prospect is the dominant influence that is shaping at this hour the policies of all the leading nations of the world. And yet, every measure they devise in the face of that prospect does but make more certain and more dreadful the very cataclysm they are so anxious to avert.

"The Sea and the Waves Roaring"

Thus far we have viewed only the present state of things political among the christianized nations of Europe ("the *earth*" of prophecy); for it is out of a combination of these, (in political alliance with apostate christianity in its final development, "the great whore"), that the last stage of beast government (that represented by the seventh head) is to arise. But for an understanding of the situation *as a whole* we must look beyond the borders of christendom, and take note of what is going on at this time among the outside nations, the restless and tumultuous "sea". For while the chief concern of the statesmen of Europe is the danger each nation has to fear from its neighbors, yet there is also a great and growing apprehension of attack from the dark-skinned peoples of Asia and Africa. For there is just now a great and increasing agitation of "the sea" of the nations.

To begin with, Russia, that land of mystery and breeding-place of horrors, must be viewed as no longer a part of Christendom. The well-posted *"Literary Digest"*, in an article entitled *"Why Russia is Outside Europe"* (June 6, 1925), shows most convincingly that the real Russia of today is a very different thing from what it is supposed, by superficial observers, to be. And in this exposure of the real Russia, we are given to see what the spirit of Bolshevism actually is. The following is quoted by the *Digest* from an informative article in *The Contemporary Review* (London) :

"Our civilization with its immense material and scientific progress is looked on as the criterion of human development. By the 'civilization' of a country or a race *we* mean its approximation to European conditions, its ability to use our political nostrums (parliaments and ballot-boxes) and our mechanical conjuring-tricks (motor-cars and electricity). All our newspapers, reviews, history-books and the like are crammed with examples of this superficial philosophy, which renders impossible a true and objective appreciation of historical movements".

But Bolshevism views these idols of Western civilization with lofty contempt. Bolshevism is a mighty reaction against the work of Peter the Great, who sought to refashion his country after the model of the states of Europe. True Russians, we are told, hated all that was representative of the Europeanization of their country, "feeling it to be artificial, almost satanic". And now the Bolshevistic revolution has swept out of Russia practically every trace of European civilization. Our authority says: "Bolshevism is purely nihilistic and destructive in its action, as all who have had personal experience of Soviet rule will agree". Yet the masses of the people, despite all their miseries, have no desire for a different sort of government. "They have a boundless confidence in the future of their country which nothing can shake. They are just waiting patiently and resignedly, and with a great confidence, for what may come". The spirit of Bolshevism, which encountered strong resistance on the West, finds the most favorable conditions for its rapid spread eastward. The present disturbances in China are due in large measure to Bolshevistic propaganda; for truly "the yellow races are turning *red*". Meanwhile the chief of the military forces of Russia says: "The Red army must prepare for action; for the moment is approaching when the Communist Internationale will lead millions of proletarians into the fierce battle of labor". What seems to be immediately in prospect is an Asiatic Alliance; and the most significant feature of the situation is that in that *Asiatic* Alliance, *Russia* is taking the leading part. As to this, a newspaper correspondent writes from Moscow:

"The corner-stone of the Asiatic block has indeed been cemented by the reinforced friendship between China and the Russian Soviet Union. . . . The leaders of Chinese thought and the vanguard of an awakening independent China are coming to feel more and more that Soviet Russia is their natural ally against the encroachments of the Western Powers. The conviction is deepening that when China shakes off the lethargy of the feudal centuries, and attempts to unify her disintegrated empire, Russia will support her in the struggle to discard Western dominion, economic and political alike".

In corroboration of the above, a British consul in China has estimated that "China will go 'Red' within five years".

Thus it is perceived that Russia now stands wholly apart from christendom and Europe, and in definite alliance with the Asiatic nations; into whose peoples, moreover, she is systematically instilling a racial self-consciousness, and fostering a spirit of deadly hatred toward the white races.

The developments of the political situation in China are becoming more and more, even as I write and revise these pages, a matter of solicitude to the western nations, who, in comparison with the dark skinned races, are a small minority. The following press despatch from London, under date of July 12, 1925, will give an idea of the seriousness of the present state of affairs in the minds of those who are best able to form an estimate thereof:—

"LONDON, July 12.—The ominous events in China, Morocco, and India apparently are the preliminary stages of an unparalleled war to death between the white and colored races, with the Pacific as the central battle ground, writes F. Britten Austen, noted English author and frequent contributor to the Saturday Evening Post and other American publications, in the Sunday Pictorial today. He firmly believes the world is almost blindly rushing into a struggle which is being incited by a shrewd Bolshevik campaign, and which will make the fall of the Roman empire look like a small local affair in the destinies of the white nations.

'The shadow of a war cloud in the east is falling darkly upon the hitherto sunny world supremacy of the white race', writes Mr. Austen. 'It is unpleasantly possible that the cloud may be cloven tomorrow or the day after, but inevitably, by the lightning flashes of war. The white man's prestige will disappear when the savage, barbaric millions from Africa and Asia can defy the white man.

'The white man has forcibly fed the ancient populations with the newest theories of education, politics, and social custom. He has fatuously presented them with thousands and thousands of cinemas showing the white races in a contemptible light. He has committed the crowning folly of leading the colored races into battle against white men. In Africa, India, Indo-China and China, tens of thousands of demobilized war auxiliaries have returned to spread the wondrous tale that the white man is not invincible.

'The colored races hate the white man, with a hate whereof we have no conception. Moscow's one great reiterated hope is that the innumerable millions of colored races will rise and massacre the white man. They have used feverish propaganda to accomplish this. They count cunningly on Japan. Although Japan is equal with the western nations in the war of commerce, the white man insultingly treats her nationals as an inferior race. Her population is desperately over-crowded, but the white man denies it an outlet. Japan could fight a war against America or Great Britain, or both with a reasonable prospect of at least temporary success. If she should, the whole world's colored races would seethe in fanatic excitement'."

Reports to the same effect come from other quarters of the Orient, specially from India and all Mohammedan countries. A student of conditions in Moslem lands writes on the theme of "Islam in Change"; and from a broad survey of the facts, he reaches the conclusion that "Christianity and Islam face each other for world decision" (meaning, of course, what *the world* regards as "Christianity").

In North Africa similar conditions prevail. The well-sustained resistance of the tribes of Morocco to the armies of France and Spain is due to the increasing hatred of the dominant whites on the part of the dark-skinned peoples. A *New York* paper puts it thus:

"That which is happening in North Africa is an insurrection against the domination of the white race. Something of the same sort is brewing in India. It is not pleasant to contemplate the possibilities of a rising of Asia and Africa against Europe, the blacks and yellows against the white, Mohammedanism against Christianity".

Therefore, whichever way we look, the same conditions prevail; and there is, moreover, a remarkable unanimity of opinion among competent observers as to the significance of those conditions. The whole world is dividing itself into two great camps; the christianized nations against the pagans; the western peoples against "the kings of the east" (Rev. 16:12); while unclean spirits like frogs, such as *Militarism, Bolshevism,* and *Modernism,* "go forth unto the kings of the earth, and of the whole world, to gather them to the battle of that great day of God Almighty" (Rev. 16:13, 14). Since that battle comes under the sixth vial, it lies near the end of the day of wrath. Therefore, by the fact that the preparations for it are already advancing rapidly, we may be sure the *beginning* of that day is close at hand.

With Russia definitely split off from affiliation with the Western nations, and identifying herself with "the kings of the East", the situation is serious indeed; for the latter outnumber the former three to one. The immediate effect is that the nations of Europe are compelled, as a measure of self-preservation, to present a united front to this combined Red and Yellow peril; and the only practical way to do this is to clothe the League of Nations with the powers of a Superstate, and to provide it with "great iron teeth".

Much more to the same effect might be adduced; but enough has been said to show that from both internal and external conditions, strong pressure is being exerted upon the nations of apostate Christendom, whereby they are being forced into the adoption of political measures which will inevitably bring about the fulfilment of the visions of Patmos, and of all that has been written aforetime concerning that great and terrible day of the Lord.

CHAPTER XV

THE MILLENNIUM

What? Where? When?

And I saw an angel come down from heaven, having the key of the bottomless pit and a great chain in his hand. And he laid hold on the dragon, that old serpent, which is the Devil, and Satan, and bound him a thousand years. And cast him into the bottomless pit, and shut him up, and set a seal upon him, that he should deceive the nations no more, till the thousand years should be fulfilled: and after that he must be loosed a little season.

And I saw thrones, and they sat upon them, and judgment was given unto them: and I saw the souls of them that were beheaded for the witness of Jesus, and for the word of God, and which had not worshipped the beast, neither his image, neither had received his mark upon their foreheads, or in their hands; and they lived and reigned with Christ a thousand years.

But the rest of the dead lived not again until the thousand years were finished. This is the first resurrection. Blessed and holy is he that hath part in the first resurrection: on such the second death hath no power, but they shall be priests of God and of Christ, and shall reign with him a thousand years.

And when the thousand years are expired, Satan shall be loosed out of his prison.

And shall go out to deceive the nations which are in the four quarters of the earth. Rev. 20:1-8.

HERE is a passage of fascinating interest, one that has, moreover, given rise probably to more discussions, speculations, controversies and contradictory interpretations than any other portion of Scripture.

If the purpose of the present volume were merely to advocate some one of the views concerning the millennium that are currently presented, the effort would be of no value to Bible readers, for practically everything that can be said in support of each of those systems of interpretation has been fully and ably presented in books that are available. Recent books on Bible prophecy are, as a rule, mere restatements of what has been previously published.

The present study of the millennium proceeds upon a different method, whereof the first rule is that all surmises and dubious inferences are to be rigidly excluded. Briefly it is purposed, on the one hand, to give full effect to what is stated in the text of the passage, and on the other, to read nothing into it. First, every statement of the text itself concerning each of its several topics (which are few in number) is to be carefully studied; consideration is then to be given to other Scriptures that deal with each of those topics; and finally appropriate conclusions are to be drawn from the pertinent information thus gathered. In other words, the plan of this study is to place Scripture alongside of Scripture and allow each passage to interpret the others and to be interpreted by them. This method has the great advantage of excluding error and of saving ourselves from guesswork.

By adhering to it, while depending upon the guidance and illumination of the Holy Spirit, we shall assure ourselves of profitable results, even though we may not find answers to all our questions. Moreover, we shall be saved thereby from erroneous conclusions, which are inescapable when scope is given to the human imagination. It is far better to leave our questions unanswered until further light is given, than to accept conclusions for which no satisfactory proof can be adduced.

Characteristics of Current Millennial Doctrines

It will be of advantage if, in embarking upon the proposed study, we have in mind the prominent features of current millennial doctrines.

Preliminarily we note that the word "millennium" does not occur in the Bible. It is a coined word, which, however, has obtained the sanction of general usage because it has proved a convenient substitute for the phrase "thousand years", which phrase occurs six times in the first seven verses of Revelation XX.

Both pre- and post-millennialists hold that the millennium is a definite era of earth's future history, a golden age, presenting the greatest possible contrast to all previous ages in that peace, health and prosperity will prevail during the whole millennial period throughout the world. Both schools are in agreement that it will be the long looked for era in which the lion will lie down with the lamb, and the nations of the world will beat their swords into plough-shares, and their spears into pruning hooks, and will not learn war any more. The only major point of disagreement is as to whether the expected age of peace and prosperity will precede or follow the second advent of Christ.

Moreover, to many of those who look for an earthly millennium, such as indicated above, it will be characterized prominently by the fulfilment of the ancient Jewish dreams of restored nationalism, the destruction of all natural enemies and world-hegemony for the Jewish nation. Those Jewish expectations, which are founded upon a miscalled "literal" interpretation of certain O. T. prophecies, include the re-birth of "Israel after the flesh"; their reoccupation of the territory promised to Abraham (from the great sea to the river Euphrates); and their national exaltation to the place of world-supremacy and lordship over the nations; the rebuilding of the temple at Jerusalem, and the restoration of the Aaronic priesthood together with the sacrifices, feasts and ceremonies of the Mosaic ritual.

As to these views and expectations it will suffice to say at this point that there is not the slightest support for any of them in the millennium passage itself, for that short passage says not a word concerning the conditions of human life on earth during the thousand years. The facts in that regard are: first, that the current millennial doctrines derive absolutely nothing from that passage except the name; and second, that the prophecies, which are supposed to predict a coming era of national glory for Israel and of blissful conditions of life for the Gentiles, contain nothing whereby that supposed era can be identified with the thousand years of Revelation XX. Therefore, the rule of procedure which governs our present study compels the exclusion of these and all similar surmises and speculations.

Dr. Benjamin B. Warfield, in commenting upon the various and contradictory interpretations of the millennium passage now current, refers to Klieforth's statement, which is applicable alike to all those interpretations, that there are "not a few passages of Scripture which seem definitely to exclude the whole conception, and which must be subjected to most unnatural exegetical manipulation to bring them into harmony with it at all"; and that "the so-called millennium . . . has been more than any other part of the book (the Apocalypse) tortured by tendency-exposition into a variety of divergent senses". Upon which Dr. Warfield remarks: "And it is to be feared that there has been much less tendency-interpretation of Rev. XX in the interest of preconceived theory, than there has been tendency-interpretations of the rest of the Scripture in the interest of conceptions derived from misunderstandings of this obscure passage" (Warfield Biblical Doctrines, pp. 643, 644).

Topics in Revelation XX, 1-10

The passage deals with the following topics and none other:

1. Satan bound and imprisoned for a thousand years, to be loosed for a little season after the thousand years should be fulfilled (vv. 1-3);
2. The first resurrection: the souls of martyrs "lived

and reigned with Christ a thousand years" (vv. 4-6);
3. The second death (v. 6);
4. Satan loosed, the gathering of Gog and Magog to battle (vv. 7-10).

We shall not discuss separately the questions, What? Where? and When? is the millennium; but will take the several topics listed above in their order, and will find that the answers to those questions will emerge as we proceed.

1. Satan Bound and Imprisoned

The great adversary is prominent in this passage, and it should be noted that he is here identified by the same four names or titles that are given him in Chapter 12:9, "the dragon, that old serpent, which is the Devil and Satan". This identical designation of the adversary is manifestly designed to link the two passages together; and, as will be seen later on, valuable help is thereby given in the interpretation of the Scripture we are studying. In it we have a brief recital of Satan's temporary imprisonment in the abyss, of his release therefrom for a little season, of his last activities and of his eternal doom.

Concerning these and other happenings to which our passage refers we propose first to inquire where—that is on which side of the veil that separates the spiritual realm from the physical—the events described in this millennium passage were to take place. For, as has been remarked above, the scenes of the Apocalypse lie some on one side and some on the other of that veil; for which reason it is most needful that, before proceeding further, we should settle the question, where do the scenes of the thousand years take place?

The indications afforded by the passage itself are clear and decisive; for they all point to the conclusion negatively that the described events do not transpire on earth, and affirmatively that they do take place in the spiritual realm. The abyss (here called "the bottomless pit") is a spiritual locality. It is the abode of the demons or evil spirits; for when Christ cast out of a man the legion of demons, "they besought Him that He would not command them to go out into the deep" (Lu. 8:31, where "deep" is the same word as "bottomless pit" in Rev. 20:1). The abyss is the source of the plague of locusts described in Revelation 9:1-11, which ravaging hosts had over them a spiritual leader, "the angel of the abyss, whose name in the Hebrew tongue is Abaddon, and in the Greek tongue is Apollyon".

The evidence warrants the conclusion that the "Angel" who bound the Devil is none other than Christ Himself. None of the angelic hosts is great enough to bind Satan (Jude 9). To the angel who opened the bottomless pit (Chap. 9:1, 2) the key was *given*; but this "Angel" *has* the key thereof; and for the interpretation of this statement we may properly refer to the declaration of the Lord in Chap. 1:18, that *He* has "the keys of hell (hades) and of death".

It follows that the key and the great chain of this vision are spiritual things; for the abyss could not be opened with a physical key or the Devil be bound with a physical chain. And in this connection let us bear in mind that things in the spiritual realm are not less *real* than those in the physical, but in fact are more real; "for the things which are seen are temporal, but the things which are not seen are eternal" (2 Cor. 3:18).

Thus it is easily and clearly to be seen that the first three verses of Revelation XX relate wholly to happenings in the spiritual realm. There is indeed one reference to the affairs of the world, and this solitary and indirect allusion to temporal affairs in a passage otherwise occupied exclusively with spiritual places, persons and things, is most significant, for it affords— and doubtless by divine intent—an indication whereby the beginning of the thousand years can be located approximately. This will be shown hereafter. That reference is found in the words: "that he should deceive the nations no more till the thousand years should be fulfilled". But even here there is no description, indeed not the slightest indication, of the conditions of human existence on earth during this period, or of the relations of the nations to each other. These words will receive consideration further on and it will be found that they afford help in determining the place of the millennium in human history. We shall return to the subject of the binding of Satan in connection with other Scriptures.

2. THE FIRST RESURRECTION, THE SOULS OF MARTYRS

At verse 4 occur the words with which the seer usually introduces a vision: *"And I saw"*. Thus we know that these verses (4-6) contain a distinct vision; but it is closely related to that of verses 1-3 by the three-fold repetition of the words "thousand years". We must therefore conclude that this scene is *contemporaneous* with that of verses 1-3.

In verses 4-6 there is no reference, direct or indirect, to earthly things or affairs. John saw thrones and their occupants. The latter are not described as persons in resurrection bodies, but as martyred souls; and they are described as in two distinct categories: first,

> "the souls of them that were beheaded for the witness of Jesus and for the word of God,"

second,

> those who "had not worshipped the beast, neither his image, neither had received his mark upon their foreheads or in their hands".

Of both these classes of the souls of martyrs it is said, that—

> "they lived and reigned with Christ a thousand years" (v. 4); and that, "This is the first resurrection" (v. 5).

In our quest for answers to the questions, what and where is the millennium, verses 4, 5 and 6 are of great importance and value. They make it abundantly plain that the vision reveals—not happenings on earth, whether after the second advent of Christ and the resurrection of the believing dead, as the pre-millennialists hold, or before those great events, as the post-millennialists hold, but—what transpires in heaven, and specially how it fares there with the souls of faithful men who have suffered death or persecution for the Word of God and the testimony of Jesus Christ.

To this subject also we will return when we come to the examination of other Scriptures. At present we are confining ourselves to the contents of the passage itself.

3. The Second Death

To this topic our passage makes only a casual reference. It is said concerning those who have part in *the first resurrection* that "on such the second death hath no power". But "the second death" is defined in verse 14. Thus the second death is placed in direct antithetical relation with the first resurrection, from which it follows that if one of those phrases refers to what is on the spiritual side of the veil the other does likewise. The second death is twice mentioned in subsequent passages (20:14 and 21:8). Therefore, it will come before us again.

4. Satan Loosed, Gog and Magog

Verses 7-10 state that at the expiration of the thousand years Satan shall be loosed out of his prison, and that he shall then go forth to deceive the nations which are in the four quarters of the earth, Gog and Magog, to gather them together to battle in countless numbers; the result of the battle being that fire comes down from heaven and consumes them, and the devil who deceived them is cast into the lake of fire and brimstone, where the beast and the false prophet had previously been cast (19:20).

It is a striking fact that "when the thousand years are expired", the description turns to events on earth; whereas no earthly happenings are recorded in the preceding verses. This further confirms the view that the visions of verses 1-6 reveal things that were to take place in the spiritual realm.

Since, as appears from the foregoing review of the passage itself, its visions do not relate to earthly events, it is not strange that expositors, who locate the events represented by those visions on the earthly side of the veil, are at odds with one another as to *the time* of their occurrence and are hard put to it to find a place in the earthly history of mankind, either before or after the second advent of Christ, where they can be located. Nor is it strange that some are driven to the despairing conclusion that there is no millennium at all.

It thus clearly appears from a rapid survey of the passage itself that it is occupied wholly with the continuation of the history of Satan—interrupted at Chapter 13:2, and with that of the souls of "the martyrs of Jesus"—interrupted at Chapter 6:11.

SATAN'S POWER CURTAILED

We now go beyond the passage itself (Ch. 20:1-10) to seek light from other Scriptures that refer to one or other of the topics we have just reviewed. In this part of our study we shall look carefully for any information whereby the thousand years may be located with relation to the course of human history. Not that we should expect to find an exact measure of a thousand years that can be identified as corresponding to the period during which Satan was imprisoned in the abyss and the souls of the christian martyrs were reigning with Christ in the heavenly places and exercising the kingly prerogative of "judgment". For we should not lose sight of the fact that numbers in Revelation have often a symbolic meaning, and that therefore some expositors regard the phrase "a thousand years" as having the indefinite meaning of numerical fulness or completeness. In that view it would signify any time-period that is rounded out and complete. An instance of this usage is found in 2 Peter 3:8, where we read that with the Lord one day is as a thousand years, and conversely a thousand years is as one day. Manifestly the lesson of that verse is that God, Who inhabits eternity, is not affected by the passage of time as we are, but is independent of all time-limitations. Hence, for the purpose of the lesson which the verse teaches, any other long stretch of years, far beyond the span of human life, might have been set in comparison with the brief space of one day. Reference to this verse is specially pertinent because the form of the numeral "thousand" therein is identical with that which occurs six times in Revelation 20; and that form, according to Strong's Concordance, is the Greek plural of uncertainty. Hence, if this learned authority is correct, we have additional reason for not regarding "the thousand years" of Revelation 20 as a measure of earthly time.

But Dr. Strong's statement, which we have cited, is not to be accepted as certainly correct, for it is questioned by other authorities. Nevertheless the idea that "the thousand years" is properly to be taken as signifying—not an exact arithmetical value applied to solar years, but—merely a relatively long period of time, commends itself to our acceptance in view of all the facts, particularly as there seems to be nothing of weight that can be urged against it.

The declared purpose of the binding of Satan is that he should deceive the nations no more until the thousand years should be fulfilled. No effect upon human life on earth other than the deceiving of the nations is mentioned. The popular surmises as to universal peace, abounding prosperity and unalloyed happiness throughout the thousand years are wholly without foundation in the text. The idea of universal peace on earth is based upon the belief that Satan is the instigator of wars. That might be in cases where wars suit his purpose. But Scripture declares, and all human experience confirms it, that "wars and fightings" come from the lusts of the human heart (James 4:1). Moreover, we must not overlook that Satan, in anticipation of his personal removal from the earthly scene, gave his power and throne and great authority to the beast. Therefore, the binding of Satan does not imply the cessation of wars and fightings. The nations need no instigations of Satan to set them at war among themselves; but when deceived by him they make war against the people of God. It was so during the "short time" between his expulsion from heaven and his imprisonment in the abyss; and when "loosed out of his prison" he will again, and for the last time, "go out to deceive the nations ... to gather them together to battle" against "the camp of the saints" (Rev. 20:8, 9).

Furthermore, the declared effect of the binding of Satan is limited to "the nations", i. e., *the Gentiles*. The text contains no reference, and nothing that could by any stretch be taken as a reference, to the Jewish people.

Finally, there is not a word or hint to warrant the idea that the thousand years were to be a period during which Jesus Christ would reign in bodily presence over the world and with Him the people of God in their resurrection bodies.

Surely if the current millennial doctrines were right as to their essential features there would be something to support them in the millennium passage itself; and conversely, since they find not a word of support therein, we are bound to reject them as unscriptural, unless other Scriptures afford clear proof that Christ and His resurrected people will reign during the thousand years over the earth peopled with unregenerate Jews and Gentiles, the Jews being restored to their ancient territory and invested with world supremacy.

But other Scriptures do speak distinctly of the curtailing of Satan's power. The binding of Satan is referred to by the Lord Himself, and He speaks of it, moreover, as something to be accomplished by Himself. The saying in which He referred specifically to the binding of Satan is recorded by Matthew, Mark and Luke. As recorded by Matthew (Ch. 12:29) the occasion was the casting out by the Lord Jesus of an evil spirit, which miracle the Pharisees attributed to the power of Beelzebub, the prince of the demons. Whereupon the Lord, knowing their thoughts, said, "And if Satan cast out Satan, he is divided against himself" (v. 26); and He went on to say: "Or else how can one enter into the* strong man's house, and spoil (or despoil him of) his goods, except he first bind the strong man? and then he will spoil his house".

The context makes it plain, as all commentators are agreed, that Christ is here speaking of the binding *of Satan.* The text shows that Christ Himself is the One by Whom Satan was to be bound; and furthermore, the Scriptures leave no uncertainty at all as to when and how the binding of the adversary was to be accomplished; for in Hebrews 2:14, 15 it is written that the Son of God became man in order that "through death He might destroy him that had the power of death, that is, the devil". Likewise in Colossians 2:14, 15 we read that, by His cross, He despoiled principalities and powers, openly triumphing over them. Also in John 12:23-33 the Lord foretold "what death He should die", and what would be the consequence thereof to the great adversary, "the prince of this world", saying: "Now is the judgment of this world; now shall the prince of this world be cast out; and I, if I be lifted

---

* The Greek text has the definite article.

up from the earth, will draw all men unto Me". Thus He declared, though in different words, the same prophetic truth recorded in Matthew 12:29.

We have seen that, in fulfilment of John 12:31, Satan was cast out of heaven when Christ ascended to His Father's throne. In confirmation of this view concerning the defeat of Satan, we cannot do better than to quote the words of Dr. J. Ritchie Smith:

> "Christ regards His work as finished, the victory won. 'The prince of this world hath been judged'. His sentence has been pronounced, his power is broken, though his complete and final overthrow may be long delayed. The death of the Lord Jesus appeared to be the hour of Satan's triumph—'This is your hour and the power of darkness'; yet through death he brought to nought him that had the power of death.
>
> How is this judgment of the prince of the world made manifest? How shall the world know that its sovereign prince has been condemned? The proof is furnished by the triumphant ministry of the disciples which rests upon the finished work of Christ. . . . For 'how can one enter into the house of the strong man and spoil his goods, except he first bind the strong man?' Every soul that is turned from darkness to light and from the power of Satan unto God is a witness that the power of the prince of this world has been broken." (From *The Holy Spirit in the Gospels*.)

The above is the more significant because it is apparent that, in writing it, Dr. Smith did not have the millennium in mind.

The Lord Jesus, after His death and resurrection, announced to His apostles that all power had been given Him in heaven and in earth. He exercised that power in heaven immediately by casting Satan out from thence. He had spoken of this in prophetic vision, saying, "I beheld Satan as lightning fall from heaven", and accompanying this with the promise, "Behold, I give unto you *power* to tread on serpents and scorpions, and over all the power of the enemy" (Lu. 10:18, 19).

We have seen that prominence is given to this great event in Revelation 12:7-17, and that passage is closely linked with the millennium passage by the fact that in both the adversary is designated by the four names, "the great dragon, that old serpent, the Devil and Satan". Thus it is impressed upon us that the casting down of that mighty being was accomplished in two stages. At the first stage "he was cast out into the earth"; and that meant "woe to the inhabiters of the earth and of the sea", for the devil was come down to them, *"having great wrath, because he knoweth that he hath but a short time"* (12:12, 13).

Here is information of great value in our present quest. We learn that the victorious Redeemer did not exercise the authority conferred upon Him at His resurrection to destroy the vanquished foe at once. His first act of judgment was to cast the adversary and his angels out of heaven, so that thenceforth he could no longer accuse the brethren before God. The adversary's power on earth, however, was not abridged at that time, but its duration was limited to what, in the divine reckoning, was "a short time". Satan himself was aware of this, and hence his "great wrath", which expended itself in the bloody persecutions of Christians that raged during the first three centuries of the gospel era. For our present purpose it is specially important to note that, during that time of fiery trial, the nations were deceived into the belief that Christians were enemies of the constituted civil government and were constantly plotting the overthrow of the throne of the Cæsars.

But early in the fourth century there was a complete change in that respect; for after the accession of the emperor Constantine to the throne, Christianity became the state religion; and from thenceforth "the powers that be" have been deceived no more as to the character of the doctrine of Christ, but on the contrary have recognized that it was a bulwark of the State, one of its cardinal doctrines being that "the powers that be are ordained of God".

In view of these undisputed facts of Scripture and of history, it will be seen that the complete change which took place at that time (the fourth century) in the attitude of the nations constituting the Roman Empire towards Christianity is in perfect accord with what the Scripture foretold as to the effect on earth of the binding of Satan. This indicates that the thousand years began at or near that time: and there is nothing in Scripture or in history, so far as this writer is aware, in conflict with that view.

This brings us to a matter of capital importance; for the main thing to be ascertained, in order to insure success in our endeavor to locate the thousand years in the course of human history, is the event or epoch that coincides with the binding of Satan. If that can be determined from the evidence available to us, the most formidable difficulty in our path will have been overcome.

Turning again to the passage that announces the expulsion of Satan from heaven, (Chap. XII. 9) we note that it goes on to describe the rising up out of the sea of a seven horned beast (Chap. XIII. 1, 2); which event is there mentioned for the sole apparent purpose of revealing the portentous fact that "the dragon gave him (the beast) his power, and his seat (throne) and great authority". The fact here revealed, and which could not otherwise have been known, is obviously of tremendous significance for its influence upon the subsequent history of the world. But more than that, it affords the very help we need at this crucial point in our inquiry. Upon consideration of the above quoted statement we would naturally ask, why did the Devil delegate to another (and why to the seven-horned beast?) his power, his throne and his great authority? The explanation lies at hand. In verse 12 of the preceding chapter it is stated that the adversary was aware that he had "but a short time" wherein to incite the nations, by means of his deceptions, to wage war against the people of God. Therefore, in anticipation of the approaching end of his persecuting career, he, with satanic astuteness, delegated his power and authority to the then dominant political system whose empire embraced the civilized world. Thus "it was given him (the beast) to make war with the saints, and to overcome them" (13:7).

This explanation is in full agreement with the fact

that, in the scenes which follow, and which depict the important events of world history (as they affect the Kingdom of God) down to our own times, Satan does not appear as an actor. He is not seen again as a participant in the affairs of earth until after the thousand years. The agents in the then ensuing warfare against the saints, in the deceptions that were to be practiced upon "them that dwell on the earth", and the oppression and bondage to which "all, both small and great, rich and poor, free and bond" were to be subjected, are the two beasts, or the beast and the false prophet.

The immense significance of this revelation for the purpose of our present inquiry is obvious; for here is strong confirmation for the view that the binding of Satan was coincident with the era of the emperor Constantine. If we accept that view we have an adequate explanation of the extraordinary change of attitude on the part of imperial Rome towards the Christian body which then took place; but if we refuse that view we cannot reasonably account for the change.

Further we note that, in the account of the activities of the two beasts, nothing is said of deceiving the nations. Instead it was given the first beast (and hence to the other also, for he exercised "all the power of the first beast before him", ver. 12) "to make war with the saints and to overcome them; and power was given him over all kindreds, and tongues, and nations" (ver. 7). This explains the persecutions of the saints of God and the spread of the secular power in league with the papacy in the centuries between the accession of Constantine and the Protestant Reformation.

THE END OF THE THOUSAND YEARS

Having thus found ample evidence and authority for the conclusion that the predicted events of the Millennium lie in the spiritual realm—"within the veil"—and having found a clearly marked epoch in human history which enables us to fix approximately the beginning thereof, our interest now centers upon the question, *when do the thousand years end?* The passage contains three references to the end of the thousand years: (1) "That he should deceive the nations no more, till the thousand years should be fulfilled" (ver. 3); (2) "But the rest of the dead lived not again until the thousand years were finished" (ver. 7); (3) "And when the thousand years are expired, Satan shall be loosed out of his prison, and shall go out to deceive the nations which are in the four quarters of the earth" (ver. 8). Verse 8 reveals also the events that are to take place after the thousand years are finished.

If we felt warranted in taking the phrase "a thousand years" as an exact measure of earthly time, there would be no need for further inquiry. For if the millennium began in the fourth century or thereabouts, it has already ended. But, as we have endeavored to show, the evidence does not warrant the conclusion that the millennium certainly began then. In any view of it, the language of the millennium passage does not require us to assume that the post-millennial events there mentioned (the loosing of Satan, etc.) begin to take place immediately upon the termination of the thousand years. What we definitely learn from the language of the text is that, from the time of the binding of Satan, whenever that might be, a full thousand years were to elapse ere he should be loosed out of his prison. This leaves room for the possibility that more than a thousand years were to elapse before the loosing of Satan.

Indeed, considering the nature of those post-millennial events, that they include calamities and woes of world-wide extent and of terrible severity, being the products of Satan's last and most virulent activities, it would be clearly in full accord with the revealed ways of God, in His marvellous forbearance toward the children of men, that He should interpose a period of delay—a suspension of judgment—before the fulfilment of this dire prophecy, which has its culmination in "the day of judgment and perdition of ungodly men" (2 Pet. 3:7).

The Longsuffering of God

The passage just quoted (2 Pet. III) supplies teaching of priceless value concerning the forbearance of God and also concerning the events attendant upon the second advent of Christ. Its sweep is stupendous, for it reaches from "the beginning of the creation" (ver. 4) to "the day of eternity" (ver. 18, Gr.); and in the survey of that vast prospect it brings into view the heavens and earth that "were" before the flood, the heavens and earth that "now are", and the new heavens and new earth that are to be. Such is the impressive background upon which the apostle unfolds the subject of "the promise of His parousia" (ver. 4), and sets before us the chief incidents that will attend and follow the Lord's return; as to all of which he appeals in conclusion to the confirmatory teaching of "our beloved brother Paul" to be found "in all his epistles" (vv. 15, 16).

In unfolding this subject the apostle makes known that in the last days there should come into prominence some who would in a conspicuous manner cast discredit upon the promised return of the Lord Jesus, appealing in support of their scepticism to the centuries of time during which there had been no interruption of the course of nature. That there was to be a long lapse of time is clearly intimated. In explanation thereof two statements are made: first, "that one day is with the Lord as a thousand years, and a thousand years as one day", whereby we are given to understand that what to men is a period of inconceivable length is to God as but a single day; and second that, whatever the hasty conclusions men may draw from the tranquil course of centuries of time, the Lord is not slack or indifferent as to His promise, "but is longsuffering toward us, not willing that any should perish, but that all should come to repentance" (vv. 8, 9).

We cite this passage primarily because it fully justifies the expectation that God would in mercy, and for the very reasons here set forth, postpone the beginnings of the predicted post-millennial events for what would be to men a long period of time though to Him it would be but "a little season". But the passage has much more to tell us that is pertinent to our subject. It is truth of immense interest and importance that the second coming of Christ will be coincident with "the day of judgment and perdition of ungodly men", and that it is for that reason alone that His coming again has been so long delayed. It is most needful we should clearly understand that of those whose blessed privilege it is to live in this day of salvation all who do not "come to repentance" ere He returns, will "perish" (v. 9). In fact, the substance of the whole passage is this: the Lord's second advent is delayed for no other reason than that it means judgment for all who are not in Christ and God is not willing that any should perish.

Most certainly the Holy Spirit could not have caused the writing of this verse if the parousia of Christ was to usher in a golden age of a thousand years' duration, at the very beginning of which all the living descendants of Jacob were to be converted and in the course of which all the nations were to participate in the light of God's truth and the blessings of the Kingdom of Christ. If such were to be the mundane conditions to follow the coming of the Lord, then the reasons which the apostle assigns as an explanation for delaying His coming would constitute the strongest possible inducements for hastening it.

The apostle, however, does not stop at verse 9, but proceeds in the next verse to make the matter even more clear and certain, saying: "But the day of the

Lord will come as a thief in the night; in the which the heavens shall pass away with a great noise, and the elements shall melt with fervent heat, the earth also and the works that are therein shall be burned up" (ver. 10). These plain words certify to us that the coming of Christ not only brings the day of the judgment and perdition of ungodly men, but heralds also the passing away of the heavens and earth, which now are, and the destruction by fire of the works that are in the earth. In the light of these clear statements it is not an exaggeration to say that nothing could be in greater contrast to the prophetic Scriptures than the doctrine that the coming of the Lord will be followed by a millennium of earthly peace, prosperity and salvation.

But it would seem that the Holy Spirit desires to leave us in no uncertainty whatever as to the truth revealed in this passage; for the apostle proceeds immediately to make application thereof to the hearts of God's people by admonishing them in respect to the holy manner of life and the godliness that should characterize all their behavior in view of the imminence of these impending events (ver. 11). Manifestly the basis for this appeal to their consciences would be lacking if a millennium of terrestrial blessedness were to ensue immediately upon the Lord's second advent. Further the apostle exhorts the people of God to be "looking for and hasting unto the coming of the day of God, wherein the heavens being on fire shall be dissolved, and the elements shall melt with fervent heat" (ver. 12), an exhortation to which they could not possibly give heed if a blissful millennium were to intervene between the present era and the coming of that "day of God".

And even this is not all; for the apostle in the next verse (13) sets forth in clear words the true outlook of God's people in this dispensation, saying, "Nevertheless we, according to His promise, look"—not for a millennium of edenic conditions on earth, but—"for new heavens and a new earth, wherein dwelleth righteousness"; and this is in perfect agreement with all other Scriptures that speak of things to come. Continuing the exhortation, the apostle bids us to account that the longsuffering of our Lord is—not the postponement of a blessing promised to all mankind in a future day but—a compassionate prolongation of the present day of "salvation"; and so desirous is he of impressing upon the minds of his readers the importance of these weighty truths that he cites the concurring testimony of the apostle Paul, in these touching words: "Even as our beloved brother Paul also, according to the wisdom given unto him, hath written you". For this teaching is not that of Peter only, but of "Paul also". Some of these confirmatory teachings of the apostle of the Gentiles will be cited below. This passage in 2 Peter III is of such nature, scope and subject-matter, that, if there were to be a millennium of bliss for Jews and Gentiles at the second coming of Christ, it would surely have had a conspicuous place therein; whereas, on the contrary, the information given in that passage is such as to exclude it altogether.

From yet another apostle we receive strong confirmation of the view here presented concerning what will take place at and immediately following the Lord's second advent. For James, in Chapter V of his epistle, writes concerning "the last days" (ver. 3) and "the coming of the Lord" (ver. 7). He too speaks of the intervening age as a period wherein God is exercising "long patience". That coming day is to be a time of judgment, and the imminence thereof is testified in the statement that "the Judge standeth before the door". Moreover, it is because the Lord is coming as the righteous "Judge", and because of the "miseries" that are then to be poured upon those who make the riches of this world their aim and "have lived in pleasure on the earth", that He exercises "long patience" and that He exhorts His people to be patient also. The long patience whereof James speaks is just another word for the longsuffering of God which Peter emphasizes.

Here again is a picture of the coming day in which no place is given to, or can be found for, the millennium currently expected by certain groups of Christians.

Deceiving the Nations

Returning to the subject of the length of the interval between the end of the millennium and the loosing of Satan, we note that with respect thereto the Scripture is indefinite, and, of course, purposely so. Likewise with reference to that "little season" of tribulation and distress which is to follow the loosing of Satan, the only indication given by the Scripture, whereby it may be known that the great adversary has been released from his confinement in the abyss, will be the occurrence of political events of such sort as to make evident that he is again exercising his arts to deceive the nations and excite their rulers to animosity towards Christians and Christianity. When such events "begin to come to pass" we may assuredly gather that Satan is again active in world politics; for occurrences of that nature have not had a place in the history of Christendom for more than a thousand years. And are not these the political conditions which distinctively characterize the governmental policy of Soviet Russia? a State which was formerly a citadel of Christian orthodoxy? And is not Bolshevism, to the consternation of all governments, making headway in other countries? particularly in the most populous and most homogeneous nation in the world—China? But this is a matter touching which the reader is well able to draw his own conclusions from the daily newspaper records of current events; therefore, we make only a passing reference to the momentous "things that are coming to pass upon the earth" under our very eyes, and will not pause to comment thereon.

"They Lived and Reigned with Christ"

This brings us again to the vision of verse 4, which will now be considered in the light of other pertinent Scriptures. Attention is first directed to the interesting

The Millennium

and illuminating fact that the enthroned company, of whom it is said that "they lived and reigned with Christ a thousand years", was composed of two divisions or groups, which are clearly distinguished from each other: first, those who "were beheaded for the witness of Jesus and for the word of God", and second, those who "had not worshipped the beast, neither his image, neither had received his mark upon their foreheads or in their hands". Those two divisions or groups belong respectively to different eras of the Kingdom of God on earth, the first being some centuries earlier than the second.

What is significant for the help it affords in determining when the thousand years began is that the first of these two groups of martyrs is seen at the opening of the fifth seal already in heaven (Ch. 6:9), and that while the second division is not then with them (for the career of the beast had not yet begun) there is nevertheless an anticipatory reference to other sufferers for the truth's sake, who would join them at a later time. It is recorded that in that earlier vision John "saw under the altar the souls of them that were slain for the word of God and for the testimony which they held". These composed the first of the two divisions that made up the company seen in Chapter XX. They were disembodied "souls", and they are identified by the same descriptive terms applied in Chapter 20:4 to the first category of martyrs there seen.

Those souls of Chapter VI were eagerly expecting some intervention of God in their behalf, the nature of which is indicated in a general way by their loud cry, "How long, O Lord, holy and true, dost Thou not judge and avenge our blood on them that dwell on the earth"? (6:10). The answer from the throne indicates clearly that their expectations were well founded, and it also explains the delay of which they complained; for "it was said to them that they should rest yet for a little season, until their fellowservants also and their brethren, that should be killed as they were, should be fulfilled". Incidentally we learn from this record the interesting fact that, to the saints in heaven as well as to those on earth, the Lord's delay to judge "them that dwell on the earth" seems inexplicably "long".

Here again is a reference to "a little season", but with nothing in the context to indicate the length thereof as time is reckoned this side of the veil. What is important, however, for present purposes, as further linking the two visions together, is that in the first the souls of those early Christian martyrs cried out for judgment, and in the second "judgment was given them". Not only did Christ, to Whom all authority in heaven and earth had been given (Mat. 28:18) execute judgment upon their enemies, but they themselves shared with Him the prerogative of His throne.

In connection with the words spoken to the souls under the altar, "that they should *rest* yet for a little season", we recall that "rest" is the blessed portion of all those "who die in the Lord" (Ch. 14:13). Those martyred souls had already entered into *that* "rest", upon their departure from this life, but they had been given to expect something *in the nature of a reward,* and the text shows that the time therefor had not yet come. Therefore, they are bidden to "*rest yet* for a little season". It may rightly be inferred that the particular reward which is here called "the first resurrection", is limited to the special classes of martyrs named in the passage, because of the fact that the time for the reward of the saints in general does not come until the sounding of the seventh trumpet; for then the elders give thanks to God, saying: "Thy wrath is come, and the time of the dead, that they should be judged, and that Thou shouldest *give reward unto Thy servants the prophets, and to the saints, and them that fear Thy Name, small and great*" (11:17, 18).

It is of interest that the Greek word rendered "rest" in the two passages referred to above, which word is of relatively rare occurrence in Scripture, is that which our Lord used in His great utterance, "Come unto Me, all ye that labour and are heavy laden, and I will give you REST" (Matt. 11:28), that being its first occurrence. Thus the vision of Revelation 6:9 gives us to see the souls of departed saints in the conscious enjoyment of that particular "rest" which our Saviour promises to "all" who come unto Him.

There is nothing in the text requiring us to suppose that the beginning of the thousand years, during which the souls of "the martyrs of Jesus" were to live and reign with Him, was delayed until the last of those who were to share that high honor had entered into rest. On the contrary the Scriptures warrant the belief that the era in which "the martyrs of Jesus" (Rev. 17:6) lived and reigned with Him began in the early Christian centuries, and that followers of Christ who subsequently in like manner suffered for His Name's sake, after the beginning of that period and throughout its continuance, were invested with royal honors and authority immediately upon their entrance by the gateway of death into the heavenly courts.

The statement concerning the souls seen in this vision, that "they *lived* and reigned", affords strong confirmation to the view that the place where they reigned is on the heavenly side of the veil and that the time thereof is before the Lord's second coming and before the bodily resurrection of the dead in Christ, which will take place then. For the word "rise" is always used where bodily resurrection is in view. "Thy brother shall rise again"; "If the dead rise not then is Christ not risen"; "The dead in Christ shall rise first" (John 11:23; 1 Cor. 15:16; 1 Thes. 4:16). The words "rise first" in 1 Thessalonians, do not imply a subsequent resurrection of believers, thus making the resurrection of those who rise when Christ descends from heaven to be "the first resurrection"; for the sense of the passage plainly is that, at that time, the order of events will be first "the dead in Christ shall rise", and "then" those believers "who are alive and remain shall be caught up together with them . . . to meet the Lord in the air", they having been "changed" in the twinkling of an eye (1 Cor. 15:52). The priority in time of the resurrection of the dead in Christ is not with respect to a subsequent resurrection of the dead in Christ but with respect to the catching up of those who are alive at Christ's coming to meet Him in the air. Further consideration will be given to this point; though the meaning of the text of 1 Thessalonians 4:14, 15, is not in the least uncertain or ambiguous. Attention should be given to the antithesis between "they lived" (v. 4) and "the rest of the dead lived not again until—" (v. 5); for it seems that "live" here connotes something more than consciously existing. Those souls, when seen under the altar, had conscious existence and were in the enjoyment of "rest"; but it is not said that they "lived". Christ came that His sheep "might have life"; (John 10:10); they already had conscious existence. So it is written: "He that hath the Son hath life"; and to define the meaning sharply, it is added: "and he that hath not the Son of God hath not life" (1 John 5:12); and again, to those who already have conscious existence, it is written: "If ye through the Spirit do put to death the doings of the body, ye shall live" (Rom. 8:13).

To the suffering saints in Smyrna Christ spake a word of exhortation, coupled with a glorious promise, saying: "Be thou faithful unto death and I will give thee a crown of life" (Rev. 2:10). If this referred only to the prospect of sharing the honors of Christ's throne in glory, which prospect is given to all His people, there would be no sequence of cause and effect between the two clauses and no point in the exhortation. But if those who were faithful unto death were immediately to live and reign with Christ for a thousand years, the aptness and significance of the words would be clear. Moreover, this passage is directly linked with the millennium passage by the promise in verse 11, "He that overcometh shall not be hurt of the second death".

We note also the promise in Revelation 3:21, "To him that overcometh will I grant to sit with me in My throne, even as I also overcame and am set down with My Father in His throne". This promise cannot without manifest accommodation be taken to mean merely that all believers will eventually be kings and priests. Christ overcame by His death, and forthwith was exalted to His Father's throne. These words seem clearly to promise to the overcomer a share in Christ's own royal glory and authority immediately upon his entrance by the gateway of death into the spiritual realm.

All Judgment Committed to the Son

Further light is shed upon our subject by the Lord's words recorded in John 5:17-29. He first refers to divine works and declares that His own works were identical with His Father's, and pre-eminently the work of quickening of the dead. "My Father worketh hitherto and I work". "The Son can do nothing of Himself, but what He seeth the Father do; for what things soever He doeth, these also doeth the Son".

He then speaks of judgment, saying: "For as the Father raiseth up the dead and quickeneth them, even so the Son quickeneth whom He will". Thus it is seen that already the Father had "committed all judgment to the Son". He continues: "For as the Father hath life in Himself; so hath He given to the Son to have life in Himself; and hath given Him authority to execute judgment also". Here is a luminous commentary upon the words "they lived", (i. e. were quickened) "and judgment was given unto them", (i. e. Christ shared His great and unique prerogative of judgment with them); and thus was fulfilled the apostle's prediction "that we shall judge angels" (1 Cor. 6:3); for beyond doubt Paul himself was one of those who lived and reigned with Christ, and who executed judgment in the heavenly sphere over angels and other celestial beings. But our Lord, after speaking of imparting life and exercising judgment, goes on to speak immediately of that which follows in Revelation XX, saying: "Marvel not at this; for the hour is coming in the which all that are in the graves (*tombs*) shall hear His voice, and shall come forth; they that have done good unto the resurrection of life, and they that have done evil unto the resurrection of judgment" (John 5:28, 29). Thus, after speaking of that which "now is" (the quickening of the dead, "whom He will", and the investiture of the Son with the sole and exclusive prerogative of judgment) our Lord reveals the future era of the general resurrection and judgment of all that are in the graves (that being the hour that *"is coming"*) which corresponds with John's vision of what was to follow the thousand years: "And I saw the dead, small and great, stand before God ... and the dead were judged" (Rev. 20:12).

"If I May Apprehend"

It is appropriate to refer at this point to the apostle Paul's intense desire and strenuous endeavor, expressed in the words, "If by any means I might attain unto the resurrection of the dead" (Phil. 3:11). Inasmuch as Paul taught, and indeed made it a conspicuous and vital part of his teaching, that *all* the believing dead will be raised and changed into the image of Christ at His coming, it is not supposable that he could have had the least uncertainty as to his own participation in *that* resurrection, or that he could have had that resurrection in mind when he said "not as though I had already attained". What then did he mean?

Upon examining closely the text and context it is observed, first, that the Greek word here translated "resurrection" differs from that used in all passages where the resurrection of the body is in view. It is a word compounded of the word commonly used for resurrection and the preposition *ek*, used as a prefix; so that the verse, literally rendered, would read: "If by any means I might attain unto *the resurrection out from among the dead*". From this it would inevitably have been understood, except for the desire to accommodate the text to an accepted doctrine, that Paul had in mind *a special resurrection*, antecedent to the general resurrection of the dead, and which was, moreover, *a reward* for some special services and sufferings in behalf of Christ. Furthermore, the nature of those services and sufferings is indicated by the preceding verses: "Christ Jesus my Lord, for Whom I have suffered the loss of all things . . . That I may know Him, and the power of His resurrection, and the fellowship of His sufferings, being made conformable unto His death"; and also by the words that follow: "Not as though I had already attained . . . but I follow after, if that I may apprehend that for which also I am apprehended of Christ Jesus. . . . I press toward the mark *for the prize* of the high calling of God in Christ Jesus".

Here is a resurrection of such sort that the apostle speaks of it as a "prize", to be "attained" only by sufferings of like character to those of Christ, and of which he could not count himself assured by all he had already suffered down to and including his imprisonment in Rome. Moreover, what the apostle so ardently sought was of such transcendent value in his eyes that no price would be too great to pay, no sufferings, loss, or torture unto death, "if by any means" he might attain unto it. Those words could not have been used if Paul was speaking of the resurrection in which all believers will share, whether or not they suffer for the truth's sake.

But if there was to be a resurrection of Christ's martyrs long before the *bodily* resurrection of His people, and if those who attain unto that resurrection of *souls* —which would be appropriately designated the "out-resurrection"—were to reign with Christ in the heavenly places for a thousand years, we have in those facts a perfect explanation of the apostle's words in Philippians (3:8-14). That there is precisely such a resurrection of souls is declared by the millennium passage; and hence those two passages mutually support and explain each other.

The writer of these pages cannot refrain from declaring the great satisfaction he feels in being relieved of the necessity of straining his ingenuity in the attempt to show that Paul, in the passage in Philippians, was expressing only the intensity of his desire to be a participant in the resurrection of the body, in which all God's people will take part at the second coming of Christ and which demands no merits and no efforts on their part to "attain". An example of that straining of the Philippian passage to make it agree with a preconceived theory of interpretation will be found on pages 578 and 579 of this volume.

"The Time of the Dead"

Further we note, in connection with the question *when* do these souls live and reign with Christ, which is identically the same as *when is the millennium*, that at the judgment of the great white throne, described in the latter part of Chapter XX, John saw "the dead, small and great, stand before God"; which plainly is what was announced under the seventh trumpet—"the time of the dead, that they should be judged" (see also 1 Cor. 15:52), and which plainly also is what is intimated in the millennium passage itself, in which, after speaking of the souls of the martyrs who "lived and reigned with Christ a thousand years", there is added immediately, "But the rest of the dead lived not again until the thousand years were finished". In agreement with this, John sees in the next vision "the dead, small and great, stand before God". That these were not the unbelieving dead only is evident from the fact that, conspicuous among the books out of which they were to be judged was "the book of life", and from the statement that "whosoever was not found written in the book of life was cast into the lake of fire" (v. 15). For manifestly there would be no use for the book of life at this judgment if all the believing dead had been raised, clothed with their resurrection bodies and made sharers of Christ's throne and glory, a thousand years previously. This reference to "the book of life" forbids the view that the words, "This is the first resurrection" (v. 5) refer to the resurrection of all those "that are Christ's at His coming" (1 Cor. 15:23) and that "the rest of the dead", referred to in the same verse, and who "lived not again until the thousand years were finished", were the unbelieving dead only.

Moreover, the saying of the elders at the sounding of the seventh trumpet, to which several references have been made above, announces not only "the time of the dead that they should be judged", but simultaneously therewith the time when God should take to Him His great power and reign, and also the time when He should *give reward* to His servants the prophets and *to the saints* and to *them that fear His name,* "*small and great*" (v. 18). The words, "small and great", constitute a special link with the vision of the great white throne, as the same words are used in describing that vision; for John records that there he "saw the dead, *small and great, stand before God*".

Some may ask whether "the first resurrection", described by John in Revelation 20:4-6, may not be that which Paul had in mind in writing that "when we were dead in sins" God had "quickened us together with Christ and raised us up together and made us sit together in heavenly places in Christ Jesus" (Eph. 2:4-6).

Such was the view set forth in the first edition of this work (pp. 518, 519). But the text will not bear that interpretation. It does indeed speak of a resurrection of believers, who are made to sit together— i. e. on thrones—"in heavenly places". But the truth declared by this passage is the union of Christ's people with Himself now, while they are alive on earth. This union, says the apostle, is such as to constitute complete identity; insomuch that even while they are in their mortal bodies, they are nevertheless, in God's contemplation, already sharers of Christ's resurrection and of His throne. That is what they already are *"in Christ"*; and the truth here revealed is of immense importance. But the millennium passage refers to what happens to Christian martyrs after death.

The foregoing discussion by no means exhausts the subject; but from what has been there advanced it seems impossible to escape the conclusion that the vision of the great white throne represents the general judgment, as has been almost the uniform consensus of opinion of Christian commentators from the beginning of the era, and that it cannot be made to harmonize with the view, now favored by some of orthodox faith, that the resurrection of all believers takes place a thousand years before the judgment of the great white throne.

There are other passages of Scripture that throw light on this subject; but in the view of this writer they all agree with the interpretation given above, particularly the great resurrection Chapter, 1 Corinthians XV.

THE PROPHECIES OF PAUL

Dr. Benjamin B. Warfield, in his volume of *Biblical Doctrines* (article, "Prophecies of St. Paul") has exhaustively discussed the predictive portions of that apostle's writings, in the course of which discussion he demonstrates clearly that, according to Paul, our Lord's Coming is to be the prelude to the general judgment. Speaking of how Paul thought of the Second Advent, Dr. Warfield says:

"Plainly to him it was above all things else the Judgment." "Every passage in which the Second Advent is adverted to in these Epistles (Thessalonians I and II) conceives of it pointedly as the Judgment Day." Christ is "the Deliverer from the coming wrath."

"The most important passage in this point of view is II Thess. 1:6-10, where the matter is not only treated at large, but the statements are explicit. Here the declaration is distinctly made that 'at the revelation of the Lord Jesus from heaven, together with the angels of His power, in a fire of flame' God will justly recompense affliction to those who persecuted the Thessalonians, and rest or relief to them."

"The apostle proceeds to declare broadly that this revelation of Jesus of which he is speaking as one giving vengeance to those ignorant of God and those disobedient to the gospel—a vengeance that comes in the way of justice and consists in eternal destruction away from the face of the Lord and from the glory of His might. And so carefully is the time defined that, to the exact statement that all this occurs at the revelation of Christ from heaven, it is added at the end that this 'eternal destruction' takes place whenever the Lord gloriously comes—'at that day' " (p. 604).

The apostle, says Dr. Warfield, goes on to declare concerning Christ's coming again, that

"The times and seasons he knew perfectly were hidden in the Father's power (1 Thess. V. 1). He might come soon. When He did come, it would be, he knew, with the unexpectedness of a thief in the night (id. V. 2).... But if, just because the 'when' was unknown, the apostle could not confidently expect the Lord in his own time, the categorical assertion that the Advent would bring 'eternal destruction away from the face of the Lord' (2 Thess. 1:9) to the special persecutors of the Thessalonians rests on his view of the advent as synchronous with the final judgment" (p. 606).

Coming to the Epistles to the Corinthians, Dr. Warfield says that in these, as in those to the Thessalonians:

"the Second Advent is represented primarily and most prominently in the aspect of judgment—as the last judgment.... His coming is indeed so sharply defined as the time of judging, in the mind of Paul, that he advises his readers to 'judge nothing before the time until the Lord come' (1 Cor. IV. 5). The connotation of 'the day of the Lord' was to him so entirely judgment, that the word 'day' had come to mean 'judgment' to him and he actually uses it as its synonym, speaking of a 'human day', for 'human judgment' ".

It would seem impossible for anyone, after considering the massive scriptural evidences which Dr. Warfield sets forth with admirable lucidity in the article cited, to doubt that our Lord's second advent will be followed immediately—not by a thousand years of edenic blessedness, but—by the last judgment.

DELIVERING THE KINGDOM TO GOD THE FATHER

In commenting upon the great resurrection Chapter (1 Cor. XV) Dr. Warfield points out a fact which, though plainly declared, is nevertheless commonly overlooked, the meaning of the passage being actually reversed. He says:

"An even more important fact faces us in the wonderful revelation we have been considering: the period between the two advents (this present age) is the period of Christ's Kingdom, and when He comes again it is not to institute His Kingdom, but to lay it down (vv. 24, 28). The completion of His conquest, which is marked by conquering 'the last enemy' death (v. 28) which in turn is manifest when the just arise and Christ comes (vv. 54, 23) marks also the end of His reign (v. 25) and the delivery of the kingdom to God, even the Father (v. 24). This is indubitably Paul's assertion here, and it is in perfect harmony with the uniform representation of the New Testament, which everywhere places Christ's Kingdom before and God's after the second advent. The contrast in Matthew 13:41 and 43 is not accidental" (p. 625).

The truth here pointed out gives special significance to the words of the Lord's prayer: *"Our Father . . .*

Thy Kingdom come". Christ's Kingdom is already come.

Incidentally, we express hearty agreement with Dr. Warfield when he says:

"John knows no more of two resurrections—of the saints and of the wicked—than does Paul; and the whole theory of an intervening millennium—and indeed of a millennium of any kind *on earth*—goes up in smoke".

And we register emphatic agreement with the remark:

"The millennium of the Apocalypse is the blessedness of the saints who have gone away from the body to be at home with the Lord" (p. 662).

The Second Death

Chapter XX of the Revelation presents a striking antithesis in two terse sentences: "This is the first resurrection" (ver. 5). "This is the second death" (ver. 14).

Here is a manifestly purposed antithesis which challenges our closest attention and scrutiny.

The first resurrection—the resurrection given to the first of the sons of Adam's race who having died the first death, "lived" again—; and the second death—which is the eternal doom of Satan and of all who have been taken captive at his will and have refused deliverance through the sacrificial death of the Lamb of God—are at opposite poles of the universe of God's dealings with mankind.

The Millennium

Furthermore, the phrase, "The first resurrection" implies a second; and likewise, "The second death" implies a first.

"For as in Adam *all* die, even so in Christ shall all be made alive" (1 Cor. 15:22). Here is the first death. It dates from Eden and is universal, embracing *all* that are "in Adam". As it is written in another Scripture, "by one man sin entered the world and death by sin, and so death passed upon all men" (Rom. 5:12). Again it is written, "it is appointed unto men once to die" (Heb. 9:27). And since this is appointed to all, as the consequence—not of their individual sins, but— of the sin of Adam, the Son of God Himself took part of flesh and blood for the suffering of death, "that through death He might destroy him that had the power of death, that is the devil" (Heb. 2:14). Thus "the power of death", is annulled for all who are "in Christ".

The devil, who had the power of the first death, is himself subject forever to the second death, which is the portion also of the beast and the false prophet (Chap. 19:20). Death and hades also, and whosoever is not found written in the book of life, are to be "cast into the lake of fire" (20:14, 15). That is for them an eternal state, "for ever and ever" (20:10).

Several of the references in the Apocalypse to the second death are couched in terms that raise a question. To the overcomer of the Church in Smyrna the promise is given that he "shall not be hurt of the second death" (2:11); and of those who have part in the first resurrection it is said that "on such the second death hath no power" (20:6). Are we to infer that the second death has power to hurt in some unrevealed manner those who are sharers of Christ's victory over death and over him who had the power of death? The language seems to imply it; but we leave the question unanswered.

Pre-, Post- and A-Millennialism Reconciled

Not the least in value of the results of the view herein advocated, which places the thousand years in the realm of spiritual realities, is that thereby a complete reconciliation is effected between the pre-millennial and post-millennial systems, whose respective view-points seem to be hopelessly irreconcilable. For according to the view of the millennium herein set forth, the pre-millennialist is fully supported by Scripture in holding that there cannot be an era of earthly blessedness before the second advent of Christ; while, on the other hand, the post-millennialist has solid scriptural support in holding that there can be no thousand years following the second advent and precedent to the final judgment and the new heavens and new earth. What brought about the seemingly irreconcilable antagonism and the apparent contradiction of Scripture by Scripture, which those mutually antagonistic systems present, was simply that the millennium was placed on the wrong side of the veil. Hence by correcting that error the long and heated conflict, by which the people of God who love and read their Bibles have been divided, distracted and confused, is brought to a peaceful and harmonious end.

Likewise the A-millennialists are right in holding that there is no earthly millennium of universal brotherhood of man—a half way state between the natural condition of man and the eternal bliss of the redeemed—intervening between the day of grace and the day of glory. This is perhaps the most distinctive feature of current millennialism and undoubtedly is the hardest to reconcile with the whole body of "the doctrine of Christ", as set forth in the Scriptures. Whether placed before or after the Second Advent, the difficulty of finding room for such an era in the future history of mankind as foreshown in Bible prophecy is not to be overcome by any reasonable process. That earth's population should be for a thousand years under the absolute sway of Him Who put away sin and vanquished death and yet be subject in a measure to both those dread powers; that the nations should be almost saved but not wholly, and other like ideas, are so incongruous and so destitute of scriptural support as fully to justify the extreme a-millennial position, were there not another view and one that avoids the described difficulty. Happily, there is such an alternative; and it is not a novelty, for its main features are to be found in the writings of able and godly commentators from very early times. But what seems to be greatly needed today is a presentation thereof in systematic form and in its relation to the crisis through which the world is now passing. To supply that special need is one of the chief aims of the present work.

SCRIPTURES CITED

Genesis	Page	Genesis	Page	Numbers	Page
bk. rf.	6	49:8	252	14:22	99
1:	5	17	184	16:19	460
"	40	22	254	25:1-3	101
"	295	24	195		
"	512			Deuteronomy	
16-18	236	Exodus		6:6-8	423
16,26	362	3:14	51	17:6	341
26	15	"	56	18:9	419
"	358	7:20,21	464	21,22	33
31	425	9:8-12	463	22	301
2:	5	23-25	283	19:15	341
"	542	10:21	473	23:18	548
1,2	449	13:21	54	28:27,35	464
1-3	425	14:30	458	45-47	276
3:15	363	15:1	458	29:18	294
"	387	1,21	185	24-28	xv
"	404	2	219	32:10,11	383
"	516	6	71	" q	384
16	365	23-25	293	22	276
24	154	16:10	54	23,42	195
"	155	33	104	41-43	233
5:27	520	19:4	383	33:3	71
9:2	71	16	63		
6	469	20:	99	Joshua	
8-17	148	18	63	6:4,6-9	358
11:1-9	494	25:8	538	10,16	359
15:6	442	18-22	157	11,13	358
16	278	23-30	160	10:11	479
"	322	30	163	24:15	xvi
19:24	448	40	150		
21:14-20	369	26:1,31	157	Judges	
22:17	394	28:15-21	536	6:5	317
25:23	xiii	30:12-15	247	7:12	394
27:34	502	34-38	270	8:9-13	284
29:32	252	38:8	166		
33	253	40:34,35	460	I Samuel	
30:8	253	38	54	4:4	159
18,20	254				
31:7,41	99	Leviticus		II Samuel	
35:16-18	256	9:7-11	276	7:2	219
37:9,10	236	15-22	276	14:24,32	543
"	295	24	277	24:1	248
41:1-7	212	10:1-3,6	277		
32	446	11:44	120	I Kings	
49	394	13:20	464	4:20	394
51	253	23:24,25	268	7:23	166
52	255	25:8-13,23	268	16:30-34	109

II Kings	Page	Psalms	Page	Isaiah	Page
9:7	507	45:	512	13:9,10	238
30-37	490	3-5	196	14:12	291
35,36	111	4	195	22:9-13	122
13:17	195	"	197	12,15	126
18:	123	10	253	20-22	126
		48:2,3	533	20-24	122
I Chronicles		12,13	533	22	121
21:1	248	69:1-4	445	24:23	165
29:1-3	220	75:8	447	27:1	395
3	127	77:17	195	13	401
		78:27	394	28:2,17	283
Ezra		79:6	460	30:21	66
2:13	427	89:28	53	26	299
		90:5	385	31:1	185
Job		94:1-3,23	472	34:2-4	237
1:6	375	20	471	40:18	74
2:1	375	97:2	159	25	407
6:4	195	103:20	79	31	384
19:2	99	20,21	269	41:15,16	289
28:22,23	283	104:5,35	506	42:4	241
29:18	394	14,15	224	44:6	75
37:1-5	275	110:	174	48:2,14	495
39:19-25	184	1	143	12,13	76
		4-6	175	20	494
Psalms		6	196	49:1,2	72
1:1-3	466	118:15,16	71	26	469
2:	172	124:4,5	385	51:5	241
"	173	127:3	438	17,22	448
1-3	404	130:6	550	52:4	400
6	15	135:4	537	4,5	495
"	143			8,9,11	495
6-12	241	Proverbs		11	496
7-9	112	2:6	424	53:11	510
9	361	20:27	78	54:	363
12	329	23:23	135	5,11,12	532
3:9	507			13	388
12:6	133	Ecclesiastes		55:1	135
17:7	71	4:9,12	341	1-4	530
14	499	7:27,29	425	57:15	120
18:13	284			20	394
14	195	Isaiah		60:9	241
19:	86	1:11ff.	339	14	299
7-11	133	2:17-19	240	18	534
23:6	127	6:1-4	153	"	535
"	538	4	460	18-20	532
24:7-10	145	9:6,7	122	19,20	299
27:4	127	13	323	61:10	134
"	538	15	313	63:1-3	512
29:3,4	275	"	367	3	70
31:14,15	71	10:24-26	401	3,4	453
33:17	185	11:1,2,10	549	65:13-17	129
36:8	542	5	67	15,16	130
9	293	13:	295	18-20	130
40:8	180	2	286		

Jeremiah	Page	Ezekiel	Page	Daniel	Page
2:1,2	92	4:16	220	9:26	385
3	438	8:2	148	10:4	394
13	293	9:1,8	461	5,6	67
3:23	241	3,4	245	7-10,19	75
4:13	185	10:1-22	154	13,20	312
31	365	20	150	14	27
5:6	393	30:	295	20,21	79
14	344	31:3	284	12:	79
7:20	284	32:1-15	238	1	284
10:7	458	33:3	14	4	49
25	460	37:11-14	523	4,10	27
12:5	185	38–39 ch.	523	7	340
15:16	331	38:9,16	524	"	373
17:7,8	466	39:4-6,8	524		
8	284	17-32	513	Hosea	
10	70	25,29	523	8:8	216
22:29	i	40:2,4	334	9:3	401
25:	448	43:2	71	17	216
10	503	47:	542	10:8	281
15-28	446	1-12	542	11:10	327
32:6-10 r	180	48:35	533	11	401
14 r	180			12:7	216
33:22	394	Daniel		13:10-14	404
46:23	317	1:5	268	14:3	185
47:2	385	12-15	99		
49:12	448	2:	397	Joel	
36	244	35	237	1:10-12	225
50:3,8,9	495	4:20-22	284	2:	295
13,15	495	5:26	248	1	267
18,23	495	7–8 ch.	400	2,20-31	296
51:1	244	7:	31	4,30	312
6,8	495	"	175	30,31	239
7,8	445	"	391	3:15,16	239
7,8,48	482	"	392	16	328
7,9	497	2	244	18	542
10	496	3	31		
13	485	7	566	Amos	
13,25	286	8	417	8:9	298
20-23	288	9	70		
25	241	"	526	Jonah	
"	287	9-14	145	2:9	507
59-64	503	"	176		
61-64	482	11	515	Micah	
		13:w, 7:13r	55	3:6	298
Lamentations		7:13	66	4:8,9	365
2:4	195	13,14	13	5:2	202
		17	30	"	365
Ezekiel		24,25	418	6:6,7	202
1:4,27	148	8:2	394		
4-28	154	5-8	30	Nahum	
5	150	9:20	286	3:11	446
7	71	24	27		
2:2	61	24-27	7	Habakkuk	
8	330	"	34	2:10,20	263

Habakkuk	Page	Matthew	Page	Matthew	Page
2:15,16	446	6:24	493	24:43	475
3:8-13	195	7:15	95	25:31-46	355
"	196	"	417	26:24	55
		8:10,11	258	53	79
Zephaniah		10:5,13,34	200	64	71
1:7	263	17-21	200	27:25	345
3:8	455	32,33	118	66	517
"	460	34-36	201	28:18	13
		35,36	202	"	76
Haggai		11:15	88	"	180
2:6	236	27	107	"	379
"	237	28	607	"	606
"	478	12:25-29	556	19,20	xvii
		26,29	591		
Zechariah		29	592	Mark	
1:8	185	13:9,43	88	4:9,23	88
10	186	24,25	227	7:16	88
12,16	333	24-30	450	16:15	xv
2:	332	25	294	19	174
1-4	496	30	17		
6,7	496	"	451	Luke	
7	337	36-43	450	2:1	207
11	333	38	306	35	256
13	264	"	439	8:8	88
3:1	375	38,39	227	31	316
1-5	374	41,43	619	"	583
4–5 ch.	217	15:26	548	10:17	291
4:1	241	16:18	59	18,19	593
2,3	343	26,27	501	33,34	225
5,13 w	343	27	526	11:21,22	304
6,14 r	343	17:5	55	12:8,9	119
7	286	18:10	77	47	277
5:	220	"	79	49-53	201
6-8	288	"	268	51-53 q	202
6-11	218	16	341	14:35	88
6:1-3,5	186	21:7	512	15:	136
1-5	244	21	287	17:20	xvi
10:10,11	401	42	220	27	498
12:10	56	22:7	65	29	448
14:8	542	11	134	19:11	233
		37	444	11-27	126
Malachi		23:32	278	12	171
4:2	86	"	279	"	451
		24:14	386	12,15	13
Matthew		"	440	17,19	540
2:	366	"	554	26	127
1-12	368	"	559	41	286
4:8-10	393	20-22	280	21:20-23	280
5:2	385	21	259	23,24	279
14,15	78	24	418	"	297
15	84	29	297	24	xi
6:13	507	30	55	"	xvii
23	319	"	56	25	298
24	xvi	31	247	25-28	xxv

Luke	Page	John	Page	Acts	Page
21:28	xxvii	14:6	107	14:22	60
36	268	18,23	125	23	81
22:38	416	29	33	15:2,4,6	81
23:27-30	280	15:5	255	18	180
30	240	24	42	17:31	441
43	449	26	341	18:9-12	89
24:25	27	26,27	83	19-28	89
29,30	138	”	551	19:8	89
46-49	192	16:4	33	13-17	90
		14	160	19,20	90
John		33	9	20:	90
1:1-3	76	17:3	120	17	81
9	73	5	70	20,27	116
”	539	6,16-18	83	25,27	555
11-13	xiv	22	537	29,30	94
18	53	23	539	23:6	353
3:3	xvi	25	53	24:15	353
29	509	18:37	53	25:4	25
34	115			26:6,7	353
4:14	293	Acts		13	73
36	41	bk. rf.	206	16	42
5:4	469	1:6	405	22	354
17-29	610	8	83	28:20	353
21-23	302	”	342	31	555
21,24-26	107	”	386		
24	526	”	551	Romans	
26	57	9	iv	bk. rf.	351
28,29	611	2:20	62	1:4	63
6:63	72	24	517	5	302
7:28	42	33	147	25-28	320
38,39	541	”	231	2:5	14
43	xiv	33,47	256	6	526
”	214	39	559	16	72
8:21	449	4:25-28	172	”	441
39,44	xiv	”	404	17-23	279
44	304	5:1-10	277	28,29	97
9:41	131	31	471	”	252
10:10	542	32	83	4:17	442
”	609	”	341	5:3	60
27	438	”	551	5	93
28	72	7:53	279	8	92
11:23	608	55	x	12	527
12:23-33	591	56	174	”	621
31	592	10:10-15	61	12-21	363
31-33	291	11:18	471	6:1-14	363
”	370	30	81	17	389
”	371	12:15	77	22	254
”	372	”	79	7:4	551
39-41	152	13:1	81	6	389
48	72	27	350	8:13	609
”	515	34	126	21,22	156
13:1	92	41	441	23,25	60
19	33	14:15	442	26-29	537
”	301	22	9	28,29	160

Romans	Page	I Corinthians	Page	Ephesians	Page
8:31	377	15:52	452	1:7	519
32-36,38	378	"	614	11	180
34	174	54,55	199	12-14	245
"	270	55-57	519	13,14	257
37	100	56-58	377	14	146
9:6-8	97	58	450	20	x
8	xiv	16:9	121	20-23	144
13	xiv			22	12
10:3	218	II Corinthians		"	14
11:	350	1:3,4	436	"	59
17-25	257	14	62	2:2	231
23,24	308	20	130	"	477
24	335	21,22	245	4-6	435
25	405	2:12	121	"	616
26	308	3:18	584	5,6	164
13:10	85	4:4	298	5-8	519
14:17	175	6	73	6	380
16:26	302	17,18	436	10	97
"	442	5:16	350	"	112
		20	83	12,19	335
I Corinthians		6:14-16	496	14	255
1:8	62	16	254	14-22	349
23,24	177	17,18	496	16	403
2:14	160	11:2	437	18	107
3:9	535	"	551	19-22	334
10,11	219	3,4	108	20	254
4:5	618	13	91	"	535
20,21	175	13,15	103	20-22	219
5:5	62	13-15	98	"	350
6:3	611	20,26	103	3:4-6	405
17,19,20	254	12:1-4	61	4-6,18	335
10:19,20	407	13	95	9	541
11:14,15	317			11	157
12–14 ch.	115	Galatians		"	519
12:4,8,9	115	bk. rf.	103	"	520
5	115	1:4	497	15	252
11,13	115	6	25	"	257
13	52	6,9	104	"	441
14:34,37	115	9	439	4:3-6	441
15:	617	2:4	103	4	52
"	619	3:7	xv	"	53
9	382	4:9	104	4-6	353
16,52	608	26	556	30	146
20	53	5:14	85	5:8	78
22	621	6:15	103	26,27	336
23	615	16	101	6:12	477
23-25	619	"	246	17	72
24,25	199	"	251		
26	527			Philippians	
28,54	619	Ephesians		1:1	81
41	113	1:	163	12	211
41,42	540	1-6	257	2:9-11	302
51,52	7	3	164	15	78
52	43	4-6	252	19,33	25

Philippians	Page	II Thess.	Page	Hebrews	Page
3:2	548	2:7,8	455	2:14	145
8-14	614	7-12	355	"	227
11	612	8-10	108	"	292
21	537	10,11	319	"	373
		12	228	"	376
Colossians				"	403
1:5,23	353	I Timothy		"	489
6	439	1:11	442	"	621
12	60	15	545	14,15	404
13-16	107	17	iv	"	591
16,17	56	2:1-8	270	4:9	426
18	12	5	53	10	67
"	53	"	269	12	72
19	115	6	248	5:8	302
2:1	128	3:1,8	81	6:1	426
9	56	14	25	7	325
14,15	591	16	405	19,20	iv
15	291	"	454	7:25	270
3:4	74	4:1	388	25,26	270
4:15	128	10	245	8:2	158
		"	274	5	150
I Thessalonians		5:6	526	9:4	104
bk. rf.	617	6:15	171	8	167
1:10	476			12	146
2:15,16	278	II Timothy		14	116
16	279	1:7	93	"	426
4:13-17	346	2:8	126	23	151
"	452	17,19,20	337	"	159
14	476	19	245	23,24	158
14,15	609	"	338	24	iv
14-17	7	3:16,17	551	27	621
"	387			10:1	158
16	374	Titus		"	420
"	434	3:8,14	112	1-12	349
"	449			19-22	167
"	608	Hebrews		"	339
16,17	556	bk. rf.	175	27	275
17	26	1:1-3	107	11:4	442
5:1,2	618	2	107	10	533
1-7	282	3	x	12	394
2	62	"	56	26	382
2,4,9	476	"	74	37-40	232
7	347	"	174	12:2	510
		8	196	2,18-24	435
II Thessalonians		10	367	15	294
bk. rf.	617	10-12	76	19	63
1:5-10	355	14	79	22	79
6-10	617	"	269	"	173
7,8	282	2:2	68	"	251
7-9	343	4	89	"	381
7-10	19	5	325	25-29	297
9	618	8,9	171	26,27	237
2:2	25	10	252	"	478
7,8	396	14	96	"	528

Hebrews	Page	II Peter	Page	Revelation	Page
13:10,15	339	3:10	525	1:1,2	46
23	25	10,11	601	1,3	26
		12,13	602	,,	546
James		13	528	1,7	iv
1:5	424	15	322	1,20	22
18	438	15,16	599	3	47
4:1	589			,,	50
4	101	I John		4	64
,,	445	1:7	437	4,5	* 50
7	377	2:13,14	380	4,8	12
5:1-6	240	20,27	134	5	86
3,7	603	3:1,2,10	xiv	,,	93
14	81	2	74	,,	260
		,,	161	5,6	* 53
I Peter		,,	537	,,	161
1:9-12	258	4:1	95	5,8	129
16	120	7	93	5,18	62
18,19	260	5:12	57	6	352
19	146	,,	107	7	* 54
2:5	350	,,	609	8,9	* 56
5,9	xiii	20	120	,,	58
7,8	220			8,11	11
10-12	354	Jude		,,	53
3:3,4	486	9	373	9	405
22	79	,,	516	10	141
,,	143	,,	583	,,	142
,,	256	24	438	10-16	* 61
,,	370			11-18	35
4:12-17	280	Revelation		13	451
17	276	bk. rf.	xii	,,	459
5:1,2	81	,,	6	13-16	128
8	376	,,	11	13,20	v
		,,	23	15,16	14
II Peter		,,	47	17-19	* 74
1:4	161	,,	48	18	226
14	25	,,	155	,,	583
19	114	,,	178	19	34
,,	550	,,	350	,,	36
2:1,2	95	,,	352	,,	39
5	457	1–3 ch.	11	,,	41
,,	498	,,	35	20	66
22	548	,,	36	,,	* 76
3:3,4,9	322	,,	269	,,	292
4	273	1–11 ch.	17	2–22 ch.	38
,,	498	1–20:3 ch.	146	2–3 ch.	vi
4,7,18	598	1:	46	,,	64
4,8,9	599	,,	87	,,	80
8	588	,,	327	2:1-7	* 89
9	499	,,	343	2	39
9,10	600	,,	511	5,16	125
9,15	235	,,	544	6	95
10	62	1	24	7,11	12
,,	238	,,	25	8-11	* 96
,,	475	,,	194	9	352

Revelation	Page	Revelation	Page	Revelation	Page
2:9,10	97	4–22 ch.	37	5:9	437
10	609	"	440	9,10	518
11	527	4:	12	10	352
"	621	"	142	11,13	168
12-17	* 100	1	vi	12	171
14	104	"	28	"	259
14,15	102	"	39	6–8 ch.	179
16	72	"	40	6–20 ch.	4
17	436	"	63	6:	186
17,29	12	"	174	1,2	* 190
18-29	* 105	1,2	* 140	1-3	193
20,21	490	2	61	1-11	182
23r, 24w	70	3	* 147	2	512
24	137	4	160	3,4 q	* 199
"	412	5	52	4	229
27	361	"	148	4r, 10w	366
28 q	550	"	149	5,6 q	* 212
3–22 ch.	49	"	276	6	220
3:1-6	* 114	6	166	"	224
3	125	8-11	150	7,8 q	* 226
3,4	475	9	143	9	165
4	116	11	vii	"	605
"	137	"	ix	"	607
6,13,22	12	"	168	9-11	* 232
7-13	* 119	5–6 ch.	173	10	470
8 q	121	"	269	"	606
9 q	123	5:	159	11	118
9,10	98	"	192	"	587
10,11	124	"	193	12,13	236
12 q	127	"	241	12-17	183
"	353	"	451	"	* 234
14-22	* 128	1	vi	"	239
16 q	131	"	325	13	296
17-19 q	132	2r, 3w	vi	15,16	55
19	135	4,6,7	vii	16	281
20	136	5	127	17	43
20,21	133	"	145	"	175
21	vii	"	549	"	242
"	x	6	ix	7:	242
"	144	"	167	"	243
"	610	"	172	"	244
24	145	"	402	"	250
4–5 ch.	ix	7	173	"	261
"	54	"	262	"	271
"	140	7-10	150	"	326
"	141	8	160	"	337
"	144	"	165	"	434
"	145	8,9	436	"	435
"	153	9	143	1-3	* 242
"	176	"	162	"	285
4–6 ch.	228	"	170	4-8	257
4–11 ch.	13	"	258	4-8,15	162
4–19 ch.	34	"	260	5	252
4–22 ch.	7	"	261	9,10	* 257

Revelation	Page	Revelation	Page	Revelation	Page
7:9,14	118	10:	271	11:15	557
11	151	"	282	15,17	329
12-14	259	"	347	15-17	262
13-17	260	"	455	15,18	289
14	9	1-7	14	15-18	271
8–10 ch.	265	1-11	269	16-18	viii
8:	18	1-17	* 324	17,18	607
1	242	3	327	18	43
"	* 261	"	492	"	272
"	359	5-7	210	"	282
1-5	452	"	211	"	347
3	165	6,7	158	"	616
3,4	269	"	508	19	153
"	270	7r, 6w	159	"	158
3-5	14	7	263	"	* 357
"	276	"	271	12–13 ch.	14
5	274	"	555	"	364
"	277	9	330	"	388
"	281	11	289	12:	1
"	282	11:	327	"	40
"	358	"	333	"	43
7	226	"	339	"	105
"	* 283	"	350	"	355
8	287	"	554	"	358
8,9	* 285	1	357	"	395
10	291	"	483	"	404
10,11	* 290	1,2	349	"	407
"	466	"	451	"	482
10-12	298	"	534	"	486
12	239	1-6	* 332	1	162
"	271	1-12	331	"	362
"	* 295	1-13	271	"	415
13	289	"	326	1,2	364
"	310	1-18	265	1,3	454
"	318	2	339	"	* 360
"	502	3	340	1-9	292
9:	314	"	389	2,3	365
1-3	516	3-6,12	434	3	487
1-11	* 311	3-12	440	4	363
"	583	6	341	4,5	* 366
2	472	7	554	4,7	367
3,5,10	313	7,8	344	5	15
4	226	7-12,15	555	"	361
"	316	8	462	6,7	368
5,6,10	311	9,10	* 345	6,14	340
7,9	317	11,12	* 346	"	383
12	318	13	267	7	390
13-21	* 320	"	346	7-9	* 370
15,17-19	322	14	324	7-17	593
20,21	267	"	502	9	105
"	323	14-18	* 356	"	360
"	326	15	274	"	516
10–11 ch.	348	"	390	"	582
10–15 ch.	18	"	508	9,12	595

Revelation	Page	Revelation	Page	Revelation	Page
12:9,12,13	372	13,17,19 ch.	150	16:12	474
10-12	* 379	14–18 ch.	15	12-14	575
11	458	14:	17	12-16	* 473
12	377	"	21	13r, 3w	417
"	380	"	434	14	521
12,17	376	"	451	14,15	475
13	* 381	1	162	15	50
14	369	"	173	15,17	461
"	* 382	"	245	17	530
15	384	"	543	17-21	* 477
"	* 385	1-5	* 432	18,19	492
15,16	373	1,14,15	15	19 q	478
16,17	* 387	2,3	151	21	479
17	388	4	436	17–18 ch.	480
"	389	5	437	17–20 ch.	481
13–14 ch.	432	"	438	17:	18
"	456	6	20	"	19
13–20 ch.	269	6,7	* 439	"	110
13:	22	6-20	433	"	113
"	31	7	441	"	390
"	229	8	* 443	"	491
"	236	"	492	1-5	* 480
"	428	9-11	* 446	2,16	110
"	446	9,13	440	2,5,18	482
1r, 7w	413	12	406	3	487
1,2	* 390	"	447	5	444
"	392	13	50	6	608
1,2,7	595	"	* 448	6,18	481
1-3	488	"	606	6-18	* 488
2	489	14-16	* 450	8	344
"	587	17-20	* 452	8,11	402
2,3	403	15:1	426	9-11	* 398
3,4	* 402	"	433	10	489
4	566	"	* 454	10,11	399
5,6	* 409	"	456	12-14	401
7	198	1-4	469	12,14	490
"	406	2-4	* 456	12,15	22
"	409	"	518	12,16	398
7,9,10	408	3,4	455	14,16	483
7,12	596	5-8	*459	15	286
9	88	8	153	"	394
10	405	"	460	"	485
"	447	"	461	16	490
11	194	16:	433	17	491
"	390	1	459	18	22
11,12	* 410	"	* 460	18:	17
" q	413	"	477	"	219
12	417	2	* 462	"	444
12,14	402	3	* 464	"	446
13-15	418	4-7	* 466	"	478
15	420	5-7	461	1-3	* 491
16,17	* 421	7	469	2	446
18	* 423	8,9	* 470	"	481
"	483	10,11	* 471	2-4	496

Revelation	Page	Revelation	Page	Revelation	Page
18:4	337	19:19-21	391	20:14	100
"	494	20	198	"	199
4-8	* 496	"	410	14,15	621
7	498	"	417	15	526
8	492	"	448	21–22 ch.	333
9-13	* 499	"	587	21:	19
12,13	221	"	621	"	336
13	105	20,21	396	1	iv
14-19	* 501	"	* 514	"	* 528
16	344	21	521	1-4	260
16,19	502	20:	xxviii	1-5 w	541
20	505	"	519	2-8	* 529
20,21	503	"	580	2,9	530
21-24	* 502	"	588	3	254
23	510	1	583	5	545
19–22 ch.	16	1,8,10	516	8	448
19:	19	1-3	409	"	531
"	390	"	480	"	586
"	432	"	* 515	8,27	540
"	515	1-4	584	9	511
1,2	507	1-6	585	9-11	482
1-4	* 505	1-7	579	9-12	* 531
1-7,11	16	1-8	* 577	10	533
4	151	1-10	581	11,23	147
5-10	* 508	"	587	12,14	249
6	436	3,7,8	597	12-21	162
"	505	4	519	"	534
6-8	528	"	525	16,17	249
8	118	"	604	18-21	532
"	134	"	605	21	538
"	510	4,5	609	22,23	16
9	50	4-6	* 517	"	* 538
"	545	4,6	518	23	73
" q	513	4-6,12	616	"	299
10	46	4,8	523	"	300
11	193	4-10	582	23,25	543
11-16	453	5,14	620	24	53
"	* 511	5,15	615	"	333
11-21	72	6	50	"	335
"	355	"	352	24-27	* 539
"	399	"	622	27	118
"	475	7-10	* 521	"	166
"	480	7-10,14	586	"	541
"	490	8,9	590	28	542
"	491	10	448	22:	155
13,16	16	"	621	1,2	542
15	70	11	524	1-5 r	* 541
"	100	"	610	1,17	293
"	396	11-15	* 525	"	530
15-21	409	12	612	3,4	128
16	53	"	614	"	130
17,18	* 513	12,15	118	3,5	543
19	401	13	465	6	26
"	483	13,14	226	6,7	546

Revelation	Page	Revelation	Page	Revelation	Page
22:6-13	* 544	22:14	* 547	22:16-18	552
7,15	50	15	338	16-21	* 548
8	46	"	339	17,19	541
"	548	"	452	18,19	89
8,9,16	47	"	547	"	107
10	27	16	60	"	551
10-12	546	"	113	19	iii
14	540	"	127	"	118
"	541	16,17	550	20	552

AUTHORS CITED

Austen, F. Britten, 543, 574

Bagster's Int. Ver., 330
Bengel, 61, 67, 132, 142, 147, 275, 323, 326, 356, 407, 417, 427, 428, 448, 449, 471, 476, 479, 489, 512, 515, 525, 529, 544
Birks, 4
Bossuet, 165, 249, 322

Clarke, Adam, 48

Darwin, Maj. Leonard, xx

Epiphanius, 148

Gassett, xix
Gibbon, 318
Gray, Lord, 567
Greene, Dr., 319, 413, 414, 515
Guinness, Grattan, 4, 318

Hartwig, 365
Havernick, 394
Henderson, 415
Hengstenberg, 3, 9, 28, 52, 62, 77, 131, 241, 249, 275, 317, 325, 331, 341, 344, 350, 351, 358, 366, 367, 376, 392, 394, 395, 399, 406-408, 419-421, 426-428, 437, 449, 463, 465, 469, 478, 489, 507, 510, 525, 528, 538, 540, 549

Howell, Edward Beach, 203

Jackson, 474

Laski, Prof., xxvii
Literary Digest, 571
Lucke, 375

Mede, 284

Newton, 4

Orpheus, 148
Osborn, Dr. Henry Fairfield, xx, xxi

Plummer, 291

Salter, Sir Arthur, i, xviii, xxii, xxiii
Seiss, Dr., 7
Smith, Dr. J. Ritchie, 592
Spengler, xix
Std. Dict. of Facts, 321
Strong, Dr., 589

Taylor, Isaac, 319
Trenchard, Sir Hugh, 569

Vitringa, 325, 351, 365, 427

Warfield, Dr. Benjamin B., 581, 617, 618-620

Zullig, 3, 164, 407

This index was compiled by
    Miss Clara Brown
    P. O. Box 22
    Sopchoppy, Florida 32358